AF248829

Southern Literary Studies
LOUIS D. RUBIN, JR., EDITOR

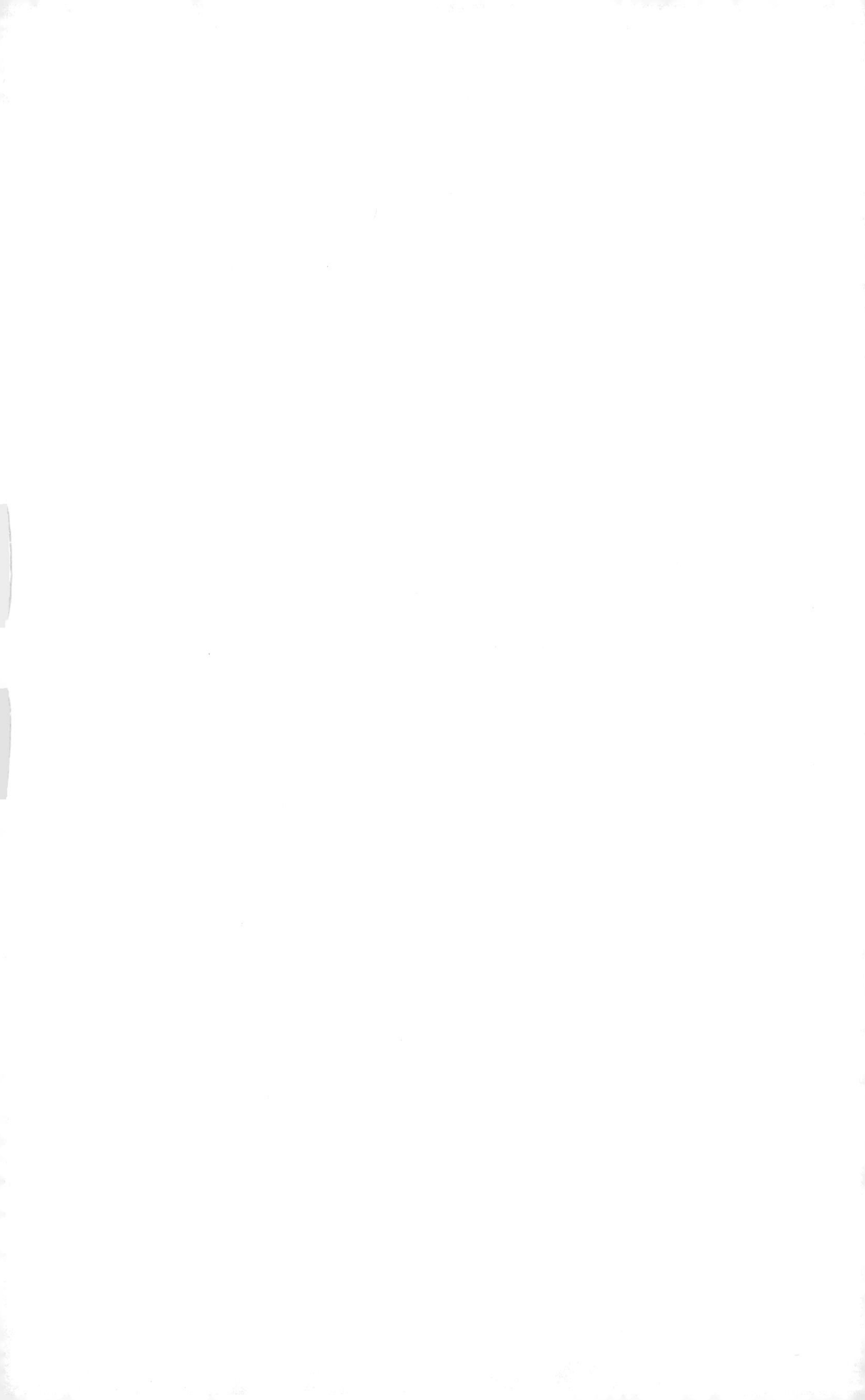

A Man of Letters in the
Nineteenth-Century South

Paul Hamilton Hayne

A Man of Letters in the Nineteenth-Century South

Selected Letters of Paul Hamilton Hayne

Edited by Rayburn S. Moore

Louisiana State University Press
Baton Rouge and London

Copyright © 1982 by Louisiana State University Press
All rights reserved
Manufactured in the United States of America
Designer: Marcy Johnston
Typeface: Sabon
Typesetter: G & S Typesetters, Inc.
Printer: Thomson-Shore
Binder: John Dekker & Sons

The editor wishes to thank the following manuscript depositories and publishers for permission to quote from their materials: the William R. Perkins Library of Duke University, the Dreer Collection of the Historical Society of Pennsylvania, the Milton S. Eisenhower Library of the Johns Hopkins University, the South Caroliniana Library of the University of South Carolina, and the Ella Strong Denison Library of Scripps College for letters of Paul Hamilton Hayne; the Johns Hopkins University Press for passages and a letter from Charles R. Anderson *et al.* (eds.), *Centennial Edition of the Works of Sidney Lanier* (1945); the University of Texas Press for passages from Daniel M. McKeithan (ed.), *A Collection of Hayne Letters* (1944); and Duke University Press for passages from David K. Jackson (ed.), *American Studies in Honor of William Kenneth Boyd* (1940) and Jay B. Hubbell, *The South in American Literature, 1607–1900* (1954).

Library of Congress Cataloging in Publication Data
Hayne, Paul Hamilton, 1830–1886.
    A man of letters in the nineteenth-century South.

    (Southern literary studies)
    Includes index.
    1. Hayne, Paul Hamilton, 1830–1886—Correspondence.   2. Poets, American—19th century—Correspondence.   I. Moore, Rayburn S., 1920–   II. Title.   III. Series.
PS1908.A44   1982   811′.3   [B]   82-271
ISBN 0-8071-1025-6   AACR2

In memory of Edd Winfield Parks

Contents

Hayne's birthplace,
Charleston, South Carolina

Foreword

Louis D. Rubin, Jr.

The reader who is interested in American literature and life during the years of the Genteel Tradition, particularly as it involved the post-Civil War South, will find much that is fascinating in these letters of the poet Paul Hamilton Hayne, which Rayburn Moore has so ably edited. As a poet Hayne is virtually forgotten today, and the same is true for most of the leading makers of verse among his contemporaries; time has not dealt gently with the poetry of Ideality that was so very popular with magazine readers in the days when *Harper's, Atlantic, Scribner's, Century, Lippincott's,* and *Putnam's* were brownstone America's leading journals and taste formers. But in his own time Hayne was a literary figure of considerable consequence. What he did and had to do in order to survive and, to a modest extent at least, even flourish as a poet in the war-ravaged and defeated South; how he approached the writing and reading of poetry; how following the defeat of the Confederacy he began repairing his literary friendships with influential writers and editors of the victorious North, even while privately typifying the way in which a thoroughly un-Reconstructed southern patrician viewed the politics and the social values of the Gilded Age: these will shed considerable light on our understanding of the South and the literature and culture of America of a century ago.

Hayne was one of the very few southern writers of contemporary importance whose career significantly bridged the antebellum and postwar decades. During the 1850s he was a leading figure among the group of literarily inclined South Carolinians who frequented Russell's Bookstore in Charleston; it was Hayne who edited the group's literary magazine, *Russell's.* Here was perhaps the first instance in southern literary life in which there existed, however briefly, a cohesive group of professional authors, men for whom literature was not a pleasant avocation but a full-time occupation to be pursued with the utmost seriousness. Hayne and his schoolmate Henry Timrod were both publishing poems regularly, as was their older friend William Gilmore Simms, a novelist and poet of widespread national reputation. Had the onset of the war not ended their collaboration, it seems possible that some important literary work might ultimately have emerged, for poets, even more so than novelists, seem to require the stimulus and encouragement that comes of close association with their fellow craftsmen.

It was not to be, however. The firing upon Fort Sumter and the resulting conflict quickly brought an end to the Russell's group. Simms lived on until 1870, grinding out reams of prose for second-rate periodicals during the last five years of his life to earn money to feed his family. His day as the South's foremost man of letters and literary spokesman effectively ended with the advent of hostilities. Though the war provided Timrod with the public theme that inspired almost all his finest work, the end of the fighting left him destitute, and he knew near-starvation before his death two years later.

Hayne was more fortunate, though only relatively so. From the wreckage of the South's downfall he and his family managed to salvage sufficient capital to enable him to build a small cottage in the pine barrens near Augusta, Georgia, where he lived during the remaining two decades of his life. His income was low, but so were expenses, and through the sale of poems and occasional articles to the magazines, he was able to keep himself and his wife and son in modest but secure comfort until his death from a stroke in 1886.

Like most professional poets both then and now, Hayne not only wrote verse but worked very hard at being a man of letters, maintaining a prolific correspondence with editors, critics, and other poets, writing and arranging for reviews, doing literary favors and receiving them. With prominent northern writers such as Oliver Wendell Holmes, John Greenleaf Whittier, and Henry Wadsworth Longfellow he traded compliments and literary observations. His English correspondents included Philip Bourke Marston, with whom he exchanged lengthy letters, and Wilkie Collins. With fellow southern authors such as Margaret Junkin Preston, Sidney Lanier, Maurice Thompson, and Charles Gayarré he not only discussed literary matters but shared his continuing outrage at the downfall of the Old South, the politics of the Gilded Age, and what he considered the vile workings of democracy.

Hayne was never reconciled to the South's defeat. Like most white

Southerners he felt no guilt over slavery, and was furious at northern efforts to educate blacks or in any way elevate them in status. Born and reared a patrician, he found nothing to admire in the industrial democracy that the triumph of the North had brought about. The observance of the centennial of American independence in 1876 disgusted him. "Ten to one," he predicted, underlining constantly as was his epistolary habit, "the *next 'Centennial' in their* sense of the word, will *never arrive*; since '*'tis a long cry to Loch* awe,' and 1976 will probably find the *ci devant* American republic split up into a half dozen mongrel nationalities."

In the years immediately following the war Hayne often found himself forced to accept rudeness, condescension, and cold disdain from editors of the northern literary magazines that were almost the only remunerative outlets for his writing. Even before the war the southern magazines were highly unreliable in making promised payment for contributions, and in the devastated postwar South little or no payment at all could be expected. Yet he persisted, and though never prosperous was able to command decent fees for his work from the early 1870s onward. In 1882, through the loyal efforts of his friend John G. James, the Boston publishing firm of D. Lothrop and Co. published the "Complete Edition" (it was by no means so) of the *Poems of Paul Hamilton Hayne*, and it was widely and favorably received.

Like most poets, Hayne tended to judge the critical standards and ethical probity of magazine editors, publishers, critics, and fellow authors in terms of their attitude toward his own verse. His literary tastes were very much those of his contemporaries. Tennyson and William Morris were among his favorite poets; he thought Browning's genius "colossal" but preferred Tennyson's poems. He admired Swinburne's craftsmanship but censured that poet's taste for sensual imagery and questionable subject matter. Walt Whitman's work scandalized him: "Think of *any mortal* coolly writing such ineffable stuff as this;—'*The scent of these arm-pits is aroma sweeter than prayer!*,'—and *then*, the big, shameless *Beast* in his '*Leaves of Grass*,' actually '*apotheosizes*,' (if I may use that term), his own *genital organs*: falls down, & *worships* them (!), as if some *visible deity* glowed in the spherical beauty of his (doubtless) enormous testicles, and equally enormous *Penis*!! (Pardon such vulgar expressions; but *apropos* of *Whitman*, one becomes necessarily, & involuntarily vulgar!)."

Oscar Wilde also outraged him; when that poet visited the United

States in 1882, Hayne observed that "by the way, *Walt Whitman* & *Oscar Wilde* ought to be made acquainted. What a lovely & congenial couple (!!)" (In point of fact Wilde did pay a visit to Whitman in Camden, New Jersey, and they got along very well together, Whitman later declaring that "I think him genuine, honest, and manly.")

It is precisely because Paul Hayne was so very much a man of his times—the America, and the South, of the 1860s, 1870s, and 1880s—that today's reader will find these letters so informative and interesting. They demonstrate what it took to be a southern man of letters in a period when the region's economic and political fortunes were at rock bottom, and the defeat of the war and Reconstruction had left its citizenry in a state of cultural and social shock. Thoroughly imbued with the values and attitudes of the Old South, Hayne and his friends found themselves confronting bewildering and to their minds abominable demands for change and reassessment. Forced to acquiesce in political reunion, they could never bring themselves to like it. The heroes of America's Gilded Age were not their heroes.

Though Hayne himself was willing and even eager to renew the literary ties and friendships that the war had severed, and on one occasion even censured those who approached literary works along sectional lines, he never really forgave the victorious Union for its defeat of his beloved South. Nor did his zeal for the cause of southern literature ever abate. "The Southern author, & scholar," he wrote to Charles Gayarré less than a year before his death, "has always been between *Scylla*, & *Charybdis*, the Scylla of Yankee *prejudice*, & *hatred*; the Charybdis of *Southern indifference*!" For those postwar southern authors who dared to criticize the region's racial and political attitudes, he had withering scorn. He took Gayarré's side in the Creole author's feud with his fellow Louisianan George W. Cable, and the two aging patricians heaped insult and abuse on Cable's head for suggesting in print that the black man was being treated unfairly.

There was in Hayne a fascinating mixture of sweetness, generosity, and nobility of spirit, and at the same time, when either his beloved South or unfavorable reception of his poems was involved, a notable capacity for outrage and vitriol. In his refusal to let the virtual collapse of his own world keep him from pursuing the career as poet that was throughout his life his foremost objective, there is something heroic. In his own way, he did manage to display the resilience and adaptability that enabled him to survive and even mildly to prosper in a confused and trying literary situation. To persevere as a poet in the South in his time was no mean feat.

These letters, carefully chosen by Rayburn Moore to illustrate the plight, and the resources, of a man of letters in the postwar South, have much to tell us about the region, its writers, its social and cultural life, the literary values of the Genteel Tradition, and the pursuit of literature as a profession in late nineteenth-century America. And Mr. Moore's lengthy, informative introduction provides the biographical information that will enable the reader to derive maximum benefit from the correspondence.

Acknowledgments

It is a pleasure to record here the obligations I have incurred in editing these letters. Without the generous cooperation of the staff of William R. Perkins Library, Duke University, this book could not have been undertaken, and I should like therefore to express my deep appreciation to J. P. Waggoner, Florence Blakely, Mary Canada, Elvin Strowd, Emerson Ford, and, above all, to Mattie Russell, Curator of Manuscripts, who for many years has made the indispensable Hayne Collection available to me even when I could not come to Durham.

Other libraries have also been helpful. The staff of the Ilah Dunlap Little Library, University of Georgia—especially Christine Burroughs and Robert M. Willingham, Jr.—have helped in various ways. E. L. Inabinett of the South Caroliniana Library, University of South Carolina, invited me years ago to use the Hayne letters there and has been unfailingly kind and helpful, as have Alan Stokes and Tom Johnson. I am also grateful to the Alderman Library of the University of Virginia, the Houghton Library of Harvard University, the Milton S. Eisenhower Library of the Johns Hopkins University, the Ella Strong Denison Library of Scripps College, the Friends Historical Library of Swarthmore College, the Library of Congress, the New York Public Library, the historical societies of Massachusetts and Wisconsin, and the Dreer Collection of the Historical Society of Pennsylvania.

I owe thanks for research assistance to James Randolph Loney, Alan C. Anderson, and Paul Schleifer and for various scholarly courtesies to James E. Kibler, Jr., Daniel Morley McKeithan, Margaret Moore, John O. Eidson, the late Charles Duffy and the late John R. Welsh. I am particularly grateful to Jay B. Hubbell, Edd W. Parks, and Arlin Turner, mentors and friends now, alas, dead, for sharing their knowledge of Hayne and southern literature and their standards of scholarship with me over a period of many years.

I am also indebted to Deans John C. Stephens, Jr., and William J. Payne of the University of Georgia for making it possible for me to devote parts of each year to this work. Professors James B. Colvert, John Algeo, and Coburn Freer, department heads in English, provided travel funds and summer support, and Dr. Robert C. Anderson, Vice President for Research, the late Dr. Charles J. Douglas, Assistant Vice President for Research, and Dr. S. William Pelletier, former Provost, all offered help of one kind or another.

For typing the hundreds of Hayne letters, I am pleased to thank Betty Hodge, John Eldridge, Kathleen De Marco, Mary Adams, Laura Mashburn, and Ann Kingston. Mrs. Mashburn and Mrs. Kingston, indeed, deserve a special word for typing the manuscript and helping to prepare the book for the press, and Mrs. Virginia Seaquist merits praise for typing changes and working on the index.

To Louis Rubin, I owe much. He suggested this project many years ago and, despite delays anticipated and unanticipated, has stayed with me to the end. No author has ever had better support from his editor.

The editorial staff at the Louisiana State University Press has been unfailingly helpful. Beverly Jarrett encouraged me even before the manuscript was completed; Martha Hall went to work with a will after it arrived; John Easterly edited the copy with diligence and dispatch; and Catherine Barton tended it through the press with care and consideration.

A Man of Letters in the Nineteenth-Century South

A Note on Editorial Principles

This is a selected edition of Hayne's unpublished correspondence, and since there are well over 1,500 letters yet to be printed in full, I have had to be rigorous in making choices. I have managed, in part, to limit the selection by focusing on Hayne as a man of letters, but, even so, I have left out many good letters for a variety of reasons. Modern editorial standards, for example, require the publication of complete texts (I have had to relax this criterion in only two instances) and quite a few letters were too long to include—there are many of thirty to forty pages in length. Still, I had God's plenty from which to choose—hundreds at Duke and other depositories that were not available when D. M. McKeithan published his edition in 1944. After several years of agonizing appraisal and reappraisal, I reduced the number to 200 and eventually to the 128 appearing in this edition.

With regard to preparing these letters for print, I have tried to reproduce Hayne's style as nearly as possible, despite its obvious eccentricities. I have changed his capitalization, punctuation, paragraphing, or abbreviations only when clarity of expression demanded it, and I have scrupulously retained his primary underscorings (a feat in itself), but have found no reasonable way to retain the numerous double and triple underlinings. I have consequently treated all underscorings the same. Any ellipsis points in the text of the letters are Hayne's, with the single exception of those noted as indicating missing lines in Letter 53. In order to avoid the overuse of *sic*, I have silently corrected a few spellings—*liesure, bretheren, d'ont* (and other contractions such as *hav'nt*). Such Briticisms as *labour, favour, criticise, emphasise,* and *sympathise* I have let stand, though Hayne is not always consistent in using them. *Shakspeare* I have also normally retained, though in some instances where several spellings of the name occur in the same paragraph I have used *sic*. There are several places where a parenthesis or quotation marks open but do not close, and I have left these passages as Hayne wrote them. Obvious slips of the pen I have corrected if retention might lead to misunderstanding. In short, I have tried to prepare a text that is faithful to the original, but one that is readily accessible to general reader and scholar alike.

Annotation is another matter. I have tried throughout to offer as much useful information in the notes as possible. The reader may consistently assume when annotation is not provided that either the information is conveniently available in desk dictionaries, encyclopedias, or handbooks of one kind or another, or that I am not able to supply it.

Chronology

1830	Paul Hamilton Hayne, son of Paul Hamilton Hayne and Emily McElhenny Hayne (and nephew of Sen. Robert Y. Hayne), born in Charleston, South Carolina, January 1.
1840s	Attends classical school of Christopher Cotes with Henry Timrod and Basil L. Gildersleeve.
1845	First verse published in Charleston *Courier*.
1847	Attends College of Charleston and graduates in 1850 with prizes in English composition and elocution.
1848	Begins contributions to the *Southern Literary Messenger* and the *Southern Literary Gazette*.
1851	Supports Robert Barnwell Rhett and secession and contributes to *Palmetto Flag*.
1852	Studies law with James Louis Petigru; marries Mary Middleton Michel, May 20; becomes assistant editor of *Southern Literary Gazette* (May) and editor in December.
1854	Sells interest in *Gazette*. Visits Boston in fall and reads proof on *Poems* (published in November but dated 1855).
1856	Accepts post as editor of *Russell's Magazine* and makes canvass of state in fall and winter to secure support for the soon-to-be-published journal.
1857	Edits *Russell's* for most of its run (to 1860); *Sonnets, and Other Poems* published in Charleston.
1859	*Avolio* published in November in Boston (dated 1860).
1860	Actively supports secession with contributions to Charleston newspapers.
1861	Aide-de-camp to Governor Francis Pickens from November until March, 1862. Poor health compels resignation.
1862–1865	Lives in Charleston, Greenville, and Edgefield, and contributes to Confederate periodicals.

1865   Moves to Augusta, Georgia, in July, serves as news editor
       of the Augusta *Constitutionalist* until November, and seeks
       to reestablish position with northern magazines and pub-
       lishers.

1866   Settles family at Copse Hill, near Augusta, and contributes
       to the *Round Table*, the *Galaxy*, and other northern peri-
       odicals.

1867   Serves as literary editor of *Southern Opinion* (Richmond;
       until 1869) and of *Southern Society* (Baltimore; until 1868).
       Begins correspondence with Margaret Junkin Preston.

1868   First letter to Sidney Lanier; contributes to *Appletons'
       Journal* and *Lippincott's*.

1870   Begins exchange of letters with Whittier. Sells first poem to
       Scribner's Monthly. With death of William Gilmore Simms
       in June, begins to assume role as leading literary spokesman
       for the South.

1872   *Legends and Lyrics*, first postwar collection, published in
       Philadelphia. First postwar verse sold to *Harper's New
       Monthly* and the *Atlantic Monthly*.

1873   Edits *Poems of Henry Timrod*, published in New York; vis-
       its Baltimore, Philadelphia, New York, and Boston (June–
       October) on first trip north since war.

1874   Renews correspondence with Maurice Thompson.

1875   *Mountain of the Lovers* published in New York.

1878   New collection of verse declined by both Holt and Putnam,
       and John G. James proposes an edition by subscription.

1879   Last trip north; visits Whittier, Longfellow, Holmes again,
       and others in New York and Boston; begins correspon-
       dence with Philip Bourke Marston.

1880   D. Lothrop, Boston, accepts latest edition of poems in No-
       vember; writes poem to celebrate centennial of Battle of
       King's Mountain.

1881   Asked by congressional commission to write ode to cele-
       brate centennial of British surrender at Yorktown; writes
       official poem for International Cotton Exposition, Atlanta.

1882   Receives honorary degree from Washington and Lee Uni-
       versity; last collection, *Poems* (Complete Edition), pub-
       lished in Boston in November.

1883　Anniversary poems for the sesquicentennial of the founding of the colony of Georgia and the centennial of the incorporation of Charleston as a city, and poem for commencement ceremonies at Smith College, Northampton, Massachusetts.

1884　Begins correspondence with Andrew Adgate Lipscomb and Wilkie Collins.

1885　Begins exchange of letters with Charles Gayarré.

1886　Honored by a series of lectures on Shakespeare delivered by Lipscomb in Augusta in March and by a reception in Macon in May. Health begins to break in late May and after a stroke in June, dies on July 6, and is buried July 11 in public ceremony in Augusta, with Bishop John W. Beckwith delivering the eulogy.

List of Abbreviations

Hayne's works (only those works frequently alluded to are listed):

Poems. Boston: Ticknor and Fields, 1855 (published 1854).   P

Sonnets, and Other Poems. Charleston: Harper & Calvo, 1857.   S

Avolio; A Legend of the Island of Cos. With Poems Lyrical, Miscellaneous, and Dramatic. Boston: Ticknor and Fields, 1860 (published 1859).   A

Legends and Lyrics. Philadelphia: J. B. Lippincott, 1872 (published 1871).   LL

The Mountain of the Lovers; With Poems of Nature and Tradition. New York. E. J. Hale & Son, 1875.   MOL

Poems. Complete Edition. Boston: D. Lothrop, 1882.   PCE

A Collection of Hayne Letters, ed. D. M. McKeithan (Austin: University of Texas Press, 1944).   CHL

Works about Hayne:

Rayburn S. Moore, *Paul Hamilton Hayne* (New York: Twayne, 1972).   PHH

Depositories:

William R. Perkins Library, Duke University   Duke

Historical Society of Pennsylvania, Philadelphia   Hist. Soc. Pa.

Milton S. Eisenhower Library, Johns Hopkins University   Johns Hopkins

South Caroliniana Library, University of South Carolina   So. Car.

Introduction

In 1873 Paul Hamilton Hayne observed in a letter to a friend that the southern writer could expect from his own section and people "nothing—unless it be contumely, and a thinly-veiled contempt," a view he had expressed as early as the 1850s and one that he would repeat frequently. Though he acknowledged, on the other hand, that the northern public was more generous in its response to him and his work, he concluded in 1885, a year before he died, in a letter to another friend that, as far as "Yankee periodicals" were concerned, the "poor Southerner" stood "at the foot of the authorial class, unless he chanced to be a *clever* and unscrupulous *Renegade*."[1] Such comments, of course, were not new in the South. William Gilmore Simms had, on occasion, been saying much the same thing since the 1830s, but Hayne's experience serves as a better illustration than even Simms's or Poe's of the difficulties faced by the southern man of letters both before and after the Civil War.

The scion of a leading Carolina family, Paul Hamilton Hayne (1830–1886) was born in Charleston, the only child of a young naval officer and the daughter of a prominent Presbyterian minister. One of his ancestors was a revolutionary war martyr and two of his father's brothers were U.S. senators. Hayne was educated at a private school and was graduated with prizes in elocution and in English composition from the College of Charleston in 1850. Always a bookish youngster, he read the *Arabian Nights* , Froissart's *Chronicles*, Shakespeare's plays, Robert Burton's *Anatomy of Melancholy*, Sir Thomas Browne's *Religio Medici*,

1. See Hayne's letters of January 16, 1873, and March 9, 1885, to Mrs. Margaret J. Preston and Andrew A. Lipscomb, respectively. All letters by and to Hayne quoted or mentioned in the introduction and in the notes to the letters are, unless otherwise indicated, in the Paul Hamilton Hayne Papers, William R. Perkins Library, Duke University, Durham, N.C. For reasons of limited space, these two letters and a few other letters quoted in the introduction have not been included in this edition.

Robinson Crusoe, the fiction of Scott, Dickens, and Simms, and the poetry of Scott, Shelley, Tennyson, and Poe. Hayne began composing poetry himself at the age of nine, and his first published poem appeared in a Charleston newspaper when he was fifteen. Shortly thereafter his verse appeared in the *Southern Literary Messenger* and other magazines, and in May, 1852, after a brief period as a student of law with James Louis Petigru, Hayne became associate editor of the *Southern Literary Gazette*. By the following December he had taken over the management of the magazine and given up the law in order to concentrate on editorial duties. Subsequently, Hayne sold his interest in the *Gazette*, and by the time the Civil War began, he had published *Poems* (1855), *Sonnets and Other Poems* (1857), and *Avolio: A Legend of the Island of Cos* (1860), and had edited *Russell's Magazine* for three years. He even spent most of the war years on literature, for his health was so poor that he managed to serve only four months on active duty in 1861–1862. After the war he moved to Georgia and devoted the last twenty years of his life to writing for newspapers and magazines and collecting three more volumes of verse: *Legends and Lyrics* (1872), *The Mountain of the Lovers* (1875), and *Poems* (Complete Edition, 1882). He was known throughout the country either as the "poet laureate of the South" or as the "representative poet of the South" and was throughout the period a semiofficial spokesman on literary matters for the region. He was on friendly terms with a number of leading writers of his day and corresponded with many of them, including Longfellow, Whittier, Holmes, Howells, E. P. Whipple, E. C. Stedman, Moses Coit Tyler, Bayard Taylor, Lanier, Simms, J. E. Cooke, Margaret J. Preston, Constance F. Woolson, Maurice Thompson, and Charles Gayarré among the Americans and Swinburne, Charles Reade, R. D. Blackmore, Jean Ingelow, William Black, Wilkie Collins, and Philip Bourke Marston among the British. More than any other southern author of his time, save perhaps Simms, Hayne was a professional writer and man of letters.[2]

At the same time, Hayne's career characterizes the plight of the southern writer during the nineteenth century. Though he was not, like Poe or Timrod, forced to grub for a literary living before the Civil War

---

2. For a more complete account of Hayne's literary career, see Jay B. Hubbell, *The South in American Literature, 1607–1900* (Durham: Duke University Press, 1954), 743–57, and Rayburn S. Moore, *Paul Hamilton Hayne* (New York: Twayne, 1972), 15–32.

(quite in contrast to his experience immediately afterwards), he early realized, as indicated, that professing literature would not be easy. Nevertheless he gave up the study of law in 1852 and took over control of the *Gazette*. Subsequently he collected and arranged for the publication of his first volume of *Poems* in Boston, where in October, 1854, he wrote his wife, Mary Middleton Michel ("Minna") Hayne, that though "the fame of the true poet" had been the "darling dream" of his life and that a "literary career" would henceforth be his "doom," he acknowledged that it (the career) must be "subsidiary to some lucrative employment."[3]

Finding such employment was not a simple matter for Hayne in the 1850s. Though interested in politics, a family tradition, he had no ambition to run for office, and he had studied law only at his mother's urging. Having already contributed to the *Southern Literary Messenger* and to the Charleston newspapers and having edited his own magazine, Hayne continued to contribute, editorially and creatively, to periodicals north and south, including *Graham's Magazine*, the *Home Journal*, and the *Atlantic Monthly*, and he managed to supplement the family income with this work. Still, without his mother Emily Hayne's assistance, he would not have been able to publish his three collections of prewar poems, and he would have been hard put to support his wife and their son, William Hamilton Hayne, who was born in 1856.

When Hayne had assumed control of the *Southern Literary Gazette* in December, 1852, William Carey Richards, the former editor and proprietor, owed him eight hundred dollars for contributions and editorial work, a sum Hayne could recoup only by taking over the periodical. Nor did it become profitable under his own management, despite his efforts to appeal to a larger audience, and he subsequently sold his interest in 1854. As Simms could have told him (and doubtless did), southern journals usually failed for lack of reader support and capital. Even when southerners subscribed to a southern magazine, the editor could not count on receiving the subscription money due, and few magazines were otherwise adequately financed and patronized. Richards had sought to deal with such a financial situation in 1850 when he moved the *Gazette* from Athens, Georgia, to Charleston and later asso-

---

3. Even as late as November 12, 1876, Hayne warned his son William not to "dream of making Literature a profession. That would under the circumstances be madness," he continued. "Even Sir Walter Scott used to speak of employing literature as 'a stick, not a crutch'. . . . A poor man, especially in this age and at the South, must have a practical business, or one recognized as such!"

ciated it with the new publishing firm of Walker, Richards and Company. This important venture linked the publication of the magazine with a house that handled books as well, including Simms's *Golden Christmas* (1852) and *The Sword and the Distaff* (1852), but collapsed when an important source of promised capital failed to materialize.[4] The failure of this enterprise underscored the problem that dogged all efforts to establish publishing centers in the South, and since it was the most significant attempt to provide a literary capital for a section that was rapidly becoming aware of itself as a political and cultural entity, its failure was therefore all the more serious. To add insult to injury, two northern firms—Harper, and Ticknor and Fields—maintained during this same decade two successful literary magazines—*Harper's New Monthly* (1850) and the *Atlantic Monthly* (1857).

Despite this unfavorable experience and the subsequent demise of the *Southern Quarterly Review* in 1857, Charleston "littérateurs" set about the establishment of a new literary magazine in 1856. Two groups, one of which included Simms, Hayne, and Timrod, were involved in bringing *Russell's* to life, and to meet the old problem of insufficient financial support, plans were made to provide for the sale of stock in the enterprise and for the editor to canvass the state in its behalf. Hayne himself was appointed "literary" editor, and with the exception of two brief periods, served mainly as editor-in-chief throughout the magazine's three-year existence. But the sale of stock was slow, and in 1857 and thereafter Hayne was forced to admit to his contributors—Richard Henry Stoddard, a young New York poet, and John Esten Cooke, a rising Virginia novelist, among others—that payment for solicited contributions would be delayed. And, indeed, in the case of Stoddard's "Herod Agrippa and the Owl," Hayne managed to pay only sixty dollars for a poem he valued at one hundred dollars, and Cooke received only fifty dollars for "Estcourt; or the Memoirs of a Virginia Gentleman," a serial Hayne had requested in six installments and had promised to pay for at the rate of fifty dollars each. Hayne was embarrassed by such conditions, and in the case of Cooke, sought for two years to persuade Cooke to allow him to assume the debt personally.

---

4. See William C. Richards' letter to William Hamilton Hayne, September 20, 1886, in the Hayne Papers, Duke. For a discussion of Hayne's editorship of the *Gazette*, see Rayburn S. Moore, "Paul Hamilton Hayne as Editor, 1852–1860," in James B. Meriwether (ed.), *South Carolina Journals and Journalists* (Columbia: University of South Carolina, Southern Studies Program, 1975), 91–108.

Hayne's comment to Cooke on April 5, 1858, illustrates the plight of both southern writer and editor:

> By Heaven! it makes my blood boil to think of the indignities to which the Literary *guild* at the South, is everywhere subjected; *you* have written a story which should have brought you $400 cash, with the reception, so far of but $50; and I have labored strenuously on a *So Magn* designed to support the honor of our Section, *for upwards of a year*, without having rec*d* *6¼ cts* in *return.*[5]

Hayne, indeed, never received any money for his work on *Russell's*, a not unusual situation for a southern magazinist before the war and one about which he and Simms and others complained to no avail.

Throughout his career, as has already been suggested, Hayne constantly protested about the treatment of writers in his own country. He felt that they seldom received their due, least of all in the South. In the 1850s he observed to Stoddard and Horatio Woodman, a Boston friend, among others, that people in Charleston and Carolina in general neither bought his books nor respected his art. "A more unfortunate home for an artist (whatever his degree!)," Hayne wrote Woodman on August 19, 1860, "could not be found in the broad circle of Christendom!" "The people," he continued, "are intensely provincial, narrow-minded, and I must add—*ignorant*. Literature they despise. Poetry they look upon as the feeble pastime of minds too effeminate to seek manly employment!"[6]

The situation after the Civil War had, if anything, grown worse (the results of the war, of course, could hardly have improved the immediate prospects for literature), and Hayne expressed himself forthrightly in 1866 to a northern correspondent who had written for his autograph:

5. This letter is printed in full below (no. 10). A few months later in the July issue of *Russell's* Hayne wrote that the "Southern literary journalist must be content with little praise and no profit" and "must be prepared for sneering opposition, shallow criticism, for a superabundance of 'kind advice,' and a beggarly meagerness of *substantial* aid." In 1885 he could still marvel "at the unconscious audacity with which . . . I coolly and cheerfully accepted one of the most difficult, exacting, and thankless positions imaginable" ("Ante-Bellum Charleston," *Southern Bivouac*, n. s., I [November, 1885], 330). The account of Hayne's experience with *Russell's* is based upon Moore, "Hayne as Editor," 94–103. For other recent discussions of *Russell's*, see Richard J. Calhoun, "The Ante-Bellum Literary Twilight: *Russell's Magazine*," *Southern Literary Journal*, III (Fall, 1970), 89–110; and Alton T. Loftis, "A Study of *Russell's Magazine*: Ante-Bellum Charleston's Last Literary Periodical" (Ph.D. dissertation, Duke University, 1973).

6. This letter to Woodman is printed in *Proceedings of the Massachusetts Historical Society*, LIV (January, 1921), 181–84.

> Here at the South a man of literary tastes is looked down upon by the gen-
> erality of people—aye! even by gentlemen of some culture and unquestion-
> able social position, as a mere *idle* Dreamer, an unpractical fool, a drone in
> the great business hive, a species of Pariah, against whom every dry goods
> Clerk and cloth-yard Apprentice is privileged to launch the small arrows
> of his scorn and ridicule! Any *little* reputation my verses may have gained
> me, I owe almost entirely to the journals and the Public of the *North*, and
> altho I trust that few surpass me in rational patriotism and a love for my
> own unfortunate Section,—yet the truth must be confessed—a more un-
> cultivated, soul-less, and grovelling set of Yahoos (so far as Letters, *poetry*
> especially, are concerned) never cumbered the Earth, than these same peo-
> ple of what is called "the earnest tropical and passionate South!!"

At times Hayne even felt that his own family (excepting, of course, his wife and mother) despised his chosen field, and he remarked to Mrs. Margaret J. Preston, the Virginia poet and an old friend, on January 18, 1873, that these relatives regarded him "half contemptuously, as a 'wool gathering,' unpractical, impecunious visionary who has somehow broken faith with his family traditions—for you must know that the Haynes pride themselves upon what they call their 'clear common sense'—which means, briefly, their blindness to all the fair world of imagination and the graces of the highest spiritual culture."

Despite such a lack of encouragement and support, Hayne had again committed himself to a literary career after the war was over, had taken a position with the Augusta *Constitutionalist* in July, 1865, and in the following year, had moved his family to a small clapboard house on eighteen acres of land near Grovetown, Georgia. There he settled into a full-time career of contributing poetry and prose to newspapers and magazines throughout the country and of serving in various edi-torial capacities on many southern periodicals.

Hayne described his situation in a series of letters to Simms in 1869. On February 23 he observed: "For myself, I continue my old humdrum existence in the pine-land Solitude, studying, and composing for such periodicals, Northern or Southern, as are able and willing to 'pay the piper' moderately."[7] By this time Hayne had contributed to the *Round Table*, the *Old Guard*, the *Galaxy*, *Appletons' Journal*, and *Lip-pincott's Magazine*, among others, in the North; to *Scott's Monthly*, the *Land We Love*, the *New Eclectic*, the *Southern Field and Fireside*, and

---

7. This letter and others to Simms quoted subsequently are printed in Daniel M. McKeithan (ed.), *A Collection of Hayne Letters* (Austin: University of Texas Press, 1944), 210–17.

the *Southern Review*, among others, in the South; and he had served as literary editor of *Southern Opinion* in Richmond and of *Southern Society* in Baltimore. Most of the northern magazines paid him for his contributions, but few southern journals were able to pay, and Hayne frequently complained about the money owed him by *Scott's Monthly*, *Southern Opinion*, and other periodicals.

On April 25, 1869, he elaborated on his literary circumstances:

> Tho not associated at present with any *one* periodical, in an editorial capacity, I contribute to nearly all: composing a story or essay today for the full-blown adult monthlies, and tomorrow entering the lists of fancy for the benefit of the Juveniles. . . . Only by becoming an absolute *free lance*, or a *Bohemian* of letters, can a man, of my *light calibre*, make his bread now-a-days. Fame, posthumous renown . . . I must leave to my intellectual betters. . . .
>
> But I have imbibed a thorough taste for the existence of the *Solitaire*.
>
> Of course, its disadvantages are patent—, but 'tis not without compensating pleasures, and *uses* too.
>
> The *money-question* could nowhere be solved as readily as it is here. Upon an income of Lilliputian proportions, one can at least be comfortable—One suit of clothes will last for indefinite periods—, and for *half the year*, one's Garden supplies all, or most, that we need to support us.
>
> There's no show, or humbug of any kind, —no necessary *social drains* upon one's scanty exchequer. Therefore, I'm settled here, for life—perhaps.

He continued in this vein on May 17.

> Indeed, I have come to consider my position fortunate. *Leisure* I can command in abundance—many of the new books, and all the best periodicals (English and American) reach me. I have nothing whatever to do with the wretched turmoil of cities, and as for politics and tyranny,
>
> "Stultorum regum, et populorum continete [?] aestus!" "the eternal rage of stupid people and stupid rulers,"—it howls afar from this quiet nook, and even its echoes—except as they reach me faintly thro the papers—are disregarded and unheard!
>
> Yes, had I but health, I should be that *rara avis*—a contented mortal. An important *desideratum*, truly, yet to be borne—with the exercise of proper patience!

His career gradually improved in the 1870s. With the death of Simms in 1870 and the publication of Hayne's own *Legends and Lyrics* in 1872 and his memoir and edition of Timrod's *Poems* in 1873, Hayne became the chief southern spokesman on literary matters, as Whittier acknowledged in a letter of February 5, 1873, shortly after the publication of the Timrod volume. "To thee and John R. Thompson," the Quaker poet remarked, "now that Simms and Timrod are gone, the

South must look for its literary leaders." (Ironically enough Thompson was struggling through his last illness when Whittier's letter was being written, and he died on April 30, 1873). And Constance Fenimore Woolson's characterization of Hayne in 1875 as the "representative poet of the South" expressed the general view of his peers north and south.[8]

The critical response to Hayne's books of the period—*Legends and Lyrics, The Poems of Henry Timrod*, and *The Mountain of the Lovers* (1875) was widespread and favorable. Hayne's first postwar collection was reviewed by Whipple in the Boston *Evening Transcript*, Howells in the *Atlantic Monthly*, Stoddard in the *Aldine*, and Mrs. Preston in the *Southern Magazine*, among others. Whipple, for example, cited the book as containing "the ripest results of the genius of the most eminent of living Southern poets," and he concluded by congratulating "the South on possessing such a poet. If it has any culture or taste, outside of politics, it must pride itself on such a product." Such a statement, of course, was thrice welcome to one who often felt his work was neither bought nor appreciated in his own region. Even more satisfying to Hayne was Howells' notice in the *Atlantic* which praised the collection but chided the poet for being too much influenced in his narrative poems by William Morris. When Hayne responded by informing Howells that all of "The Wife of Brittany" and most of "Daphles" had been completed before Hayne had read Morris, the editor of the *Atlantic* issued a correction in the next number of the magazine. Hayne observed to Mrs. Preston on May 19, 1872, that the monthly had "absolutely been guilty of a piece of *pure justice*." The most generous praise of *Legends and Lyrics* came from Mrs. Preston, who wrote Hayne on February 1 that she had tempered her praise in her review for fear of editorial change but that she actually thought the collection "the truest book of poems that has ever come from a Southern singer. There is none," she continued, "in the range of my knowledge that can compare with it in fine, polished artistic work—real poet-work."[9]

8. Constance Woolson's letters to Hayne are in the Hayne Papers, Duke, but are quoted in part in Jay B. Hubbell (ed.), "Some New Letters of Constance Fenimore Woolson," *New England Quarterly*, XIV (December, 1941), 715–35.

9. Whipple's review of *Legends and Lyrics* appeared in the *Evening Transcript*, February 5, 1872; Howells' in the *Atlantic* for April, 1872; Stoddard's in the *Aldine* for March, 1872. For other contemporary comment on this collection, see Maurice Thompson's review in the Indianapolis *Journal*, November 14, 1874, and Sidney Lanier's article in the *Southern Magazine*, January, 1875.

Yet Hayne had sent the manuscript of *Legends and Lyrics* to several houses which wanted substantial subsidies before publishing the book, a fairly normal arrangement for a northern firm that was considering a collection of poems, even when the subject matter was not controversial, by a former Confederate officer. Finally, J. B. Lippincott in Philadelphia agreed to bring out the volume if Hayne "assumed the initial expense of publication" and would be willing to share any profits that might accrue.[10] Hayne accepted the terms, borrowed money from his mother, and discovered to his dismay, eighteen months after publication, that his share of the profits amounted to five dollars. His reaction was to characterize "the Lippincotts" as "complete scamps" in a letter to his wife of July 13, 1873. Despite such treatment, Hayne admitted that the criticism of *Legends and Lyrics* had advanced his reputation without increasing the size of his pocketbook.

The reception of *Poems of Henry Timrod* was also favorable, though much of the attention was focused on the editor's biographical and editorial contribution and on the poet's constant struggle to make a living. Indeed, in a letter to Hayne of April 20, 1873, after a second edition had appeared, Mrs. Timrod noted an "absence of criticism" in many of the notices, and Hayne acknowledged to Mrs. Preston on April 15 that "my life-sketch of the poet did—as you intimate—secure the public attention and deep pity, and, so, these feelings moved them to read his verses with an indulgence, and almost a loving gentleness, which could not otherwise have been elicited." John Greenleaf Whittier, on the other hand, was concerned that Timrod's genius should be recognized at the same time that Hayne's editorial tribute should be appreciated. "I hope and believe," he wrote Hayne on February 5, 1873, "that the time has fully come when no sectional feeling will interfere with the recognition of his genius." Eventually the edition was even reviewed in the London *Literary World* on January 9, 1874. Hayne's "labor of love" had succeeded indeed.

Though *The Mountain of the Lovers: With Poems of Nature and Tradition* was well received by the critics, Hayne had again had difficulty finding a publisher. Osgood, Roberts Brothers, and Lippincott's all were willing, according to Hayne, to "undertake *half the expenses* of the work, and offer a fair per centage on sales," but, he wrote Mrs. Preston on October 24, 1874, "I had hoped they would take *all* the risks at

---

10. Moore, *Paul Hamilton Hayne*, 56.

this late day (the 11th hour of my artistic existence!)." A few weeks later he commented on other "rebuffs" in a letter of December 1 to Mrs. Preston:

> One of these days I'll outline for your amusement and edification the long *series of rebuffs*, disappointments, neglects and contempts to which I too have been subjected! Only recently my poetical *MSS* (arranged for publication in book form) have been unceremoniously rejected by *every* prominent *belles lettres Publishing* House in the *U. States*! Yet, as you observe, they accept the performances of the Nora Perrys, the Miss Hudsons, the whole "mob of gentlewomen and gentlemen that 'write with ease' (but furnish heavy reading), as if they were of the 'few, the immortal names, that were not born to die!'" Confound their ——— taste!

All this, of course, despite Hayne's growing reputation and standing. Finally, early in 1875, E. J. Hale and Son, a firm owned by North Carolinians in New York City and publisher of Hayne's edition of Timrod's poems, agreed to publish the collection on the basis of an "advance" from Hayne with the understanding that this sum would be returned to the author from the first sales and that subsequent sales would be shared on the usual terms.

The Mountain of the Lovers was widely reviewed, notably by Whipple and Maurice Thompson in the Boston *Evening Transcript* and Indianapolis *Journal*, respectively, and by the *Aldine, Appletons' Journal*, the *Atlantic, Harper's New Monthly*, and *Scribner's*. Whipple characterized the collection as Hayne's "best" because it "exhibits his genius in the maturity of its power." A reviewer in the Boston *Daily Advertiser* asserted that Hayne was "now without question" the "Poet of the South," a view that Thompson also expressed in describing Hayne as "our only truly representative Southern poet." Moreover, a number of the critics, including Thompson and those in *Appletons' Journal* and *Christian Union*, thought that Hayne succeeded best with nature and with the "scenes and incidents" of his own experience. Several reviewers also maintained that the collection reaffirmed Hayne's position as a writer of sonnets. Thompson, for example, concluded that, with the exception of Lowell, Hayne was the "best sonneteer in America." On the whole, Hayne's work in the 1870s and the critical response to it contributed to his establishment as the leading literary spokesman of the South, though his reputation failed to guarantee him a stable livelihood.[11]

11. For reviews and notices of *The Mountain of the Lovers*, see the Boston *Evening Transcript*, June 22, 1875; Indianapolis *Journal*, May 29, 1875; *Southern Magazine*, Sep-

Even more important, however, to Hayne's literary position was the critical reception of the last collection of his *Poems* in 1882. This so-called Complete Edition, hardly complete since Hayne left out many early poems and did not, of course, include any poems written after the summer of the year of publication, provided an occasion for an appraisal of his canon, an opportunity which many reviewers readily embraced.

In the beginning a subscription book, the Complete Edition attracted the attention and support of many of the leading poets and writers of the day—among them Longfellow, Whittier, Holmes, Whipple, Stedman, Boker, Tyler, and Lanier—but since it was difficult to find reliable canvassers (around two hundred mail orders were received), John G. James, a Virginian who had migrated to Texas after the war, had become president of Texas A & M College, and had persuaded Hayne in 1878 that a subscription sale with James in control of publication might work, decided eventually to try to get the book published in a more conventional manner. D. Lothrop, a reputable Boston firm, agreed to assume all risks and to undertake its publication on a modified subscription basis in 1880, and two years later the Complete Edition appeared in time for the Christmas trade.

The reviews were slow in coming out, for Lothrop was chary of sending out many review copies before the book was widely distributed, but Hayne himself sent out some copies and reviews followed.[12] Several important considerations of the collection appeared in March. The *Literary World* in Boston examined the book in its March 10 number.

> The uniform excellence of his work is something remarkable; he took
> a lofty standard from the first, and has kept it throughout his entire career
> and while it is easy to trace a growing thoughtfulness and a more complete
> mastery of expression in his later poems, the earlier show no deficiency in
> imaginative power, in ideal perception, or in lyric grace. This is no doubt

tember, 1875; *Aldine*, September, 1875; *Appletons' Journal*, June 26, 1875; and *Christian Union*, July 14, 1875. The comment in the Boston *Daily Advertiser* is from Hayne's clipping file, Duke, and the date has been cut off.

12. Two years later Lothrop was still reluctant to send out review copies. Daniel Lothrop himself informed Hayne on June 25, 1884, that the sale of the book had "been quite limited," but that he planned to advertise it in "some of our magazines in the fall and also send to some English periodical for review." On December 29, Mrs. Ella F. Pratt, one of Lothrop's editors, wrote Hayne that the firm still wished to "defer" sending copies to reviewers, though she promised that copies would be readily available when a new edition appeared.

due to Mr. Hayne's inherent genius, which is descriptive, and not philosophical. He does not undertake to solve the problems of the universe, although these problems come to him as they must come to every thinking man. These he formulates in a mystic fashion of his own, as if he were pleased with their very mystery, and passes on to seek his inspiration in the external aspects of nature.

From this point the writer goes on to take up individual poems and to conclude that Hayne is entitled to an "honourable place among the minor American poets."

A more generous critique of the Complete Edition had appeared a few days earlier in the Chicago *Sunday Times* for March 4. Written by an old friend, James Maurice Thompson, a reconstructed southern lawyer, poet, and writer who had removed to Indiana after the war, the article characterizes Hayne as a "lyrist of no uncertain power" and ranks him, along with Holmes, Lowell, and Whittier, as one of the four best living poets in America. "At many points," Thompson adds, Hayne "is not surpassed by any American poet." This is, of course, the partial judgment of a friend, but it is a view that Thompson expressed on several occasions during Hayne's lifetime—even after the two had quarreled over the merits of Thompson's novel, *A Tallahassee Girl*, in the summer of 1882—and one that changed only after Hayne's death and after modifications in poetic tastes had occurred.[13]

A more judicious notice, at least as far as mid-twentieth-century views are concerned, appeared in *Harper's New Monthly* in June, 1885. Charles Deshler, editor of *Harper's* "Literary Record," praised the "maturer poems" for their "melody, impassioned poetic feeling," and for their pictures of nature's "changeful and glowing features," but he was not unmindful of the mixture of virtues and limitations in some of the poems. "Many," he acknowledges, "are immature, many are defective in some detail of form or spirit," but, he also maintains, "in all there is visible a sensitive and loyal conscientiousness begotten of their author's ever-present idea of the loftiness and dignity of the poet's calling, with the effect of curbing the vagaries of his rich and versatile fancy and chastening his active imagination."

Hayne's correspondents were even more enthusiastic about the Complete Edition. Moses Coit Tyler, a onetime member of the editorial

13. For a more complete discussion of the Hayne-Thompson relationship, see Rayburn S. Moore, "The Old South and the New: Paul Hamilton Hayne and Maurice Thompson," *Southern Literary Journal*, V (Fall, 1972), 108–22.

staff of the *Christian Union* and subsequently a teacher at Michigan and Cornell, acknowledged receipt of a presentation copy of the "noble and beautiful volume" on November 22, 1882. "How glad I am," he remarked, "to see all these exquisite poems gathered together in so stately a form. It seems to give body and might to your fame; and to your circle of readers—immense extension and perpetuity."

A later member of the staff of the *Christian Union*, Hamilton Wright Mabie, wrote on March 3, 1883: "I am drinking in your volume and finding it full of the bouquet of genuine poetry. You have certainly lived deeply if not widely, and that is the main thing in life. A true poet, whose roots strike into the mysterious soil below consciousness, is always a wonder and a gift from heaven."

A few days afterwards, on March 15, Maurice Thompson reiterated the generous opinion he had expressed in his review, but he urged Hayne not to "become sectional or local," for such a stance would "hinder your just recognition as a national poet." "Stand by the nation and the world," he commented. "Forget, as a poet, that there ever was a so-called Confederacy. A poet must have wide visions, and you have. You are a noble poet, and I wish to see you take your true place."

On April 7 Philip Bourke Marston, the English poet and a friendly correspondent, commented on Hayne's "unfailing" instinct for the "loveliness of nature" and on the "wide range" of his "powers." "It is seldom," he observed, "that one finds an imagination so agile, so able to pass from grave to gay, from the sternesses of philosophy to the fragrant delicacies of love."

But the most favorable comment of all came from the best-known American critic of poetry of the time, Edmund Clarence Stedman. "On the whole," he wrote on December 20, 1882, "your 'Complete Edition' is a beautiful success—in every way such a voucher and witness as an American poet may be proud to bring forward. There is something in dimensions, as Landor has asserted, and one now sees, for the first time, how important and genuine your life-long [*sic*] has been. Nor is there an affected, careless, untrue piece of workmanship in the entire collection." Too fulsome, surely, but indicative on the other hand of Hayne's increasing stature in the American community of poets.

At the same time, Hayne's enhanced reputation did little for the sale of the Complete Edition. Not only was Lothrop reluctant to send out review copies but Hayne received no royalty on the volume before he died in 1886, almost four years after its appearance. William Hamilton Hayne, indeed, went to Boston in 1887 and collected "'nearly a hundred dollars,' the first payment from the publishing house, the officials of which promised for the fourth or fifth time to bring out a new and cheaper edition in which all the errors of 1882 would be corrected," an edition that never appeared.[14] It is clear, then, that Hayne made no money from the sale of his collections of verse but that, nevertheless, the critical reception of his books was important to his reputation and that he made his living after the war by selling poems and essays to northern periodicals and eventually in the 1880s to some southern journals—*Home and Farm* and the *Southern Bivouac*—that were able to pay.[15]

Throughout the 1870s and 1880s Hayne also helped to affirm his literary reputation by corresponding with many of the leading writers in the North, especially Whittier, Holmes, and Longfellow, who, in turn, responded genially to the warm and respectful notes of a litterateur located far from the centers of literary and intellectual activity.

In 1870 Hayne launched a correspondence with Whittier that blossomed into a warm friendship and lasted until his death in 1886.[16] In 1873 and again in 1879 Hayne visited Whittier (Mrs. Hayne accompanied him in 1879), and the two poets, despite differences in politics, grew closer as the years passed. Hayne's relations with Longfellow and Holmes were less intimate than those with Whittier, but he knew them both over long periods—Holmes from 1854—visited them also on his trips to the North in 1873 and 1879, addressed poems to them on occasion, and corresponded for years on very friendly terms. Longfellow sought Hayne's help and advice on the collection and editing of the volume on the southern states in the series of *Poems of Places*, and Holmes

14. Moore, *Paul Hamilton Hayne*, 178. Incomplete royalty figures for 1892 to 1917 show that 483 copies were sold, but no statements of sales or royalties for dates prior to 1892 are in the Hayne Papers.

15. Richard W. Knott, the editor of *Home and Farm*, a Louisville semimonthly, and subsequently one of the editors of the *Bivouac*, another Louisville journal, sought Hayne's contributions in 1882 and thereafter paid him well for poetry (frequently forty or fifty dollars for a poem of fifty lines or more) and prose (five dollars per page).

16. For an account of the Hayne-Whittier friendship, see Max L. Griffin, "Whittier and Hayne: A Record of Friendship," *American Literature*, XIX (March, 1947), 41–58. Some of the correspondence between the two poets is printed in John Albree (ed.), *Whittier Correspondence from the Oak Knoll Collections, 1830–1892* (Salem, Mass.: Essex Book and Print Club, 1911); John B. Pickard (ed.), *Letters of John Greenleaf Whittier* (3 vols.; Cambridge: Harvard University Press, 1975); and McKeithan (ed.), *A Collection of Hayne Letters*. Other letters are in the Hayne Papers, Duke.

encouraged Hayne to write poems stressing the reconciliation of the sections after the war, a theme Hayne developed in "The Stricken South to the North" (1878) and dedicated to Holmes. When Hayne died in 1886, Whittier wired Mrs. Hayne on July 9: "The North joins the South in lamenting the death of her honored poet and in sympathizing with his family." On the following day, he offered his opinion of Hayne's character and reputation: "He leaves an honored name behind him, a true gentleman, a generous unselfish friend, a poet whose pure, lofty verse is now known and loved wherever the English language is spoken—he will have a place in the Valhalla of the country, with Longfellow and Bryant and Taylor who while living were his friends." On the whole, Hayne's cordial relations with Whittier, Longfellow, and Holmes—not to mention other prominent northern writers—helped considerably to solidify his literary reputation throughout the country.

Hayne's relations with less important northern writers were also vital to his reputation. His friendship with Moses Coit Tyler may be cited as a case in point. As an editor of the *Christian Union* in 1873–1874, Tyler had recommended that a number of Hayne's poems be accepted for publication. Later, after the publication in 1878 of his own *History of American Literature During the Colonial Period*, he recommended Hayne's poems to his own publisher and praised his work to friends and acquaintances in Boston and New York. On January 15, 1881, he characterized Hayne as a friend:

> I can hardly tell you, my dear friend, how heartily I respond to all your words of affection and friendship. You seem to be almost unique among men of this time in still indulging in the luxury of downright friendship, and in having the boldness to say so. . . . I must say that I cannot help being on rather better terms with myself for finding delight in a nature like yours, a nature that seems almost an anachronism in our cynical and mercenary age. I am hard driven by work and it is not likely that I shall be able to write to you as many letters as I should like. So let this letter testify to you across all the continent that lies between us of a friendship that will defy not only space but time.

Finally, there is strong evidence of Hayne's standing in the various honors he received during the last decade or so of his career. In the 1870s and thereafter he was elected to honorary membership in literary societies at Emory, Princeton, Davidson, Sewanee, and the Citadel; and to corresponding membership in the historical societies of Alabama and Georgia. He was invited to deliver an address at Emory, a series of lectures at Vanderbilt, and to serve as a member of the board of examiners at the University of Georgia. He was awarded an LL.D. by Washington and Lee University in 1882. Literary circles and clubs in Alabama, North Carolina, and Georgia bore his name, and shortly after his death in 1886, a school in Birmingham was also named for him. He was warmly received by Whittier, Holmes, Longfellow, Whipple, Stedman, Stoddard, Tyler, and others in New York, Boston, and New England on his trip north in 1879 and was "royally entertained" by Rowland G. Hazard, the wealthy Quaker industrialist, and Charles A. Coffin, a well-to-do Massachusetts manufacturer. Nor was he neglected at home, where he was feted at Charleston, Montgomery, Augusta, Atlanta, Macon, and Savannah. He was frequently appealed to for autographs and copies of his poems from lovers of poetry throughout the country, and he was asked, especially during the 1880s, to commemorate various public occasions with odes and lyrics: the centennials of the Battle of King's Mountain in 1880, of the British surrender at Yorktown in 1881 (for this occasion he was appointed "odeist" by the official commission of Congress), of the incorporation of Charleston as a city in 1883, and the sesquicentennial of the founding of the colony of Georgia in 1883 (for which effort he was given five hundred dollars, the largest honorarium he ever received for a poem). He was also asked to provide suitable verse for ceremonies at Smith College and the International Cotton Exposition in Atlanta; for birthday tributes in the *Literary World* to Emerson, Whittier, Longfellow, and Holmes; and for a variety of functions and memorials honoring the Confederacy and the Lost Cause.

Hayne's work, moreover, was not unknown in Britain and Europe. Swinburne praised some of his lyrics, Tennyson thought well of his sonnets, Victor Hugo commented favorably on his poetry, and Hermann Grimm reviewed the Complete Edition in 1883, praised Hayne's poetic "spirit," and translated one of the poems into German.[17] R. D. Black-

17. For Swinburne's opinion, see Cecil Lang (ed.), "Swinburne and American Literature: With Six Hitherto Unpublished Letters," *American Literature*, XIX (January, 1948), 348–49. Tennyson's view of the sonnets was frequently quoted in the 1880s. See, for example, A. A. Lipscomb's observation in the Richmond *Christian Advocate* for August 12, 1886: "Tennyson pronounced him [Hayne] the finest sonnet-writer of the age." In 1881 Hugo was quoted in several American newspapers as mentioning Hayne's poems favorably. Maurice Thompson refers to Hugo's opinion in two letters—October 10 and October 20, 1881. Grimm's review appeared in *Deutsche Rundschau* (May, 1883) and was translated by Charles W. Hubner, an old friend of Hayne's, and reprinted in the At-

more, the author of *Lorna Doone*, also thought highly of the Complete Edition and dedicated his *Springhaven* (1887) to Hayne. Wilkie Collins, like Grimm and Blackmore, was impressed with the Complete Edition, and when he learned of Hayne's death, he wrote Mary Hayne on November 13, 1886: "It is not possible for me to tell you how shocked and how grieved I was, when I opened your letter and read the first lines which told me that your husband's silence—as my dear and welcome correspondent—was the silence of death." Altogether, Hayne's stature was considerable in his own day, a situation all the more remarkable since his subsequent standing has declined so noticeably. This is not to suggest that Hayne's work and his reputation have not received justice from critics and literary historians, though it is true that neither has been given full attention, but it is worth remembering that, despite ill health, poverty, and a strong commitment to southern letters, in his own day many competent judges in America and abroad thought well of both poet and man. And his work and career may still serve as an example of the plight of the southern man of letters.

II

Hayne was a prolific writer of letters. He kept up a steady correspondence, especially after the war, with editors, publishers, and other writers and considered it his duty to encourage young writers, particularly southern ones, and to promote reconciliation and understanding between authors of the two sections. Letter writing he considered not merely as a "conventional mode of exchanging a few formal facts and ideas, but [as] a blessed means—if we choose to avail ourselves of it—of exchanging the best cordialities of the heart, and the truest thoughts of the mind." By 1877 he was averaging "from 6 to 700 [letters] per annum." He obviously felt his isolation in the Georgia pine barrens and yearned to keep in touch with other literary folk at home and abroad. Thus it is not strange that he wrote many prominent authors in the North, in his own section, and in Britain. As I have already noted, he corresponded with Longfellow, Whittier, Holmes, Bryant, Lowell, Whipple, Howells, Stedman, Stoddard, Taylor, Fields, Tyler, Constance Fenimore Woolson, Harriet Waters Preston, Charlotte Fiske Bates, among others in the East and New England; with Simms, Timrod, La-

---

lanta *Southern World* (September 1, 1883). See also Hubner's letter to Hayne of August 27, 1883. Grimm translated Hayne's "A Character" into German.

nier, John Esten Cooke, John R. Thompson, Maurice Thompson (in Indiana after the war), Margaret Junkin Preston, Andrew A. Lipscomb, and Charles Gayarré in the South; and with Tennyson, Swinburne, Charles Reade, William Black, Jean Ingelow, R. D. Blackmore, Philip Bourke Marston, and Wilkie Collins in England.[18]

Margaret Preston thought Hayne the "prince of correspondents," and Marston, Lipscomb, and Gayarré, among many of the aforementioned, also praised his letters. Though he never met Mrs. Preston, Hayne corresponded with her for almost twenty years, and his epistles to her reveal many facets of his personality and aspects of his literary artistry and career.[19] The style is sometimes pungent, sometimes florid, sometimes periodic, sometimes idiomatic, but always fascinating and interesting. The topics are mostly literary and personal—talk about books, authors, editors, publishers, magazines; discussion of and comment on manuscripts of work in progress; and descriptions of the personal situations and homelife of two formerly affluent members of prominent families now fallen on hard times and circumstances. Mrs. Preston herself once characterized his letters as "full of pleasant talk and sentiment and nice criticism," and on February 3, 1873, she remarked: "Madame De Stael somewhere says, that after she became a writer of books, she never troubled herself to take the least pains with her letters. You do not follow her example—being willing to expend upon my gratification and entertainment as much time, eyesight and mechanical labour of writing, as would finish with a magazine article. This is exceedingly good of you." Hayne, in turn, acknowledged how much her epistles meant to him and his household. "It is hardly necessary for me to say how welcome they were," he wrote on September 9, 1872, in reply to two letters she had written, "and how eagerly we devoured their contents. In truth, separated as we are from the world of society—living the lives of almost veritable *hermits* in the shadows of great woods, *letters* are to us *inexpressibly* dear; i.e., of course when they come from *congenial friends*." As the years passed, the friendship

18. Hayne's letters to several of the British writers, Miss Ingelow, for example, are no longer easily found or readily available.

19. The correspondence between these two poets is too full to exemplify adequately in this volume. Mrs. Preston returned to Mrs. Hayne approximately 150 of Hayne's letters after his death, and this total apparently did not include all he had written her. Accordingly, the exchanges between Hayne and Mrs. Preston (as well as the equally long ones between Hayne and Marston, Lipscomb, and Gayarré) can only be represented and illustrated in a selection of this type.

deepened and Hayne frequently expressed his gratitude for her letters. "I must answer your beautiful and affectionate communication at once," he informed her on July 26, 1878, and after acknowledging that it had "deeply touched" him and was "dear" to his "heart and understanding alike," he took up the topic of death that she had introduced in a letter of July 21. On January 15, 1880, he characterized her letters as "beyond price," and a year later commented, as he had before and would again, on the literary benefits of their correspondence. "It is a sweet thought to me," he wrote on March 22, 1881, "that you and I—lonely workers in the field of Southern literature—can exchange (as it were) such artistic and poetic confidences." And on February 9, 1884, he paid her the ultimate compliment: "What you have been to me, O! dearest of Friends, as a literary Adviser and invaluable Critic in the by gone years, is known only to God, & to my own grateful & affectionate Heart!" Mrs. Preston, on her part, was equally grateful to Hayne. Despite frequent illness and gradual loss of eyesight, she criticized his poems in manuscript, reviewed *Legends and Lyrics*, published articles on Hayne in the magazines, penned an introduction to the Complete Edition, invited Hayne and his wife to Lexington, secured a scholarship for Hayne's son, William Hamilton, to Washington and Lee, and successfully recommended Hayne for an honorary degree at the same institution. And when Hayne was near death, she wrote Joseph A. Hill, Hayne's neighbor and old friend, on July 5, 1886, the day before Hayne died: "How fully I can enter into all you say about our dear friend. Such bravery, such high-heartedness, such uncomplaining endurance, such steady persistent [*sic*] in his honorable path—where shall we look for their like?" On July 9 Mrs. Preston responded to Hayne's death in a letter to Mrs. Hayne: "The world to me seems the poorer now that this friend has left us. How I shall miss his letters, his unvarying sympathy, his tender and kind words! I never had as true a literary friend, nor one I verily believe, who was so interested in me. What a deep regret it is to me that I never saw his face! And now, it never can be; we can only meet on the Hitherward Shore."

Philip Marston, the blind English poet and friend of Rossetti and Swinburne, also thought highly of Hayne as a correspondent, and though they were separated by the ocean, the two men became good friends over a period of seven years. Their letters usually were long, journal-like accounts of activities and opinions, frequently reaching a length of thirty or forty pages. Marston gossiped about the current literary scene in London and Hayne about literary matters in the New World. Hayne initiated the correspondence through Mrs. Louise Chandler Moulton, a Connecticut writer and a mutual acquaintance, in March, 1879. The two poets quickly took to each other, valued each other's letters, and published lyrics in each other's honor. On January 1, 1884, for example, Hayne thanked Marston "for the beautiful sonnet you have addressed to me" and urged him never "to stand upon ceremony" concerning immediate replies to his letters. "There are few persons, even blessed with every material sense and convenience of life," he continued, "who can compare with you as faithful correspondents. For the rest, it is pleasant to learn of the value you place upon my own letters, penned tho they may be in the remote backwoods of America; and you may be assured that so long as I retain the strength to lift my right hand, I shall continue to write to you, for this is to me, God knows, a genuine labor of love."[20] Marston's opinion of Hayne as letter writer had already been expressed on December 27, 1882: "Your letters are all charged with your own individuality, and pass so swiftly and naturally from grave to gay, are so varied, so full of anecdote and reflection, as to form delightful reading." In a long letter of thirty-eight pages begun on March 6 and concluded on March 31, 1885, Marston remarked: "As long as I am [able], it will always be one of my pleasures to write to you, and I fear only that my letters are such inadequate returns for your own brilliant and interesting communications, but in affection I think they are equal." When Hayne died in 1886, Marston wrote Mrs. Hayne on July 22 of his "passionate regret" concerning "the death of my dear friend your husband." "My regret," he continued, is

> all the more poignant because for weeks past I had meant to write and of course should have done so but for ill health which quite disqualified me from getting through any of my own work, besides being much worried in mind. Of course I had no idea that anything so dreadful was imminent and now too late I find that it was. Alas my very dear Mrs. Hayne I can say nothing except that my heart is with you in the dreadful night of desolation which must have come upon you. I dare hardly think of how black that night must be. . . . Only do not forget to remember how though we had not met I loved him and delighted in his letters which being gone will leave a very big void.

20. Marston's sonnet, "To Paul Hamilton Hayne," was later collected in *Wind-Voices* (1883) and subsequently in *The Collected Poems* (1892). Hayne's poem in honor of Marston, "Philip My King," a double sonnet, was collected in *Poems* (Complete Edition, 1882).

Another valued correspondent was Andrew Adgate Lipscomb, well-known Methodist divine and onetime chancellor of the University of Georgia (1860–1874). Lipscomb began the exchange of letters in 1884, and quickly became one of Hayne's most cherished correspondents during the last two and a half years of the poet's life. The topics discussed were usually of a philosophical, religious, or literary nature. In his first communication of January 25, 1884, Lipscomb, a "confirmed invalid," sent a "brother's greeting" and some verses and sermons he begged Hayne to accept "as a mark of my very high appreciation of your genius and admiration of your character." Hayne responded on February 7: "I am indeed proud and happy to have rec'd such a communication from one whom to know is to honor." He then discussed the sermons particularly and characterized them as "essentially prose-poems" in a style "at once virile and tender" and enclosed one of his own poems, presumably "Seed-Visions," as a means of expressing his thanks "for the pleasure and instruction derived from your productions." Moreover, this immediate rapport between the two was based not merely upon a congeniality of intellectual interests and opinions but also upon an empathy resulting from years of chronic ill health on the part of each writer. On April 22, 1884, only three months after he had inaugurated the correspondence, Lipscomb wrote: "Pencil or pen, your letters are always welcome. Nothing breaks the monotony of my chamber-life so pleasantly and so profitably, and the constant feeling of my heart is that Providence has added you as a gracious gift to my soul. Friends come to us at different eras of life, divinely suited to existing needs, just at the right moment in God's secret calendar, and they soon become one by laws that will be read and understood hereafter. For a long time, I yearned to know you. At last you have come and I am satisfied! Heaven bless our friendship!" In the following September, Lipscomb managed to visit Hayne at Copse Hill, and by the end of the first year of the correspondence, Lipscomb frankly acknowledged his debt on January 24, 1885: "You have revived my interest in life. You have been a lesson and an inspiration to my heart, and I am the stronger intellectually and the better spiritually because of the year's close fellowship with you." And Hayne had been no less moved. On December 3, 1884, he observed: "Your letters are indeed a great benefaction; I may go further & say they have assumed the importance to us here of an *Institution*! Could you see *how* they are welcomed, you would acknowledge that the above is no mere idle compliment, or vague figure of speech." Shortly thereafter in an article for the *Christian Advocate*, Richmond, Virginia, March 5, Lipscomb offered his view of Hayne the artist.

> Mr. Hayne is the best exponent of Southern literature we have had; and I say this in full recognition of Poe, Simms, Timrod, and Lanier. All these were men of genius . . . and yet, in point of original capacity, versatility, breadth of action, and exquisite naturalness combined with spontaneity, to say nothing of education and culture, it can scarcely be doubted that [Hayne] has given utterance to the Southern heart as no one else has done. I do not refer especially to his "War Poems," but to "Legends and Lyrics," and to "Later Poems" in the complete edition, 1882.

At the end of the year Lipscomb reiterated his gratitude for Hayne's friendship: "I often thank Providence that you came to me with so much beauty and blessing when I most needed heart and hope." And when Hayne died six months later, Lipscomb was prostrated with grief. He wrote Mrs. Hayne on July 12, 1886, six days after Hayne's death: "Such days as the last week, I have never spent in any season of affliction, outside my own household. I am overpowered. I cannot divert my mind, nor indeed would I, if I could divert it, from the precious recollections I have of him." The next day Lipscomb published a final tribute in the Augusta *Evening News*.

> The poet made good his "claim on our appreciation and homage," but still more the man evoked a finer regard and a sublimer reverence by virtue of the heroic manhood, which never once faltered or quailed in the most unequal struggle with the adversities of ill health and outward ills, I have ever witnessed. . . .
>
> Marvellous indeed it was that he did so much work, more marvellous that he did it all so well, and most marvellous that the friction of worldly circumstances and the vexations attendant on his earthly lot seemed to leave his creative power untouched. It is not the Poet but the Man that explains this mystery. . . . "In himself was all his state."

Unlike his friendships with Mrs. Preston and Marston, Hayne actually met Lipscomb on three or four occasions (Lipscomb paid at least two visits to Copse Hill), but in the main the Hayne-Lipscomb relationship was established and cultivated by correspondence.

Charles Gayarré, the Louisiana historian and man of letters, was the last correspondent to exchange an important series of letters with Hayne. On January 18, 1885, Hayne initiated the correspondence by writing the elderly historian (just turned eighty) about the first of his two rejoinders in the New Orleans *Times-Democrat* to George W. Cable's articles on the Negro in the *Century*. "It is right, it is *imperative*,"

Hayne maintained, "that a man of your exalted service and intellectual position should thus vindicate the character of his People against attacks from men who are far more dangerous than any *aliens* could possibly be because such persons are aliens in *heart, soul, affection,* and *principle,* while pretending to be 'to the manor [*sic*] born.'" Gayarré responded on January 23: "Commendation bestowed on me derives its value from the source whence it comes. The clear and sparkling stream that flows from the mountain top has always been the most pleasant to my eye." From this point the two "literary cavaliers," as Charles Anderson has called them, quickly grew intimate over matters social, political, and intellectual.[21] Hayne expressed on February 4 his "satisfaction at having formed your acquaintance as a Correspondent, even at the 11th hour" and soon set about seeking "full justice" for the almost penniless but very proud Gayarré. He spent considerable time and effort trying to see that his friend was properly honored in Louisiana and the South. "It seems to me *infamous*," he fulminated on November 3, 1885, that "such a People who owe you so much should refrain from making your last years comfortable, easy, and independent. By heaven! my brain grows hot, my heart furious, my blood boils when I reflect upon such atrocious ingratitude." Consequently, Hayne penned an article on Gayarré that appeared in the *Southern Bivouac* for June, July, and August, 1886, and for which he read proof less than three months before his death. Gayarré, in turn, assured Hayne on April 17, 1885, that "to have acquired your esteem and friendship is not the least of the few consolations which remain to me," and two weeks later the reserved octogenarian admitted to Mary Hayne: "There is so much intuitive congeniality between Mr. Hayne and what remains of my self that I keenly regret the distance which separates us. He reminds me of my noble friend Gilmore Simms whose loss I never can cease to deplore." On August 13 Gayarré acknowledged Hayne's intention to take "public notice" of his work and concluded that such notice was "compensation" enough. A month later he was urging Hayne to "nurse your health, husband your physical and intellectual resources and try not to allow yourself to be killed by *necessary* work, as Walter Scott and Simms have done. Old age has not yet closed for you the career of usefulness and fame."

21. For Anderson's consideration of the two writers, see "Charles Gayarré and Paul Hayne: The Last Literary Cavaliers," in David K. Jackson (ed.), *American Studies in Honor of William Kenneth Boyd* (Durham: Duke University Press, 1940), 221–81.

But old age in the sense of three score and ten was not to be for Hayne, and when he died in July, 1886, at the age of fifty-six, Gayarré wrote Mrs. Hayne on July 8: "I thoroughly believe that outside of his immediate family circle it is impossible to have had a keener appreciation of your husband's merits, whilst living, than I did, and to mourn more painfully for his loss. His friendship was the consolation and the pride of my old age. He was my last friend, and he is gone!" But Gayarré was not willing to give up Hayne completely. He had saved his letters and suggested to Hayne's son on August 31 that he (Gayarré) extract from these in order to show "the beauty of your father's soul and the richness of his intellect." "It would be," he continued, "Paul Hamilton Hayne painted by himself and what artist could do it better." Encouraged by the Haynes, Gayarré completed the article and sent it to Mrs. Hayne on December 19, 1887. It has never been published, but is a useful record of a literary friendship of the 1880s that reveals the plight of two old-fashioned gentlemen of the Old South trying to deal with their changed and changing circumstances in a new and less desirable day. Gayarré's conclusion, the partial opinion of a friend, notes the "chastity" of Hayne's mind and heart and the "purity" of his poems, an insight not without its irony in the context of Hayne's castigation of Cable and the people of Louisiana for their "atrocious ingratitude" to Gayarré.

> What may be said more specially for him than any other writer, as a very rare characteristic, is that he was gifted with a wonderful chastity of heart and mind which is strikingly apparent in his writings. There is in his poetical productions the modesty and purity of virginity. Each of his poems is a cameo Madonna. He seemed to be one in whom was incarnated Christian love. In an age when literature is tainted with so much impurity, this love was a vestal who sat by and watched over the fire of his inspiration. He has not penned a line which would shrink from being transcribed on an angel's tablets. Clothed in the imperial purple of poetry, each thought of his presents itself with the humility, the tenderness, the soothing physiognomy of a sister of charity. There was a sort of evangelic atmosphere around this apostle bard. It was his hard lot, by the apparently stern decree of Providence, but no doubt for some benevolent purpose in the end, to be cast on this earth, endowed with a spirit which could find in it but little congeniality.

III

Paul Hamilton Hayne, in summary, was the leading man of letters in the South after the death of William Gilmore Simms in 1870. Known as the "poet laureate of the South," "the representative poet of the

South," "the best of Southern poets," "the Longfellow of the South," "the foremost man of letters of his section," and "the most conspicuous figure of contemporary Southern literature," he took his reputation seriously and served as a literary spokesman for the South in periodicals throughout the nation.[22] His correspondence with other poets and writers in this country and abroad also manifests the usual interests, activities, and intellectual concerns of the man of letters who devotes himself to his craft and professes literature as a means of livelihood and as a way of life. At a time when such devotion and professions were rare in the South, Hayne, despite a long period of poverty, chronic ill health, and professional disappointment, single-mindedly made literature his end-all and be-all, and though he frequently complained about lack of public support, about editorial treatment and decision, about having to write for pay, he nevertheless committed himself to the literary life in a way few of his American contemporaries contemplated. "The few genuine men of letters in our section," he affirmed to Lanier on January 10, 1871, "ought and must stick together" since there were "but few poet-artists, South." Poetry, after all, as he pointed out on another occasion, was "its own exceeding *great reward*." "Never despair," he wrote Mrs. Preston on August 6, 1877, in an effort to persuade her not to give up writing poetry. "Never dream of 'giving up' what, after all, is the crown and glory of your earthly existence; nor of the *earthly existence only*! *Thro poetic thought spiritualized*, we pass from earth to heaven!" This view, in spite of periods of discouragement, he maintained throughout his postwar career, and it may well serve, in cameo, as a summation of his attitude toward literature as a profession and as a goal.

22. Hayne gave his occupation as "Literature" in the 1870 U.S. Census and "Poet" in the 1880 listing.

Selected Letters of
Paul Hamilton Hayne

*Copse Hill, Hayne's
home from 1866 to 1886*

To Mary Middleton Michel Hayne   MS Duke

Charleston Friday Dec. 31st 185[2]

Dear wife:

I was much disappointed in not receiving a letter from you on Thursday. I know you have written, but I suppose the mail has failed. I rejoice to tell you that the business which has so long worried us both is at last happily & satisfactorily arranged. I have, after mature deliberation, consented to take the "Gazette" at $800, knowing that I shall get that amount back in no other way.[1] I send you my notice to the Public but beg you, as I have done *them*, not to consider the first issue as a specimen of what the "Weekly News & Lit. Gazette" *will* be. I intend now to devote every energy I possess to the furtherance of the interest of my journal. I *must* make a living, nay! more, I must make a *comfortable* living. I cannot bear to think that my darling Minna should be put to inconvenience in any way from the lack of "dirty lucre"—& "dirty lucre" I shall therefore honestly try to gain. I had a long conversation with Alston yesterday upon the subject of my plans. He *entirely* approves them, & thinks I have acted with prudence, & good sense in not giving up to mother's whim ab't the Law—[2] I am *very* anxious to know how you propose to come down—not dearest! that I wd. wish to hurry you, but because I wd. like to arrange my plans accordingly. You don't know how desolate our room looks without you; and at *night* I am completely lost in our rambling bed that seems ab't three quarters of a mile too large for me. The old man is well but still desponding.—How fares it with the old lady? Charleston is if anything more dull than usual—however, as my fate seems irresistibly cast in the abominable place I must abide it. With my dear little wife to soothe my labours, & aid them too, I shall be happy & contented. I trust that my conduct hereafter will render her happy also—The thought shall never rise in her mind again that Hamilton does not love her! How is "Stupid"? Tell her I attended *John's funeral* the day before yesterday; and that she had better try her best now to secure Hamlet. Her former flame is married, so she has no chance in that quarter. How are they *all* at Mrs. Wilkinson's. Is

the dear old lady in her usual health & spirits—? & cousin Sep &
Dan'l, & Frank & all of 'em—how are they? My love to the whole fam-
ily.[3] And now, darling! being in a great hurry I must close this wretched
scrawl wh' I hope you can make out, with the assurance of my tenderest
love, & the hope that I may soon *hug* my *dear, dear,* "Small" once
more—

> Now, as I have *ever* been,
> Your deeply attached—
> Hamilton

1. W. C. Richards (1818–1892), editor and owner of the *Southern Literary Ga-
zette,* owed Hayne this sum for contributions and editorial assistance offered since the
previous May. As the title in Hayne's next sentence suggests, he combined the *Gazette*
with the *Weekly News* and changed the name accordingly.
2. William Alston Hayne (1821–1901), son of Robert Y. Hayne and therefore Paul
Hayne's first cousin. Though Emily Hayne (1806?–1879) had long cherished the hope
that her son would be a lawyer and though Hayne had studied law with James Louis Peti-
gru, one of the leading legal minds in the state, he had always preferred literature to
"Chitty and Blackstone."
3. Mrs. Hayne is visiting the Seabrooks at Grahamville. "Cousin Sep" Seabrook is
Mary Hayne's cousin and a close friend. The Wilkinsons, of Adams Run, are also related
to the Haynes. Mrs. Emma Wilkinson is the mother of Daniel and Frank.

2

To Mrs. Hayne   MS Duke

Boston Sep 2nd 1854

Dearest Minna;

Were I not so well acquainted with the character of the U States
mail, I should feel uneasy at the non-reception of letters from home dur-
ing the last week, but knowing as I do what a careless vagrant Uncle
Sam is in this particular, my fears are quieted. I wrote you at length on
Wednesday last about my progress in the composition of the Poem
which is to be the "leader" in my volume; since then I have arrived
within *fifteen verses* of the conclusion; think of that—Shortly every-
thing will be ready, & I shall get hold of my proofs—Ah! the latter will
be a glorious feeling. An author with his *first* proof-sheets is like a
mother with her first baby (By the way, how is *our* baby, the dear crea-
ture?) & generally makes a fool of himself over them.[1] Dearest, I sleep
with your likeness under my pillow, & whenever I wish to compose a
line particularly good, I give it a look, & a kiss—My life here is of the
quietest kind—I keep mostly to my room, work very hard, & spend as

little as I can—Ramsay, I learned yesterday from his friend, Mr. Dana, has *already*—much to my disappointment made his visit to this city—[2] Therefore I am all alone—Now it is that more than ever, I appreciate what my lot *would be* without you—When I come home Minna, I humbly trust to make you happier than hitherto—In the meantime, believe me I am scrupulously careful of myself—It seems to me, I am a good deal stouter than usual—& perhaps I shall return to Carolina quite a Falstaff—Be prepared to enlarge the borders of my garments. Fields says there is one verse in my longer Poem, which is grand—I wrote it in his store, while he stood by, defying me to compose a syllable in the noise, & confusion.[3] It describes the degradation of sensual passion, & comparing the soul to a tree, sapped of its green core, adds:

> "Thro whose dried branches to decay resigned,
> *Remorse rushed howling, like a hollow wind—*"

I like the last line, it expresses the idea accurately. The preparation of my book is about the hardest thing I ever attempted to do, but still I progress famously—How are they all at home—?. I am certain I shall hear to morrow; if not the mail will be subjected to certain hard terms. The cholera has disappeared almost entirely from the city—People are talking more of the yellow-fever in Savannah than of any local disease—

Do give my love to mother, (whose health I hope, is *entirely restored*), as also to Amelia, Myddleton, & everybody, who happens to care for me—[4] The instant I receive a letter from you I shall reply *in extenso*—Bear in mind that this is the *sixth* time I have written (counting the letter to mother) since my absence, which makes up the average of *three* times a week precisely—

God bless you my darling;

Believe me as Ever
Your affectionate Husband,
P H Hayne

1. The chief poem in the volume is "The Temptation of Venus." The reference to "our baby" is to Hayne's library, a point clarified in his letter of September 30, where he also observes: "My poems are progressing. I am adding several additional ones to the volume. You don't know how tremulous I feel about them. A hundred faults unnoted before, spring up like so many accusing ghosts."

2. David Ramsay, a classmate of Hayne's at the College of Charleston. Mr. Dana is presumably Richard Henry Dana (1815–1882), though Hayne himself knew Richard Henry Dana, Sr. (1787–1879), and later wrote a poem to his memory— *Youth's Companion*, LII (March 13, 1879), 86.

3. James T. Fields (1817–1881), a partner in Ticknor and Fields, the firm which published Hayne's *P*.

4. Amelia is an old family servant and Myddleton [*sic*] is William Middleton Michel (1822–1894), Mrs. Hayne's elder brother.

3

To Mrs. Hayne

MS Duke

Boston, Oct. [10] *1854*

My Dearest Minna;

Upon hearing of the death of my poor aunt, whose soul I trust is now at peace—I immediately wrote a postscript to a letter I had prepared the day before for Aunt Mary, & despatched the communication by the next mail. I do most sincerely trust she will receive it.[1] This morning I had the great satisfaction of receiving yours of the *2nd* inst. It is sad news you tell me of the death of Mary Seabrook.[2] True, I knew her but slightly, yet even in the partial acquaintanceship I cd. perceive how sweet, & endearing a woman she was. I shall write to cousin *Ben* to morrow, directing the letter to *your* care, in order that he may see that I sympathize, & sympathize deeply in the affliction of the family. They have been very, *very* kind to me, & I feel that I have not shown the gratitude I ought. Alas! & alas! how I have blundered on thro life! Circumstances, temperament, education, have all united to drift me down unfortunate currents of thought & action, but all may be amended, may it not? Your heroic attempts at disguise my dear wife cannot conceal from me the fact that you are very uneasy, & nervous about me. Your letters are sweet, & show a spirit of patience, & resignation, but I know you have been wretched all the time. Cheer up my little Minna, & think still of our meeting. And now, for a piece of good news. Whipple has seen parts of my main poem & pronounces favourably upon it, & Fields whose taste is very fine, says "it is full of the richest fancy & that portions of it are *grand*"—I use his own words—from no vanity Heaven knows, but in order that you may see what are my chances of success.[3] I feel quite light-hearted, & happy about it. Fame, the fame of the true Poet has been the darling dream of my life.[4] I have a dedicatory Sonnet darling to you, which I hope you will like. Every word in it leaped forth from the heart. I told you I think that I had added 2 or 3 new poems to the vol—Altogether the pieces will make some hundred & *twenty* pages—much more than I had any idea of—The cost of the book will be therefore a good deal more than was anticipated, viz. $180. To morrow I shall write to mother stating the facts, so that she may let me have something additional. I am sorry for this, but can't help it. Fields believes the volume will sell, in which case, I shall of course repay mother in full. By the way I have definitely made up my mind to enter into some *remunerative* business when I return. I shall continue of course to write for the "*News*," but with the stock of health I have now got laid up for 3, or 4 years (I am really stout & well) I can do a great deal more & by the beard of the Prophet I will *not* be a dependent.—And so Ben & Margaret, & the other servants have been doing well. Tell the former he shall receive "lickings" in abundance when I return, as I have grown very crabbed, & ferocious.

My love, dearest, to mother, & all my friends.

God bless you—Ever yrs;

Hamilton

1. Sarah Hayne (1800–1854), a sister of Paul Hamilton Hayne, Sr., had just died. Mary A. Hayne (1797–1875) was another sister of Hayne's father.

2. Mary Hamilton Seabrook, the daughter of a former governor of South Carolina and a relative of Mrs. Hayne's, had died on September 15.

3. E. P. Whipple (1819–1886), well-known literary critic and friend of Hayne. He reviewed *P* in *Graham's Magazine* for February, 1855. See Letter 4.

4. On October 27 Hayne wrote: "I think, my dear wife, that a literary career is henceforth to be my doom, not exclusively so perhaps (for I must make it subsidiary to some lucrative employment) but still in a great measure my heart & soul shall be in that work."

4

To Mrs. Hayne   MS Duke

Boston Nov 11*th* 1854

My Dearest Minna;

I rec*d* 2 letters from you yesterday. In one of these you speak of being very uncertain as to my movements. The last *three* letters which I despatched South, *one* of which you must have rec*d* ere this, will explain in full my situation. I am very *very* sorry dear wife to perceive how distressed, & low-spirited you are. It could not be otherwise. My absence has been protracted beyond all bounds. The reason you now know, & I think upon a calm review of the circumstances you can hardly blame me. I have been the victim of the lack of good faith in another. However, if I *do not* receive Mr. P[axton]'s remittance in a day or two, I shall despite all obstacles leave Boston next Wednesday, take the land-route probably—& be in Charleston by the 20*th* of this month. Before the reception of this letter, mother will probably have sent me a remittance in the form of a check on one of the banks here—That will make not the slightest difference—I have friends in the city, who will attend to the business for me—Do not think, my dear wife that I have not divined the *agony unspeakable* which you have suffered on my account this summer—Your letters have been *heroic*, but I know the feelings they have tried to mask. Let the Past be to you as a horrible dream—a nightmare that has departed forever. Before we meet let me tell you that I have been during the entire season systematically *careful* of my *health*. A rapid recovery from his late attack will return the wanderer upon your hands in much better condition than he expected—Ah! & then, we shall not part again, until one of us be called to the "undiscovered country from whose bourne no Traveller returns"—My book is done—& will be published very shortly. Whipple got a number of the proof-sheets from me a week since, & has I understand reviewed me most flatteringly in Graham.[1] But I expect, & am perfectly prepared for notices of a very different kind. The vol is not what I cd. wish it—ay! within fifty degrees—But I have been told that many of the Poems denote *promise* & that is all I care for—I will rise yet, dearest, & carry you up with me. Did you not receive the letter enclosing *your* Sonnet?[2] or has that too miscarried?—

On the 20th then, dear Minna, if Hamilton is in the world at all, he will be in Charleston[3] —May Heaven bless you—Love to Mother—

Your affectionate husband—
P.H.H.

1. See Letter 3, n. 3.

2. Hayne had mentioned the "dedicatory sonnet" in Letter 3.

3. In a later letter —November 16—Hayne described his plans again, and his arrival in Charleston had been delayed until Tuesday, November 21.

5

To Mrs. Hayne   MS Duke

Columbia Dec 6th 1856.

Dear Minna;

I have had no opportunity as yet of writing you in full as to the success of my lecture—What I said in the letter to mother yesterday presented a very imperfect outline indeed of the affair. The audience as I told you was small, but exceedingly select, all the *belles lettres* professors being present. When the address was over, Mr. Rivers (whose kindness I can *never* forget) came to me, his face all aglow, & said that I had at last laid the foundation of *real reputation in the State*, that among the Professors there was but *one* opinion as to the ability of the address, & lastly that he had *never* known a Columbia audience whose attention had been kept so firmly fixed, & who really seemed so deeply interested.[1] The next morning the "Carolinian" designated the Lecture as "masterly"—in a word, my success has been beyond expectation, & all who love me should feel encouraged, & gratified—

Dr. Thornwell I met yesterday. He wishes me to incorporate our new Magazine with the So Quarterly, & pledges himself to do all in his power to advance the project. I like his manners, & bearing—In fact, there is a heartiness about these upper-countrymen very refreshing to a Charlestonian.[2]

My chief reason for giving up the trip to Savannah, is, that there will be *no* chance of lecturing, or even canvassing for the magazine. I am assured by men of experience, that nothing but the material interests of the South are attended to at these Conventions.[3] I have just come from Rob*t* Barnwell's lodgings—He is *very* anxious that when I make my January tour thro the State, I should bring you & Willie to Columbia.[4] He will then have entered on his professional duties & will of course have a house in the "Campus." His sisters are to stay with him. He says that if it suits you, they will be *very glad* that you should remain with them while I am absent—

Expect me positively upon Monday morning—I have opened a subscription list which progresses famously—

By the way, cousin Isaac, Gen. Martin (!!) and cousin *Eliza*, attended my Lecture.[5] *The former* spoke very cordially to me afterwards, but I thought that cousin E—— looked exceedingly horrified at my unorthodox sentiments. That however, is a good sign.

Most Affectionately;

P H Hayne

1. Hayne was lecturing in behalf of the recently announced but yet-to-be-published *Russell's Magazine*, of which he was editor. William J. Rivers (1822–1909) was a professor of Greek and ancient languages at South Carolina College from 1856 to 1873.

2. James Henley Thornwell (1812–1862) served on the faculty and as president (1851–1855) of South Carolina College. In 1856 he became a professor of theology at the Presbyterian Seminary in Columbia and editor of the *Southern Quarterly Review*. Hayne declined his proposal to merge the *Review* with *Russell's*.

3. The Southern Commercial Convention was scheduled to meet the next week in Savannah.

4. Robert Barnwell (1801–1882), another former president of South Carolina College and a leading southern politician of the 1850s and 1860s, had known the Haynes in Charleston. Willie—William Hamilton Hayne (1856–1929)—was only nine months old.

5. Isaac W. Hayne (1809–1880) at this time was attorney general of South Carolina; Gen. William E. Martin, the husband of Eloise Mary Hayne, another cousin, was clerk of the state senate; and Eliza P. Hayne (1823–1863) was the oldest daughter of Eliza P. Hayne (1795–1875), one of Hayne's father's older sisters.

6

To Mrs. Hayne   MS Duke

Saturday 17th Jan 1857.

My Dearest Minna;

I mentioned last night the reception of your affectionate letter of the 10th, & the *great* relief wh' it afforded me. In travelling, (I know not why), the time passes slowly; a week seems almost like a month, one month like *two* or *three*. Thus, altho I have been absent from Charleston but *10 days* I have travelled so rapidly, & seen so much, that there is a singular disproportion between the *real*, and *apparent* lapse of the hours.[1]

At ½ 4 o'clock I reached *Charlotte* wh' is the *only* N.C. town I design visiting. I am exceedingly pleased with the appearance of the *place*—There is a neatness, and air of prosperity about everything, which to be candid, one misses in *So. Carolina*—Having armed myself with numerous notes of introduction, I trust to enlist popular favor in behalf of my magazine, my lecture, & myself—There's a string of Egotisms for you. I am glad that the major portion of Stoddard's new vol. pleases you—He is in my poor opinion the *Keats* of America. His delicacy of imagination, richness of coloring, & general Artistic power are *very* remarkable—[2] Uncle Arthur—if I may dare contradict so grand a seigneur—is wrong in regard to Winsboro'—The place is a poor place, & I have made up my mind to *cut it*—[3]

I have been quite amused by the surprise which is generally expressed in the up-country when I declare myself a *married* man. People seem to expect a *hoax*. At the same time it is rather disgusting to be mistaken continually for a *boy*.

On Monday evening next I hope to be able to deliver my *Lecture* here—The North Carolinians are somewhat jealous, (the Lord knows

why), of their S*o* Carolina neighbors; besides they are violent *Whigs*, &
these two causes uniting *may* procure me doubtful reception. Blessed
are those who expect *nothing*!!

I send by the mail of to day a letter to *mother*. Pray, if you have not
yet decided, decide at once to visit *Sep*. I *may* be detained beyond a
month. Here are my plans in a nutshell.

I lecture *here* upon Monday *the 19th inst*. On *Tuesday* I go back to
Columbia—On *Wednesday* I take the cars for *Greenville*, at wh' town I
shall arrive on the *afternoon* of the same day—*Thursday* , *Friday, Sat-
urday* & *Sunday*, (4 days *neither more nor less*) I expect to spend *there*.
On the ensuing Monday (the 25*th*) I travel to *Newberry*—on Wednes-
day (the 27*th*) to Laurens—(on *Thursday* 28*th*), to Spartanburg—On
Saturday (30th) to *Union*—Afterwards to *Cheraw, Camden*, & perhaps
one or *two* other villages—[4]

This will occupy my time until (probably) about the 12*th* or 13*th*
February—

Love to Mother & Amelia—Should you still remain at home, if not
love to *Sep*., cousin *Ben*, & *all* the kind friends with whom you are now
living—[5]

What would I not give to see *you*, and my *dear* little son at *this*
moment!!! May God bless you dear wife; & Believe me

Every Faithfully & truly *yrs*
Paul H. Hayne

1. Hayne had left Charleston on January 6 to canvass again for *Russell's*. He had
already visited Winnsboro, Chester, Yorkville, and other villages by this time, and he de-
scribes the rest of his itinerary in this letter.

2. Richard Henry Stoddard's *Songs of Summer*(1857). Hayne had met Stoddard in
New York in 1854 and had corresponded with him frequently. Hayne's characterization
of Stoddard as the Keats of America is a view he maintained consistently throughout his
career.

3. Arthur P. Hayne (1788–1867), one of Hayne's father's older brothers and U.S.
senator from South Carolina in 1858. Hayne had visited Winnsboro on January 7–8 and
considered it, as he wrote Mary Hayne on January 7, the "least favorable of *all* the places
I intend visiting."

4. A quick glance will indicate that Hayne's dates, beginning with "the ensuing
Monday (the 25th)," are off by one day. Monday, of course, was January 26 and Saturday
the 31.

5. The Seabrooks in Grahamville. See Letter 1, n.3.

7

To Mrs. Hayne

MS Duke

Newberry 6th Feb '57

Dearest Wife;

I have been detained here for a day & a half by the non-arrival of the cars from Greenville—It makes *no difference* however as to time of my return—I shall *positively* come home on *Monday next* (the 9th inst)—

I have a great deal to tell you with regard to my success in the up-country—In many respects it has been peculiar—Its prospective advantages cannot be overestimated—My life is now dedicated to a purpose —the building up of a So. Literature, so far as the work may be accomplished by the energy of *one man*—[1]

> God bless you all
> Expect me soon
> Ever affectionately yrs.
> P.H.H.

1. This is the first statement of this "purpose," a goal Hayne consistently maintained before him, despite disappointment, discouragement, and disillusionment, for the next thirty years. Having just turned twenty-seven and having brought out his second collection of poems—*Sonnets, and Other Poems*—Hayne was preparing to edit the second important southern magazine he had worked on during the decade, and he was more sanguine about the possibilities of southern literature now than he ever would be subsequently.

8

To John Esten Cooke[1]

MS Hist. Soc. of Pa.

Charleston Feb. 14th 1857

My Dear Sir:

I had the pleasure of receiving yesterday the second installment of "Estcourt," with the cordial note accompanying it.[2] The story progresses admirably. Not only is it *per se* a fine work of art, but it possesses in an eminent degree that general power of compelling the reader's interest and attention which in a serial magazine tale, is *so* important. I mean that *every* chapter entertains. You have not satisfied yourself with a tame beginning, with the design of working out a striking *denoue-*

ment. "Estcourt" *will* be of great value to us, & we thank you heartily for the zeal with which you have prosecuted the work.

I am mortified Mr. Cooke, at not being able to fulfill *my part* of the engagement as promptly as you have executed *yours.* As intimated in my last communication, my colleague Carlisle has been, & indeed *is* in bad health & during my lecturing tour he could not labor energetically.[3] Consequently the pecuniary affairs of *Maga* have been put back. I assure you *only* put back. The Joint-Stock is *now* accumulating, & I pledge myself to pay for "Estcourt" as soon as practicable. You will understand me when I say that *my honor* is pledged to this. So great was my chagrin at the delay referred to, that I very nearly quarrelled with Carlisle upon his lack of energy, (the result I am bound to say of temporary sickness). I am quite glad that my poems please you.

Commendation from a judicious source is worth all the magazine & newspaper puffery in Christendom.

With the present letter I mail you a copy of certain "Sonnets" of mine just published. Pray let me know if the vol. reaches you.

To stand well before the Virginia public is a matter of serious solicitation with me.

To morrow (the 15th) I shall send you a packet of *Circulars,* which perhaps may be used to advantage.

I must again thank you for the warm & generous interest you have manifested in the magazine.

Very Truly yrs

Paul H. Hayne

P.S. Will you oblige me by saying to your younger brother St. George that *I have just* recd his M.S. story & poem sent me nearly 6 weeks ago. I left the city before its arrival, & it has remained in my box at the P.O.

P.H.H.

P.S. No. 2 As we are now getting up Clubs & agencies, can you recommend any respectable agents in the towns & cities of Virginia?

1. On September 16, 1856, Hayne had requested from Cooke (1830–1886), a rising young Virginia novelist, a "brief serial novel (*upon your terms*) to run through 6 numbers" of *Russell's.* See *CHL,* 67.

2. "Estcourt" began in the first number of *Russell's* (April, 1857), continued for *seven* issues, and was concluded in October.

3. W. B. Carlisle, a Charleston journalist, served as political editor for the first two numbers and was thereupon succeeded by John Russell, the owner of Charleston's chief bookstore and a principal financial supporter of the magazine. Hayne had promised to pay fifty dollars an installment for "Estcourt" and had not yet been able to pay for the first

one. The payment for this novel continued to be a problem, as subsequent letters indicate, and Hayne on several occasions offered to assume the debt himself. See, for example, his letter to Cooke of November 4, 1859, in *CHL*, 84–85.

9

To John Esten Cooke   MS Hist. Soc. of Pa.

Charleston Feb. 27th 1857

My Dear Sir:

Yours of the 21st I rec*d* the day before yesterday. The kind expressions which it contains in reference to my dwarfish vol. of verses have greatly cheered, & encouraged me. The Sonnet is so unpopular a structure that the book I fear has had little success, but the commendation of men of taste, and education is all I desire.[1]

There is one thing you say about it which especially pleases me. In every notice of the work which has yet appeared, the poem called "The Island in the South," has been abused or laughed at, as "morbid, unwholesome" stuff—*the* inferior poem of the collection. Having taken some pains with that performance, I was naturally mortified—but your approval has re-instated the piece in my esteem.

Thanks for your liberality in reference to "Estcourt."[2] As intimated before, our joint-stock scheme has been *delayed*—and *that* is all. The magazine progresses admirably.

The 1*st* no. which is to appear in about 2 weeks will be labelled "April," so that we may always have the work, *before*, and not *behind* time. Let me give you an abstract of the Table of Contents.

Leader—A Reply to the strictures of the Ed[inburgh] Review upon
   So. Society.

2nd—"Estcourt" &c

3 The Tress of Hair

4 The Flower-Girl of the Rue de la Harpe

5 Sonnet. A Character

6 Ione

7 Beranger

8 Poem on the Death of Kane

Editor's Table

Putnam's Mag. on So Literature. Comic version from Juvenal.

Dr. Dewy & the N.Y. Ev. Post—3 epigrams—Fraser Gallery &c

Book Notices
A Trio of Poets—Boker, Stoddard & Matt Arnold—His. of Mysticism & some half dozen other works—
I am anxious & fearful in the extreme about this first number—People are expecting altogether *too much*, & that looks *squally*. However *Nous Verrons*.

Believe me my dear Mr. Cooke, Ever Truly Yrs.
P. H. Hayne

1. Yet Hayne wrote R. H. Stoddard two and a half years later: "In 1857 . . . I published a small book (chiefly of *Sonnets*). . . . *Three hundred copies* were issued by Messers. *Harper & Calvo* of this city, *more* than *100* of which now burden the shelves of my library" (August 28, 1859, *CHL*, 35).
2. See the previous letter to Cooke, Letter 8, and the next one, Letter 10.

10

To John Esten Cooke   MS Scripps College, Claremont

Charleston April 5th 1858

My Dear Mr. Cooke;

I cannot permit *one moment* to pass before I answer your *frank, generous, and noble* letter of the 1st inst, just recd. I felt a glow of gratitude as I read it. I thank you for the kind, and ready comprehension of *my* position, and also for the magnanimous terms in which you refer to *my* share in the unlucky pecuniary difficulty which has arisen in reference to "*Estcourt.*" Let me at the outset relieve you of a misconception of the meaning of my last letter. I *did* not design (God forbid), to insinuate that you had ever *dunned me.* If any such construction could be placed upon my hastily written words, I heartily regret it, and solicit your pardon. Your courtesy to me throughout this affair has been almost unexampled, and I should prove myself a *beast* & an *ass*, if I failed fully to acknowledge it.

And now, one word with regard to Mr. [John] Russell & his conduct towards yourself. I repeat that his reputation for probity (& Simms I am sure will confirm my assertion), stands high in this Community. I *know* that he has acknowledged the justice—the *perfect* justice—, of your claim, & Mr. Simms stated to me, that Russell declared his intention of paying you, whenever he could secure a surplus—i.e. anything *above* the mere *expenses* of the Magazine.[1]

This, however, is no excuse for his most discourteous refusal to answer your letters. *That*, I can neither understand, nor defend.

In the confidence of the friendship, with which you have honored me, I will be candid on this point. Russell is not only a *careless*, but a somewhat arrogant man. His store has, for years, been the fashionable literary resort of the people of Charleston. Altho possessed of considerable cleverness, R. lacks *ballast*. He thinks himself the Moxon, or the Murray (whichever you choose), of this Ilk. He is occasionally so conceited, and dogmatic as to offend his best customers, and most faithful friends. In fact, he does not properly appreciate his position. I myself have found it a difficult matter to get on amicably with him; he has sometimes assumed a manner I did not like; & could hardly tolerate. On last Saturday afternoon he was so outrageously rude to me, that I immediately went home, and wrote him a note dissolving my connections *at once*, & *forever* with "*Russell's Magn*"—*This* brought R——— to his senses; he gave an ample explanation, which in accordance with the advice of friends, tho (let me confess it) sorely against *my own* inclination, I *accepted*, so that I have to retain my *unprofitable post* as Editor. By Heaven! it makes my blood boil to think of the indignities to which the Literary *guild* at the South, is everywhere subjected; *you* have written a story which should have brought you $400 cash, with the reception, so far of but $50;[2] and I have labored strenuously on a So Mag*n* designed to support the honor of our Section, *for upwards of a year*, without having rec*d* 6¼ *cts* in *return*.

I am tempted, Mr. Cooke, to *turn* ——— Yankee, and write exclusively for Yankee publications. All this talk about *So* patriotism is gammon & moonshine. May the Devil seize the *whole* of the degenerate *race*!

I am compelled to bring this letter *to an abrupt* close; but hope to be able to write again in a day or two. Of course, what I have said about Mr. *Russell*, I have said in strict confidence.

Believe Me, Most sincerely yr. friend,
Paul H Hayne

1. For John Russell's position with the magazine, see Letter 8, n. 3.

2. This is all Cooke ever received of the three hundred dollars Hayne had agreed to pay for "Estcourt." For Hayne's other efforts to resolve this matter, see *CHL*, 84–85.

11

To Mrs. Hayne   MS Duke

Woodlands,[1] Dec 4th 1860

My Dear wife;

I arrived here *safely* yesterday morning at 10 o'clock, (after a comfortable ride in the cars,) to receive the warmest of country welcomes, & to feel myself *at once* established, as if, in my *own* home.

There is no company here just now, but Mr. Simms expects a housefull of visitors in the course of 3 or 4 days. The climate is delicious, & notwithstanding the season, everything looks cheerful, even spring-like.

Large clumps of evergreens surround the dwelling-house, & what with immense pine-knot fires *within*, and bright sunshine *without*, one would indeed be misanthropical, not to feel any unusual sentiment of joy and exhilaration.

Last night I went to bed at half past 7 o'clock, and slept for *12 full hours* the sleep of the *just*. This morning I woke, with my throat, & voice *much better*. It seems that the *cold* which troubled me, is about to retire before the dry atmosphere, & genial influences of *Barnwell*.

By the way, this place is 25 miles distant from the Court-House, so that a visit to *Susan Hayne* is *impossible*. On Thursday the 7th (*election* day) we are all going in state to Bamberg (a small village in the neighborhood), to attend a political gathering. Mr. Simms, & Gen*l* Jamison[2] are expected to speak, & both these gentle men are trying to persuade me to do likewise. As my voice has returned, perhaps I *may* address my "fellow countrymen" of these "diggins"!; that is, with *your* permission, for—as you know—I *dare* not act, or talk, without *your* sublime endorsement!

I've just finished reading the Charleston papers. How gloriously everything is progressing!!

To show in what manner, the secession excitement works in one important respect, I may mention the fact, that yesterday the Cars contained (between Charleston & Midway), but six passengers altogether!! This is a significant circumstance. Our yankee "bretheren" [*sic*] (confound them!) are very chary about travelling over So *Rail* Roads! Perhaps, they fear being compelled to ride upon *rails* of a somewhat different description! (I expect you to applaud this original, & striking pun).

I have the prospect before me of a pleasant week. *Game* is not wanting, and as the Jamisons own a *pointer*, probably, I shall bring some partridges, & wild ducks when I come back. Please answer my note immediately, & tell me how you all are. I'm *especially* anxious, of course, about *Willie*,[3] and your "dear little self"—

Kiss the boy for "*old bugger*," over, & over again. Say, that "papa" will try his *best* to shoot a squirrel for him, and to bring down the skin, *stuffed* if possible.

Tell Amelia that I am luxuriating on country fare; fine *fresh* butter, turkeys, crisp roast pig, *bacon* both rich & delicate, hams of superlative quality, the fattest sort of tender fowls, sausages spicily seasoned, turnips, & sweet potatoes that melt in the mouth, *cream* (as rich as any English pastured cow *ever* produced)—, honey taken from the woods, (the flavor of which has made me comprehend for the first time, the appropriateness of the Scripture promise about a land "flowing with milk *and honey*")—, game, consisting of venison, wild-duck, (including English, teal, "canvass-back," & widgeons), partridges, *woodcocks*!, black-birds, larks, robbins [*sic*], & huge *sparrow* pies; & also,—in the way of *dessert*—, plum-puddings, plain-puddings, mince pies, jellies, syllabub, *tarts* of every conceivable description, & native sweet oranges ad-libitum!, not to speak of nuts, such as *ground nuts*, prepared in several delicious ways, hickory nuts (roasted), and walnuts, &c &c &c. Of course, all these delicacies haven't been placed before me *yet*, but they are *certainly forth coming*.

When you write, give me an account of Miss Dewees' wedding, (*don't fail to attend it*), and say in what spirit my note was rec*d* by her *papa*.

With renewed love to *Willie*, and to *yourself*, also to *mother*, & Amelia, I

remain, *dear wife*, as Ever,
Your sincerely attached,
Hamilton

P.S. I must *particularly* beg you to mail *all* my letters, & *all* the Northern journals & magazines that may reach me, thus,—P. H. Hayne, care of W. G. Simms, &c *Midway, So Ca*

No matter what the *post marks* of my letter may be, send them all up.[4]

---

1. William Gilmore Simms's plantation, near Midway, S.C. Simms (1806–1870) and Hayne had been associated in the plans for and publication of *Russell's* and had known each other since Hayne's college days.

2. Gen. David F. Jamison (1810–1864), the owner of Burwood, a neighboring plantation, and a former member of the South Carolina legislature.

3. William Hamilton Hayne (1856–1929) was four years old.

4. At the top of page one of the manuscript, Hayne added: "I send you an envelope franked by W. P. Miles [an old friend of Simms]; Mr. Simms gave it to me."

12

To Mrs. Hayne   MS Duke

Fort Sumter, Friday 28th Feb. [1862]

Carissima,—

I *think* I hear you say; "well: if Hamilton *was* attentive before, he is surely making up for his long letters *now*, by never deigning to address me at all!"

Oh! my darling!, forgive me! Believe, that your "own Alexander" has *really* & *truly, truly* & *really*, been much engaged during the last 6 days.

The ancient poetical "afflatus" has strangely come over my spirit again, so that I have been composing all sorts of lyrics, chiefly of a patriotic order. You may have read some verse, called "The Blockaders," in the "Mercury." [1] They possess *no merit*, I am aware, but the merit of simplicity & truth; being in an artist [*sic*] point of view quite faulty. Never mind! I am now composing a more ambitious performance, which perhaps, you may pronounce, respectable. *How can* I thank you for your thoughtful kindness about the "Song," which was *murdered* in the "*Mercury*"? [2] Do you know, I strongly suspect that pretentious blackguard Courtenay (who hates me with a "perfect hatred") of tampering with my MSS. On several occasions, while he was at the office, (for, as sub-editor & writer, he must be there continually),—I have observed the queerest misprints in my poems. A year, or two (perhaps 3 years) since, this creature meeting Simms, told him that he (Courtenay) could observe some merit in Timrod's pieces, but as for my unlucky self—he thought me a humbug.—Simms, with all his faults, is not indifferent to your husband. He rushed on Master C. in his usual bull-like fashion & made of him an enemy for life!!! Thus; you will comprehend my sole fear in sending articles to the "Mercury" is, that they may (if not yet in proof), come under the kind supervision of Mr. Ashmead C. Thus, *entre nous*! My last recent poem was so clearly penned, that I am obliged to suspect the scamp! [3]

Pardon me in regard to *Willie*;—"*please do*"—(!!!) I *could not*, positively, resist the poor little fellow's pleadings, he was *so* anxious to see Fort Sumter. Besides, what *real* danger was there? I regret my young Hero's reticence "anent" a matter, which *might* have been so easily attended to;—nevertheless, it shows the lad's *hereditary modesty*—!!,— I mean, as derived from his *Father* (!!).

Thanks, for your extracts from Paul Seabrook's letter. I confess it to be a *manly, well-written communication*, so much so, that *I* forgive Paul (for this once) the familiar style of address; "*My Dear Little Rocks*."—Ah, but the extract from Myddleton's letter to your Father, pleased me *inexpressibly*!!—

So, so, he has *at length* discovered that his sister is a "true woman"? He was somewhat slow in finding out so patent a fact,— but—, God knows I blame *not* my brother. Let me rather look to *myself*. With *many* superior opportunities of judging, how long was it before *I* (the mule-headed, and the leaden-hearted)—, began to see, "dimly, as thro a glass," the treasure bestowed upon me by Providence;— &c. God bless you a *thousand times*!! I love you *not only* with truth & fervor—I love you *madly, wildly sometimes*!!—Richard, you observe has been *in town*.[4] Frankly, I don't wish to meet him just *now*. *Much* as I love Dick, I *can't* stand his "Jeremiads" at a crisis like *the present*. It affords me pleasure to be able to say, that *Ransom Calhoun's* command of the Fort *promises* to be a change for the better! He seems a *thorough soldier*!

I have just been re-perusing the last paragraph of your epistle! Oh, Minna, *how* you love me! *how we love one another*!!—*Will* not the merciful Father spare *us both, thro* this terrible war? I *trust so*, Yea, I *believe* he *will*. Thank & *kiss* Willie for his pretty letter. Say "pa pa" will soon reply. Best love to Mother, Amelia and all at home. I am studying *hard* in *military matters*.

Forever yours,
Paul H Hayne

1. Charleston *Mercury*, February 27, 1862.
2. Charleston *Mercury*, February 25, 1862.
3. William Ashmead Courtenay (1831–1908) was a member of the printing and publishing firm involved with the production of *Russell's*. He later became mayor of Charleston (1879–1887). During this period he was not only responsible in 1883 for inviting Hayne to write a poem celebrating the centennial of the city's birth, but he also offered in 1882 to pay for a voyage to England and back for Hayne. Long before this period, Hayne acknowledged that Courtenay was a friend, and Courtenay had realized Hayne was a much better poet than he had thought.

4. Richard Fraser Michel, another brother of Mrs. Hayne's who, like his father and elder brother Middleton, also was a physician. After the war, he moved to Montgomery, Alabama, and became a leading physician in that state.

13

To Mrs. Hayne   MS Duke

Sunday, Aug. 6th 1865

My Darling:

It is now just *two* weeks since I entered the Constitutionalist Office, & having fairly tested the business, I am glad to say, that it suits me much better than I expected it would.[1] I am rapidly mastering all needful details, & consequently begin to feel at home in my work. And as regards *health*, I stand astonished at myself. Altho my labors extend over a period of about *10* hours a day,—altho the weather has been often terrific, I am actually *far better* than usual; my digestion improved, & my spirits good. I think this is partly owing to a constant exercise of the mind, & also, to the glorious feeling of *independence*. No human being, (not even *you*—, with all your keen perceptions,) could imagine what I suffered of torture & humiliation at the Gov'n's house, & having known what it is to eat the bitter bread of dependence, my exultation at escaping from such bondage is only the more intense.[2]

But away with this subject! As intimated before, I am very comfortably situated. Mr. McLaws & his wife treat me precisely as if I were one of their family.[3] The *latter* is an exceedingly pretty brunette, as lively as any lark, & prodigiously curious in reference to my family. I could hardly get her to believe that I was married at all; in fact, I don't think she believes it yet. "When I *see* your wife, Mr. Hayne," she says, "then I'll give you credit for veracity on this point!" Mrs. M—— has a daughter about 11 years old, who is a perfect *picture*. Her beauty is of a very singular kind, being perfect as to feature—& striking one like a clear painting in light oils. She is very clever, & thoroughly spoiled.

Four days ago, I rec*d* a letter from Mr. Poujaud, which I enclose for your perusal; also, a letter from our eccentric friend, Cohen, wherein he says that if I can raise a capital of $5,000 (!!!), he would advise me to purchase a share in the "*Bulletin* & Crescent" [*sic*] newspaper of N. Orleans, & thus make myself independent for life!

The generous old fellow adds, "if I had the money, you should get it from me at once!!"—*Apropos* to Cohen, I shall, early to morrow morning, visit the store of his *sons*, & buy the *ribbands* you wrote for. When young Allen came down, his arrival being unexpected, & his stay short, I had no opportunity of procuring these things. By the way, I have now on hand, some excellent green tea—& *white* sugar, a little good soap, & one or two kinds of medicine, (rhubarb, soda &c &c), for Mother & yourself—

Magnesia, just at present, I can't procure. Yesterday afternoon, I went to every Apothecary's store in town, asking for it, but they were all unable to accommodate me.

Do, *my darling*, write, & let me know *what* you need most & what mother needs likewise. I am trying to live economically, so as to help you *both* in every way. In a short time, (i.e. after this month) I hope to be enabled to put up *money*, & *then, I have a plan to propose which will please you.*

Pray give my *best* love to mother, cousin Susan, & the whole family. Did Capt Lipscombe receive the various papers I sent him? He may depend upon getting as many journals as I can procure, whenever the opportunity occurs of communicating with *Newberry*—

You spoke of having sent me my *valise*. I can't imagine where it is. It was neither left at my former lodgings, nor at Dr. Steiner's.

Among the things I send is a parcel of *candy* for my dear little boy. I thought the poor little fellow would enjoy such a treat, & couldn't resist the temptation of procuring it. Kiss him *over* & *over* for "papa," & say I'll write him a letter soon, all for himself.

Remember me especially to Miss *Minnie* & to the Simkins family—Read particularly the note I send in regard to Maria &c.

And now, God bless you, my dear little one! *Be perfectly easy about me. I am progressing admirably.* Say to Cousin *Sue* that, if there is *anything* I can do for her here, she must not scruple to command my service. And say too, that her kindness to my family shall *never be forgotten*; Perhaps one of these days, (who knows) I may be enabled to return it.

Your affectionate
Hamilton

P.S. Thus far, I have escaped the taking of the Oath. It is sad to observe how thoroughly our People have been conquered. As for *Editors*, they occupy the *tightest* of straight jackets. If you see anything in the "Constitutionalist" which displeases you, remember I am only *news-Editor*, & in no way responsible.

P.S. (no. 2)

I have not *as yet* written to Gov. P——., but of course I shall do so, with as much courtesy as the case demands.[4]

I recognize the necessity of keeping upon good terms with him, alive, (as I said in *my last letter*); I would urge upon mother & yourself *not* to visit his house again, *if you can help it.*

Fifty notes of recommendation written in the spirit & for the purpose which characterized his note to Col Gardner, could not make up for the indignity with which he treated me, while at "Edgewood."

I *never* wish to see the man's face again. At the same time, be assured that I will act towards him with proper judgment & discretion.

In 10 days, I have recd more real kindness from the McLaws' family here, than I expect to receive from "King Francis" in the whole rest of my life.

Have you heard any further from Myddleton? Present my love, & congratulations, when you write.

1. Hayne had moved to Augusta, Georgia, in July and accepted a position for twenty dollars a week as news editor of the *Constitutionalist*, a local newspaper owned by Colonel Gardner and managed by John L. Stockton. Governor Francis Pickens recommended Hayne to Gardner.

2. Francis W. Pickens (1805–1869), a relative of Hayne's mother and governor of South Carolina, 1860–1862. From November, 1861, to March, 1862, Hayne served as his aide-de-camp. Pickens' home near Edgefield was called Edgewood. Despite what Hayne says later in this letter, Mary and Willie Hayne and Emily M. Hayne, Hayne's mother, lived at Edgewood in much of 1865 and early 1866 until they moved in April to Copse Hill, their new home near Grovetown, sixteen miles from Augusta.

3. McLaws, an Augusta lawyer, as Hayne notes in a letter of July 30, 1865, was also a brother of Gen. Lafayette McLaws, the well-known Confederate leader.

4. Despite the heat of these remarks about Francis Pickens, Hayne acknowledged a month later on September 9: "*He* (cousin F——) could never comprehend *me* in any one important respect, & I may be equally at fault as regards *his* character. If he is kind to you & the poor old lady [Emily M. Hayne]; I can ask no more." Later in this letter Hayne lists some gifts for those at Edgewood, including "one bunch cigars for Cousin Francis."

14

To Mrs. Hayne   MS Duke

Monday Nov 20th 1865

My Beloved Minna:

I had not heard from you for nearly 3 weeks until your most welcome letter of last evening, sent by Cousin F[rancis Pickens]. For 12 or

13 days I have been in the Country with one of the kindest friends it has ever been my lot to make, preparing material for several other Lectures. M*r* Redmond[1] (the great So Agriculturalist) is my friend, & his Library (a superb one in the ideal departments), is the only library I have access to here. In my next letter—and upon Wednesday, I shall write in full—I shall tell you all about the *important plan* to which I referred. I think its details will both astonish & delight you. It will also charm mother. Every practical man in Augusta whom I have consulted concerning it, declares that to neglect such an opportunity would be simply—madness! Wait & learn![2]

I was terribly provoked yesterday by receiving a curt note from a man named Williams to whom just before leaving town I had entrusted 2 (two) *long letters* to mother & yourself because he declared he was going straight thr*o* Edgefield—saying that he had changed his mind, & that the letters were sent back to my lodgings! Alth*o* these epistles will be stale I shall still send them to you by the next chance, so that you may know I did not neglect either mother or yourself. Pardon the great haste of my last notes. I have been deeply engaged in study & composition even before I left the office.

As for the reason why I left the *"Constitutionalist,"* M*r* Cole's assertion of "too hard work," is all *wrong*! I quitted it because M*r* Stockton the Manager, & I, could *not* agree upon the manner in which such a journal should be edited. *He* complained I was *too literary*, my style altogether too "high" (his very word), for the "local" department, whilst I in my part, (I *can* be *quietly* obstinate, you know) refused to yield my Editorial rights, especially the right to exercise my own judgment in Selections.[3] *Soon I shall get an engagement with the Transcript*; meanwhile I am not only engaged in the plan hinted at, but writing besides &

Health good; am doing
admirably. Must close in a hurry.
Expect to hear soon.
Ever your Faithful
PHH

---

1. Dennis Redmond, the owner of a large nursery and plantation near Augusta, also knew Simms. See Mary C. Simms Oliphant, Alfred T. Odell, and T. C. Duncan Eaves (eds.), *The Letters of William Gilmore Simms* (5 vols.; Columbia: University of South Carolina Press, 1952–56), IV, 615n.

2. The "important plan" is fully described in Letter 15.

3. For a consequence of Hayne's refusal to "yield" his "Editorial rights," see Letter

16, in which he reports that Stockton has just asked him to "create a Literary Department" for the *Constitutionalist*!

15

To Mrs. Hayne   MS Duke

Constitutionalist Office Nov 29th 1865

My Dearest Minna;

Thank Heaven I have an opportunity of writing you *in full* at last. The fact is, that for *30* days past, I have been *more busy* than at any period since my arrival here—writing for the *Transcript*, sending literary papers to 2 Georgia monthlies, & doing as Dard used to say in [Charles Reade's] "White Lies" all sorts of little "odd jobs"—Your *last letters* reached me long after date, especially the one asking for *Willie's shoes, medicine* &c &c—Those matters I'll at once attend to; & send the articles up by the very next chance. I saw Mrs. Rosa S., cousin Susan &c, but at the time, I was so thoroughly occupied in procuring a room for my Lecture, & in canvassing for an audience that I could not attend possibly to any other business. Previously, I had been for sometime in the Country at Mr. Redmond's place, 16 miles from Augusta, preparing a *second Lecture*, which I am taking prodigious pains with. It is on "Heroism," but, much *fuller* than the poor affair delivered at Greenville. Nevertheless, I want you to send me by the *first opportunity* that address, parts of which I shall retain.

As for the 2nd delivery of the Lecture on "Imaginative Literature," it was very successful, only the Theatre took off *so many*, that of course, I was disappointed in the numbers attending. But *substantial* reputation has been gained. Again, the People were *more* than attentive.

By the way, before I forget it, one word in relation to the *valises*! Capt. Lipscombe's is safe at my apartment, and I'll send up my summer clothes in it. The *only* difficulty about communicating with Edgefield now, lies in the fact, that I am *not*—I *cannot be,* (owing to *other* engagements), so often at the "Constitutionalist" Office as before, thereby missing many chances.

Still direct *all* your communications to this office, as follows; viz: P H Hayne, Care of J*no* L. Stockton, "Constitutionalist Office," Augusta &c—

As for my *own* valise (found at last), *"the man"* Mr. Coles refers to, has made an *utter* mistatement [*sic*] No body ever whispered a word to me concerning the valise, which some negro must have placed in a dark corner, & then, (to excuse himself), lied out of the *difficulty*.

And now, *Dearest*, about that plan of mine. Pray *give* it your *best* attention, for the future welfare of the *whole family* depends upon its being carried thro, as promptly as possible.

Frequently, in my letters I have mentioned the name of Mr. Redmond, who among many kind friends, made by me here is beyond measure, the kindest. All over the South, he is known as a *Horticulturalist* of great *practical* knowledge, & as a gentleman of the largest generosity, & the most *unselfish character*.

Now, as remarked above, I went during the 1st week of Nov. (after repeated invitations) to stay with him at his country place, & to consult his admirable Library. While there, I met with Mrs. *Bonitheau*, & in the course of a long conversation with her upon the results of the war &c, as affecting Charlestonians, she earnestly recommended me to advise Mother to settle in Georgia. "Speak," she said, "to our dear friend, Mr. Redmond, on the subject, & see what *he* advises."

I *did* so, & the result was, that Mr. R——, (who owns a fine saw-mill in the neighborhood),—has offered to build us a small Cottage, (but most comfortable), on one of the *healthiest* locations in Ga., (near his *own* house)—, that he will let me have 18 acres of *fruit land*, which he will himself superintend the planting of, as long as I choose, that our fruit in less than *one* year will bring in a regular income, annually increasing—, that for *all this*, (the building of the Cottage, the planting of fruit trees, the value of the 18 acres &c &c), only $1000 of ready money is required, while the balance of the cost, (which is $3,000) I am to have no less than *three years* credit upon. In one word, we can all get a comfortable home to be finished in the *Spring*—, for the price of $4,000 in *toto*—& upon $3,000, the credit stretches to *three years*, at the end of which time we can begin to settle by installments (if needful), altho by then, our Bonds will certainly be settled & the value of the Farm *doubled*.

At any period, taking the most *prosy* view of the case, our Cottage could be sold for *more* than *cost*, so, that, in effect, we are buying upon a *Certainty*, & not going into *debt at all*.

Now, I *beseech* you *solemnly*, as you desire *a home*, comfortable, healthful, surrounded by pleasant neighbors,—as you desire *me* to engage in a delightful employment, the details of which under Mr. Redmond, I can soon learn—, & *which* will lengthen *my life*, I know, for years—, as you desire to be freed from a humbling dependence, do *not* reject this plan but give me leave, (as the head of the family now), to carry it out.

One thousand dollars is wanted, *as soon* as possible, simply to procure the iron work, glasses, & many other things necessary to the erection of the cottage. Now, how is this sum to be procured? Probably *I* can raise it here, upon some of *our Bonds* under the advice of certain practical, business men, if you give me due authority; & if *not* (so urgent is the case), that doubtless, the Gov. will let you have part of the $1,800 owing you, (I address *mother* here of course), & thus, the work can *at once proceed*. Let me say that I have *fully laid* this plan before some of the *best farmers*, & most experienced merchants of Augusta, & they *declare unanimously* that it would be *absolute madness* to reject it![1]

As for *Mr. Redmond*, everybody gives him the *loftiest character* for integrity—& in point of generosity, he is a sort of "brother Cheerable" [*sic*].[2]

Pray, don't think that I am led away by a foolish enthusiasm—5 months rough contact with the world has knocked the nonsense out of me, & even *if* you *won't believe me*, respect, at least, the opinion of those practical men I mentioned.

God has been kind to us; he gives us an opportunity of once more living under our own roof—; shall we throw the opportunity aside? In my next I'll send you a *plan* of the Cottage, which will have 6 good rooms at least—:

Remember too, that a *fruit-farm* is more lucrative, & *more* rapidly lucrative than any other—, we shall, of course have a vegetable garden, a cow &c—& I can enjoy the necessary liesure [*sic*] for literary work.

Consider, mother & my dear wife, all I have said in this letter. Don't let any apparent (temporary) difficulty, embarrass you. *We must* get a home, & here is one almost ready made to our hands.

This Letter I leave at the *"Constitutionalist" Office*, (with a bundle), & should anybody call from Edgefield, the Clerk here, has orders to deliver *both* to him.

I may have to go into the Country for a few days *shortly*, to take some survey of the 18 acres, & to hunt up authorities for my Lecture, & also for a Poem I am composing. Be assured, Darling, I'll write you just as *often* as *possible*.

The enclosed likenesses I send to mother & yourself.

Kiss my dear boy again & again for me— & *best love* to *mother*,— Love to the Gov & all his family.

i was shocked at what you told me of Jeannie.

Always your devoted
Hamilton

P.S. Cousin F[rancis] *never* has said *one* word as to my visiting him, & unless he asks me (terrible as this separation is), I shall *not* intrude upon his presence.

    1. With the financial help of Emily Hayne and Governor Pickens, the land was purchased, the house was built according to the plan described, and the immediate Hayne family moved in the last week of April, 1866. Emily Hayne followed early the next fall. At first Hayne called it "Hayne's Roost," but quickly changed the name to "Copse Hill," since the house was built upon a knoll in an area of pine forests.

    2. Edwin and Charles Cheeryble appear in Dickens' *Nicholas Nickleby* (1838 −39).

16

To Mrs. Hayne   MS Duke

Hopewood (Mr. Redmond's place),
(on the Ga. R.R.) Dec. 23rd 1865)

My Dearest Little Wife;

I am here with the kindest friends that ever a man had, for the Christmas Holidays; I term them holidays, altho every morning finds me at work on some literary article or another.

For example, I have just finished re-writing a paper on Hartley Coleridge, for *Scott's magazine*,[1] & I shall immediately set about another essay to be sent to the N. Orleans "Crescent," or a monthly they have lately started, (with capital) in Baltimore City. By the way, referring to my writings &c—, I had quite a *little triumph* the other day, which I must inform you of. [John L.] Stockton of "the Constitutionalist" objected, you'll remember, to me, *because* as he expressed it—, I *was too literary*!

What then was my surprise, amusement, & (let me confess it!) *triumph*, when he came to me on Wed last, & actually engaged me to create a Literary Department in his journal, giving me *carte blanche* as to the nature of the pieces I am to send him!! So, I'm again connected with "the Constitutionalist," as sole Literary Contributor, & every Sunday morning there shall be issued in that magnificent paper, a column, or more of purely Literary matter, (varied by *moral* essays &c, under my *proper name*, the appearance of the *latter*, (as Mr. Stockton has kindly intimated), being in some sort essential to the success of the articles!!

The fact is, *my darling*!, that the Lecture I delivered here altho *pecuniarily* (as regards the net results of both lectures), I must acknowledge it a failure—*almost*—, procured for old Hamilton a degree of reputation which is beginning to bear some substantial fruits. Evidently, influential people (I know not whom), have been talking to Stockton, & urging him to procure my services, & thus, give to his journal a more interesting tone, particularly upon Sundays. (This last sentence has a conceited smack about it, which I pray you, forgive—The words slipped off my pen unawares)—

I am steadily extending my Literary connection. And now, with Mr. Redmond's fine Library at my disposal (particularly rich in the periodical literature of 30 years past), I have the necessary authorities at hand, & can write on every topic which comes within the scope of my peculiar tastes & talents—such as they are!—We have here, indeed, no heterogeneous, topsy-turvy, pell-mell, scatter-brained, & wretchedly naked *sans culotte* of a collection of books, shivering like denuded beggars, upon worm-eaten shelves of a remote, & undefined antiquity, but *such* a library as one can regard with a keen satisfaction, entirely released from the apprehension that all sorts of creeping things, & vermin with disgusting forepaws, & slimy antennaë, will certainly crawl up one's sleeves, & insinuate themselves in one's cravat, (hatching instantaneous eggs of a mouldy odour there), the moment a person ventures to open the leaves of the forlornest of works in the dustiest of cases!!! No!, but *all* of England's Immortals are ranged in due order upon plain, but clean, & substantial shelves, & their grand "countenances," (as Milton expresses it!) "look out" upon one, with a grave and lofty decorum which (to wind my sentence up with a flourish), is decidedly agreeable, and—pretty!!! In all seriousness, I have not encountered so well assorted a collection of writings since I glanced last, ("wo worth the day!"), upon mine own fat shelves, or the still more corpulent ones of our friend, W. Gilmore &c!

And now, a word on business. A lucky opportunity occuring [*sic*] on Tuesday evening last, I was enabled to send some *Magnesia* to *Mother*, (the right sort!)—, a dress & 9 yards of shaker (why shaker?) flannel to my darling; also, a box of toys to be divided (don't let them quarrel over it), between Willie, & Douschka.[2] These things I sent, by what seemed a perfectly *safe chance*, but there are a few other articles (no matter *what*!), which I design as Christmas gifts for my dear mother, & yourself, but which I may not be able to send up until after Christmas, thus making of them a kind of Anachronism in the way of presentation.

You rec*d*, I hope, the nail-brush, the soap, & the *flesh gloves*. You'll find the *latter* a most admirable invention, since it is *soft*, yet quite strong enough to produce the healthiest glow upon the skin. I remember how partial you were to *gloves* of this description. And let me say, *en passant*, that if either mother or yourself stand in need of *ordinary* gloves, I can readily procure them for you. By giving these merchants a brief *business notice* (which does them far more good than a regular advertisement)—, they—many of them, at least, show their appreciation by handing over various things to the Editor, or *writer*, (who ever he is) "scot-free"! The arrangement is an old-established one, & perfectly fair. Thus, I have procured many valuable articles.

As I said, *darling*!, in my last letter—, *how long*, & *weary*, this separation of ours *does* seem! *Never*, since our marriage—, have we been parted for a *period so protracted*. And when I think, that cousin F[rancis], has not *even hinted* to me a desire that I should come up, (were it but for a *single day*), & see my *loved ones*, again,—it *does* appear *cruel*, oh, and, and unfeeling!! And he *knows* too, how uneasy I am still about *Willie*. At all events (if he placed himself in *my* position), how *could* he fail to understand the *yearning desire* at my heart to see *you all*? I presume, however, that he really looks upon himself as the type of a modern "good Samaritan," & of course, I *cannot forget* that he has given you *food and shelter*, for nearly a year—that (to employ his favorite word!), he has honored you with his—"charity"!—[3]

But, I pray you, keep up your courage, & *beg* my poor mother to keep up hers! Thank God! I have *friends*—real, unselfish, disinterested friends in Georgia—, upon whom *in extremity*, we may *all rely*.

Reflect also, that your obligation to cousin F[rancis], can continue (absolutely) but a few months longer! We are exerting ourselves to have the cottage up as soon as practicable. *Lumber* is being sawed, carpenters (the best in the neighborhood), have been engaged—, & by the *last* of *March*, I hope to introduce you into our humble, but *Heaven* grant!, our *happy* future home! Mr. Redmond will make a great effort to complete the Establishment for us, by *that date*.

How is cousin *Lucy*, & has Jenny returned to *Edgewood* [?] I missed seeing the *latter* thro no fault of my own. Going down on the

Cars to visit her, some 5 days ago, I met Miss Dearing, who informed me, that after quite a brief visit, Jenny had departed. Please give her my *sincerest love*, & tell her that "cousin Paul" *very very* often thinks of her with kindness, & affection. My *earnest love* likewise to *Cousin Lucy*. Beg her to drop me a note, (care of Jno L. Stockton, "Constitutionalist" Office), stating what *new novels* she would like to receive, & I'll gladly attend to the commission. (I have some excellent stories for *mother* & *yourself*, by the way, awaiting *transportation*).

I met in Augusta, on Tuesday afternoon (the 19th inst.), our little friend, Miss Simmons, & her sister Eliza? *She* (the former) promised if she saw you, to tell you of my *welfare*. I must not forget, in conclusion, to thank you *my Darling*, for the *shirts* [you] sent me. The Lord knows, they were sorely needed.

Mr. Lipscombe's *valise* will arrive soon. He must pardon the delay.

I must now go to my *lonely bed*, where, (ten to one), I will *dream* of my wife. It is strange that I have dreamt of you *3 times* in *succession*. But the dreams were pleasant ones.

Does my Love *ever* dream of me?

Looking (after our many sad trials), with a trustful soul to the Future, & sending many kisses to mother & yourself—& *Willie*,

I remain
Your ever faithful
Hamilton

1. "Hartley Coleridge," *Scott's Monthly*, I (February, 1866), 154–61. This essay is a slight revision of "David Hartley Coleridge," *Russell's Magazine*, IV (February, 1859), 433–42.

2. Douschka is the young daughter of Francis W. and Lucy Holcombe Pickens (the "Cousin Lucy" referred to later in this letter and Pickens' third wife).

3. For Hayne's opinion of Francis Pickens, see Letter 13 and n. 4 under it.

17

To Editor, *Southern Society*[1]   MS Duke

Augusta Sat 21st Sept 1867

My Dear Sir:

I acknowledge your note (just rec*d* with the order for $25). Accept my *sincere thanks* for your courtesy. The trifles I mailed you, have been most liberally paid for. I'm glad that you like them, alth*o frankly*, these verses hardly approach the *artistic* standard I would always wish to arrive at. Hereafter—God giving me health—I trust to do something of real importance for your work.

Meanwhile, in the columns of the "*So Opinion*,"[2] you will *soon* find a notice of your undertaking, to be followed by an article in one of the "*Augusta papers*."

The "S.O." will be *regularly* mailed you.

By the way, *accept* I pray you, the enclosed *Sonnet* of a descriptive nature.

It will serve to fill some vacant corner in your "*weekly*."

With renewed thanks, & an earnest desire for *your complete* success.

I remain Most Truly,
Paul H. *Hayne*

P.S. No pains shall be spared on my part to increase the circulation of "*So Society*"—[3]

1. *Southern Society* was published weekly in Baltimore, and Hayne is addressing either W. J. McClellan, Porter Morse, or E. L. Didier, the editors. The periodical became the *Leader* on April 18, 1868, and ceased publication with the October 10, 1868, issue. Hayne wrote Didier on December 13, 1867, that he would "contribute regularly."

2. During this period Hayne was also literary editor of *Southern Opinion* (1867–1869), a Richmond political and literary weekly.

3. This was a part of Hayne's plan—a quid pro quo as he characterized it. Since he regularly contributed to newspapers in Augusta and Charleston and to magazines all over the South, he could easily afford to say a kind word in one of them about a new periodical.

18

To E. L. Didier[?]   MS Duke

Monday 13th Jan. 1868

My good Friend;

To morrow I send you a careful *review* of Miss Crane's "Opportunity."[1] If you know this lady personally, pray give her my respectful compliments, & say, that her book seems to me a remarkable one, & that I think she is destined to do *great things*.

Tell me, if my review suits your taste. It embodies what to my mind is simply *the truth*.

To morrow I'll mail you, likewise, another *Editorial* which shall be quickly followed by book notices &c.

May I ask a favour?

If not inconvenient, I would thank you for a few more copies of the "S.S," containing "*Fire Pictures*."[2] And by the way, can you send me *per Express*, (or thru the P.O.) some common writing paper, & envelopes; also some stamps?

I'll *fully* make up the expense by contributing every now & then, essays, poems *et cet*, outside the Editorial department.

Paper is enormously high in the little picayune town of *Augusta*, beyond exception the most Yankeefied place in the South.

All your *Circulars*, I have disposed of.

Depend upon my using every practicable exertion to benefit your journal.

Always Faithfully,
Paul H. Hayne

1. Anne Moncure Crane, *Opportunity: A Novel* (1867).
2. "Fire-Pictures" had appeared in the last issue of December, 1867.

19

To Editors of *Southern Society*   MS Duke

Private   9th Feb. 1868

Gentlemen;

I have this moment recd your note of the 4th with check for $15.

Its *contents* have inexpressibly *annoyed* me,—the *more* so, as I am *almost* tempted to believe that you suppose me guilty of what in *my* view, as an honorable literary gentleman, would be an ineffable meanness.

Now, *both* the poems to which you allude, were sent you in *perfect good faith*.

I had *no more idea* that *either* had seen the light in print, than that any verses of mine had appeared in the journal of Uranus, or the Moon.

Upon consideration I can account for the circumstance only as follows.

Two years ago I sent on to Richard Henry Stoddard of N York a small batch of poems ("The Lotus & Lily" amongst them)[1] begging him to *sell* the pieces, if he could, as I was ruined by the War.

He promised to do so, but subsequently, he informed me (thro Mr. Simms), that the literary market was glutted, & that neither my rhymes nor poor Timrod's, (the *latter* had sent him certain productions of his own), *could be sold*.

I then immediately wrote him withdrawing my pieces altogether & if any have since been issued in N York, or anywhere else, *it has been emphatically without my knowledge*, co-operation, or consent.

As regards the *Sonnet* which—for the 1st time—I learn, appeared in Scott's Mag*n*, I am excessively *indignant* , because in *this* case the Ed. of that monthly has been guilty of *more* than impertinence.

Why, Gentlemen, the Rev. Mr. Scott *now* owes me for articles in prose & verse, a good round sum, which I never expect to receive.[2]

The Sonnet *in question* more than *18 months* ago was sent him as a *free contribution*, under the *express condition, that he should at once pay me* the *amount* previously *due at a specified period*.

He *did not pay me*, & I wrote *requesting in emphatic words* the *return* of my *MS*.

It was *not* returned (with a solitary exception) & no no. of his confounded monthly has since reached me.

How could I dream that the Rev. scamp has presumed to publish my *Sonnet* after this?

These are *simple facts* which if needful, can be demonstrated.

Indeed, it does appear as if *Fate* had especially marked me out as a victim either of mistakes, or imposture.

Only 3 days since the Edts. of NY Home Journal addressed me to the effect that somebody in their city had actually *forged my name*, both to a note, and a *poem*, which I had never seen!!

Occasionally, I have given copies of original poems to friends, simply for *their personal perusal*—, & it has happened that these friends (without a word to me) have undertaken to publish them.

Mr. Simms (entre nous!) did this thing once, & involved me in a disagreeable scrape.

Henceforth, in writing for your paper, I *solemnly promise that nothing* shall be sent you, which by *any mortal possibility could have crept into print before*.

Let me hope that this will prove *satisfactory*.

Respectfully,
Paul H. Hayne

P.S. To prove beyond all possibility of *cavil* that my *sincere* wish is to make up to you for this disgusting error, I will *not* accept another cent for "Fire Pictures." Consider that debt *cancelled* now of course.[3]

In addition I will as intimated above, mail you 2 original poems of *value*.

You have been *perfectly-fair* in your dealing with me, and I am ready to make *any sacrifice* rather than seem ever grasping, or *selfish*.

The cause of *So* letters is *too near* to my *heart for that*.

You will have recd "Fire Pictures" therefore, for only $11, which is not *very dear* I imagine.

When my Editorials fail to come, 'tis no fault of mine, but the mails', for I send them regularly. You *ought* to have now, 4 or 5 Editorials, & as many book-notices. Still, the loss or delay of my compositions, *I* must suffer for, not *you*—

Let me know promptly whether you are not in copy—

1. "The Lotus and the Lily" was collected in *LL* and *PCE*, 144–46.

2. William J. Scott (1826–1899), editor and owner of *Scott's Monthly* in Atlanta.

3. In Letter 20 Hayne acknowledges receipt of nineteen dollars to cover "'Fire Pictures' & *last Editorials*." The editors accepted his explanation and generously declined to accept the poem for only eleven dollars.

20

To E. L. Didier [?]   MS Duke

Augusta, Georgia 25th April, 1868

My Dear Sir;

Thanks for the 2 no*s*. just recd of the "*So* Leader." I have read the paper with *great* attention, & honestly, it seems to me admirable—, much more likely to succeed than the "Opinion," which addressed itself chiefly to *scholars*, while the "Leader" must interest everybody.[1]

We know each other well enough by this time, to justify me in making a proposition.

It is simply this—I will send you about 2 *columns* of *original* prose-matter every 7 days, (say, *one* Editorial on *Politics*, & a column of critiques), besides *giving* you now & then a perfectly original poem, for the sum of $8 (eight) dollars *payable weekly*, or (*minus* the poems) $6 weekly—[2]

So many *notes* of an interesting & important nature are by me now—collected in the first place, for "So. Society," that I am anxious to use them for *your* benefit.

Tell me what you decide upon!

By the way, did you receive my acknowledgment of the $19, sent (thro a *P.O. Order*), for my "Fire Pictures," & *last Editorials?*[3]

I am *peculiarly grateful* for your *prompt* courtesy in this matter.

Ah! heaven! *what* a contrast it forms to the general policy of So. Editors towards their contributors!!

Please write soon, & Believe [me]

Your obliged friend,
Paul H. Hayne;
P.O. Box, 260, Augusta, Ga.

1. It is possible that Hayne means that the *Southern Leader* is more likely to succeed than *Southern Society*, its predecessor, for the *Southern Opinion* was still being published.

2. The *Leader*'s first issue appeared April 18, and the editors accepted Hayne's proposal, though the weekly lasted only through the issue for October 10.

3. See Letter 19 for payment for "Fire Pictures," a long poem of 250 lines.

21
To Sidney Lanier   MS Johns Hopkins[1]

"Copse Hill," Ga R.R. (16 miles from Augusta)
Sep. 7th 1868

My Dear Mr. Lanier;

Thanks for your *exceedingly* pleasant, & entertaining letter. I like to receive such epistles. They warm one's heart up, acting like a kind of spiritual (not *spirituous* liquor), & producing as Holmes says, the "true, champaigny, old-particular, brandy-punchy feeling"!

You tell me, that I ought not to curse *Destiny*, or to call *her* a "harridan" who has "placed laurels upon my brow &c"!

My kind friend! I really am grateful for your compliment, but alas! I know that *my* place is at the very bottom on *Parnassus*, & that in an age like ours, so fruitful of great thought set to majestic harmonies, the music of *my* poor little pipe is not likely to survive a single year after the humble minstrel has departed.

It surprised me beyond measure to hear that *you* are a sufferer from *ill-health*. How a man with the insubordinate "stomach" you describe, *could* have written "*Tiger Lilies*" is to me, the most puzzling of problems!!

Why, the animal life of that tale is superabundant. I pictured its author to myself as a young Giant—hale, healthful & happy!

Certain I am that your constitution is sound at the *core*; & that these "megrims &c" will disappear like foul mists of morning.

Apropos of the "R. Table" I fear we have *both* been a little unjust. With all its manifest faults, & shortcomings, this *weekly* is the only periodical of its class in America, which a thoughtful person can read with the certainty of being interested, often *instructed*.

Disagreeing "*toto caelo*" with some of its *general* principles, & regarding not a few indi[vid]ual articles as equally impertinent & unjust,—I have nevertheless, come to estimate the "R.T." as a sort of "institution," the destruction of which would sincerely afflict me![2]

Have I seen *Bulwer Lytton's* "new Poems"?—Yes, & perused many of them with great care. They show an immense versatility of fancy, multifarious scholarship & an elaborate artistic conscientiousness; but the impulsive glow & fervour of *genius* are wanting. Compare him with Swinburne, for example. Truly as I detest the foul imagination of the *latter*, there can be no question as to the vast superiority of his *poetic genius.*[3] B. Lytton is however, a *gentleman!* he deals with no "Petronian abominations," & would scorn to wallow like a hog among the atrocious conceptions of the *nastiest* beasts that ever breathed, I mean, the so-called Poets of the latter Roman Empire!

As for *Wm Morris*, I, for one, consider him as beyond doubt, the *purest, sweetest, noblest narrative* poet G. Britain has produced since *Chaucer*! *This* may sound exaggerated; nevertheless 'tis simply *true*!

By all means, procure his works—"Jason," & "The Earthly Paradise."

(By the way, let me remark, that "*Not Dead,*" was composed, in part, before I knew that such a *man as Morris existed*! The stanza is an old *English stanza*, & the *refrain* of course, may be regarded as one of the most common of artistic points).[4]

Please tell *your wife* how proud I am that any verses of mine attracted her notice & praise. With best regards to *her*, & hoping that you will write soon, I am as Always,

Faithfully yours,
Paul H Hayne

1. Though this letter has been printed in Charles R. Anderson, *et al.* (eds.), *The Centennial Edition of the Works of Sidney Lanier* (10 vols.; Baltimore: Johns Hopkins Press, 1945), VII, 394–96, it seems appropriate to reprint it here. The text is based upon a photoduplication of the manuscript. Hayne apparently started the correspondence earlier in 1868 (not 1867 as he once claimed) with the usual motive—to encourage and stimulate southern writers and writing.

2. The *Round Table* (1863–1869) published contributions from Hayne and Lanier.

R. H. Stoddard served on the editorial staff. See Hayne's letters enclosing poems to Stoddard for the weekly: *CHL*, 43–45.

   3. Hayne consistently maintains this view of Swinburne, though he was careful not to comment on Swinburne's morality when he corresponded with him in the late 1870s. For Swinburne's side of the correspondence, see Cecil Lang (ed.), "Swinburne and American Literature: With Six Hitherto Unpublished Letters," *American Literature*, XIX (January, 1948), 336–50.

   4. "Not Dead. To J. A. D." was written to Jeanie A. Dickson, a longtime friend of Hayne's, an early admirer of his poetry, and a daughter of Dr. Samuel H. Dickson, the well-known Charleston physician and teacher. The poem was collected in *LL* and *PCE*, 142–43. For another comment about Morris' possible influence on Hayne, see Letter 41.

22

To Oliver Wendell Holmes[1]   MS Duke

Augusta Oct. 13th 1868

My Dear Doctor:

   I remember reading in the papers, some time ago, a paragraph stating that your late distinguished Gov. Andrews,[2] quoted a few days before his death, with earnestness & feeling a little poem of which he was fond, "the production" (here we borrow the words of the journalist), "of an obscure So. poet, named Henry Timrod"!

   Well, the works of this Henry Timrod,—so "obscure" at the North—are widely known, & admired here. He possessed *real* genius, & had health & life granted him;—but poor fellow! he is dead, & the enclosed verses are dedicated to his memory.[3]

   As a little vol. of his, (Timrod's), was published by Ticknor & Fields in 1860, & favourably noticed by some of your critics—may I beg you to have "*Under the Pine*" re-published in the "Transcript," "The Advertiser," or any of your dailies?

   It will not, I suppose, give anybody much trouble, and yet I am assured the reappearances of the piece in Boston will gratify the dead Poet's wife and family. Hence my request![4]

   Let me hope, *Dear Sir*, that you continue well, & fortunate, I was about to add, "happy," but such a wish would be superfluous in the case of one who in promoting all his life the happiness of *others*, could not, by an infallible law—have failed to secure his *own*!

   If you see Mr. Fields, pray give him my *sincere regards*, & Believe me, Always Faithfully Yours,

Paul H Hayne
P.O. Box 260, Augusta, Ga.

[P.S.] Is it not sad to think that *Timrod* died partly from the want of the absolute necessaries of life? His disease was aggravated by coarse improper *fare*,—& *now* his family are nearly *starving*—(literally), among neighbours in Columbia, (S.C.), not much better off than themselves. Many parts of the South are beginning to resemble Ireland after the failure of the Potato crop!

    1. Hayne had met Holmes while in Boston in 1854 and corresponded with him occasionally before the war. He had resumed the correspondence prior to the penning of this letter, and he subsequently visited Holmes on trips to Boston in 1873 and 1879.

    2. John A. Andrews (1818–1867) was governor of Massachusetts from 1860 through 1866 and a leading spokesman for antislavery opinion in his state.

    3. "Under the Pine (To the Memory of Henry Timrod)," *Lippincott's Magazine*, II (October, 1868), 414–16. Hayne later collected the poem in *LL* and *PCE*, 103–105.

    4. Holmes replied on October 21, 1868:

> It is not so easy for a good poem to escape the eyes of a Boston Editor as you seem to think. I read the poem you sent me a week or two ago in the Transcript if I am not mistaken. . . . I would send it to the [*Advertiser*] with the greatest pleasure if I did not think that the editors do not like to print a poem which the other paper has put before so large a proportion of its readers. The poem struck me as musical, tender, thoughtful, and chastened to that tranquil form of beauty which we sometimes think is oftener found under our cold northern skies than in the fierce sunshine of the south. I like it all the better for this contemplative calmness.

But Holmes could not miss an opportunity to make a point. Noting that Timrod's poems were not "much known at the north" and that neither Timrod's nor his father's names were in *Appleton's Encyclopaedia*, he observed: "I do not know whether the fancy some of your authors have had of building up a distinctively Southern literature is responsible or not for some of our ignorance, but any such ambition must to some extent interfere with the growth of a truly national reputation." Typed copy, Duke.

23

To Margaret Junkin Preston[1]   MS Duke

"Copse Hill" Ga R.R.
Sep 5th 1869

My Dear Mrs. Preston:

My answer to your *last* kind, generous, & *more* than appreciative letter, was very hastily mailed; that is to say, it was perforce entrusted to the care of a certain reckless "Ethiop"; who at times manages the accommodation Train, running between this *pine* barren, & the town of Augusta.

Therefore, I am half afraid that my prior epistle miscarried, a piece of ill-luck which would place me in the unenviable position of a *thoroughly ungrateful dog*; at least for the time being.

So, please comprehend that I *did answer* you, and with all the *sincere* gratitude, elicited by one of the most encouraging letters I have ever rec*d* in the whole course of my life! What is that old Latin proverb about the delight of being praised by one who has himself deserved, & rec*d* the praises of mankind?[2]

I can't recall the *words*, but the *sense* is sufficiently plain, & thro your kindness I have really been made to feel its truth deeply.

Moreover, your commendation has helped me to bear up under a rather mortifying "snub" just administered to my self-esteem by the gentleman who plays the part of "Critic" in the NY "*Nation.*" Apropos of 2 *Sonnets* of mine issued by *Lippincott* (in his mag), for Sep—, the "Nation" remarks, that "to speak plainly, Mr. Hayne has never penned a verse worthy of *more* than a moment's *notice* !"

How this would have stung, & humiliated me once, coming as it does, from a journal of ability!. But *now* I have learned to understand these critics better. Few are at once honest, & *capable*. As for the *Jupiter* of "*the Nation,*" *nothing* seems to satisfy *him*!

He is afflicted evidently with *chronic* intellectual *jaundice*, & looks forth upon the world of *Art, thro* a green, & yellow medium! Well! I *survive* his *bolts*, & am not even *deafened* by his *thunder,*—for during the last 5 or 6 days, I have composed the greater part of a story in verse, which finished late on Sat. night, numbers some *600 lines* in the *heroic* measure—not of *Pope*, but of Chaucer, & after him Keats, Hunt, and Morris! It is called simply, "*Daphles*"; and the time, & characters are *Greek*.

I hope—I almost venture to *believe*, that you will like it. If possible, I contemplate publishing it in the "*New Eclectic,*" or perhaps—*the "So. Review."*[3]

Since my last letter, I have been studying with greater care your little *classic* Poem of "Rhodope"—and I find that it *grows* upon me, the more I read it.

The *compactness* of the verse, and a general air of *reserved* powers, are, to *my* mind, *particularly* striking.

As for the *rejection* of a piece by a Yankee mag, *that* goes for just *nothing*—nothing whatever! Most Mag. Editors indeed possess a real genius for blundering!—Edgar Poe's wonderful "*Ulalume*" (wonderful as a rhythmical study, & as a piece indefinably & weirdly *suggestive*) was rejected by 4 prominent periodicals of his day—,[4] and "The Burial of Sir John Moore," modestly contributed by its author to an obscure county paper was *returned* to him with ridicule, & coarse contempt!

But eno' of this! I am writing almost in the dark, & must now abruptly close.

Won't you drop me a line when this letter reaches you? And pray, *dear Madame,*

Believe me

Always Faithfully yrs.
Paul H Hayne

1. Hayne apparently began this correspondence with the Virginia poet (1820–1897) on December 31, 1867; on that date he praised her poems "Jackson's Grave" and "Poor Carlotta" and inaugurated an exchange of letters and friendship that was vital to both poets. The text of the letter is printed in Elizabeth Preston Allan, *The Life and Letters of Margaret Junkin Preston* (Boston: Houghton, Mifflin, 1903), 243. Mrs. Preston was the daughter of George Junkin, president of Lafayette College, Miami University, and Washington College (1848–1861; later Washington and Lee University), the wife of Col. John T. L. Preston, ranking member of the faculty of Virginia Military Institute, and sister-in-law of Gen. Thomas J. ("Stonewall") Jackson. She had published *Beechenbrook: A Rhyme of the War* (1866) and her first collection of poems, *Old Song and New*, would appear in 1870.

2. Laudari a laudato viro. (Cicero, *Epistolae ad Familiares*, xv, 6).

3. Hayne began "Daphles" on September 10, 1864, and subsequently worked on it in 1868 before completing it as described herein. It appeared in the *New Eclectic*, VI (March, 1870), 257–69.

4. Hayne is wrong about "Ulalume." The poem was commissioned by C. P. Bronson, an elocutionist who had no objections to the publication of the poem, and Poe was able to place it with the second magazine he tried—the *American Review*, where it appeared in December, 1847. See Thomas O. Mabbott (ed.), *Collected Works of Edgar Allan Poe* (Cambridge: Harvard University Press), Vol. I, *Poems* (1968), 409–13.

24

To Sidney Lanier   MS Johns Hopkins

Near Augusta, Sat 11th Dec: (1869)

I am too *unwell, Dear Friend & Poet,* to write at any length, but 'tis not in my nature to keep silent—were I "under the ribs of Death"—concerning *such* a poem as your last, "Nirvâna." Once upon a time I made that curious, & in many respects—*sublime* Hindu religion, with its Buddhas, & Brahmas a *special study*, and therefore, the subject of your verses is much to my taste! And the verses *themselves*, are *exquisite*! I like their subtlety, their terseness, their fine, clear-cut imagery, together with a certain *inner* harmony of thought & rhythm, difficult to define!

I'm disposed to look upon "Nirvâna" as, thus far, your *ablest* Poem! Of course, it is a work for *Thinkers*; your "Psalm of Life," and "Star-spangled banner" people, would gape at the very *names*![1]

Have I seen Prof. Davidson's critical publication?[2] No! But I am tolerably well acquainted with its *materiél*! What do I think of *him*, & it?—Well! *mon ami*, (for your *private ear*), I think that D—— is a *windy ass*, with just eno' of half-spurious cleverness, ill-digested information, & *Twilight taste* to deceive himself—& perhaps a "select few"! (Since he's sharp on *me* in some respects, tho decidedly, & unduly eulogistic in *others*, my verdict may be deemed partial).

Occasionally he writes a fair essay, (like that on poor Timrod),—but on the whole, is unsufferably *crochetty*, and dogmatic to a laughable extent. As an *English scholar*, he is shallow as a—*saucer*!

For years he labored along—(critically) with *Poe upon the brain*, and even now one can see how he tries to imitate Poe's *style*, a dangerous experiment in third-rate genius!

Did you know that D—— himself wrote poetry or a species of stuff so-called? to say, that it is *hideous*, affecting one's nerves, like a monkey-ground organ—is to employ the *mildest* of expressions!

(Pray *burn these words*, for I don't want to appear ill-natured; moreover, I once actually wrote D—— a *complimentary* letter "anent" his criticisms, judging the whole, *imprudently* from a single paper!)

—One final illustration is not to be resisted! You remember Dame Quickly's saucy boy in Henry V? You remember his anecdote of Bardolph's nose? "I saw upon that nose," quoth he, "a flea & it looked like a *black soul* burning in Hell fire!" Now, I regard the *critical soul* of Mr D—— as so very diminutive, that I'm sure it could be transferred to the descendant of the Bardolphian "Flea," could take up its habitation therein, and yet find an abundance of—elbow room![3] *Basta*! for *this* topic!

Two stanzas in "Nirvana," are *particularly fine*: The one beginning; "*The Silence ground my soul keen like a spear*" and the concluding verse: "*The storms of Self below me rage & die*": Indeed, this last *sticks* to my memory: Half-consciously I find myself repeating it, especially when *musing* in bed!—

What has become of your narrative poem of the "Jacquerie"? Don't let it remain a fragment—, *Law or no law*—

For myself, you'll observe that my recent verses are purely *domestic*. Circumstances carried me into that humble department. Still—, are there (in some aspects), any nobler, sweeter themes for the Poet than the *affections*? I wot not!!

At the same time, I like the transcendental, & the subtle,—little as you might think it. Write soon, & Believe me your friend Ever

> Paul H Hayne
>
> PO Box 635 Augusta, G*a*

Do you ever see Burke's juvenile paper? Glance over a trifle of mine in the Jan. issue; 'Tis called "The Life of a *Robin Redbreast*."[4]

1. "Nirvâna," *New Eclectic*, VI (March, 1870), 294–96. The poem had apparently been written in November or early December of 1869 and enclosed in a letter that is now lost. See Anderson, *et al.* (eds.), *Centennial Edition of the Works of Sidney Lanier*, VIII, 50n. Part of Hayne's letter is also quoted in the same note.

2. James Wood Davidson (1829–1905), *The Living Writers of the South* (1869). Hayne is even more forthright about Davidson a few weeks later in a letter of January 2, 1870, to Simms. Davidson, "a very sufficient ass" who has managed "to *humbug* the *Yankee* Publisher," alludes in the book "impertinently" to Simms and his poems, and Hayne continues: "The evil, mean, bitter *animus* of his articles is even more apparent than their *stupidity*. Such a scribbler would have deserved no sort of notice if he had not committed the folly of trying to perpetuate his pestilent nonsense in *book-form*. Now,— he must receive no quarter" (*CHL*, 228). Hayne later modified his view of Davidson the man and admitted in a letter to Maurice Thompson (see Letter 40) that he had "made up" with Davidson "a long literary feud . . . wherein I confess myself to have been much in fault."

3. This scene is often quoted by Hayne, especially when he wishes to indicate the diminutive size of something. For other references to this scene, see Hayne's letter to Philip Bourke Marston, January 1, 1884, and Letter 78 below.

4. "The Life of Robin Redbreast," *Burke's Weekly for Boys and Girls*, III (January, 1870).

25

To O. W. Holmes   MS Duke

> *"Copse Hill" Geo R Road*
> *July 21st 1870*

My Dear Doctor;

It is a *long* time since I had the pleasure of writing you, and now I merely write to inquire how you are, & to enclose a little poem the *ground-thought* of which was suggested by a passage in your *"Autocrat of the Breakfast Table."*

It seems to me that this idea is *profoundly* true. *Who* has not *some-*

times experienced a sort of inward spiritual convulsion at the discord which seems to prevail between the mystic soul of *Nature*, and the soul of *man*? Such is the conception I have *tried* to embody in "*A Summer Mood.*" *You* comprehend it, & have given utterance to it, more than once.[1]

If the papers speak truth, *what* a terribly hot summer you must all be having, *North*!! You'll envy me when I say, that here among the *pine* Barrens, (considered generally intolerable as *Hades*!) we seem to live, environed by eternal breezes. The thermometer has seldom ranged, since June—above 78 or 79°; and after 8 o'clock at night, it often becomes so cool, that the windows must be shut.

You have heard probably of the climate of *Aiken* in So Ca;—of— the peculiar lightness, & dryness of the atmosphere which will make that place world-famous in the course of time. Well! *our atmosphere* is still dryer, lighter, and more wholesome.

Indeed, were I a man of capital I would convert this neighborhood into a watering-place; for in addition to the excellence of the climate, we have the best *water* that an invalid of the consumptive class could desire.

Meanwhile, however, the woods remain desolate, the streams are lonely & unsought. You can hardly realize—the tenant of a large City—, how completely isolated are immense tracts of country at the South—, even tracts—like ours—which border upon flourishing and long-established towns.

May I venture to inquire, *Doctor*, whether the report is true that you are engaged upon another story! Honestly, I hope it is, for *you* are among the very few authors—American, or English—whose system of art has chosen the medium of fiction to convey some of the noblest truths, of the fair presentation whereof humanity stands in need.[2]

The world is to be turned topsy-turvy again, it seems, because of the vanity of a single man. Napoleon to preserve his dynasty is determined to sacrifice *millions*. The old fashion of *tyrants*!!

A letter reached me yesterday from a most able & well-informed friend, (now in London), which says, that many persons of sagacity maintain, that this war between France & Prussia (if *once* fairly inaugurated) *must* result in the involvement of all the other Continental Powers of any importance.

Nous Verrons! How charming for the *Philanthropists*, who were beginning to look upon the *speedy* advent of the *Millenium* as a thing absurd?

Believe me,

Always Faithfully yrs

Paul H Hayne

P.O. Box, 635, Augusta Geo.

P.S. My best regards—if you see them—to Mr. *Horatio Woodman*, & Mr. *Whipple*.[3]

1. "A Summer Mood" was subsequently collected in *LL* and *PCE*, 106. The epigraph, by the way, is not from the *Autocrat* but from Thomas Heywood. Lanier remarked in a letter of August 9, 1870, that he had read the poem to a group of approving friends (including Jefferson Davis) and concluded: "I like it better than anything you have written: it has in it the *magnetism* which distinguishes genuine poetry from culture-poetry. Write me some more like this, good Friend!" Anderson, *et al.* (eds.), *Centennial Edition of the Works of Sidney Lanier*, VIII, 94.

2. This was not idle flattery. Hayne had favorably reviewed Holmes's *The Guardian Angel* (1867) in *Southern Opinion* and managed at the same time to say some good things about *Elsie Venner* (1861) and the "Autocrat and Professor essays" (1858, 1860). His general opinion is that "Dr. Holmes is the brightest and most catholic of the New England *literati*. With marked powers of metaphysical and philosophic disquisition, he possesses a breadth of sympathy, and a warm genial humour, which, it must be confessed, are not usual characteristics among the writers of his section." Undated clipping, Hayne Papers, Duke.

3. Hayne had met Woodman and Whipple on his trips to Boston in 1853 and 1854 to arrange for the publication of and see through the press the first collection of his poems. Though not a writer, Woodman was a member of the Saturday Club and was frequently present on social occasions with groups of the literati. Hayne wrote him a series of revealing letters in the late 1850s and early 1860s that have been printed in the *Proceedings of the Massachusetts Historical Society*, LIV (January, 1921), 178–84. E. P. Whipple, the well-known critic and essayist, had favorably reviewed *P* and *A* when they appeared in 1854 and 1859. See Letter 4. Whipple's review of *A* appeared in the Boston *Evening Transcript* in November, 1859.

26

To Sidney Lanier[1]   MS Johns Hopkins

"Copse Hill" Geo R.R. Jan 10th 1871

My Dear Poet;

Some self sufficient Roman, some "stuck up old cuss," as our California brethren would express it, used to say, that he was never "less alone than when alone"—, but for *my* part, I must confess that I yearn sadly at times, in this my Robin Crusoe solitude, for intellectual society—the attrition of mind with mind, the exchange of artistic experiences, even the careless competition of good natured jest, quirk, & repartee! But then, *Freedom* is a compensation for all losses, & oh! *how thoroughly independent* I am, in my woodland cabin! Could I induce my friends to *write* more frequently & fully, I almost think that the *yearning* above mentioned, would possess me seldom, if at all; and among my friends, I've long counted *you* & have been most proud to do so.

Even a brief note however, like your last (of the 7th inst) gives me a peculiar satisfaction, enhanced by the extracts from your Poem, which it rejoices me to perceive, you are "buckling to" in good, hearty earnest.

Once—months ago—I told you how noble a subject it seemed to me you had chosen in "*the Jacquerie*," and all the extracts I've seen, prove that you understand the right mode of treating it.

As for the two *Lyrics*, now before me, I think them *perfect*—each after its kind. The *first* is a true mediaeval song, the sentiment, & quaint terms of expression showing your familiarity with antique ballad poetry, and having so to speak—a *smack* of the old dead centuries about them; and the second, is *exquisite*; a thing not [to] criticise, but feel![2]

Go on my son! go on, and conquer!

Remember too, if you please, that as your Poem ('twill be a tolerably elaborate work I suppose) as your Poem progresses, I would esteem it a privilege to see *fragments* thereof, preluding the completed strain. God knoweth, we have but few poet-artists, South;—shall we not hail them when they appear? At least, the few genuine men of letters in our section, (you I *know*, are one, & let me humbly *trust* that I may be reckoned another) ought, & must stick together; encourage each others' [*sic*] efforts, and support each other's fame! So don't forget my hint, and send a *soupçon* of your performance, every now & then, as the labor of love advances.[3]

I'm writing this long after *midnight*, and the involuntary drooping of the lids, and a mistiness of sight, warn me to stop, and go to bed.

But *insomnolence* has recently attacked me to a painful degree. I know too well that the moment I'm carefully tucked up from the cold, all disposition to slumber will have vanished, and there I shall be forced to lie for hours, "chewing the cud of fancies," few of them "sweet," and a vast no. disgusting! O! for a *nepenthe*!

Nevertheless, I must throw aside my pen, and bid you "good night," and "God bless you!"

Always Faithfully Yours
Paul H Hayne
PO Box 635 Augusta, Geo

P.S. I hear that that ineffable donkey I termed J. Wood Davidson has been assailing me tooth & hoof in the NY papers, *apropos* of the "*Wife of Brittany.*" How the fellow *does* hate me! I suppose because I've called him a "Peter McGrawler" [?] & dared to doubt his *critical* wisdom. Great God, Lanier! what fools many of our so styled scholars and authors here in the doomed South seem to be—always like Dogberry writing themselves down—"asses"—

1. Part of this letter is quoted in Anderson, *et al.* (eds.), *Centennial Edition of the Works of Sidney Lanier*, VIII, 137n.

2. The editors of Lanier's letters, Charles R. Anderson and Aubrey H. Starke, conjecture that these poems may be two of the "Songs for 'The Jacquerie,'" though they admit that the two could also be dialect poems (*Ibid.*, 135n).

3. This is one of the clearest statements of Hayne's approach to the encouragement of southern writers and the promotion of southern literature throughout the postwar period.

27

To Sidney Lanier   MS Johns Hopkins

"Copse Hill," Geo R Road
Thursday, 23rd, March, 1871.

My Dear Poet;

You have done me an *essential service*, & in the very *kindest* manner too, in your letter of the 20th inst. Thanks! a *thousand thanks* for the trouble you have taken about "Fire Pictures." That (*upon the whole,*) you should like this poem so *much*, is a great comfort, & encouragement to me. *All your suggestions* I will *carefully* study, & I *haven't* the *shadow of a doubt* that they will help me to a clearer, finer presentment of thoughts which perhaps are not wholly unworthy of *artistic treatment*.

I see with *rare delight*—that the passages concerning the "*twilight asphodels*," "the *lady-Lily*" &c, have *not* been penned in vain. Hereafter, I will write more in detail, touching your corrections, emendations, hints &c &c. And at the same time, I'll return the MS of "*F.P.*," which you will *honor me by retaining*.[1]

—Don't fancy, meanwhile, that I've forgotten *your* far more important, elaborate, & ambitious poem on the "*Jacquerie*." I am in sooth, *examining it line by line, syllable by syllable*, as under a species of *mental microscope*; and my admiration *deepens* as I go further & further into the *minute* heart of the narrative—, the ripe, rich core of the *mediaëval* romance, so strange in its *inceptions*, its progress, its *denouement*.

Your blank verse has all the air of *genuine* originality in *construction*; & the story *itself* possesses a noble *quaintness*, a weird "*strangeness*" (in the sense of that word, indicated by *Lord Bacon*; see his *Essays*). When done with them, *I'll carefully* remit your Mss *by Express*.

Believe me,

Always Faithfully,

Paul H. *Hayne*

PO Box 635 Augusta Geo

I have a number of suggestions to make about the *minutiaë* of your Poem. Just now, I can only express my great admiration of its fine, subtle irony. "Your" *fool* or Lord "*Raoul's*" is *superb*!

---

1. Lanier's criticism of "Fire Pictures" has to do mainly with lists of mechanical flaws on the one hand and of beauties on the other. He concludes: "Nothing you have ever done has pleased me so entirely: and I believe the verdict of after-poets will support me. (Anderson, *et al.* [eds.], *Centennial Edition of the Works of Sidney Lanier*, VIII, 145–49). Many of the same points are made again in Lanier's review of *Legends and Lyrics*, "Paul H. Hayne's Poetry," *Southern Magazine*, XVI (January, 1875), 40–48 (also in Anderson, *et al.* [eds.], *Centennial Edition of the Works of Sidney Lanier*, V, 322–33). Hayne was revising "Fire Pictures" for another appearance. See *Harper's Weekly*, XV (November 11, 1871), 1066. The poem had originally appeared in the last issue of *Southern Society* for December, 1867, and was subsequently collected in *LL* and *PCE*, 111–13.

28

To Margaret J. Preston   MS Duke

"Copse Hill," Geo R Road

August 29th 1871

Dear Mrs. Preston;

Both your last letters—need I say how welcome?—have reached me, and I earnestly thank you for them. Thanks too for so promptly returning the MS of "*Cambyses & the Macrobian Bow*," a poem which I'm *charmed* to see you really like. Yes! the *subject*, as you observe, is *very* striking, full of picturesque & tragic capabilities.

I first encountered the narrative in a novel by [G. A.] *Lawrence*, the gallant English gentleman who came over to fight for the "Confederates," but was unluckily taken prisoner by the watchful Yankees, soon after he entered Virginia, confined for months in a *Washington jail*. It's a delightful thing to know that, upon the whole, you rather admire my blank verse, & of course, I shall *profoundly* consider your advice about composing my next long narrative poem (if I am spared to write one!) in *that* measure.[1]

You give us a graphic picture of the "Springs," & of the existence generally passed at watering places. I recognize the truth of what you write, for in my younger days I used to visit Saratoga, Newport, & the various Virginia *spas*; and *vividly* do I recollect most of them, and the amusements prevalent thereat.

The "*Sweet Springs*" *Va.* are associated in my mind with a tragic occurrence which took place at the *table d'hôte*, the *shooting*, namely, of one man by another, & the almost immediate *death* of the wounded person whose appearance— as they carried him by me on a couple of planks—I can never forget, despite my own tender age at the time of only 9 years.

As for the *recreations*, & the mode of spending one's leisure & money at these "*Springs*,"—I look upon them as the mere desperate resources of a Conventionalism, the laws of which would be "more honored in the breach, than the observance!" So *thorough* a Barbarian have *I* become on account of my long sojourn in the woods, and among the free untrammelled hills, that I would find it simply insufferable— this *dressing*, and *redressing*, this subservience to forms, & ceremonies, this weary round, (in brief) of fashion, as narrow, and disgusting as the journey on a tread mill.

But—with reasonable prudence—*health* may be gained at these "*springs*." For example, I cannot but fancy that *your* strength & spirits are much improved by your sojourn among them.

You write *more* cheerfully; your very *calligraphy* looks firmer, and *clearer*. Am I not *right*?

The escape from housekeeping *alone* must have proved an ineffable kind of relief!

Good Heavens! *What* a picture your words suggest, in regard to the troops of visitors who descend upon you so often in Lexington!! It is absolutely *terrible*! My *wife* declares that *she* especially sympathizes with you upon these household difficulties, and the marvel to *both* of us is, that despite *such* constant drawbacks, such interruptions & material obstacles of every sort, you can nevertheless, compose so *frequently*, and compose so *well*![2]

I would like to see the *hymns* you have just written.

With *all* my soul I agree with you upon the immense difficulty of composing *devotional* poetry. *Once* in my life I tried this species of composition and failed—ignominiously, utterly, completely, disgracefully. The *conventional* style of *Hymn* appears to me the *flattest*, & most doleful of commonplaces.

Devotional Sentiment is crushed thereby into a "straight waistcoat," & its contortions *distress* instead of *elevating* the spirit.

Chaucer alluding to his noble, pure young *Prioress*, says that her psalms or hymns were,

"Entuned thro her *nose* full sweetily" but the *nosy twang* which accompanies the vast majority of our Christian hymns, whether they be simply *read*, & we consider their rhythmical & metrical effects, or *sung*, and we listen to the *air* which hath married the *words*, is assuredly, *not* "entuned sweetily," however undoubted its connection with "Noseology." *Some* hymns of course are exquisite; but I speak in a general way.

What a criticism you've given me on Browning's style in a couple of sentences!, so terse, philosophical, and discriminating—a *critique*, I call it, "in a nut-shell"!!

As for the *native genius* of the man, it is *colossal*, with more *weight*, and *breadth* in it than *Tennyson*'s, yet *who* does not prefer Tennyson?

"He," says Edgar Poe, "who in *poetry* neglects *music*, and the combinations of musical effect, is mad, *theory-mad* beyond redemption," and in *this* Poe is *right*.

With the *highest* appreciation of that marvellous "*Book and Ring*" or "Ring & Book," I would rather be the author of "*Guinevere*" in "*Idylls of the King*," than the author of a score of such *wonders*!

I saw the paper on Salerno, (in "New & Old") to which you refer. I delight in *such* articles. In fact, *all* well written accounts of travels & of foreign places are most interesting to me.

It was my *dream* once to visit the old World, and linger among the scenes of the *Orient*;—to sojourn particularly in Scotland & England, and S*o* Italy—but the dream *can never* be fulfilled *now*, and I must e'en content myself with liberal draughts upon imagination, while I absolutely try to *bury myself*, (as it were) in the pages of such writers as Howells (see his admirable books on *Venice*, and his "Italian Journeys"!), and Kinglake & quaint old *Hué* whose "China," and "Tartary & Thibet" are pictures, clear & keen as photographic likenesses![3]

O! how I delight also, in the reading of the "frozen North"!—of accompanying Hays [*sic*], and Bush among the arctic seas and the lakes of Siberia!![4]

Only in the *latter case* I prefer going in *spirit*;—it must be simply *horrible* to live in an atmosphere 30° or 40° *below* freezing point, & in contact with filthy Kamskatkians [*sic*], or yet filthier Esquimaux!!.

By the way, the friends you mention who have become so captivated with *France*, that they can't abide this "rude" land, are at least, lucky inasmuch as they possess the *means* of going back to their beloved Gaul!

Nor am I surprised at their feelings! We are all, more or less, the creatures of *habit*; and my experience is,—or I should rather say my *observation* leads me to assert, that *nobody* who has resided in *Paris*, or any prominent French city for a *decade*, can be happy or contented in America.

We speak loftily of our *immortal* souls, & "a' that," but *most* people are wretchedly dependent on "materialities," on food, fashion, dress, the tables we sit down to, and the beds we sleep in!! Well! *one* comfort of *poverty* is, that *perhaps* (who knows?) *Fortunatus* may visit us with his purse before "the end of the chapter," whereas if that "purse" be already ours, overflowing with *sovereigns*, or *greenbacks*, there is no outlook beyond the present; we have *all* we need, or the *means* of procuring all we need.

Despite, therefore, what I have written a page or two back, it *may* be in my power yet to row up the *Bosphorus*, and to view the ruins of the Acropolis, and smoke the "Sacred weed" in the streets of Damascus, & among the *bazaars* of Cairo & Constantinople!!

Apropos of this topic, I possess a few stained letters, old and weather beaten written by my father to his sisters, & dated, one *Smyrna*, another Constantinople, a third Naples, (my father was an officer in the U.S. Navy), and I can't tell you how oddly it makes me feel to glance over the *signature* to these epistles, (Paul H Hayne), written in a calligraphy so much like my *own*, that 'tis startling!! Yes, *he*—my father—, saw all the wonders of the world; and came towards home, 2 years only after his marriage, to perish of yellow fever at the miserable town of Pensacola in *Fla*!! And I—I cannot even remember his appearance!! He died at the age of 29, & his face always shines upon me thro a cloud of romance and mystery.[5]

But I must pause. My *wife* sends you her earnest love, & my boy entreats Mr*s* *Preston* *not* to forget him.

> Believe me Faithfully yours
> Paul H Hayne
> P.O. Box, 635, Augusta Geo

1. The novel by G. A. Lawrence remains unidentified. All considerations of Cambyses, of course, are ultimately from Herodotus. The poem was collected in *LL* and *PCE*, 116–18.

2. Mrs. Preston was often beset by household duties occasioned chiefly by "Virginia hospitality," as Hayne expressed it. She often explains her approach to literary matters in terms of the brief time she has to devote to composition and artistry in the midst of the "mysteries of Sally-Lunn" or "company to breakfast, ditto to dine, ditto to tea." And yet she did not wish to be Susan B. Anthony's "compeer." "I scorn to see a woman, who confesses even to very positive literary proclivities, turn with contempt from, or neglect the proper performance of a simple woman's household duties. Let them come first, by all her love for husband and children; by all her self-respect; and if a margin of time is left, then she may scribble *that* over, to her heart's relief" (Allan, *Life and Letters of Margaret Junkin Preston*, 246).

3. Alexander W. Kinglake (1807–1891) was the author of *Eothen, or Traces of Travel Brought Home from the East* (1844) and Fernand Hué (1846–1894) also wrote about the East.

4. Isaac Israel Hayes (1832–1881) was an arctic explorer whose most recent book, *The Land of Desolation* (1871), Hayne had probably heard about or read.

5. Paul Hamilton Hayne, Sr. (1803–1831), was the thirteenth of the fourteen children of William and Elizabeth Peronneau Hayne; at the time of his death on September 14, 1831, he was a lieutenant in the U.S. Navy and twenty-eight years old.

29

To Sidney Lanier	MS Johns Hopkins

Private & Confidential

> "*Copse Hill*" *Geo R Road*;
> *September, 8th 1871*

My Dear Lanier;

Thanks for your long and interesting letter. The details of your sickness I have read with great attention, and *frankly*, my dear fellow,

I'm sorry to see that things are worse than I expected. *Not* that you ought to be discouraged; for Consumption is not a cureless disease, & moreover it is certain that, as yet, you cannot be properly said to have consumption.

Still, all your symptoms point to great feebleness of the lungs; & the muscular & nervous disorganization you mention, is significant & serious enough. Then, your *average* weight being near a hundred & fifty pounds, you only weigh a hundred & *twenty two* at present, (which, by the way, is *my* average *precisely*).

What *should* be done in view of these considerations?

I can only tell you what cured *me*, after I had become a mere shaking & rattling *skeleton*.

My Physician—an English Doctor, & an eccentric, whom some persons laughed at—informed me, that my chances of life were just represented by the biggest of big *Osts* [*sic*], in fact were absolutely *nil* & that I was a good patient to experiment upon.

"Experiment away!" said I, "what the deuce does it matter, since I'm booked for Charon's boat?" "Now," cried the Doctor, "I'll *kill*, or *cure* you!" Whereupon he took me in hand, and made me drink from 2 to 3 *strong milk punches* a day, (generally 3) and beginning with a 5th of a grain of *morphine*, pretty rapidly increased the dose to *1,—2,—3,* & lastly *4 grains*!!

Opium, quoth *Aësculapius*, is "absurdly miscomprehended by the Profession, both in America, & Europe. It is, rightly administered, a *great tissue* saver; & acts *indirectly* upon *diseased lungs*, in rendering the system impervious to *colds* &c.

"No opium eater ever dies of consumption; and it is a remarkable fact that in China, the *mandarins* who take *small specified doses of the drug daily*, arrive as a Class, at extreme old age!

"When, therefore, the consumptive patient comes to me, declaring that the other Doctors have given him up, I treat, and have often cured him, with *milk punch* and *morphine*. The taking of the *latter* may *generally* necessitate a *partial* subservience to the medicine *ever after*; but *that* is better than death, despite the howlings of Coleridge and De Quincey, who *abused* a great blessing, and were punished accordingly."—Thus far my D*r*!! In a *desperate* position, he resorted to a *desperate* remedy,—and in my case—*succeeded*!!! Should the *Leeches* begin to shake their heads over *your* Condition, follow my advice, *Lanier*, and at least *try* the course recommended.[1]

—God grant you may get well, *without* it, however, & pursue your life course brilliantly & successfully to the end.

Well may you refer mournfully to Literature, above all, to Poetry, as the means of gaining one's bread!

Bitterly myself do I feel the degradation, when *forced* to manufacture verses for the *Market*. But with *debt*, & *starvation* staring a man in the face, he is driven to "little" expedients, & loses a portion of his squeamishness, (alack! that it *should* be so!) as time rolls on![2]

As regards *yourself*, I *can't* help believing that if *circumstances* drive you into *Literature, as a profession*, you will *unequivocally* succeed; & I could almost find it in my soul to rejoice if you *had* to become an author. "*'Tis thy vocation, Lucius!*"

You are going positively to N. York City. Would to Heaven I could spare the time & cash to accompany you! But Fate sternly sayeth, "*no!*" as She *always does* manage to say, whenever I specially desire to do something agreeable, & after mine own heart.

Think of it! *Lanier*, since 1866, I have never been more than 10 miles from my cottage home! I who *delight* in movement, travel, adventure!, & who *previous* to *that* period had been accustomed to rove from *Carolina* to *Canida* [*sic*], from Manhattan, to the *great West*!!

I ask of *Destiny*, "Stern *Mother*!, what sin hath thy son committed, that he should thus be "cabinned, cribbed, confined?"—But, the "oracles are dumb," and perforce I must *endure*.

'Tis harder than ever, when I read the poems ("*Songs of the Sierras*") of the new celebrity *Joaquin Miller*, who despite his infernal name, is I assure you a *true Genius*, evincing the Strongest imagination, veined all over with the rich, ripe blood of youth & passion!

The fellow sings what he was *seen*, and *heard*, and *acted*, and so, there's a *reality* & *vim* about his tales, and metrical pictures, very striking & effective. The London *guilds* have gone mad over him, & in this Country some critics, (*women* critics especially) are trying their d——t to ruin him; but *Miller* has the true *afflatus*, & may refuse to be ruined—*artistically at least*.[3]

—To return to New York! Shall I send you the letters of introduction *there*, or *at once* to *Marietta*? Have you time to inform me? "*Cambyses*" was mailed you in a very rough state, & you have made but little of the poem, I fear. Yet the legend is *striking*, and in the right hands would have come out gloriously.

God bless you *my friend*, & may the *Angel of Health*, re-visit you. She is an Angel *I* have not seen for a quarter of a century.

Always Faithfully,
Paul H Hayne
PO Box 635, Augusta Geo

1. There is a question about whether Hayne was actually cured of tuberculosis. On several occasions subsequently he was examined by physicians who informed him that he had no "tubercles on his lungs," but he had some form of occasional lung trouble and recurrent hemorrhages throughout the rest of his life, though he apparently died of a stroke and not tuberculosis.

2. Hayne maintains consistently this view of "writing for bread" throughout his career, but he made no serious effort after the war to turn to any career apart from writing.

3. For a different view of Miller, see the next letter (no. 30), where Hayne admits to Mrs. Preston that he had been taken in by the writer and the poems and had "overrated" both.

30

To Margaret J. Preston   MS Duke

"Copse Hill," Geo R Road Dec 15th 1871

Your letter of the 15*th* ult, *My Dear Friend*, (& a most *charming* letter, I can tell you), gave me the greater pleasure, because it found me sick, struggling against the worst cold & cough I had caught for 20 years, and just in sore need, consequently, of *some* consolation from *without*!

How kind it was of you wearied by the duties of Hostess, protracted to an unusual degree, to think of [writing] to me at all and how deeply, when your communication arrived, I . . *all* here—appreciated, & enjoyed it![1]

I doubt, indeed, whether you can form the remotest conception of the real value I place upon your correspondence. To do so, it would be necessary that you should come here, and examine my home, and its surroundings, behold the isolation *of both*, and the precise manner in which, tho still *in* the world, I cannot claim to be of it!

Then you would comprehend *what* my friends' letters are to me!

You have written *graphically* of the feelings of an author,—especially a Poet, who is engaged in correcting & arranging his proofsheets—: clothing and daintily adorning the children of his brain, sentiment, fancy, imagination, philosophy, before finally dismissing them to be criticised by a callous Public. A decade ago, my own sensations in regard to the publication of my *2nd* vol, were exactly such as you describe;—but *now, now,* many an artistic illusion has melted into thin air. I have come to know both others & myself better; to realize the fact that no vo*l* of *my* composing can long keep its head above the tide, the terrible o'er whelming tide of Time:

"What ever 'scaped Oblivion's subtle wrong, Save a few clarion names, and golden threads of Song!"

No verse of mine, alas! can enter into the warp or woof of that "golden thread" whereof the Poet speaks!

Fully contented shall I be, if my rhymes are of a sweetness and thoughtfulness sufficient to keep their place in the hearts of loving friends; and for a season, to murmur harmoniously in the depths of kindred spirits!

Every foolish idea of an extended *fame,* had a *long, long* since abandoned me; therefore, I looked over the proofs of what I composed, in a humbled, chastened temper, with far more of melancholy, than exultation; unvisited, I fear, even for one fleeting moment, by the delightful mental "titillation" to which you allude! But I am sick of my own Egotism! Please forgive me.

Like myself—I perceive that you all get the various new books, of any account, as they issue from the *Northern press!* You mention *Stoddard,* and Winter! *The former* is an old acquaintance of mine, with whom I have corresponded upon intimate terms (at intervals), for 16 years.

Perhaps a *personal* feeling may somewhat influence my judgment, when I declare that his last work is, to my taste, one of the *subtlest,* sweetest contributions to the world's poetry, that has appeared for a quarter of a century! His *Eastern Songs*—exquisite as many of them are—I admire less than the *longer* pieces contained in the first *half* of his vo*l*; for example, his noble " *Ode*" to *Shakespeare*, his terse, simple, forceable [*sic*] lines upon the death of Dickens; & above all, that wonderful "*In Memoriam*," which possesses an almost awful beauty and tenderness!

Neither Tennyson nor any other master, has excelled *some touches* in that long wail of desolation & grief!

One stanza especially affects me; I mean the verse which runs thus;

> "Pale fathers pass me in the street,
> Where little sons like mine are dead;
> I *see it in the drooping head*,
> And in the wandering of the feet:"[2]

What simple pathos, heart-broken, ineffable, comes to one, in these unambitious lines, at once so homely, and so true!

There are, however, some 4 or 5 productions in S's book, which as a Southerner, I find it hard to peruse with anything like patience.

Those "Homeric" *lines* on *Lincoln* (for instance), *may* be good, but I see continually between each stanza, a gaudy, coarse, not over cleanly, whiskey drinking, and whiskey smelling Blackguard, elevated by a grotesque *Chance*, (nearly allied to *Satan*), to the position for which of all others, he was most *unfit*;—and where memory has been *idealised* by Yankee fancy, & Yankee arrogance, in a way, that *would* be ludicrous, were it not *disgusting*, & calculated, finally, to belie the facts of History, and hand down to future times as Hero & Martyr, as commonplace a *Vulgarian* as ever patronized bad Tobacco, and mistook *blasphemy* for *wit*!

I declare, this *monomaniac Apotheosis* of Lincoln is unaccountable! That (after Stoddard) a man like *Lowell*, in a poem of the scope, power, & genius of his grand "Commemoration Ode" should designate the Illinois pettifogger as "the *first American*," confounds one's sense of right & wrong, & produces a chaotic condition of the brain!

Apropos of Lowell, is it possible, as you say, that any Critic has been stupified to compare *Winter's* productions with *his*?[3]

The latter, (Winter), is a *careful* versifier, no more, and his book, like *Miller's* has been outrageously overrated. Let me frankly confess, however, that these "*Songs of the Sierras*" took me in, completely deceived me, *for a time*.

Their frequent resonance of rhythm & picturesque force & beauty, blinded my judgment; and I formed an opinion of the writer's talents, which every subsequent perusal of his work has led me wofully to modify.

Bret Harte (to whom you refer) I think very highly of, as a *prose* writer, a sketcher of rough Western scenes; but as for his "*Heathen Chinee*,"—which everybody North, and even in London seems to have gone crazy over,—I can't read it with any pleasure whatever. It appears forced, and vulgar too! (My *own* fault perhaps).

How *right* you are concerning *Emerson*, and his transcendental opinion of *Plato*, and Aristophanes!! It is all the *merest humbug*; the fanatical view of a man whose genius th*o* acute, & often profound also, is sharply limited! When he wanders beyond its keenly defined boundary, then, he grows, feeble, erratic, and preeminently untrustworthy!

The cold weather from which you have been suffering, has visited us at last!

Day before yesterday, we had a severe storm; yesterday it still blew and rained at intervals, but to day is clearly cold, *bitter* indeed, and demanding huge pine-knot-fires!

Ah! these blessed "*pine-knots*!" They are our winter "*stand-by*"; and it was the gorgeous flames *they* produced, which suggested to my fancy, the poem, called "*Fire Pictures*," published recently in Harper's "Weekly," and enjoying a popularity which has amazed me.[4]

Excuse the rude handwriting of this letter. Despite the fire, my fingers are dreadfully numbed.

My wife & boy unite with me in best love to you.

Write soon, and

Believe me,

Always yr true friend,
Paul H Hayne
PO Box 635, Augusta, Geo

P.S. I don't know *when* my book will be out! The title is simply: "*Legends, & Lyrics*."[5]

It would give you *real delight* to know *how highly* my wife appreciates your poetic genius. She has your book in hand *continually*, & has memorized many pieces.

Which of Mr Preston's *two* daughters was *married* the other day? We would so like to know.

1. All ellipsis points in the text of the letters, unless otherwise noted, are Hayne's.

2. Richard Henry Stoddard's long poem is in memory of his second son, Will, who died "almost at his birth." It later was collected in *The Book of the East and Other Poems* (1871).

3. William Winter (1836–1917) published several books of verse, one of which— *My Witness*—appeared in 1871, but he is better remembered today as the drama critic of the New York *Tribune* (1866–1909).

4. This passage suggests that Hayne may have forgotten that he had sent Mrs. Preston in an earlier letter (December 31, 1867) a version of "Fire Pictures" that had just appeared in *Southern Society*.

5. *Legends and Lyrics* appeared in January, 1872.

31

To Sidney Lanier   MS Johns Hopkins

near Augusta March 6th (1872)

My Dear Lanier;

I was *both* pleased, and freed from much anxiety, by the reception of your kind letter of the 1st, just now resting on the desk before me. I learn *two* things from it! *Firstly,* your *health* has at least rallied so far, as to allow of your returning to the toil of business, and very onerous labor too, as I can't help perceiving. This is news only the *more* welcome, because somewhat unexpected. The fact is your hurried note from N York, referring to *relapse* startled me considerably. I almost began to fear it was all up with you; and the pain caused by such a feeling I would find it hard to exaggerate. Apart from our *personal friendship,* I have always—despite your necessarily *practical* profession—to take [*sic*] a vivid interest in your *literary* prospects & have looked to *you* to do the South rare honor in the bright fields of *imaginative art,*—and so, the prospect of *Death* drawing his black, oblivious pall over all your hopes & mine, saddened my *heart* and *mind* alike!—Thank Heaven! the prospect lightens! But be careful of *thyself,* O Poet, and friend!

A word ab't my book! How charmed I am that you should *specially* have selected the *Mockingbird "Sonnet"* for commendation[,] of all the *Sonnets* my *own* favorite!

As for your promise to review "*L & L*" in the Macon "*Telegraph*" or "*Somewhere else,*" I am *more* than *pleased* at *that*—, I am *deeply touched.*[1] That you should amid your press of *business* engagements, turn aside to *think* and to *write* on my behalf is a kindness I am never likely to *forget.* And let me say what I hold to be simple truth. You are gifted with a *subtlety* of critical, (or I should rather say) *imaginative perception,* wedded to equal power of subtle expression, and analytical judgment, which would cause me to select *you* from among all the writers I know to bring out any hidden or occult meanings, any spiritual suggestiveness that may possibly lie beneath the surface of my verses. Think then with what unaffected eagerness I must look forward to your review. Only—I would not (for a moment), be so *selfish* as to wish you to over fatigue yourself in any way. When leisure comes, you must tell me about your MS poem "*The Jacquerie.*" (And ab't my own vo*l Lanier,* of course I want you to find as much fault with it as your *artistic con-*

science may tell you is right. You are not the man to compose nor am I the man to ask for a *puff*!! God forbid.) In haste but always y'r *true friend*.

Paul H Hayne
PO Box 635 Augusta, Geo

1. A few weeks earlier on February 15 Hayne had written to ask if *Legends and Lyrics* had arrived. "Should your strength allow," he continued, "I would like above all things to have a candid review from your pen in 'The Telegraph'—or elsewhere." For reasons not entirely clear, Lanier had a hard time placing his review, but it subsequently appeared in the *Southern Magazine* for January, 1875, three years after the book had appeared. The text is reprinted in Anderson, *et al.* (eds.), *Centennial Edition of the Works of Sidney Lanier*, V, 322–33.

32

To Margaret J. Preston   MS Duke

"Copse Hill," Geo R Road April 9th 1872

My very Dear Friend;

I must lay all my work aside for the moment, and tell you of the *heartfelt satisfaction experienced* by all the members of my little family, when your letter of 3rd in*st* reached us, yesterday afternoon! Great was the *"hullabaloo,"* (to borrow a childish expression) in this cottage on the hill! It would have pleased your sympathetic & generous heart to see Minna's delight, and mine, also the *boy, "Will's"* who is by no means backward in offering you his juvenile allegiance.

Per Hercle! but the news *is glorious*! That notice of *"Sandringham"* by Gladstone on the floor of the *Parliament House*, is *alone worth* all the critiques of North & South put together, even if every paper in America had been loud in your praise!

Perhaps as the Premier read your beautiful lines, he thought of the years that are gone, of the So Confederacy, struggling, & alone against fearful odds; anxiously casting her eyes across the water for *some* symptom of practical help from *England*; & perhaps too, the idea struck him that the only voice of *genuine sympathy* from this Country, touching the illness of England's "Crown Prince" came from a Southern quarter, and was emphasised by the passionate sincerity of So genius. I marvel whether some slight pang of *self-reproach* shot thro the Politician's care-hardened bosom, while he pondered over your verses?

Still more a matter of congratulations is the letter of thanks from her Royal Highness, the Princess of Wales, to the Ed: of the "*London Cosmopolitan*" for re-publishing your piece. This fact, so pertinent *in itself*, and so honorable to *you*, & to Southern letters, I shall take special pains to have noticed in *every So journal*, or *Magazine* I can *possibly* reach, and influence.

We owe it to your position, and genius, and to our Section too, that this much should be done. Of course, the *Gladstone notice* shall be mentioned likewise.[1]

Surely these things *my friend* must encourage, & *greatly* stimulate your artistic *ambition*! I am so glad—so *heartily rejoiced*!—and as for my wife—she's *lilting* like a canary or thrush, all over the house in pure delight of soul at your glorious recognition.

Now, *what am* I to say in response to such unselfish kindness as *yours*?

Then, I find you, (after having done my book a *world of good* by your *first exquisite critique*), actually composing & sending off a *second* review!![2] I am deeply *touched* by *such* consideration, & can hardly trust myself to thank you aright. But your *more* than kindness will never be forgotten.

Barron Hope I knew *once*, years on years ago—i.e. as a Correspondent, about the period of his acting as Ed: of a journal called, (I think) "*the South*."[3] His *prose articles* I was often charmed with, the style being lucid, strong, and scholarly. His poetry (*sub rösa*!) I never *could* admire,—excepting some *few individual pieces out* of his general manner of rhythmical composition. Hope's verse to my mind lacks *simplicity* and symmetry; it is frequently very ambitious, resonant, sounding—but just a trifle *hollow* in regard to *genuine thought* too much, (in brief)—like a—*drum*!! Yet I respect his talents, which are unquestionable, and somebody—[John R.] Thompson I believe—told me he was, and *is* doubtless—a most worthy and high-toned gentleman.

You inquire concerning my sketch in "*Appleton's*."[4] The whole article tells the *literal truth* about our troubles with servants, and outlines—barely *outlines*—our sad, forlorn poverty-stricken condition in many other particulars. The *denouement* alone—is purposely exaggerated, or rather invented "out of the whole cloth" (to use a cant phrase), for purposes of effect—an exhibition of bad taste I must frankly acknowledge.

No such negro as the one mentioned had waited upon us, and *par consequence*, no such negro was shot!! But apart from the conclusion, my picture is *underdrawn,* not *overdrawn*!! One of these days, when the chance occurs, I will write you a full, true narrative of our early trials in *Georgia.* Our really terrible position in the "back woods" for months and indeed upwards of a year, *sans* money, *sans* friends, *sans* hope, *sans* Provisions, & *sans*—everything! Even now, we live in a *house* and a *style* which to most people born as we were, & comparatively opulent once—would seem intolerable.

The house, *per se,* would make a man of *the most* moderate aspirations on the subject of a family dwelling—*look blue* and disgusted; and the *bare sight* thereof would cause a *petite maitre* [*sic*] to faint dead away upon the spot!!

'Tis a small *white-washed* Cottage & execrably built; and even more execrably *planned.*

So loose is the *flooring,* that it *creaks,* and "warbles" at every step one takes. The gaping voids between the planks are clumsily filled up with *laths,* and as for the ceilings & walls,—especially the ceiling and walls in my chamber—they exhibit the oddest & most grotesque combination of *figures,* and *faces*; the result of the dropped and eternally dropping *plaster,* which process has converted the room into a species of rough "*Comic Annual*"!! There's the head of a *woman* (for instance) just over my bed which represents "Little Dorrit's" friend *Maggie* in all the splendor of her dirty but voluminous cap with frilled borders, and her extraordinary *bonnet,* pushed back from a face of flat features, and an amazed & *amazing* vacancy!!—

And—but I must not attempt to describe our Cottage at length.

As for the *style of living here,* altho my wife has *educated herself into the* position of first-class practical housekeeper, and *substantial* comfort (thank God!) is not wanting—yet the entire *ménage* would cause you, I'm sure, to start back with astonishment!

—Certain mines of Cornwall are *strongly* represented, at "Copse Hill," for bright as many of our plates & drinking utensils may seem, they are *not silver* but *tin*!

But the air is healthful, and we can enjoy in these woods perfect independence,—*social* and *political*!!

Moreover, the small income which *house rent* & *taxes* would swallow up in a *City,* suffices for our humble wants.

In any *town* whatever I should have no choice but to become a *local Editor* or Clerk in some mercantile establishment—a molasses & bacon store probably—, whilst here I am free—as the clouds & the rain, and if the great advantages of intellectual attrition are denied me,—at all events, I have *nature* as a friend, and these undisturbed opportunities for commune with *her*, and with the noble-minds of the Past, so eagerly looked for, and vainly looked for, by men *in all other* regards, more fortunate than myself.

Let me revert to some items of interest suggested by your letter of the 26*th* March—the last but one rec*d* from Lexington. You mention our ex-vice-President, [Alexander H.] *Stephens*, who has, you say, written you a friendly letter. I really think that M*r* S. has every desire to honor *Southern Literature*, but he stands, a noteworthy, conspicuous example, of the *aesthetic ignorance* of our So Statesmen & Politicians!! He praises in the "*Atlanta Sun*" your "*New Song & Old*";—my poems too, are praised in the same journal—together with Miss Fisher's "*Valerie Aylmer*," & "*Morton House*"—, but alack! taking all artistic force, and significance from the commendation of *such* a *Critic*—we find him—M*r* Stephens—growing enthusiastic over the merits (!!!) of a *novel*, like "*Heart Hungry*," by a M*rs* *Westmoreland of Atlanta*,— which he calls a "characteristic So work," "an extraordinary effort," with the *tragic* force in parts of a *Shakspeare*, and heaven knows how much pestilent twaddle besides!

And *this* is the mode adopted by M*r* S.. to advance the glory of So letters!!*⁵*

By the way, if you have not enjoyed the rare good fortune of reading "*Heart Hungry*," now in its 4*th* edition, & about to be acted on the *stage*, let me observe, *that* the vilest trash that ever issued from the "*Minerva press*," in the latter portion of the 18*th* century, would compare favorably with its coarse *morale*, its characterization, at once extravagant, & feeble, and its entire atmosphere of silly sentimentalism, unredeemed by a single grace of composition, or a single trait, natural, and unconventional!!

I am pleased to see that my friend Miss Fisher's letter charmed you, as it appears to have done! She is indeed, a remarkable young woman; full of genius, and energy, and will & ambition, with sound common sense to *back* all her endeavors. I predict for her a *brilliant* future!*⁶*

A word about "*Appleton's Journal*" & its Editors. When 3 years ago the journal was started, I rec*d* from the Proprietors an invitation to become one of their *Contributors* & ever since, I've written *more* for "*Appleton*" than for any other periodical. The *Chief Editor*, is M*r Robert Carter*, assisted by Mr. O. B. *Bunce*; both of whom have treated me with invariable courtesy, kindness, and *liberality*. But on several occasions *Carter* has not hesitated to return poems, and prose essays I had sent him, with no further explanation than that involved in the remark, that "they *did* not suit him"!

It is often, in truth *not* the literary *merit* of a piece which causes its acceptance;—so much as its probable *popularity*.

And, in like manner, pieces of *great merit* are rejected frequently, because they fail to treat of a popular topic in a popular manner.

Do I receive "*Scribner's,*" you inquire? Yes, and almost *all* the other Magazines, and papers, issued in America. My room looks continually like an Editor's "*Sanctum,*" covered with "exchanges" of every conceivable kind. By the way, your dramatic poem in "*Scribner's*" on the *boy* who wanted to be shot with his "*back*" *to the wall*, is a *noble* performance, terse, suggestive, powerful!! It has made its mark already. The papers everywhere are copying it!

You surprise me not a little, *apropos* of your Poems, by saying that Co*l* Preston rather encouraged the notion of simply a "*private* circulation" of the book; and that he is averse to a woman's "*rushing into print*" &c—No man could by *any* possibility desire to see all the delicacies which surround your sex, more carefully preserved, than I do,—*but there is no sex in genius*, and, I would, with my dying breath uphold a woman's *right* nay! her solemn *duty*, (to God, & her own nature), to appear before the world as a *Teacher* & *Consoler*, thro the force, or beauty of her *thoughts*, as presented in *poem, novel, essay,* or drama!!

In *such* a case, the *writer herself* appears not *at all*; her conceptions, her ideas, her imaginations speak for her.

And the history of Literature shows, that many of the most *gifted women*, the most *voluminous* as well as *luminous* female authors have been accomplished *housekeepers*; full of practical experience, efficiency, and power.[7]

Your mention of *Hand Browne's* contemptuous allusion to *Whipple* reminds me to say, that I by no means agree with *B's* policy, or rather his petulant habit of crying over all genius and reputation "*north* of the Potomac," or at least, north of Maryland.

I think this sort of thing *childish*, and unworthy the good sense, and keen intellectual vision of a Thinker like M*r* Browne.

As I told him in a recent letter, I never inquire (e.g.) *who* has *written* such & such a poem, or critique, but is such a poem, or critique *good*—is it full of imagination, & feeling, or of logic, and sound argument? If it *be*—let us acknowledge it, tho the *Devil himself* may have been the author.[8]

The "Sonnet" dedicated to yourself you have kindly commended; but I regard it as utterly *unworthy* the *subject*.

—Contrary to the general idea, *inspiration* in *poetry*, does *not always keep pace* with *feeling*, however deep, and sincere.

—Often & often I have *tested* this matter, and I think a very subtle, and suggestive essay could be written on the subject.

What think you?—The Editor of "*The Atlantic Monthly*" has actually accepted & payed for, a little poem of mine ("*Aspects of the Pines*," which I sent you a copy of!!)[9]

Is the world coming to an end? It looks fearfully like it!!

Receive—in conclusion—the united love, & felicitations of all my household.

Minna is so firm & enthusiastic an adherent of monarchy; she loves the English People & government so truly, that she was vastly delighted with the honor you had rec*d*, and ran down stairs, clapping her hands, and genuinely excited, to read the paragraph (from the "*Cosmopolitan*"), to my *mother*, and a *friend* who happened to be visiting us at the time.

My wife begs you to offer her congratulations to *Col Preston*, who must feel—she knows, as *proud* as *she herself* would feel under similar circumstances.

Believe me Always Faithfully

> Your friend,
> Paul H Hayne
> P.O. Box 635, Augusta, Geo

By the way, did Lippincott send your books to *England*, or did you yourself mail it to some friend there? I have found the *Lippincotts* very polite &c, but *wofully* [*sic*] *careless* in regard to advertising my work, or sending it to Edts &c—Many copies (at great expense), I have had to *send myself*.

---

1. This comment is characteristic of Hayne. Not only does he appreciate the honor to Mrs. Preston, but he is aware that recognition of her work reflects credit upon "Southern letters," and he takes it upon himself to spread the news throughout the South. This is another instance of how seriously Hayne took his self-appointed duty as literary spokesman for the South. Mrs. Preston, of course, is a friend, but she is also a southern poet

whose work has attracted appreciation from the highest levels in England. "Sandringham" had originally appeared in the *Albion* for January 27, 1872, and was subsequently collected in *Cartoons* (1875), 186–88. For an example of Hayne's effort to spread the news about the response to Mrs. Preston's poem, see his letter to E. P. Whipple of April 13, 1872, in which Hayne informs Whipple that he has "ventured to persuade Mrs. Preston," a "woman of genius," to send Whipple a copy of *Old Song and New* and suggests that he notice it in his literary column in the *Globe*. Then Hayne describes the reaction to "Sandringham" in England and concludes: "Any evidence of intellectual improvement at the South, especially in *art*, and belles lettres, I like you to see, since your heart is so generous, as your brain is full of imaginative pith, and the rich marrow of wisdom!"

2. Mrs. Preston's first review of *LL* appeared in the *Southern Magazine* for March, 1872. Her second review, according to Hayne's letter of July 3, 1872, was in the *Old Dominion Magazine*, a journal no longer readily available for examination.

3. James Barron Hope (1829–1887), Virginia journalist, editor of the Norfolk *Virginian* and later the *Landmark*, and author of two volumes of verse by this time, had corresponded with Hayne in the late 1850s.

4. "Southern Country Life," *Appletons' Journal*, VII (March 16, 1872), 284–89. A fictional account of servant troubles in Georgia in 1865, Hayne's sketch is climaxed by a scene in which the narrator shoots a male servant who is robbing his house.

5. Stephens and Hayne had been friends for years and had kept up a desultory correspondence, but Hayne had to admit that a statesman he honored had little discrimination about literature. Ironically, later in 1872 Stephens asked Hayne to contribute "critical articles" regularly to his newspaper, the Atlanta *Sun*, and Hayne agreed. Hayne's real feeling for Stephens is expressed in "Alexander Hamilton Stephens: In Memoriam," a lyric published on April 1, 1883, in *Home and Farm*, shortly after Stephens' sudden death and barely a month after Stephens and Hayne had appeared together in Savannah as orator and poet of the sesquicentennial celebration of the founding of Georgia. Hayne paid his respects to writers like Mrs. Maria Westmoreland and novels like *Heart Hungry* (1872) in "Literature at the South: The Fungous School" in the *Southern Magazine* for June, 1874.

6. Frances C. Fisher (1846–1920), a North Carolina woman who wrote under the pen name of Christian Reid, had also received encouragement from Hayne, who had written her late in 1870 or early in January, 1871, with praise of *Valerie Aylmer* (1870), her first novel.

7. Hayne was indubitably a gentleman of the old school; indeed, on occasion, he referred to himself in the 1880s as an "old fogy." But the views he so eloquently expresses about the right of a woman to write are ones he maintains throughout his career, and they stand out in strong contrast to those of Colonel Preston.

8. William Hand Browne, the editor of the *Southern Magazine* in Baltimore, was far more unreconstructed than Hayne was, and he bombarded Hayne and Mrs. Preston alike with the need to oppose "the Yankeeisation of the South" on all fronts, political and cultural alike. See, for example, his letters to Hayne of July 30, 1870, and September 11, 1871. The literary standards Hayne describes are those he had tried to maintain from the beginning of his career.

9. "Aspects of the Pines," *Atlantic Monthly*, XXX (September, 1872), 351. For discussions of Hayne's experience with the *Atlantic*, see Rayburn S. Moore's articles: "Paul Hamilton Hayne and Northern Magazines," in James Woodress, *et al.* (eds.), *Essays Mostly on Periodical Publishing in America: A Collection in Honor of Clarence Gohdes* (Durham: Duke University Press, 1973), 134–47, and "'The Absurdest of Critics': Hayne on Howells," *Southern Literary Journal*, XII (Fall, 1979), 70–78.

33

To Margaret J. Preston   MS Duke

"Copse Hill" Ga R. Road.
(Jan: 18th 1873.)

Hardly had I given up, (last evng) my long letter of some *28 or 30 mortal pages* (!!), together with a couple of chromos, and a copy of Barry Cornwall's Poems, (all addressed to you!), and seen them carefully deposited in the Bag Master's Box, preparatory to their being delivered to the P. Office at *Berzelia*,—than opening my day's mail, lo! the very *first* communication that appeared was your *kind note* of the 13*th* Jan!!

Ah! *how kind* it is!! What a *real* interest you take in me & mine!; an interest I appreciate the more deeply, because (outside my little *home circle*) I haven't a single *blood relation* who cares *three straws* whether I live or die; nor *one* in whose eyes I am not viewed half contemptuously, as a "wool gathering," *unpractical*, impecunious *visionary*, who has somehow broken faith with his family traditions—for you must know that the *Haynes* pride themselves upon what they call their *"clear common sense,"*—which means, briefly, their blindness to all the fair world of imagination, & the graces of the *highest spiritual* culture.

One lady of this family, writing to another lady—connected with the family *by marriage*, rebuked the latter for complaining that her eldest son showed *no literary turn*, and said; "so far from *complaining*, my Dear! you ought to be thankful! Only look at *Paul*, for example—, (meaning your humble servant), & see what has come of poetry, Literature, & such stuff!" What these final words mean, except that I *am poor now* & not likely to become a Cröesus in the future by any *mental* toils of mine, I can't well divine!

My isolation only draws me the nearer in gratitude to those, who like yourself, have given me not merely intellectual recognition, in largest measure, but personal affection.

You can fancy then, how I smiled over the paragraph, in your note, suggesting that *"the Atlantic Monthly's"* favor had absorbed & temporarily *alienated* my spirit(!!!)

O! ye "ancient Heavens"!!, I wouldn't give a *scratch* of *your* pen for all *"the Atlantic's"* that ever *were,* or *may be* published.

Surely, you know *this!*—

We are grieved—*all* of us, to hear of your sickness, and confinement to your chamber. Dreary indeed, must it be in this bitter weather, to have the four walls of a room continually around one;—*unless* your chamber owns an open fire-place, and you can pile up the oak & hickory therein!

You inquire about Timrod's vo*l*. I *haven't* seen any bound copy of the Poems, but I know that the work is *fairly out*.[1] *Hale*, the Publisher, a No Carolinian, (and a generous, gentlemanly *old fellow*!) writes, that he will send me, as Editor of the book, *any number of copies* I choose to mention, which is very handsome, very handsome indeed! Of course, I shall not *abuse* his liberality; but still, his offer enables me to secure as many copies as I need, both for myself, and friends. I'll mail the vo*l* to *you*,—so soon as I receive it—, and *oh! my friend*—if your physical condition permits, I would be more than grateful for a brief notice in the papers from *your pen*![2]

I'm *so* anxious this book should succeed; for the sake alike of the *dead*, and the *living*! (by the *latter*, I mean Timrod's *widow*; a young Englishwoman, struggling by herself in Washington.)

And won't you *buy* a copy too, and induce your friends, to follow suit?

Since the whole matter is with me, a *labor of love*, I can make these requests.[3]

You seem to have a good many foreign Correspondents. Two letters from distant China, and on the same day! Then, there's another letter from England; from the same friend, I conclude, who has just married, and whose name I asked you to tell me, in my last long epistle.

How did you feel in receiving those precious *leaves* from the grave of *Mary* Russell Mitford? I know that I should have *kissed* them, with a reverent, and thankful heart. Miss Mitford is a prime favorite of mine—, not as a poet, or dramatic writer; but as the author of "*Our Village*," and still more, as the sweetest, and noblest *woman* of her generation. Tho it makes one furious, in a certain sense, I know of nothing so pathetic as her life-long illusions concerning that scampish father of hers; & the heroic unselfishness of her devotion to him.

We are having terrible weather here! Yesterday at 12 N. the atmosphere was mild as spring; and now, the ice coats everything; and the Wind howls, like a Dragon in awful agony!

By the way I expect some extra copies of the *Jan*: "*Atlantic*," & will mail you the number.[4]

We respond to your good wishes for the coming year, with *all our hearts*! Pray write when you can, &
Believe me,

> *Always Faithfully yours,*
> Paul H Hayne
> (P.O. Box 635)

P.S. Did you ever read *such stuff* as the enclosed verses by "*Bret Harte*"? Now do tell me, *am* I mistaken? or are these verses really—*poetry*? Say how you like "*Barry Cornwall.*"

    1. *The Poems of Henry Timrod*. Edited, with a sketch of the poet's life, by Paul H. Hayne. New York: E. J. Hale & Son, 1873 (published 1872). In a letter from Hale received by Hayne on January 7, 1873, Hale announced that the book was out.

    2. Mrs. Preston may have written several notices, but her main review appeared in the *Southern Magazine* for April, 1873.

    3. Hayne is quite consistent in referring to the edition as a "labor of love," but his characterization of it in a letter of September 9, 1872, to Mrs. Preston is even more to the point: "The more I study my poor friend's poems, the *more* I perceive what a marvellously *delicate* & *beautiful genius* his was! As for his 'life,'—the consideration of its trials, and privations, might draw tears from a stone!"

    4. This issue (Vol. XXXI, p. 53) contained Hayne's "The Voice in the Pines."

34

To Sidney Lanier   MS Johns Hopkins

> *"Copse Hill," Ga. R Road*
> *Thursday, 27th March (1873)*

My Dear Poet;

Your note of the 12th inst—with its precious "MSS" enclosure, duly reached me, but I have had no leisure to reply until *now*.

Good news it is to hear you say, that your strength has *measureably* returned, and that henceforth you intend devoting much time and energy to *art*!

I think so highly Lanier! of your powers, especially of the *delicacy* and marvellous opulence of your *fancy*; and of your sense of *rhythmic harmonies*, and *verse-music, without* which the *greatest poems* seem harsh, and the *greatest poets uncouth* (if indeed great poems *are*, or great *poets* possible without this sense), that I hail the determination you express to *snub Law* for *Literature* with *real* delight!! And let me add, that *hereafter* I shall look for & shall *confidently* expect to hail brilliant artistic performances on *your part*!

If you *disappoint* me "*odd's! zooks!* and *boddikins!*" [*sic*]—but I'll manage to torment you in some fashion!

And now for the "*June Dreams in January*":[1]

Very attentively, and *half* a *dozen times* over, have I perused this poem, quite a remarkable composition in many respects.

Firstly, I stand *amazed* at the lavish imagery, and the rich overpowering Orientalism of the piece!

Why *Hafiz* might have written it, or *Firdusi!*—Only *one other* English speaking bard ever sang in *this* precise *style*, and that was Alex: Smith in his "*Life Drama*," a production *enormously* overrated, no doubt, *at first*, but most unjustly depreciated *now*.[2]

Your "*June Dreams*" belong to a section of the "*Arte Poetique*," I have never myself affected, and *were* I to do so, heavens! *what* an ass I *would* appear in the eyes of the judicious!!

Don't conceive me as *depreciating* this Oriental magnificence of metaphor, this rapid, magical reproduction of rainbow-blue similes, and bright verbal ingenuities.

On the contrary, there are moods when such things both dazzle & charm me.

And in *such* a mood I read your last poem!

Let us come to *particulars*: (*1st Stanza:*) Your *friend's* objection to this, as "improper," (i.e.) "*Swinburnish*," & too voluptuous, is with due deference—perfectly *absurd*! I like the stanza because it opens the poem nobly, gives at once the *key-note*, and moreover, the personification is equally bold and clear.

2nd Stanza; 1st line reads *haltingly*, why don't you leave out, "*while th'intense hours* &c ["] with its needless *elision* and substitute the following—

"*Throb Beautiful! the fervid (fervent) hours exhaled &c &c*" The idea of the "*kisses* faint-blown from June's *finger-tips* up to *the Sun*," has a certain *prettiness*, but I can't help thinking it a little *artificial* too.

3rd Stanza: Altogether *lovely*!!—with its mellow picture of the "tender darkness," and "crushed day flowers" &c (By the way do you like to put so much stress & emphasis upon the last syllable of a word like *flower*? thus; *flow-ér*) I *don't*!!

4th & 5th *Stanzas both fine,* very *fine! One* expression only I would alter, "And *short-breathed* winds &c"—'Tis horribly suggestive of the *asthma*, or *consumption*!! At *best*, it brings up *prosaic*, not *poetical* images; such as the figure of a burly tourist panting up a mountainside; or a fat *Adonis* like *Joseph Sedl[e]y* (*vide "Vanity Fair!"*) on his knees panting & perspiring before some coquettish Becky *Sharp!* And *these stanzas,* (*4th* & 5th) are too beautiful to be marred even by a trifling *mal-apropos* phrase like the one I've pointed out.

6th Stanza: a *little* extravagant isn't it?

7th Stanza: The *first couplet exquisite.*

8th: The line beginning, "*Or clambering*" &c, affects my imagination with a peculiar feeling of *quaintness,* a remote, fantastic quaintness. As for the 9th & *concluding* verse, it is not merely the artistic & appropriate winding up of a poem, sweet and ardent as the June *marvels* it describes, and the rich June *atmosphere,* which surrounds & interpenetrates every line—, but *in itself,* how musical, how suggestive, how *perfect*!!

Indeed, *such* a stanza might have arisen, (like the bubbling of fresh waters from some secluded fountain, flower-crowned), out of Edmund Spenser's *heart,* and been at once glorified by his divine imagination, in the days of his golden youth, before disappointment, & the "*hell it is in suing, long to bide,*" had done their wild work upon his sweet, exalted nature!![3]

These lines have sunk into my memory, and are likely to remain there. They differ in *quality* of *tone* & *sentiment* from all the preceding verses, and still they *harmonize* with them!

In regard to the little story outlined in *blank verse,* I think it a rather happy conception, and see nothing to specially amend, or alter:

"Come *Name,* come *Fame,* and kiss my *Sweetheart's* feet!," I *like* exceedingly.

To wind up—in "*June Dreams*" you have happily embodied a quaint, fantastic, alluring, and richly fanciful topic,—;—there is the "*lush,*" *juicy richness* of the season *itself* in it, and *all* thro it!![4]

Let me tell you as a somewhat *odd coincidence* that *just previous to* the arrival of your "*June Dreams*" I had myself completed a poem upon "*Midsummer in the South,*" the general style whereof I *do* think or *hope* at least, you may be pleased with:

It opens *thus*:

> "I love queen August's stately sway—,
> And all her fragrant South Winds say,
> With strange, mysterious meanings fraught,
> Of half-articulated thought:—
> Those winds in charge of gloom & gleam

Seem wandering thro a golden dream—,
The rare midsummer dream that lies
In humid depths of Nature's Eyes,
Weighing her languid forehead down,
Beneath a fair, but fiery crown;
Its witching rules o'er earth & skies'
Fills with divine amenities
The bland, blue spaces of air,
And smiles with looks of drowsy cheer,
Mid hollows of the brown-hued hills,
And in the tongues of tinkling rills,
A softer, homelier utterance finds,
Than that which haunts the lingering winds![5]

But I have no leisure to proceed. I'll send you extracts *another* time. Ever (in haste) but Faithfully

Paul H Hayne

P.S. Send me your photograph.

1. Though Howells rejected "June Dreams" for the *Atlantic* in April, 1873 (Anderson, *et al.* [eds.], *Centennial Edition of the Works of Sidney Lanier*, VIII, 337n) and it was also declined by the *Galaxy* and *Scribner's*, it was finally published in the *Independent* in September, 1884, three years after Lanier's death.

2. Alexander Smith (1830–1867) published *A Life Drama* in 1853.

3. "Mother Hubberd's Tale," line 896.

4. Lanier accepted some of Hayne's suggestions and declined others. See Anderson, *et al.* (eds.), *Centennial Edition of the Works of Sidney Lanier*, I, 338–39.

5. This is only the introduction to the poem as it is printed in the *Christian Union*, VII (May 14, 1873), 382. It was collected in *MOL* and appears with verbal and mechanical changes in *PCE*, 192–93.

35

To Sidney Lanier   MS Johns Hopkins

my address is PO Box, 635 Augusta Geo
"Copse Hill" Ga Central RR
(Saturday afternoon) March 29th 1873:

My Dear Lanier;

I wrote you at some *length* yesterday, enclosing at the same time the "MSS" poem you had kindly given me the chance of reading *before* the general public could catch a glimpse *thereof*.

I have frankly told you in what manner the poem affected me, pointing out here & there some trifling blemish, but upon *the whole* expressing *warm* admiration of as pretty a piece of rich, fanciful, *Oriental* composition, as ever came to my notice—not excepting *Alex Smith's gorgeous*, and really striking passages in the "*Life Drama.*"[1] (By the way, I have *never* ceased to wonder *how*, and *why* it was that *Smith*, whose *poetic youth* blossomed so *luxuriantly*, failed in every sense, to carry out its *superb promise*).

What in *your* "*June Dreams*" particularly charmed me, *was* or *is* the *lush*, juicy, overflowing richness & vitality of style & fancy, a species of half *sensuous*, and half *intellectual abandon* to the sweet *impulses of a poetic mood*, which was common with the un-artificial Elizabethan *Singers*, from Shakspeare, down to Phineas Fletcher, but which now-a-days, the *trim, careful* Muses are evidently afraid of &c &c.

When fairly published, send me *half a dozen printed copies* of your "*Dreams*"; I shall have *good uses* for them! Enclosed, you'll find a rough copy of "*Midsummer in the South.*"[2]

Please read it *critically*!

You are the only man—*South*—now *living* to whom I would come in this way, asking counsel, and *free*—nay! the *freest* criticism! Perhaps by an exchange of *poems* (in *course* of composition) *thus*—we may mutually benefit one another. I know that your *hints* as to my "*Sunset in the Pine Barrens*," were *pregnant* with *meaning*; as you'll perceive, when the poem entirely *re-written, because* of your suggestions—is sent you in its *last* form—printed!![3]

Write me *very soon*, & Believe me Always Fraternally & most Faithfully Yr's

Paul H Hayne

P.S. You write in a way not altogether satisfactory ab't *your health*. What do you mean, (*for example*), by saying, that the "*moderate degree of strength*" you have attained, will be devoted chiefly to "*artistic labors*," since "it seems *fated* that you are *not* to practice your profession of the *law*"? *Why* fated? Because while your physical "*strength*" admits of moderate "*art-labor*," it is insufficient for the exacting duties of the Lawyer? Is *such* the *case*?

1. For Smith, see Letter 34, n. 2.

2. Only the introduction had been enclosed in the previous letter.

3. Lanier had written his wife about criticizing "In the Pine Barrens" on February 16, 1873 (Anderson, *et al.*[eds.], *Centennial Edition of the Works of Sidney Lanier*, VIII,

330), and Hayne had acknowledged his help on February 27, 1873: "You have done me more, far more than 'Yeoman's service' in your hints, suggestions, and alterations touching my poem of the Sunset" (MS Johns Hopkins).

36

To Sidney Lanier   MS Johns Hopkins

Address PO Box 635 *Augusta,* Ga
"*Copse Hill,*" *Central Georgia R Road.*
Friday 2nd May; (*1873*)

Dearly Beloved Poet;

I think, nay! I am all but *certain* that *yours* of the 11th ul*t* remains unacknowledged![1]

The letter I mean, was despatched from Brunswick.

Thanks again, and heartfelt thanks too, for the trouble you vouchsafed to take with my "*Midsummer in the South*"—

'Tis encouraging to be informed, that taking that piece *as a whole,* you decidedly like it, and so feel disposed to rank the verses among my *best.*

Yet, *twice* has the poem been rejected, (albeit with *mellifluous* excuses!), by certain Yankee Editors; *a fact* I mention in order that you may not yourself deem it singular that "*the Atlantic*" returned the MSS of your "*June Dream.*"[2]

Of about 8 carefully written poems of mine, sent to *Howells* during the past year, just 4 were accepted, and subsequently *published.*[3] And verily, you must know, that such rejection by no means invariably signifies *inferiority, apropos* of the verses dismissed. Length, elaboration, has a great deal to do with it!

'Tis no *mere* excuse likewise, but a *fact* the *Edt's* are often *buried almost* under accumulated *loads* of *rhyme*; and that they *must decline* poetry even of a *high* order, when thus oppressed.

Recently I mailed to "*Scribner's*" *two* poems, one a *legend* of Scandinavia, the other a trifle of 5 stanzas, a brief lyric in fact! Holland *returns* the "legend," and (as a very special *distinction* I'm disposed to believe), accepts the *song,* at the same time, calling my attention to certain pencil marks upon the outside of my rejected "*copy.*"

I look, and to my *amazement,* decipher the figures, 2,756(!!!) indicating that just that number of poems are now on hand, *unpublished*, and many *unexamined*, in the drawers of the "*sanctum*" bureau!!⁴

Discouraging isn't it?—

And next, comes my good friend O. B. *Bunce*, (do you know him?) the present Ed: of "*Appleton's Journal*," who in a half-despairing note, *begs*, & entreats me almost on his knees, metaphorically—to spare him for months to come; (i.e.) to forward him no more verses!!

Poetry—he cries, with a most plaintive outcry,—"will be my *death*, if things go on as they *threaten* to do! All verse-mongers are not reasonable, like yourself—" (that's *me*, you must know!) "On the contrary, here am I, up to the *neck already* in reams of metrical "MSS," flooded with a fresh tide of inspiration from these four well-known *litterateurs*, the rejection of whose pieces, will bring on my devoted head, God knoweth how much abuse, & detraction!"—

And all this is the Gospel truth! We must sympathise a little with the Ed'ts, no less than with their *victims*(!!)

If I can dare to *advise*, I should tell you to put by for the nonce your longer poems—as far as the Magzns are concerned, and to elaborate with *immense* care a series of *short lyrics*, "Swallow flights of song" &c. Put all your richness of fancy, and all your gracious art into these efforts, and my word for it, they'll bring you substantial results both in *repute* and *greenbacks*!!

Try the experiment!!

I'm sorry to hear about your *health*, and the necessary abandonment of your profession; but still, *Art and Letters* may gain *thereby*!!

Have you any acquaintance with a young man, named Fred: Williams, a Lawyer of Augusta? I ask, because he mailed me a vo*l* of his verses 2 weeks agone, requesting my "*candid opinion*" in regard to "their merits or demerits!" As *kindly* as possible, I wrote and told him what I thought, viz, that his verses, (generally), were insufferably bad! Now, 'tis whispered in mine ear, that a *literary clique* in *Augusta* feel assured of my *narrow, mean,* and *envious* (!) temper!

I would fain put down a fiery genius; lest perchance—but you know what is meant!—

Again, they *persecute* me with copies, by mail, of a tale called "*Clifford Troup*," (Mrs. Westmoreland author), and then, when I criticise it, as a *worthless, & stupid production,* which it really *is*—I am threatened with intellectual and literary extinguishment!!—

—By God, Lanier! it is *disgusting*—this attempt to bully men like—yourself, (for ins:) and your humble servant—into bepuffing and beplastering every ambitious fool, whether, man or woman, of the South, who chooses to reach after literary honors!

I am sick of it, and if they bother me in the papers much longer, I'll wax savage—for once—; and speak the plain truth in tones *not* to be miscomprehended. What right have mere society-women, like *this*— what the devil's her name?—to come forward, but pshaw! "the game's not worth the *candle*" &c.[5]

Basta! *Basta*!

In a fortnight's time, I start (DV), for the *North*; hope to visit Philadelphia, N York, Boston &c &c. You are going too, this season—but *when*? Write, & tell me![6]

Ever Yr's sincerely
Paul H Hayne

[P.S.] Return "*Violets*" when you are done with the piece! I know 'tis full of *artistic faults*; yet perhaps there be lines in it, you'll like well enou'!

1. Lanier's letter of April 11, 1873, is lost. See Anderson, *et al.*(eds.), *Centennial Edition of the Works of Sidney Lanier*, VIII, 338n.

2. "Midsummer in the South" appeared in the *Christian Union* (see Letter 34, n. 5). For the rejection of "June Dreams," see Letter 34, n. 1.

3. Howells presumably rejected "Midsummer in the South" and most assuredly declined "In the Pine Barrens. Sunset" in February, 1873. Meanwhile, Howells published nine poems by Hayne in the period 1872–1876, though he also returned at least two of his best—"Cambyses and the Macrobian Bow" and "Muscadines." For Hayne's annoyance with these rejections, see his letters to Mrs. Preston (December 23, 1873) and F. B. Stanford (January 10, 1878; *CHL*, 194), a member of the staff of *Sunday-School Times*, Philadelphia. These matters are also discussed in the two articles cited in note 9 to Letter 32. Both poems were collected in *MOL* and reprinted in *PCE*, 192–93, 194–95, respectively.

4. Josiah Gilbert Holland, editor of *Scribner's*, had accepted one of Hayne's poems as early as December, 1870, but Hayne's first appearance in the magazine did not occur until August, 1875, by which time Holland had accepted at least three of Hayne's poems. The "legend of Scandinavia" referred to is "Frida and Her Poet," *Southern Magazine*, n.s., VI (June, 1873), 661–64 (collected in *MOL* and *PCE*, 202–204). The "song" cannot be identified and may never have been published.

5. Hayne had already commented on Mrs. Westmoreland's *Heart Hungry* (1872) in a letter to Mrs. Preston (see Letter 32). His views are echoed in Lanier's reply of May 26, 1873 (Anderson, *et al.* [eds.], *Centennial Edition of the Works of Sidney Lanier*, VIII, 347–49): "God forbid we should really be brought so low as that we must perforce brag of such works as 'Clifford Troup' and 'Heart Hungry'." Hayne, of course, eventually waxed "savage" about such writers and writing in his "Literature at the South: The Fungous School" (see Letter 32, n. 5), where he ridicules "Mrs. Duck-a-Love's 'pathetic

and passionate romance'" and "Mrs. General Aristotle Brown's 'profound philosophic novel.'"

6. Hayne went north in June and returned around the first of November, and though Lanier had planned to be in New York City from early July to the middle of October, he did not make the trip. The two friends, consequently, did not meet in New York, nor did they ever meet in Georgia, though Macon and Augusta are only 125 miles apart.

37

To Margaret J. Preston   MS Duke

"Copse Hill," G*a* R Road
Sat; *10th May* 1873.

My *Beloved Friend*;

I am *indeed* your *debtor* for a most thoughtful, & feeling action! You have by your beautiful note of the 5*th* inst: enclosing the remarkable letter from M*rs* Dodge—, been the means of affording information I greatly needed concerning the final hours of one, who—after Gilmore Simms' death in 1870, was the *oldest*, & among the very *best*, of my literary & personal friends![1]

Towards Thompson I entertained a peculiar tenderness.[2] As far back as 1848—49, Timrod & I began to contribute verses to the "*So. Lit. Messenger*," and naturally thus we formed the acquaintance of its *Editor*. In the *Spring* of '49, (I being then a *mere* lad at College), and *Timrod* a Law Student in *Petigru's* office,[3] *Thompson* visited *Charleston*, and for the *first time* we beheld him "in the flesh"!

How vividly I recall his appearance! Just 26 *years* old, slightly, but elegantly formed, with a *manner* far quicker & more vivacious, than it was in after life—, dressed in the *height of the prevailing mode*, with light-twilled pantaloons, and a blue coat, brass buttoned,—he shone upon us "hobbledehoys"—a somewhat *radiant* vision of a man partly *litterateur*, and partly dandy! We liked him none the less, however, for this touch of the *petit maître*, and from that spring morning in the month of May 1849 when his acquaintance was made—until the end of *T's* career—*I* at least, can affirm, that our friendship continued uninterrupted, growing *warmer*, despite many a year of separation, for our Correspondence was never wholly broken off, until within a few months of his decease!

Not since my poor Harry left me, have I been so afflicted as I am now, for with *Thompson* the ambitions, hopes, purposes of youth, and early manhood, were so inextricably associated, that a part of *myself*, my very *soul* and *mind,* seems to have gone down with him into the grave! What a *tremendous* realization of the *uncertain, almost phantasmal* nature of human existence, these losses bring to one's consciousness! They *emphasize* the meaning of the *great* poet's words, "life is a walking *shadow,* a poor, poor player who struts his hour upon the stage, & then is seen no more!"—[4]

Out of the impenetrable darkness, a ghostly Hand appears to flash! It seizes our comrade on the right, or our comrade on the left (as the case may be) and he disappears suddenly, mysteriously, awfully; no voice comes back from the Hadean gloom,—no faintest outline of the beloved face or form, reappears on earth! All is silence & the bewilderment of deep darkness!—unless the promise of Christ come to support & soothe. *Then*—as you remark—, "all is *well!*" One is transported in thought & imagination to the "ineffable Glory," and the "grandeurs of an immortality of youth," I will try to believe—nay! I *must* believe that such a "*glory,*" such inconceivably sublime an "*immortality*" awaits *him* we have lost! If indeed, it *be reserved* for any of mortal race, *he* must have attained it—; for Mrs Dodge is *right* in alluding to *Thompson* as among the *purest* of the *pure*—; a *practical Christian* thro life, and a patient, long suffering *faithful martyr,* thro *later years* of pain, and sickness, and bitter suffering!

Ah! well, his life-story has ended as *yours* and *mine* must, to morrow, or to morrow, or to morrow—. When our *little* sand has run!—

And I, who mourn him, would leave this world, to day, to be with him—(wheresoever that may be), for, "*I am tossing,* tossing at sea—, he is in port!"—

From her letters, I have formed a *very high* opinion of the *talents,* and the good feeling of your new *friend & Correspondent*—Mrs Dodge!

As an *author* I knew her long before! Some of her poems in the Magazines, are remarkably fine;—I would instance that called "*A Spring Idyl,*" in a recent no. of "*The Christian Union*"!

Her last epistle, so touching, and womanly, and sympathetic, I *return,* in accordance with your desire.

My wife, and *all* here at "*Copse Hill*" send you *love!* God *bless,* & *keep* you!

Always Yr' *true friend,*
Paul H Hayne
PO Box 635

(P.S.) I am winding up many a tangled *skein* of *business &c &c*, in order that I may leave my home, & visit the Northern States: (partly on *business*, partly for my *son's health & my own*) about the 25th of the *present* month!![5]

I do *so wish* that Lexington lay along our *route*, or near it! But alack!—'tis not so.

Why should the place be so "*remote*"?

I'm disposed to think that the *Doctors* who sent poor Thompson, *almost* at his *last gasp* on a journey of thousands of miles, to *Colorado*, and thus *intensified* his *suffering* a *hundred fold*, ought to be *hung*—or at *least*, "*bastinadoed*" in true *Turkish fashion*! They treat consumption thus (the cold blooded Empirics & Quacks!) first to save *their* precious reputations, and to put aside troublesome *patients*—the *Brutes*!!!

1. Mrs. Mary B. Dodge, New York journalist and poet, was introduced by Mrs. Preston to Hayne via correspondence. Mrs. Dodge also knew John R. Thompson, one of Hayne's oldest literary friends.

2. John R. Thompson (1823–1873) edited the *Southern Literary Messenger* from 1847 to 1860 and was literary editor of the New York *Evening Post* from 1868 to 1873.

3. In 1850 Hayne also studied law with James Louis Petigru (1789–1863), attorney general of South Carolina (1822–1830) and a leader of the Union party in the state from 1832 until his death.

4. The text of *Macbeth*, V, v, 24–26, actually reads: "Life's but a walking shadow, a poor player / That struts and frets his hour upon the stage / And then is heard no more."

5. Hayne finally left Copse Hill on June 5.

38

To Sidney Lanier   MS Johns Hopkins

"*Copse Hill*," Geo R. Road
Near Augusta, March 21st 1874:

My Dear Lanier;

What has become of you? For *months* not a ripple of news has reached me, as to your "*whereabouts*," your present condition of health, your prospects, literary and artistic, your plans, wishes, or employments!! Last summer, for the first time in a *score* of years, I went *North*; my health utterly broken down, and my spirits at *zero*. Well! all went "merry as a marriage bell" for 2 months (I was fairly out of my troubles) when an evil and malignant *Fate would* have it that what I had gained in strength &c, in the course of *months*, should be nullified almost in a single day! My *left* leg, *or ankle* rather, was severely injured; the *pain* first, and *lameness* afterwards laid me up; my general condition of body deteriorated; I became well nigh *desperate*—and was going to the Devil *fast—fast—*when summoning up all the will & energy which *sickness*, & unspeakable agony had left me,—I took passage by sea, and returned to my *"Pine Barrens,"* as soon as practicable. *Great* care, since then, has brought me "standing" again. *Bref*—I'm tolerably well, and a harder Worker than ever before—as may be proved (DV) in a few months hence!—[1]

—By the way, how did you dispose of your criticism on *"Legends & Lyrics?"*[2]

That no Northern periodical would have taken it, I could have told you before hand; and at the *South* there exists, you know, but *one* monthly of any account, viz—Hand Browne's "*So Magn.*" Now as *Browne*—, altho he calls himself my very *dear friend, et cet, et cet—*, refused a brief & clever notice of my *Works*, (!) (pardon so absurdly big a term!) some time ago, I've no reason to conclude he would accept *your* critique, or any body *else's*!! Yet, he calls himself a *Patriot*; swears by the dignity and integrity of *So Letters*; thinks no *Southerner* should contribute to Yankee journals &c &c, and finds fault, I understand, with poor John R. Thompson & others, who preferred *living* in *Eng:* or *NYork*, to *starving* in their *native quagmires. (All this is strictly entre nous*!!)

My Boy! *Will* you allow me to send for your perusal & *strict* criticism, *private criticism* I mean, a Poem of mine just completed, of a legendary nature, & numbering about *500* lines? You are the only friend I possess now, to whom I cd. entrust so delicate a task.[3]

Horrible *egoism*, this! But please pardon me. Have you read the great work of the hour "*Forster's Life of Dickens?*"[4] It impresses me with some admiration of the Biographer's talents; and great contempt for his vanity, diffuseness, and self-importance. As for *Dickens*, one puts down the record of *his* life existence, with a sentiment of wonder, and grief. God! *What an imaginative genius! & Artist!* Yet, what a *mean spirit inherently*!! Judging him by his *own* letters, his conduct towards his *Wife*, was such, as *must* meet with the indignant scorn of every heart, uncorrupted, & manful.

His *fine sentiments* were all *intellections*; his *tenderness* was the offspring of delicate *nerves*, not of a noble *soul.*[5]

How different from the great *Sir Walter*!!

Ah! *"noblesse Oblige!"*—'Tis a motto that can never lose its significance!

And now, *Lanier*! Write me at once!!! I am *really, earnestly* anxious to hear of your present condition; your health, pursuits—everything!— With *affectionate regard*, I am as Ever, *Faithfully*

> *Your friend,*
> Paul H Hayne
> *PO Box 635 Augusta (Geo)*

1. Early in September in New York City Hayne injured his ankle in stepping from a streetcar, and as a consequence, he spent six weeks in bed and had "two surgical operations." See especially his account of his troubles in a letter to Mrs. Preston of November 10, 1873, shortly after his return home.

2. Ironically enough, Lanier's review appeared in the *Southern Magazine* for January, 1875. It may now be read more conveniently in Anderson, *et al.* (eds.), *Centennial Edition of the Works of Sidney Lanier*, V, 322–33.

3. Since Mrs. Preston was reading and criticizing Hayne's poems regularly during this period, this statement is a bit exaggerated, though Hayne sincerely appreciated Lanier's critical insights. The poem is presumably "The Mountain of the Lovers," but it was not forwarded at this time because Hayne "reperused" it and found that "much remains to be done," so much that Hayne decided not to "submit it even to your friendly criticism" (June 1, 1874; MS Johns Hopkins).

4. John Forster (1812–1876), friend and biographer of Dickens (1872–74).

5. Yet Hayne truly loved Dickens' fiction and refers consistently to Dickensian characters and their tag lines throughout his correspondence. See, for example, his reference to Mark Tapley in Letter 39, to Mrs. Preston.

39

To Margaret J. Preston   MS Duke

> *"Copse Hill,"* Ga R Road.
> *Tuesday, 12th May 1874.*

Dear Friend;—

I must at once answer your letter of the *6th* inst, rec*d* yesterday afternoon.

It *grieves* me to perceive how low-spirited you are; how discouraged th*o* Heaven knows! *most naturally*, most *inevitably discouraged*—, by Osgood's letter, and by the disgusting apathy of our own People to every manifestation of art & Letters.[1] Perhaps *no one* in this country can enter into, comprehend, or more fully appreciate your present condition of feeling, than myself! Indeed, it would be strange, were this *otherwise*; since repeatedly I have had to endure the sort of mental despondence which proceeds from "hope deferred," and an ever strengthening conviction that the Southern writer—particularly, the

Southern Poet, must be content with only *partial* recognition from the *Litterateurs* of the North, who distrust whatever may "come out of Nazareth"; while as for the *Southern* public, the sooner he ignores, and dismisses their *very existence* from his mind, the better!

And yet, *Dear Mrs Preston*, both you and I, have much to live and work for, despite our imperfect recognition abroad, and our *no* recognition at home. Take all the circumstances of the case into consideration; consider the many serious difficulties which beset your literary path (e.g.) from the beginning; and apart from all even *natural* egotism; ask yourself whether you have not accomplished *a vast deal*; enough aye! *more* than enough to fire ambition anew, re-knit the sinews of effort; and wing *Inspirations* you cannot quell (because come they will & must), with that *enthusiasm*, which gives to them a thrice vigorous vitality! Your name is so widely known & respected among the proprietors of Northern Periodicals, that they never hesitate to accept your verses, & to give a material "*quid pro quo*"; and even across the Ocean, *you* probably are the sole female poet of *Southern* birth, whose genius is not utterly unknown.[2] *Bref*: your literary position is assured; and being in the noonday of your powers, you must not speak, write, or *dream* of "*giving up*"! "Giving up"!!! with two-thirds of the journey along Parnassus gloriously accomplished; and the full power in you to accomplish what remains!! A hundred thousand times, *no no*!! *no*!! *Resolve as I* have done, in *my own case, solemnly,* to have your volume published sooner or later at whatever cost of time, labor, patience, trouble, and *temporary* humiliation! And for God's sake, don't *de-preciate your own* genius, & performances. I tell you, that your "*Cartoons*," will add not merely to their author's reputation, among real thinkers, but to the substantial mass of the world's Literature; that species of Literature which "hath a smack" of something better than "*ambrosia*," about it; being founded in the immortalities of imagination, sentiment, and passion. I'm not trying to flatter with fine words, and what may *seem* high-sounding phrases. On the contrary, I express the merest *truth*; truth of which I feel absolutely assured.

As for *Osgood's* letter—bah! let it pass! Why, when I was struggling to secure a Publisher for "*Legends & Lyrics*," I believe that at least *6* or *8* Firms refused to even *entertain* the *idea* of undertaking my volume! Some were absolutely rude in the manner of refusal. And a little volume, I now have on hand, (a "MS" vol, of course), about which I *sounded* recently *one* Publisher, to begin with, has encountered the same difficulty in its effort to enter the world of Published Poetry![3]

These be hard blows; they irritate, & depress by turns. Often under their sting, or weight, I roam the woods in furious mood, indulging I'm afraid a strain of remark that might come under the "Sandlapper" category of "mighty hard *cussing*"; or, for hours, perhaps *days* I can't rouse my discouraged mental energies, but *mope,* and *moan* about; muttering sullenly, "*cui bono?*" and even disposed to "snap up" my little Lady of "the bonny brown hands," when she would soothe & comfort her consort, changed for the nonce, into a *bear*!!

Yet, Lord bless you, (as *Mark* Tapley was fond of exclaiming), "I don't noways *abide* in them humors; hating fustiners, and mustiners; and finding violence bad for a body; specially—arter, *meals!*"[4]

The disgust, anger, or depression wears off;—I take juster views of my own powers, & position; and vow to fight out the battle to the end.

Instead of putting aside your "*Cartoons,*" as your threaten, and leaving them to your "*boys'* care," to see the light long after your own death, perhaps; let me beg you merely to "rest upon your oars; to wait for brighter times, and a fairer opportunity."

What Osgood says is really, for once, & tho it *did* come from a Publisher—*true*! This particular period *is* dreadfully unpropitious; & then only glance over the enclosed slip of paper, cut from "*the Boston Globe,*" & remark, how crowded the Publisher's summer list of new books is! No! dear friend, *both* of us must simply curb impatience; defy the fiends of discouragement, and "*bide* our time." Never fear; it will duly arrive. Meanwhile take care of those precious "*Cartoons.*" They may *seem* dull & colorless to *your* eyes, just *now*, but you behold them thro a morbid, somewhat "jaundiced vision."

Intrinsically they are noble poems, and the world will so pronounce them yet!—"We will see!"

Your praise of "*Timrod's Grave,*" I take deeply to heart.[5] It consoles; it greatly encourages me. As for *Mr* Hand Browne, were I in your place, I would behold him in—ahem—*Jericho,* or *Coventry*—, before condescending to furnish him with another line. The notion of his arrogating to himself the privilege of telling you that such and such of your pieces, [were] "*unworthy your powers*"!!! *What* confounded impertinence!! Certainly an Editor has the right to *reject* any article sent him; but unless he is *personally intimate* with a writer, *there* his rights stop. He is not required, (unasked) to enter into special criticisms.

The fact is, I utterly mistrust this fellow, *Browne* now; and the firm of Messrs *Turnbull & Bros,* are about as patriotic, I believe, as a broomstick, or a scare-crow! They have shown the "cloven foot" in their conduct concerning the progress & establishment of the "So His. Society," of which their monthly claims to be "the organ." From an English gentleman, (by birth, tho a So by adoption), *Mr Henry Eubank* who acts as the agent of the "Society" and Mag*n*, I lately learned many things, (while M*r* Eubank visited me,) which are conclusive in regard to the selfishness of this House.

And oh! the petty meanness of the scamp!!—but—*such* topics are "not for edification."[6]

I frankly confess, that with the *South*, I, as a literary man, have *done* forever! No longer shall I attempt to the utmost verge of my humble ability to sustain her periodicals, extend her knowledge of art, defend her people, vindicate her character!

The only *real art-friends*, (excepting, of course, some *very dear* personal friends like *yourself*), I ever found, are *Northern* men;—when I found myself sick, & helpless, almost pennyless at the *North*, last summer, every appeal by letter to *Southern* generosity failed; and probably, I should have died in a land of strangers; if these *very* strangers had not suddenly shown themselves my brethren; and recognizing me as one of themselves by the subtle ties of *art*—, done *all* that *could* have been done, in my behalf!

Is it in human nature to forget such things? I reck not!!

But I am growing prosy. Think over what I have ventured to say so frankly; and *never* allow your courage to cool, or your determination to sink below the right mark.

You are a *born Poet*; and a *made Artist*;—write! sing!—you cannot help yourself there; but believe, that despite appearances, you have not thought, or sung, in vain!

Minna joins me in *affectionate remembrances*, & *Willie would* do so, but he is just now in town, falling in love, I presume, with some pretty girl, or another, after the fashion of lads. God bless you!

Ever most faithfully
P.H.H.

P.S. Minna wants to know to whom Miss Preston is about to give her "*heart & hand*," and also, *something* of the little motherless babe, grand-daughter of your husband?

She bids me say, further, that she for one—*isn't* at all willing that you should "give up," as you express it; turn your back upon *those Muses*, whose inspiration breathes so sweetly, or so powerfully thro almost *everything* you have composed.

1. James R. Osgood, head of a Boston publishing firm, has apparently discouraged Mrs. Preston from publishing *Cartoons*, though the collection of poems was brought out the next year by another Boston house, Roberts Brothers.

2. Mrs. Preston was born in Pennsylvania and came to the South with her father, George Junkin, in 1848 when she was twenty-eight years old. Hayne forgets this fact frequently because his friend is so consistently loyal to Virginia and the South.

3. By the time this letter was written, Hayne's "Mountain of the Lovers" manuscript had been rejected by Osgood, Hurd and Houghton, and Roberts Brothers in Boston, by E. J. Hale in New York, and by Lippincott in Philadelphia. Yet Hale had published Hayne's edition of Timrod's poems in 1873 and Lippincott had brought out *LL* in 1872. Eventually Hale agreed to publish the volume. The problem was that all the publishers, according to Hayne, were willing to "undertake *half the expenses* of the work, and offer a fair per centage on sales" (see his letter to Mrs. Preston on October 24, 1874), but Hayne needed full support.

4. Mark Tapley appears in Dickens' *Martin Chuzzlewit* (1843–44).

5. "By the Grave of Henry Timrod," *Christian Union*, IX (June 10, 1874), 452. Hayne received twenty-five dollars for this "in memoriam" on his friend, the second such elegy he had written. See also "Under the Pine." Both poems were later collected in *PCE*, the former on pp. 198–200 and the latter on pp. 103–104.

6. Despite the intervention of other nouns and pronouns, Browne is the "scamp."

40

To James Maurice Thompson[1]   MS So. Car.

Augusta, Georgia
May 20th, 1874

My Dear Sir;

Many and many years have passed since last I had the pleasure of hearing from you.

Since then I have written you, *twice* I think, but doubtless my letters miscarried, since they were addressed to your old Georgia home; and now, I learn that you moved some time ago, to Indiana.

I have not, as remarked above, heard from you *personally*; but in another way, I have, in common with the Lit. world, heard from you very pleasantly indeed.

Really, Sir, I must be allowed, as one of the very few *Southerners* devoted like yourself, to letters, to congratulate you upon the success of your poems; especially those published in "The *Atlantic Monthly*." I am not alone in my admiration of these pieces.

Last summer while travelling thro N. England, renewing *old*, & making new acquaintances, I heard your verses, ("*At the Window*"), and other similar performances, spoken of *in high terms*, by men whose commendation is *more* than ordinary fame. And only a week or two since, a letter reached me from one of the first art Critics of America, in which incidentally he referred to your "Atalanta" in terms of enthusiasm.[2]

I write these things from no design to *flatter* (men of any sense of delicacy don't *insult* each other in that way), but because, the *victor* is worthy the *Crown*; and the *So man* who succeeds in getting a foothold among the acknowledged art representatives of the North, has achieved a feat, deserving recognition, especially from his own *brethren*. And yet, I'll wager a good deal that the note you are now reading is the first communication of the sort you have rec*d* from any *So* source! It maddens me sometimes to think of the supineness, and intellectual toadyism of our own People; but what would you? "Whom the Gods would destroy &c &c"

I wish you could have accompanied me last season. I dined with Longfellow; saw Holmes more than once; had many hours of converse with my old friend *Stoddard*, and had the pleasure of following up a charming correspondence of years with *Howells* by knowing him *individually*, and liking him heartily. In N York I saw *Davidson*, who is now engaged upon the "Ev. Post" newspaper, in poor Jn*o* R Thompson's place and made up with him a long literary feud (which threatened personal quarrelling), wherein I confess myself to have been much in fault; (in the *feud*, not the "*making up*" of course).[3]

If this letter reaches you, I'd be very glad to receive an answer at your earliest convenience.[4] Tell me something about yourself; your literary prospects &c.

Luckily you have made literature, simply your "*staff*," as Scott called it, and *not* your *sole* support; for even in the *West & North*, mere writing could hardly support one, unless a vein of immense Popularity were struck; and *popularity* I rather distrust, don't you?

Some tremendous public favorites in this country are in point of the *higher art*, just—*nowhere*!

In 1872, I published a vo*l* of Poems, (in Phil*a*), which has had considerable success, *North*; and even attracted some favorable notice in England. Shall I send you a copy? But here I must pause.

With best wishes, believe me,
Faithfully Yours,
Paul H Hayne
P.O. Box 635, Augusta, G*a*

1. Thompson (1844–1901) was born in Indiana, though he had family in Georgia and had fought in the Confederate army. He had returned to Indiana after the war and established a law practice in Crawfordsville. He had accepted the verdict of the war and had no illusions about defending the past; and in his own way he would soon become about as "reconstructed" as George W. Cable. The future of the friendship between Thompson and Hayne might be construed from the very beginning as having considerable possibilities for volatility.

2. Both poems appeared in the *Atlantic*, "At the Window," XXXI (April, 1873), 461, and "Atalanta," XXXIII (May, 1874), 615. The reference to "one of the first art Critics of America" is presumably to E. P. Whipple.

3. See Letter 24, n. 2.

4. Thompson replied genially on May 23 and the correspondence continued, despite occasional squabbles, until after Hayne's death in 1886. For a full account of this relationship, see Rayburn S. Moore, "The Old South and the New: Paul Hamilton Hayne and Maurice Thompson," *Southern Literary Journal*, V (Fall, 1972), 108–22. For Thompson's literary experience, see Otis B. Wheeler, *The Literary Career of Maurice Thompson* (Baton Rouge: Louisiana State University Press, 1965).

41

To Sidney Lanier   MS Johns Hopkins

"Copse Hill," Ga R. Road
Wed: 19th Jan: 1875.

My Dear Lanier;

"Figure to yourself," (as the Frenchmen say), "figure to yourself" that I take your hand, nay *both your hands,* and wring them *very hard,* as a material sign of the *inward* satisfaction, & gratitude I experienced, upon reading your wonderful critique in "*The So Magn*"; the *subtlest & most searching review* ever suggested by my verses.[1]

When the *heart* is full, *words* refuse to come! Once for all, most *earnestly,* let me thank you for this "labor of love"; for such indeed I consider it.

Now as to details: Your argument provoked by that *Morris Sonnet,* (which, *en passant,* you've taken *too literally,* and given too great a prominence to), is full of cleverness & vigor; and many of the points made, touching the *radical* differences between the elder & younger Poet, strike me as *unanswerably true.*

Some *particulars* of *likeness,* however, have escaped your attention; particulars which go far towards justifying my Tribute, exaggerated as it may seem (on the surface).[2]

These I shall mention, when I am able to command the leisure for a longer letter. Candidly let me say that that [*sic*] the *one* portion of your noble review which I regret somewhat, is this *too close & frequent juxtaposition* of the names of *Morris & Hayne*, with the clear inference that the *latter* has permitted himself to be injuriously influenced, if not dominated by the *former*! Dear friend!, There is *not* a single elaborate narrative poem *in "the Legends & Lyrics,"* ("the Wife of Brittany," "Daphles," *et id omne genus*), which was not composed *long before the very name of* W*m* *Morris was known in America*!

But you go further than this! You appear to think it is an artistic mistake to choose any of the old world legends, (akin to that of the "Franklin's Tale" &c), since after all, *what* do they embody, *what* can we find in them, but *"a titillation of the Unreal"*? *Substance* here is compounded with *Shadow*; the *externals & environments* of a Theme with its inner, vivifying *spirit*. So clear is this to my mind, that I actually have the vanity to believe I can induce a *modification* of your views, at least, when Time is granted me to produce my arguments *in full. How ungracious*, it seems, my cavilling thus, tho mild the protest!! But just *here*, all objections end! Every *other point* of censure urged against my poems, I unconditionally acknowledge as right. The superfluity of adjectives, the too frequent *"lapses"* of the thought &c &c! I've not the feeblest shield of defense to raise against your critical arrows thus directed. I can only endeavor to amend. *Au reste*, that any work of mine should have been made the text for an article so profound in insight, so suggestive, and altogether able, as this of yours, must ever yield me a keen delight. Then, if your *conclusions* be correct, (as I would fain believe), may I *not* exclaim, even were *Death* to claim me to morrow, *"behold! I have not lived utterly in vain?"*—

Again & finally, I thank you with *"heart, soul,* and *strength"* for what you have written! The Gods reward you, for it!

The Fe*b* *"Lippincott"* publishes *"Corn"* I perceive. Last night I read, re-read, studied profoundly this remarkable *"Ode."* My first impression, after a perusal of it in "MSS," has been strengthened & confirmed. It *ought* to make you a name; aye! Many a poetic reputation has been founded on single compositions *far far* inferior to this. In noticing *"Lippincott,"* I'll mention *"Corn"* as it *deserves* to be mentioned. See how fairly y'r literary path opens towards the Future!

Being *very busy*, I must stop now. *Write the moment after* this reaches you, (if possible). Always y'r obliged & faithful friend,

Paul H Hayne

PO Box 635, Augusta, Geo

1. *Southern Magazine*, XVI (January, 1875), 40–48. Reprinted in Anderson, *et al.* (eds.), *Centennial Edition of the Works of Sidney Lanier*, V, 322–33.

2. Lanier begins his essay by citing Hayne's sonnet "To William Morris" in which the point is made that Chaucer's "rich bays" have been passed to Morris and "Hence the ripe blood of England's lustier morn / Of song burns through thee." He disagrees with this resemblance and sees Hayne's dependence on Morris as "the only natural quarrell" he has "to pick" with Hayne. Hayne's response in the letter is similar to the one he made to William Dean Howells, who made a similar point in his review of *LL* in the *Atlantic* for April, 1872. Hayne immediately remonstrated with Howells, and the editor admitted in the May issue that he had been unjust. See *PHH*, 60–61.

42

To Maurice Thompson   MS So. Car.

Always address me   *PO Box 635*
"Copse Hill," *Ga* RR. *Augusta (Geo)*
June 21*st* 1875

This little breeze of a discussion, *Dear Thompson*, originating in a *single paragraph* of your subtle & scholarly critique, has blown itself clear away; and even the slight under "*sough*" is heard no longer; its last murmur being dead forevermore![1] But oh *Thompson*! *Thompson*, Thompson: how *could* you think, nay, *dream* for the fraction of a second, that you had "*lost me by it*"? say, *rather* "*gained*" *me*, for, *sincerity & candor* are the *rarest qualities* nowaday—in criticism; and these *high qualities* in *you*, *none*, I venture to observe, *could* appreciate more profoundly than I!—"*Send that review to the deuce!!*" 'Quotha'!! Excuse me! I shall cherish it, on the contrary, among my valued *literary* treasures.

Your last letter *touches* me in a tender point! A *big faithful heart*, hast thou, my son, and Hayne understands it, to its "golden deeps." Am I *so* rich in friendships, that I, of all mortals, can afford to reject the "pure metal, ringing sound & true"? *Never! Never! never!!!*

A *hundred* thanks for your cordial invitation: There is hardly *anything*, (and please believe, that I am writing *unconventionally*), hardly *anything* that would delight me so much as a visit to the *West*, and above all, a month's sojourn at your hearthstone.

But inexorable Fate binds me here, as with limbs of iron. The ill health of an aged mother, (who may at any *hour*, be called away), and the narrowness, just at present, of my domestic means, together with certain other difficulties needless to particularize; all combine to *tie me down* closely and immoveably. It is *too* bad! Not the less however, do I appreciate *your* generous courtesy; and also your *wife's*. *Thank her for me*; and add, that (DV!), we may yet meet this side the "Mysterious Shade," and enjoy many a pleasant talk, and perhaps *ride*—, together![2]

Is Mrs Thompson a horsewoman? (Inform her, that 20 years agone, I courted my own wife, then (*can't* I be *forgiven* for saying it?), *then* the prettiest brunette in C*a, on horseback*; and in her agitation, I presume, my sweetheart *switched me* instead of the *animal*! By Jove! how it hurt! and how desperately I tried to look—charmed! Subsequently my "*ghastly smile*," on the occasion, was made, *most inhumanly*, the subject of much chaff, and of many jokes!

It was very characteristic of my Publishers, to send you a note of thanks, and some of their *books*.[3] They are, in a high sense of the term, *gentlemen*! As for their *considerateness*, & generosity towards myself, *never can I forget it*!

By the way, a letter has just reached me from *Messer Lanier*, postmarked *Savannah*. He speaks of being in *Augusta* to *morrow*, or next day; & wants to see me. (We *never* have met *personally*). A *really fine & noble fellow* is *Lanier*, as I have *every reason* to believe, and of his *genius* there can be no question. But tell me—, we *are literary brothers, henceforth, I trust*—, tell me what your critical opinion is, touching his "*Corn*," and the later poem in "*Lippincotts*," called "*The Symphony*"? (*Everything* that passes between us, of this kind, I shall hold *sacred*).

The truth is, I desire, for *special reasons*, to know what estimation *you* have formed of these two pieces, before I give my own opinion.

Lanier, (like *yourself*), has a bright intellectual *future*! When I—after doing my "little best," under innumerable difficulties—, shall be sleeping quietly beneath the pine trees, yonder,—you *two* "brave Minstrels" will be in the prime of your powers & inspiration!

Perhaps I may catch the echoes of your fame, even in that lowly dwelling place!!

Pardon this "rambling" letter! An attack of dysentery, or something like it, has made me weak & giddy;

And Believe me
Always Your true
& loving friend,
P. H. Hayne

(P.S.) "*One* last *remark* I wish to make; *one* last explanation I wish to offer," (*vide* "*Little Dorritt*"), *apropos* of my long letter, directly preceding this. My purpose was *not* the *mean & childish* purpose of trying to overwhelm *you with mere authority*, (as might have *superficially seemed* to be the case), but to express my sense of *bewilderment*, between so many *cross fires* of *Criticism*!

Believe this, I *entreat*!!

So *away* with *that topic forever*!!

    1. Thompson reviewed *MOL* in the Indianapolis *Journal*, May 29, 1875. He praised Hayne's lyrics, cited him as "our only truly representative Southern poet," and concluded that *MOL* was a "more worthy volume" than *LL*. But he admitted that Hayne "fails" when "he attempts strong dramatic effects," and this is the view that occasioned Hayne's remarks in this paragraph.

    2. A few years later, in November, 1881, Thompson and his wife visited the Haynes at Copse Hill.

    3. E. J. Hale & Son, New York.

43

Mary L. Booth[1]   MS Duke

"*Copse Hill*" (near *Augusta*)
Oct: 6th *1875*

My Dear Miss Booth,

Thanks for your kind note of the 1st Oct, enclosing Check ($10.00) for "*The Vision by the Sea*"![2]

I am especially glad that the little poem "found favor in your sight."

It is *not* a fancy sketch; but the record of an *actual* occurrence.

In the summer of 1873, at "*Nahant*" I beheld, (in the way, and at the hours described), the *loveliest girl* conceivable, "*standing between the blue sky & the sea*"; and *truly* she has occupied my *Brain* ever since, irradiating there from memory "like a star."

Odd romance, you'll say, for a middle aged rhymster! But, you see, *dear friend*! that girl was—a—*stunner*!

Your health, you inform me, is "*fully* restored." Ah!, *that* is indeed excellent news. If you ever carry out your half-formed design of coming *South,* so far as Georgia; we must get you up among the pine barrens, the great, gaunt old hills, and the forests which seem stretching away with eternity. "*Copse Hill*" would welcome your appearance enthusiastically.

In haste, but Ever Faithfully
(PO Box 635) Paul H Hayne

1. Mary Louise Booth (1831–1889), the editor of *Harper's Bazar* (1867–1888), accepted poems frequently from Hayne in the 1870s and 1880s.

2. "The Vision by the Sea," *Harper's Bazar*, VIII (December 25, 1875), 830. The poem was collected in *PCE*, 240.

44

To Sidney Lanier   MS Johns Hopkins

"Copse Hill," Geo R. Road
Oct. 23*rd* 1875

My Dear Lanier;

Yours of the 16th inst is before me! I have been *much touched* by its perusal. The earnest, affectionate tone of the whole communication, shows how high *your nature* is above the nature of those damnable human curs, who, the moment they begin to rise in the world, drop old associations, repudiate old friendships, and tell old Allies, that having no further use for them, they may go straightway to the Devil!!

Now my dear boy! it is *very very* different with *you*; and I rejoice to know it.

With *pride* no less than *pleasure*, I hail your really brilliant success in Literature. Some fools in this quarter of the world have thought proper to express *surprise*, at your waking up one morning (after the publication of "Corn")[1] and "finding yourself famous." I gave one of these a piece of my mind (last Tuesday) in Augusta, and rather amazed him, you may be sure! O! these miserable Southern people! *Since* the war they have partially lost many of their former characteristic virtues; and are becoming *Yankee-ized*, day after day, upon the meanest Yankee models.

The *Augustanians* fell down, and worshipped *Saxe*(!), when he lectured to them, (for $100 per night); but they can't understand that *Lanier*, being a Georgian, *has*, or *could* have any *real* claim to artistic distinction![2]

You may thank God, however, that you are wholly independent of your own section.

I see that your labors on the *Florida* book have been *tremendous*!;[3] *far too* great & protracted, 'tis evident, from their effect on your physical health. A *Titan* could not work for *12 or 14* hours daily, without paying for such an outrage on nature.

But I know these Northern literary taskmasters, as cruel, and inflexible as those of Egypt. They *killed* poor John R. Thompson, working him down to skin & bone in "*the Ev: Post office*"; and then paid his expenses *Westward,* that he might die—I presume, in the wilderness!

Be careful, *Lanier!*, in *this,* the bright morning of your fame; don't allow the "silver cord to be loosed, & the golden bowl broken" prematurely, & needlessly.

Send an early copy of your Fla. book to me. Rely *not* upon the Publishers, but mail the vo*l* with your own hand. I shall do all I can for its success in this quarter. By the way, your 2 papers on Fla in "*Lippincott's*" are very remarkable productions; both seem to me *prose-poems*; exquisite in thought, imagination, & description. *Certain sentences,* alluding to the effect upon your fancy of the deeply shadowed streams & lakes, *thrilled* me by their beauty!

You kindly inquire after my *health*; ask what I am doing &c?

Let me be frank! For *months* I have not known a single *hour* of *peace*; nay! hardly five minutes together, free from pain, or languor. The shadows are closing about me, my friend! A few more autumn seasons, (perhaps!) and "*hic jacet*" will be all that remains of *Hayne.* Were it *not for wife & son,* I—care not a *straw.* (But, "there's *the rub*; there's *the rub*"!!)

Now, *should my presentiment come true,* I shall *tax your peace* in one way. *Supposing you survive me,* don't let my memory *wholly die out, do for me what I tried to do for Timrod.* You understand! Upon *you only* can *I depend* in *this matter.* (And *Lanier!*, *keep* [this] letter. It may serve as your authority hereafter). There! my mind is relieved!

Write me, as soon, as you can. And Believe me, Always Y'rs Faithfully

Paul H Hayne PO Box 635 Augusta, Geo

P.S. Read my last *vol,* when leisure permits. The "nature pieces" *may* please you.

1. "Corn," *Lippincott's,* XV (February, 1875), 216–19. This was Lanier's first appearance as a poet in an important northern literary magazine. The *Round Table,* where he had published twelve poems in the period 1866–1868, was not in the same literary league with *Lippincott's.* Hayne, of course, is intentionally exaggerating the comparison between the reaction to Lanier and "Corn" and that to Byron and *Childe Harold's Pilgrimage.*

2. John Godfrey Saxe (1816–1887), a popular New England journalist, lecturer, humorist, and poet.

3. *Florida: Its Scenery, Climate, and History* (1875).

45

To Margaret J. Preston   MS Duke

"Copse Hill," Ga R Road
Monday, Oct 25th 1875.

Dear Friend;

Yes: you have *caught* me *fairly*! The letter of Miss Woolson had *not* been returned as I fancied, *thro* mistaking, possibly, some *other* letter by her (resting on my desk), for the epistle in question. I am glad that she sent you her book, & rejoice to find that you so perfectly agree with my own high estimate of its freshness, originality, & real artistic power. If true to herself, that young girl is destined to become a "bright & shining light" in our literary firmament. Her *letters*, of which she has penned me about half a dozen, are unaffected, modest, & altogether *charming*; with *not* the remotest tinge of literary *conventionalism* in them. And by the way, she writes *poetry too*; and of the *genuine sort*, let me assure you! Her taste in this department leans evidently towards the *Dramatic*; and several of her dramatic lyrics,—notably *one*, (the scene of which lies in So Ca, the hero being a Blacksmith, ruined by the war, & lamenting the death of his gallant boys &c &c), struck me as full of "*grit*," vigor, and almost *manly verve*.[1]

Would you mind, *dear friend,* my copying what you have written me about Miss W's tales, and sending your words of encouragement in my next communication to her? Such *spontaneous* praise would greatly delight & encourage the young author, I feel sure.

How curious ab't your "*Cartoons*"! Why, my *Willie* saw them noticed as "just out" on the *2nd* Oct, in a book list of Roberts & Br*os*, issued in "*the Boston Lit: World*." Perhaps the notice was a trifle premature? Only let me get firm hold of the precious vo*l*; and I'll do *all* for it that *one person can* accomplish in a barbarous country like this!

As for the paragraph in "*The Independent*" it was taken from a *private* letter of mine to the *Editor*: and it was *misprinted* besides! Had I anticipated his action of course I should have prepared something *fuller & better*.

The beautiful *Oct* days are with us now, and the keenness of the atmosphere encourages work, *out* of doors & in. Having a good day at last, I've taken up my ancient *rôle* of *hunter*; and thus far have had *miserable* luck; but my "hand is out," and the birds, (partridges) are rather young as yet.

What a shame it *does* seem, this slaughtering of God's tender &

lovely creatures, just to procure for a man some hours' excitement *abroad*, and a luscious *entrement* subsequently, at home!! But we are *two thirds animal*, and the hunter's *furore* is like the old Berserker's, *not* to be appeased by sentiment, or eradicated by pity.

In *literary matters* I stand aghast at the variety of tasks before me. Here is *Harper* engaging me to compose an elaborate prose paper for his mag*n* upon the old Revolutionary battles in Georgia, (provided I can put him, (*Harper*), in the way of procuring "*illustrations*" for the article without which he does not want it written!); [2] and then I've a biography to prepare of my old friendly correspondent, *F. O. Ticknor* (the poet); [3] and a long novel in "MSS" by an Orangeburg (S.C.) man, to correct,— besides criticisms of every kind & degree, for "the *Wilmington Star*," & Gen*l* D H Hill's "So Home," issued in Charlotte (NC). [4]

Moreover, I *must* repeatedly be composing verses; not *inspired verses*; hot from the brain & heart, but, (oh! shameful prostitution!!), rhymes for the trade, the hucksters in literary wares, for Poverty is a hard "taskmaster," and insists even upon "saddling Pegasus," and putting the Muses into harness!—*Here* behold the *true* reason why I compose so *unevenly*! Ah! my friend, 'tis a hard case; yet when I compare my fate with—*Timrod's* for example—; I exclaim, "*who* am I, ungrateful fool! to complain"?

Starvation, at least, we need not fear; nor any absolute hardships, of the *material sort*; only my poor little wife is being half worked to death sometimes. Indeed with a *single servant* to help her, (& often with our cottage full of guests), you can imagine what *her* toils must be! Your *ennuyed* [sic] fine ladies of NY. and Boston & Paris & London, ought to be made to take a few weeks' "*turn*" with her! By *Venus*! how they would groan, lament, and weep; calling upon all Gods & Goddesses to come down to their help! It might teach them a good lesson, nevertheless. How many really need it!

I see young girls, among our guests here not out of their "teens"; who *ought* to be strong & serviceable; yet they *complain* eternally of this thing, that thing, or the other thing from a sore throat to a finger ache; and wonder how "*cousin* Minna," or "M*rs* Hayne," (as the case may be), *can stand the* "*awful* work" she accomplishes daily.

My wife tells me to thank you gratefully for the specimen of Jackson's handwriting. 'Tis invaluable to her, and to *me* also. Yet Minna says, that had she *dreamed* of your being forced to look over old letters to find it, and thus opening the half-scarred wounds of grief afresh—, she *never* would have made the request she did. [5]

Pardon her, *won't* you?—
With earnest love from all my household, *I am* as Ever,
> Faithfully yours,
> Paul H Hayne
> PO Box 635, Augusta, Geo.

1. Constance Fenimore Woolson (1840–1894), a grandniece of James Fenimore Cooper, had published her first book—*Castle Nowhere: Lake-Country Sketches*—in the spring of 1875. For her correspondence with Hayne, see Jay B. Hubbell, "Some New Letters of Constance Fenimore Woolson," *New England Quarterly*, XIV (December, 1941), 715–35. For a critical consideration of her literary career, see Rayburn S. Moore, *Constance Fenimore Woolson* (New York: Twayne, 1963). The poem Hayne refers to is "At the Smithy. (Pickens County, South Carolina, 1874)," *Appletons' Journal*, XII (September 5, 1874), 289–90.

2. When Hayne could not procure illustrations, the commission was withdrawn.

3. Hayne's biographical sketch of Francis O. Ticknor (1822–1874) appeared in the *Independent* for September 26, 1878, and was reprinted as an "Introductory Notice" in *The Poems of Frank O. Ticknor, M.D.* (1879).

4. Hayne contributed essays and notices of books to the *Star* throughout the 1870s and 1880s. He respected the editor, Theodore Bryant Kingsbury (1828–1913), and had praised his editorial principles in *Russell's* in 1858. Gen. D. H. Hill (1821–1899), former college teacher and Confederate leader, had edited *The Land We Love* (1868–1869) before taking over the *Southern Home*.

5. Mrs. Preston's younger sister Eleanor was Thomas J. Jackson's first wife.

46

To A. H. Dooley[1] MS Duke

March 8th 1876

My Dear Sir;

Your *kind* note of the 28*th* ult. would surely have been answered *sooner*, but the fact is, that I am still under the clouds of sickness; and while this uncertain *weather continues,* I don't believe that I can recruit either my strength or *spirits*!

It is the failure of the *latter* that I particularly regret. One can endure philosophically mere *physical* weakness; but when it comes to a general *blue atmosphere* enveloping the soul; *per Hercle*!—'tis no joke; but a *real, grave,* almost "immedicable misfortune"!

However, I have no design of succumbing to *any* torments, blue, black, brown, green, or yellow; but shall *die,* if die I must, fighting; and "girding" to the very last!

About my *photograph*: you shall have a *likeness as soon as prac-*

ticable; & if one of Timrod's *be* procurable, which I *doubt*, you shall have *that* likeness.

No! I have not seen Walt Whitman's new book; nor, to be *frank*, do I care a "*button*" about it! The world, or rather a few *artists*, English & American, have gone mad, touching the characteristics of this odd *Writer. One thing is certain*! If Mr. Walt Whitman really *is in any sense*, or to *any degree*, a genuine Poet; then, *all the canons of poetic Art must be reversed*; *and their most illustrious expounders* be consigned to oblivion, from Job to Homer; from Homer to Horace, from Horace to Shakspeare, from Shakspeare to Tennyson.[2]

The admiration for this false, shallow, feculent *Eccentric*, is either *half affectation*, or *complete madness*! Were an Angel from Heaven to praise him to me, I would think it more probable that the Angel was a *false spirit* than that his commendation was *just*.

Good God! My Dear Sir., think of *any mortal* coolly writing such ineffable stuff as this;—

"*The scent of these arm-pits is aroma sweeter than prayer*!,"—and *then*, the big, shameless *Beast* in his "*Leaves of Grass*," actually "*apotheosizes*," (if I may use that term), his own *genital organs*; falls down, & *worships* them (!), as if some visible deity glowed in the spherical beauty of his (doubtless) enormous testicles, and equally enormous *Penis*!! (Pardon such vulgar expressions; but *apropos* of *Whitman*, one becomes necessarily, & involuntarily vulgar!).

Perhaps W's poems are a species of "*Palimpsest*,"—that is to say, profoundly *mystical* compositions, with an *outside layer* of filth, & *revolting bestiality*; but *beneath these*, wonderful thoughts of power, sweetness, and exceeding beauty!! If so, I, at least, have not been able to discover the merit which lies *au fond*; & am naturally sceptical as to its existence!—

Fawcett & Thompson are remarkable men, *both*!—Did you see the former's recent poems, in "*the Atlantic*" & "*Appleton's*"?[3] Exquisite!

Equally good are Thompson's verses in the "*Jan Atlantic*" called "Aoede." I cannot *begin* to rival these younger Poets in grace of expression, and imaginative delicacy. In sooth Hayne's day is over; a sad & bitter reflection, *my friend*, when the *thought really strikes home*, and is not the *mere product of a moment's discouragement*.

Excuse so egoistical a letter. Write when you can; & Believe me

Always Truly
Paul Hayne
PO Box 275, Augusta, Ga.

1. A. H. Dooley in 1875 operated a bookstore and stationery business in Terre Haute, Indiana, and in 1878 established the *Modern Argo*, a literary weekly in Columbus, Ohio. He also corresponded with Maurice Thompson.

2. Hayne's opinion of Walt Whitman had been expressed as frankly in *Southern Opinion* in 1867, *Southern Society* in 1868, and elsewhere, though in language, of course, more suited to public print. See Rayburn S. Moore, "The Literary World Gone Mad: Hayne on Whitman," *Southern Literary Journal*, X (Fall, 1977), 75–83.

3. Edgar Fawcett (1847–1904), a New York poet and playwright, had corresponded with Hayne since 1874, and James Maurice Thompson had resumed a correspondence with Hayne in the same year. See Letter 40.

47

To Sidney Lanier   MS Johns Hopkins

June 29th 1876

My Dear Lanier;

You rec*d*, I hope, my last letter. I was perfectly candid, you'll remember, concerning "The *Centennial Cantata*";[1] but sure I am that you are *not* the man to take offence at such frankness. *Have* we not known each other for ages? And where have *you* a *sincerer* art-comrade & *a truer appreciator* than I?

Now, let me be equally candid about your *"Psalm of the West."*[2]

I have studied this Poem *profoundly* ; & can only say it is an *amazing* production.

It contains the material for 20, nay! 50(!) ordinary odes; the wealth of imagination, oriental luxuriance of imagery, the crowding, brilliant metaphors, the star-like fancies, and the strong, dramatic *vraisemblance*, altogether marking it as among the *strangest*, (recall what Lord Bacon says of this element of "strangeness" in connection with certain forms of "Beauty") the "strangest," and most noteworthy works of recent times. Owing to a certain *abruptness* of *execution*, inseparable from your general plan, the *conception* (just at *first*) was hardly as *clear* as I could have wished; but this finally *dawned* upon me in all its originality.

Then, I was enabled to appreciate the separate sections, verses, lines, phrases, &c.

Wonderful are many of these! The *initial* stanza, for example; the verse beginning,

"O, Darkness! *tawny twin* &c," *the whole passage* descriptive of Columbus' doubts, and his superb resolution, with its crowning tri-

umph; and the concluding lines, which have a *simpler strength* than perhaps, any *other* portion of the "*Psalm*."

In brief, altho the almost *painful superabundance* of imagery, & the *gorgeous Orientalism* of style, in your poem are opposed to my *individual taste*, which leans daily, *more* & *more* towards simpler, & sterner models; yet I repeat my conviction that "*the Psalm*" is an *astonishing performance*; bewildering from the *very opulence* of *its beauties*, & leaving an effect upon the fancy akin to that which follows the perusal of many passages in "*Festus*."[3]

—And now, I *congratulate* you *heartily* upon *all* the good work you have wrought during the last *2 years*; and rejoice to think that my prognostications (ventured long ago), as to your poetical powers, and their final recognition, are being so vividly verified.

Write to a poor devil Invalid, & Believe me

Ever most Faithfully

Paul H Hayne

1. Lanier's "The Centennial Meditation of Columbia" (sometimes referred to as "The Centennial Cantata") was published in the New York *Tribune*, April 12, 1876. See Anderson, *et al.* (eds.), *Centennial Edition of the Works of Sidney Lanier*, IX, 355n. This poem was requested by the Centennial Commission, set to music by Dudley Buck, and performed at the opening exercises of the Centennial Exhibition in Philadelphia on May 10, 1876. For letters and annotation on the composition, performance, and the controversy aroused by the "Cantata," see the *Centennial Edition*, IX, 299–382 *passim*. In his letter of June 13, 1876, Hayne acknowledges that the poem can hardly be discussed apart from the music, but since Lanier has "expressly asked" for his opinion, Hayne agrees to comment on the lyric "in its strictly poetical sense." "It is not," he concludes, "one of your happiest efforts. On the contrary, the performance, (poetically), appears to me uncharacteristic of your usual style, and your higher genius; and such I am bound to confess, is the opinion of many of my literary correspondents, some of them individuals of widely recognized reputation" (MS Johns Hopkins).

2. "The Psalm of the West," another centennial poem, was commissioned by *Lippincott's Magazine* and published therein in XVIII (July, 1876), 39–53. Hayne continues to comment on the poem in his next letter (no. 48).

3. *Festus* (1839) is a long poem by Philip James Bailey (1816–1902), a British barrister who had retired in order to write this version of the Faust legend. Hayne corresponded briefly on several occasions with Bailey.

48

To Sidney Lanier   MS Johns Hopkins

July 3rd 1876

Certainly, *My Dear Poet*, your "*Psalm of the West*" was composed during a flood-tide of inspiration![1]

Yet further study of this wonderful piece, not only *confirms*, but deepens my first favorable impression, already conveyed to you.

Indeed, your poem will "cap the climax of a fame," most *rapidly* won, & most richly deserved.

Let me adopt on this occasion the words of *Lord* Jeffrey to *Tom Macaulay* just after the publication of the latter's "*History*["]—They will hardly come amiss from your *senior* by possibly a decade; & from one whose interest in the development of *So* genius has always been *intense*.[2] "Your own brother could scarcely feel happier & prouder than I do, at this outburst of your serious fame! I have long had a *brotherly* interest in your glory, & it is now mingled with a feeling of deference to your intellectual, & artistic superiority!"

These be *true, heart-felt words*, my son! *Believe them! Remember them*! And thank God!, such sentiments are unmingled with the *remotest tinge of that* mean—, Devil-engendered, sneaking species of *envy* at your superior success, which alack! is too common among our *genus irritabile*! My own poor "career"(!!) is over!—Very soon the words which *Keats* so erroneously dreamed would serve as *his* epitaph, may *truly* be quoted as *mine*.

"*Here lies one whose name was writ in water!*"[3] But what matter? "*Dying* even," I can find it in my soul *cordially* "*to salute you.*" May your fame brighten & brighten towards the perfect Day!

Ever Yr's   Paul H Hayne

1. Hayne began to remark on the poem in Letter 47.
2. Francis Jeffrey (1773–1850), Scottish judge and one of the founders (and first editor) of the *Edinburgh Review*. Macaulay's dates were 1800–1859. Hayne was twelve years older than Lanier.
3. Actually "Here lies one who writ in water."

49

To Maurice Thompson   MS So. Car.

"Copse Hill," Geo R Road.:
November 28th 1876.

'Tis a long time, *My friend*, since I have written you more than a mere note; or read anything *from* you of the dimensions of a letter. The reason on *both sides* is obvious! You have been wrapped up in *Politics*,[1] and I have been *busy* in *Literary* departments. Yet of late, the *political* fever has actually mastered *me* also. I wonder at myself!

Not once since that dreadful April day (in 1865) which closed our hopes as *Southerners* forever, had I bestowed the slightest attention upon American public affairs; refusing for a whole decade to vote for any man, Democratic or Republican, great, or small; not from any mean, narrow, or sullen sentiment of revenge; but merely because I regarded myself as "*a Man without a Country,*" as desolate & forlorn, in *that particular*, as any human creature could possibly be.

But recent events dispelled my lethargy, and I have labored, *honestly* by *act and pen*, to promote *Tilden's* election. That he *has been* elected, *everybody knows*; but whether the Radicals will permit his peaceful installation, is *more* than problematical. Everything depends upon the temper of the Northern Democrats. Let *them* exhibit the *slightest signs of weakness*; of trepidation, of *uncertainty*, & the game is up, *finally* up!

Even *Tilden's* successful and tranquil inauguration, I would consider as only "a sop thrown to Cerberus!" (ie) I believe that *no Administration, however conscientious and able*, can permanently save a Country like ours! Its enormous size, the variety of material, and moral interests, the rapid diversions from *homogeneity*, the freedom of the ballot box granted to millions of ignorant black barbarians, fast reverting towards *fêtishism*, and blatant "heathenesse";—together with a general *laxity of principle*, from one end of this continent to the other,—all seem to be hurrying *us to the Devil*; and the *only* question, perhaps, remaining is,—*how long are we likely to occupy the downward road; the facilis descensus Averni?* It is lamentable, and pathetic, to turn back to Washington's time; nay, to a period of only *30* or *40 years* ago, and read the confident prophecies of our Statesmen, and Orators concerning American freedom, & its perpetuity.

One can understand *their* patriotic Optimism; but *now—, now* it puzzles me past all expression to comprehend how *thinking* persons, with the history of the antique world before them; with all human experience pointing so clearly in *one* direction; can nevertheless, indulge in glowing prognostications of American glory; brightened by visions (God save the mark!) of the *next Centennial* advent, the magnificence whereof is (of course) to be unsurpassable!! Ten to one, the *next "Centennial"* in *their* sense of the word, will *never arrive*; since "'*tis a long cry to Loch awe*," and 1976 will probably find the *ci devant* American Republic split up into a half dozen mongrel nationalities; as worthless and disorganized as the States of Spanish So America, or the Provinces of what Joaquin Miller[2] is pleased to style "glorious *gory Mexico*!"

(About the "goriness" there can be no dispute; but for the "*glory*"—the "least said" the better!)

Perchance my detestation of all *unlimited Republics*—indissolubly associated in my mind with the "*bonnet rouge*," and *sans Culottism—may* darken my judgment in this *special* case; but, I'm afraid *not!* Do we not behold *Republicanism* carried to its legitimate results, in the present condition of S. Carolina!? Even as I pen these lines, it is quite probable that Grant's bayonets occupy the State House hall in Columbia, for the purpose of installing a set of legally defeated *Thieves* & *negroes*, in preference to the choice of the *Christian gentlemen* of that unlucky Commonwealth,—*Hampton and his allies*!!

But a *truce* to this discussion![3]

I have read with *lively interest* your paper on the "*Game Birds*" in the last "*Appleton*"; and I am anticipating your other article on "*Archery*," (with illustrations) in "*Scribner*." By the way. I wish that you could examine a *Bow* I have managed to buy, which originally came from one of the "*South Sea Islands*." 'Tis *7 feet and a half* long, & the *wood* seems almost as hard as *iron*. Ten arrows came with it, pointed with a species of "*lignum vitae*," and all of them *poisoned*. This curious weapon I procured from M*r* W*m P. Brown* of the "*Curiosity Cabinet*" *Establishment* in *New York* City! He *sent it by "Express."*[4]

Enclosed, you'll find a *likeness* of myself, which is *Mrs. Hayne's present to you*. "Tell M*r* T." she says, "that I *confidently expect his photograph in return!*" The enclosed likeness is remarkably *faithful*; only the *right* eye looks smaller than the *left*, as if it had been "banged up" by a rather severe blow. Bating this solitary defect, we think the photograph (as I have said) more than "passable." *Yesterday*, I heard at some length from *Fawcett* again. He writes of my "*Muscadines*" (in *Harper's*), that they "*afforded him great pleasure*;"—that the piece is full of a "*delicate vigor*." Now, I value *F's critical judgment, especially in poetry*.[5] He is himself a *wonderful poetic artist*. Tell me *frankly* whether you too like the "*Muscadines*." (I've a *particular reason*, *Thompson*! for inquiring; and *I know you will be candid*). Your "*Garden Statues*" (*did* I tell you?), are as *clearly & beautifully cut* as the original *marble* triumphs of which they *sing*. Write soon! Ever Faithfully,

Paul H Hayne.

---

1. In addition to his law practice and work as a civil engineer for a railroad, Thompson in 1876 "campaigned all over the state for the Democratic party, and in 1878 he was

a successful candidate for the legislature." Wheeler, *The Literary Career of Maurice Thompson*, 25.

2. Joaquin Miller (1839–1913), a poet whose *Songs of the Sierras* (1871) had brought him to the attention of a national audience. Hayne at first was enthusiastic about Miller's work, but later changed his mind. See Letter 29, n. 3, and Letter 30.

3. Though Thompson made no effort to hide his political views, Hayne was not yet aware of the true nature of his friend's opinions about national politics. Hayne would probably not have been as forthright in this case if he had realized that Thompson did not fully agree with him.

4. Hayne eventually gave the bow and arrows to Thompson.

5. For Fawcett, see Letter 46, n. 3. "Muscadines," one of Hayne's best poems of the period, appeared in *Harper's New Monthly*, LIV (December, 1876), 127–28.

50

To John Esten Cooke   MS Duke

"Copse Hill" Ga R.R (16 miles from Augusta Ga)
March 16th 1877

Dear Old friend;

Your P.C. came yesterday, & I at once write to acknowledge your cordial communication.

Somehow, the *briefest note* of yours always inspirits me! There's a *tonic* in the very wave of your pen;—& a geniality not to be repressed, or mistaken, trickles, as it were, out of your ink stand, carrying warmth & encouragement to your far-off friends!

I'm heartily glad you liked my S.C. lyric;[1] *heartily glad & grateful* to find that you think I've "*done my literary devoir*" gallantly! . . . But the idea of your saying that "you yourself are doing *nothing*"!

Why, you work like "20 *horses rolled into one*"! No man in America can show a fuller record! Novels, essays, biographies, histories, miscellaneous tales, poems &c &c—flow from your brain with a magic facility.

Indeed, your industry amazes me!

I felt sure that "*the Craniologist" must be* your work! Let me tell you that therein you have "made *a decided hit*,"—the entire story being of its kind nearly perfect. "*Canolles*," I'll read, you may be sure, with avidity.[2] Nay! I'll do *more* than *that*. I'll *notice* the work, and try to increase the sale in this section of Country.

Thanks again for your kind invitation to visit you. Alack! my dear *Cooke*. I would *fly* to *Millwood*, were the thing possible; but I could as reasonably expect, just now, to fly up into heaven!

But we'll hope for better days!

My wife joins me in thanking you for all your unselfish courtesy, & kindness *to her husband*!

She often talks of *Mr Jno Esten Cooke*, as one of the *very few real Southern gentlemen, left to show what the manners & morals of the South once were*!

By the way, I enclose for your amusement two political trifles.[3]

Thinking of the Country, & its degradation, one feels simply *desperate*! Thus much for *Republics*! Jefferson, Washington, *all* of them, were mistaken! Republics are *impossibilities*!

Ever affectionately   Paul H Hayne.

1. Presumably "South Carolina to the States of the North," a passionate comment on the treatment of South Carolina after the presidential election of 1876, which had appeared only two months earlier in the Augusta *Constitutionalist*.

2. "The Craniologist" appeared in *Harper's New Monthly* for January, 1877. *Canolles* (1877) is a romance set in Virginia during the colonial period.

3. The "trifles" are "To the Life" and "Hampton! and Right Forever!" The original appearances of these poems have not been located.

51

To O. W. Holmes   MS Duke

Augusta, April 6*th* 1877.:

My Dear Doctor,—

I trust that the years as they pass, deal kindly with you; that in body & mind you are as well & cheerful as a mortal can be!

Just now, I wish to enclose for your perusal two poems of my own, which perhaps may interest you, th*o* in very different ways.

The *political* lyric embodies the passionate protest of my unfortunate compatriots, touching the monstrous tyranny of the Grant administration, which until 4 days ago we feared might be perpetuated; the second piece explains itself.[1]

For almost the first time since the close of the war, the people in S.C. begin to breathe a little freely. Oh! Sir, if you could only imagine a *tenth part* of the anguish, the suffering, the *unmitigated torture* to which Carolinians have been subjected under "Carpet Bag" & negro rule, you would even now stand aghast. It has been ancient *Imperialism, plus* modern *Bashibazoukism*. Why, the *white* ladies & children of such a City as Charleston cannot or could not until *Hampton's* victory, walk the public streets without gross insult from the negro rabble, spurred on by cowardly white villains.

Think of your *Mass* mothers, your daughters, & sisters being daily assaulted in Washington St, or on the Common, for example, not merely by the basest epithets from the foullest lips, but by actual *blows & physical insult*!

At length, our women (in C*a*) had either to remain in doors when no male escort was near, or to go abroad *armed*. Of course the *vast majority* chose to remain at home, *virtually imprisoned* in a Country called Republican.

I desire you, Doctor, as a fair minded man, to know these facts. They explain the *furor* over *Hampton*, who alone has the power at present, to govern his native State, & bring some order out of Chaos.[2]

He is quite as much the Negro's friend as the white man's. As for Chamberlain, tho a man of talents, & education, he has miserably succumbed under temptations, & allowed himself to make assertions, & justify actions, whereof he ought to feel increasingly ashamed, if his life continued for a hundred years to come![3]

There is no prejudice in this;—once I believed in Chamberlain; but his *own words & deeds condemn him.*

Is *Wendell Phillips* quite mad?

I've just read a report of one of his *Lectures*, which for *shameless* vituperation, bloodthirsty malignity, and downright, deliberate falsehood "Out Herods Herod"! *Where* was he during the *war*, when *bullets, not words* were abroad? Did he command an Army, a brigade, a regiment, a company? If so, I never heard of it.[4] Pardon such a hurried "screed," & Believe me

Now as Always
Faithfully Yr's
Paul H. Hayne
PO Box 275

1. The political lyric referred to is "South Carolina to the States of the North."

2. Wade Hampton (1818–1902), South Carolina planter and commander of the Confederate cavalry after J. E. B. Stuart's death, was elected governor of South Carolina in the disputed election of November, 1876, and took office when federal troops were withdrawn on April 10, 1877, four days after this letter was written.

3. Daniel Henry Chamberlain (1835–1907), a native of Massachusetts who settled in South Carolina in 1866 and was elected governor in 1874, was Hampton's opponent in the contested election of 1876. When the federal troops withdrew on April 10, 1877, Chamberlain left the state.

4. Wendell Phillips (1811–1884), a disciple of William L. Garrison and a rabid Ab-
olitionist before the war, continued to lecture on political and social topics afterwards.

52

To Sidney Lanier   MS Johns Hopkins

Address, PO Box 275 Augusta (Geo) (Private)
"Copse Hill," Geo RR July 19th 1877:

My Dear Lanier;—

Your last letter, while relieving me of the fear that *my own* former
epistle had miscarried, has somewhat shocked & distressed me.[1]

It is clear from what you say, that another of those vile pulmonary
attacks threatens you, or has already made its devastating assault. The
whole tone of your communication shows the natural, the *inevitable*
despondency which comes of a diseased physical condition; and then,
'tis equally evident that you have been over working yourself, & playing
the Deuce with an exceedingly delicate system of *nerves*. I cannot dis-
guise from myself that this long-continued, & apparently incurable irri-
tation of the lungs, forebodes evil; & *poverty*, (accursed poverty!!)
being added as you remark, to physical weakness, *must* produce a gen-
eral condition of things the reverse of agreeable. And yet *Lanier*, my
impression is, that you possess unusual *resiliency* of constitution; &
that from blows which would prove fatal to *apparently* stronger men,
you are destined to arise triumphant again & yet again!

Touching *literary* success, it is evident that you take too low a view
of your own position, & prospects.

Why, the *very stir & turmoil* which your decided style & man-
ifestations of original thought, have created, are *positively* demonstra-
tive of the life, vigor, and suggestiveness of your endowments.

Opposition, even the *bitterest opposition* to the first works of a
Poet, may often be regarded as *the most favorable of symptoms*.

Need I point to illustrations; need I mention the careers of such
men as Keats, Wordsworth, L. Hunt, & Tennyson?

Remember too, that you have *admirers*, quite as earnest as your
detractors. And take into account above all things, the fact, that few of
your *adverse Critics, have really studied the peculiarities of your mind
& temperament*!! Either thro the operations of constitutional descent,

or thro the subtle processes of what may be called *spiritual whim—*, your intellect, especially on the imaginative side, partakes largely of the *Teutonic element*; is, in brief, almost as much *German* as *Saxon*. Are you not a devoted student of *Heine*? If *not*, even if you never read a line of his works, your mental *attitudes* continually remind one of *Heine*. You have his grotesqueness, his fantasy; and *involuntarily*, these appear after a fashion, which the major portion of your American Critics can't be made to comprehend. I myself find such ebulitions [*sic*] of yours *charming* at *certain* times; and again, to be frank, I don't like them.

For example, in your "*Fla*," that extravaganza suggested by the sailor's "*yawn*," is *Heine* all over, *at his best*;—("*Florida*," by the way, tho written in prose, is one of your *truest poems*);—but in "*The Psalm of the West*," your somewhat abrupt transition from the brilliant & dramatic, to the *grotesquerié* of the Tournament between "*Brain*" & "*Heart*," deserves, I'm afraid, the censure of "the Nation," (in many *other* respects, *as wrong as wrong can be!*)

Reviewing the whole matter, your *general* literary success seems to me *wonderful*. In little more than a year, to have made your name known among literary societies everywhere; to have gained the position of Poet in Chief to one of our first class periodicals; & to have issued, (during this short period), *two* noteworthy books—; why, *per Hercle*? few could show *such* a record!

A few words more upon " *Florida*": 'Tis among the most delightful works of the sort, I have ever seen. Seldom have the *Poetical* & the *Practical* been so harmoniously blended.

Science & sentiment, love & liquor, trade & tenderness; hard history & romantic rumor; delicious descriptions of the liquid weirdnesses of the water, & the solemn solidities of the shore—; fact & fancy; disagreeable flurry, and fascinating *dolce far niente*; pictures of the peculiarities of animated Nature, from tom-tits, & tortuous water-turkeys, "all neck," up to the most gorgeous feathered tenants of semi-Tropical woods;—each & all, have been presented to "the mind's eye," vividly, and vigorously;—moreover, *some* of the Chapters are truly eloquent in a higher way; as, for instance, that wherein you defend the *lowland Pine*, with an acuteness of observation, force of illustrative reasoning, and flowing grace of phraseology, which one cannot too earnestly admire. Cheer up, therefore, *my Friend*, despite *poverty*, & despite *sickness*.

You are the most gifted man, now hailing from the *South*—, as a *Litterateur*; and your *wise* resolution to reside, henceforth, in NYork, will bring you to opportunities of progress, not to be found in these semi-barbarous latitudes for a century to come!

My career (such as it is) draws rapidly to a close; but I look confidently *to you* to uphold the aësthetic banner, & to win both for yourself & section, a *true renown.*

In addition to your more liberal gifts of nature, you will enjoy chances which never have approached within a thousand miles of me;—and if *Fate* only condescends to give you *health*, there's no predicting what you may not accomplish. As for *Critics*, if they seem earnest, & capable, *respect* them; but if *au contraire*, they merely attack you, to exhibit a malicious cleverness, let them go to the Devil, by the shortest cut!

The author of true power, & true resolution, is sure to survive an *army* of *mere detractors*. Think of "gad flies" attacking a knight armed *cap á pie*. How their little stings must rebound, crushed & smarting, from contact with the indomitable steel!!!

Again I say, preserve your *health*, if possible, and *all shall be well*!

Answer this at your *earliest convenience*; and believe me Always Faithfully

Paul H. Hayne.

1. Lanier's letter, now lost, apparently was written in June and reflected the kind of depression clearly expressed in a comment to Gibson Peacock on September 27, 1877: "Altogether it seems as if there wasn't any place for me in this world, and if it were not for May I should certainly quit it, in mortification at being so useless." Anderson, *et al.* (eds.), *Centennial Edition of the Works of Sidney Lanier*, IX, 475–76.

53

MS Johns Hopkins

To Sidney Lanier

Address PO Box 275, Augusta, Geo
"Copse Hill" Ga RR.
July 25th, 1877

My Dear Lanier;

I hope that you rec*d* my long letter of a few days ago.[1] That letter must show you the deep interest I take in you, and your *literary progress.*

Now, don't misunderstand, or be offended, *Lanier*, if I have a small, and not particularly "black crow to pick with you," concerning a passage in your able book on *Florida*, a passage which has just caught my attention.

Involuntarily, no doubt, your criticism on Timrod's poetry does it less than justice, at least, in the particular of *art*.

One but slightly acquainted with his verse, or who had never read it, would derive from your remarks the impression that he was a half rustic-Bard, who never in the course of his thirty eight years of mortal life, had enjoyed the opportunity of associating with men eminent in letters, & was wholly ignorant of the great rules of poetic art.

"It is *thoroughly evident* from these, (his lyrics)," you say, "that he had never had time to learn the *mere craft of the poet* , the *technique of verse* & that a broader association &c &c."

I must confess my *astonishment* at such a view as this!! Glancing over the many critiques, English & American, which were published on his vo*l*,[2] I find a remarkable agreement upon *one* point, (viz), in the language of "*The Athäeneum*," "the singular delicacy & *finish* of T's versification, the unpretentious, but *exquisite art which conceals itself!*"

Are "*Ethnogenesis*," "*The Cotton Boll*[,]" "*Katie*," "*The Exotic*" and many other pieces, *not* admirable illustrations of the truth of this opinion?

Moreover, let me tell you, that I have heard Timrod, for hours, discuss with scholars of the "first water," such men as Prof: Gildersleeve, formerly of *Göttingen*, now of the U. of Virginia, the *profoundest* questions associated with both *English* & *Latin prosody*; displaying a subtle & minute acquaintance with his subject, which surprised those with whom he conversed.[3] Excepting *Edgar Poe*, I don't believe the Southerner, nay, the American has ever existed, whose knowledge of the "*technique of verse*" surpassed Timrod's. It is exemplified in his . . . it, to invest your notice with . . . well . . . *what* shall I call it? . . . a certain air of *posthumous patronage*, as if you had said, "come here my bonny lad; my clever "child," and let me pat you on the head!—do you know that your "native wood-notes wild," are very graceful & musical? they please me much; but ah! my sweet boy, what a pity it is you sing so completely by ear!"[4] If you had only been blessed with the chance of learning that poetry is not altogether confined to spontaneous bird-warblings! Oh, dear! how sad to reflect, that, probably, the "*technique of verse*," is a phrase you but dimly comprehend!"[5]

Upon my soul, *Lanier*, such is the *impression* produced by your notice, not on my mind merely, (you may deem me *prejudiced* unduly in T's favor), but upon the minds of several highly cultivated persons— *Northern* men of letters—, to whom I showed your paragraph.

And now, you'll forgive my candor, I'm sure; and believe that you have few really better friends anywhere, than

Yours Always Faithfully,
Paul H. Hayne

1. See Letter 52.

2. Hayne presumably means the *Poems of Henry Timrod* (published 1872) and not the collection that appeared in 1860.

3. Basil Lanneau Gildersleeve (1831–1924), a native of Charleston and schoolmate of Hayne's and Timrod's who had become a leading classicist of his time, went in 1876 to Johns Hopkins University, and would soon found and edit the *American Journal of Philology*. Lanier may have known Gildersleeve by this time, though it is not clear exactly when Lanier met Gildersleeve in Baltimore. There is, however, no doubt that he knew him by reputation at this time and that within a year or two he was on terms of friendship with him (Anderson, *et al.* [eds.], *Centennial Edition of the Works of Sidney Lanier*, VII, xlvi–lii).

4. Several lines of page 3 of this letter have inadvertently been removed from the manuscript, as indicated by the first ellipsis.

5. As a result of Hayne's comments, Lanier changed these passages. See Hayne's letter of January 5, 1878 (MS Johns Hopkins): "Your alteration—, in some measure, of those passages upon Timrod's poetry, shows that you possess a magnanimous spirit, for which no man can honor you more truly than I do. Some persons, nay very many writers, would have flown into a passion with me for my too frank statement of the impression to be drawn from your original critique; but you, (and I thank God for it!) are 'every inch a man.'"

54

To Maurice Thompson   MS So. Car.

"Copse Hill" Geo RR
Oct 10th 1877

Dear Thompson;

Your note of the 1*st* inst., just rec*d*., is the first communication from you, since your return from the summer holidays.

How rejoiced am I [to] hear of your success at the Bar! *One Hundred Cases*, between yourself, & brother, at a single term!! By heaven, but isn't this glorious?

Evidently, my dear boy, you are making your way with about equal rapidity & success in the domains of Literature & those of Law.

I take a *real brotherly* interest in your progress.

About the delay in your reception of the South-Sea "*Bow*," I have *already* explained.[1] Doubtless, by *this time*, however, the weapon has reached you. (Tell me about it!)

By the way, *apropos*, of *Griswold*, 'tis evident that you are some-what in the dark as to the *actual* character of the man.[2] Harsh as my sentence may *seem*, on the surface, pronouncing him in H——, it is *not* a *whit too* harsh, *under the circumstances*!

There are some crimes compounded of deliberate treachery & meanness unspeakable, which (*to those fully acquainted with their de-tails*)—place a man *outside* the charity embodied in the proverb of "*De Mortuis nil nisi Bonum*!" unless, indeed, the Judge chances to be a mere milk & water Sentimentalist!!

Years ago, *Thompson,* I knew, at *one* period, knew *well*, Miss Car-oline *Griswold*, the Dr's intelligent & estimable daughter; & thr*o* *her* friends certain facts about the father came to my knowledge, which demonstrated his infamy beyond the shadow of a doubt!

He was a malicious serpent in human shape! Over female inno-cence & purity, he left his loathsome trail. He spoiled the life of *one* woman, and broke the heart of another, & his crimes seemed *deliberate*!

Now, to deceive the gentler, nobler, more confiding sex, after *this fashion*, is to *my* mind, "*the one unpardonable sin*!"

Moreover, the man was steeped to the lips in hypocrisy! A minister of *Christ*, he enacted the part of *Iscariot*.

His atrocious Record, with its *Q.E.D.* of accomplished & brazen infamy, seems to stand forth in letters, compounded of blood, fire & poison!

Don't tell me that such a wretch, because of the mere "accident of death," deserves consideration, tenderness, or mercy! Can one feel par-ticularly benevolent towards a *slain Snake*, puffed out with venom; venom which before the monster's decease, had been injected into the veins of the innocent & helpless?

"My brethren," said sturdy old Sam*l* Johnson, "above all things, let us divest our minds of *Cant*!"

—Gill, acquainted with the facts I have alluded to, felt them natu-rally *re-act* upon him in his estimate of *Griswold's* connection with *Poe*. So far *as it goes*, his case *versus* the *former*, appears to me a *very power-ful* one. And, upon my soul! I don't *see* how, with the lights before him, he *could* have written differently.[3]

Of course, as a *general* principle, what you say concerning the "*meanness*" of *assaulting* the Dead, is beyond all dispute; but let me *repeat* that *exceptional* Cases exist, to which the charitable *Rule* applies *not*! *G's case is one of these*!

In one of your generous notices of my poems, you said, that, "*Hayne was sincere to a fault*!"—This perhaps is true. My *bluntness* has *sometimes* offended people; but (generally), they have been persons with more conceit than brains; or adolescents, delicate, emasculated *Dilettanti*; frail intellectual *Eunuchs*, ready to "Die of a *rose* in *aromatic pain*!" Now, *You* have a pre-eminently *virile* genius; & when I differ on any question from *such* a friend, & express my views *strongly*; I well know *he won't* misunderstand me![4]

But eno' of this.

After the "*Bow*" reaches you, you may expect *soon* to receive such of the arrows, as are fit to send.

Enclosed, I despatch a poem, which please *read carefully*; and at *once return*. Altho I composed this piece under strong emotion, & took much pains with the rhythm & wording,—who shall say whether I have succeeded?—

Ah! *you* shall say it.

Tell me frankly how the verses strike you.

Will *not Mrs Thompson* (to whom I offer my *best regards*) send my wife her *likeness one of these days*?

In haste, but Always Truly & affectionately Yr's

Paul. H. Hayne.

1. The bow is described in Letter 49.

2. Rufus W. Griswold (1815–1857), editor, anthologist, and Edgar Allan Poe's literary executor, wrote an infamous memoir of the dead poet and supervised the first collected edition of his work (4 vols., 1850–56).

3. William F. Gill's *The Life of Edgar Allan Poe* (1877) presumably is the source of this discussion of Griswold. Gill, by the way, was associated with the Poe Memorial Committee in Baltimore, and he exchanged letters about Poe with Hayne on several occasions in the late 1870s and early 1880s.

4. Viewed in the light of future misunderstandings over Hayne's criticism of Thompson's fiction, this passage seems particularly ironic. It is even possible that Hayne is trying to alert Thompson to such possibilities, but, if so, the warning had little effect.

55
To Charles Warren Stoddard[1]   MS Duke

Address P.O. Box 275, Augusta, Ga.
"Copse Hill," Geo RR
December 24, 1877

My dear Mr. Stoddard:—

At length, I enjoy a few hours of leisure, and these I shall devote to you.

Let me hope that my brief pencilled note of the 19th, and the vol. called "*The Mountain of Lovers*," reached you safely.

En passant, I must inform you that the only poems I myself like in the book mentioned, are the *poems of Nature*.

The chief narrative piece was composed in a very unlucky vein, and I *bitterly* regret its publication.

Indeed my *Legends and Lyrics* issued by Lippincott in 1872 contain the only *two narrative* poems I really value.

Now, for yourself! *Again* & *again* —I have perused your letter of the 11th inst., & while I perceive from it, that you are the *same frank spirited, warm-hearted man as ever*, it really *grieves* me to perceive also, that in the very bloom and flush of manhood, you seem broken down, *ennuied*, and utterly despondent!

Now, may I take a friend's privilege and offer you some counsel?

It appears to me that I *fully* comprehend your frame of mind; and that the remedy for your intellectual & moral sickness is too patent to be neglected.

Five years ago, under the pressure of deep affliction, you became a wanderer, and ever since like the "Ancient Mariner," you have roamed from land to land, seeking peace, but finding it *not*!

And now, returning to your native country, a dreadful depression, —the result of certain *reactionary forces*,—has taken possession of your soul. Forgive me! but may not this condition of things be owing *partly* to *physical causes*?

A long observation of life, above all my *own* experience, convinces me, that many of the more *serious* ills of our poor Humanity (don't start at the *apparent bathos*!) have their roots deep down among the fibres—so to speak—of a diseased *Liver*!

On one side of his nature, man is *wholly Animal*; when the *body* is out of gear, how can the mind work properly? Possibly—forgive me *again*!—you have, like so many persons of your ardent temperament— sought consolation from time to time, in those stimulants, which give such marvellous *temporary* relief, only to revenge themselves (finally) upon every nerve, in ways impossible to describe; and all but intolerable to the harassed sufferer. And the Devil of it is, that under such severe punishment, the *bravest* man is apt to grow *desperate*; and thus, to hurl away all chances of recovery by *again* and yet *again* resorting to the perfidious enemy, where insidious poison has already undermined & weakened the very sources of his existence!

The *first* thing to be done in such a case is to seek *physical re-cuperation* by abstenance [*sic*], & a fair share of that obtained, then let the patient address himself to labor, *engrossing work of some sort!*

Unless absolute organic disease has begun, he is sure to recover, to be his former self once more!

In virtue of my 47 years, and of some *horrible personal experiences besides,* I have dared to throw out these hints, *God knows* how well & kindly meant.

Certainly, I *may* be on a false track; certainly, you may be enabled to laugh at my advice as needless, and my anxiety as misplaced; but if— if it be not so, then my *dear Boy,* you are the last person to be offended, or to accuse me of officiousness.

I am no Pharisee! I write (this in *sacred confidence*), as one who has been plunged into the depths of *Hades*! Basta! it is enough! you will understand.[2]

To pleasanter matters! By all means, send me your *"South Sea Idylls."* From what chance has enabled me to see of your *prose-style, I like it exceedingly.*

You possess genuine imagination, & often your *Prose* is *rhythmic.*

As for the condemnation of *"The Idylls"* in England, & the relega-tion of the book to the "street stalls," that circumstance affects me but little.

I recollect Byron's saying (*true* for once), that the English are often seized by periodical fits of *squeamish morality.*

Today they condemn with horror, what tomorrow, is eagerly sought after, and as eagerly devoured!

You *never* write *poetry* now, you tell me!

Well! never mind! *never* be discouraged! If, as I believe, the *"root of the matter*" be in you; a second, & probably, more splendid poetic day is yet destined to dawn over your path.

To compose true, *artistic* verse, one *must* have a certain degree of quiet,—of repose.

Don't forget your promise to answer this letter *soon & fully.*

And now, with the very *best* wishes for your welfare in every *conceivable way*, please believe me

> *Always Faithfully yr friend*
> *Paul H. Hayne*

P.S. Glance over "Scribner" for once & tell me, frankly, how my "Unveiled" strikes you? I was *pleased* to read what you sent me concerning "Muscadines." *Swinburne* also wrote me very kindly & enthusiastically about that poem.[3]

1. Stoddard (1843–1909), author of *Poems* (1867) and *South-Sea Idylls* (1873), had initiated a desultory correspondence with Hayne in 1866 which was now being temporarily renewed after a lapse of some years.

2. Hayne's own years of experience with ill health often led him to offer avuncular advice to correspondents—especially to his juniors—who were depressed or in poor health. Lanier's example comes immediately to mind. See Letter 29.

3. "Unveiled," *Scribner's Monthly*, XV (January, 1878), 383–86. Dr. Josiah G. Holland, the editor, said in his letter of September 10, 1877, to Hayne that this poem was "much the best, largest, most strongly and evenly sustained piece of work I have ever seen from your hand." And Hayne himself later agreed that it was his "high-water mark." Swinburne commented on "Muscadines" (*Harper's Monthly*, LIV [December, 1876], 127–28) in a letter of 1877 (quoted in *CHL*, 366).

56

To Margaret J. Preston   MS Duke

"Copse Hill" Geo RR July 26th 1878.

My Dear & Valued Friend:

I rec*d* your last letter (of the 21*st* in*st*) yesterday afternoon. Being somewhat better in health, I *must answer your* beautiful & affectionate communication at once. Ah! *it* has *deeply* touched me! Its thoughtfulness, its concern for my welfare, bodily & spiritual, its profoundly religious tone, which I appreciate, as once I could hardly have done, all these things combine to make your letter a memorable one, dear to my *heart*, & understanding alike.

As for the solemn subject upon which you dwell so *feelingly*, let me tell you that not a single day has passed over me, from my *9th* year, until now, when I am 48, some minutes at least of which have failed to be occupied, tho involuntarily perhaps, of reflections upon *Death*! In every possible phase, dark and bright, has this topic come up for consideration,—thoughts innumerable, some sceptical, others full of faith have grouped themselves around the central *idea*; but of course all speculation is worse than vain. How could it be otherwise? God designed to make a Mystery of Death, to surround it with clouds and *darkness* thro which, however, a *wonderful* illuminating light shines now & then!

I declare very seriously that death while invested, to my mind with unspeakable *awe*, carries with it *terror* in only two aspects. The first and lowest, refers to physical pain. I *hate pain*, shrink from and abhor it, tho upon occasion I may endure as well as another.

The *second* (*and here is*, indeed, the rub) refers to the *spiritual pang* of parting from those we *love*. Doubts & fears will assail one touching this inestimably important point; but thank God they are merely temporary. My *settled conviction*, that conviction of all times of insight, and spiritual inspiration is, that heaven would not be Heaven robbed of the presence of one dearly Beloved on earth. No! the concluding stanza of "A Thousand Years from Now" expresses my unalterable faith in reunion beyond the grave.[1]

Like yourself, I am not ashamed to walk (spiritually) in the footsteps of *my fathers*! not ashamed to confess my dependence upon the aid & love of that *Divine Master who* has been the stay of Poets & Martyrs and Prophets in all ages, the adored of Genius & Greatness, no less than humble, struggling *Poverty*, the beneficent Lord whom Bacon, in the utmost contrition of sin & abasement, so pathetically invoked, and whose holy name rises like an incense flame, from the dark *Will* & Testament of the grandeur of uninspired mortals, one who having seen higher, deeper, broader, than any other of woman born, could *yet humble* himself and his all but supernatural intellect before the majesty of divine meekness & incarnate Pity.

The Christ of Shakspeare & the wisest of *inductive* Philosophers may well be your *Christ* and mine!

Let Huxley argue, and Darwin teach 'his religion of dirt & degredation'; let Tyndall thunder about the potentialities of Matter, and *Clough, with his school* of iconoclastic Infidels, declare that "Christ has not risen!" I only know that he *has risen for me*; & that about the antique faith, there gathers a *reverence*, a sacred pathos, a divine purity of hope, which Modern Philosophy, backed by all the Sciences, can never dim, far less weaken & destroy.

Such being the case, why as poor little Amy says in Tennyson's "May Queen," "*why* make we such ado," at the approval of AZRAÏL, the dark Angel of redemption. A brighter world beyond; re-union with friends & lovers! What more can we desire, or dream of?

And for the terrors of the mysterious Valley, why think how the lowliest woman, the feeblest children have passed thro the shadow before us undismayed, and shall we coward-like shrink back?

To turn to other topics.

You refer to Bryant's death & poetry.[2] You think it was scarcely worth living 84 years, to have his genius dissected as it is being dissected now by the Press, & his claims as a first-class Poet disallowed!

Well! my friend!—I don't altogether agree with you here. Bryant—like *most true* Poets doubtless found that "poetry was its *own* exceeding great reward." Possessed of an eminently philosophic temper, he wrote far more for his own satisfaction, than the applause of others; and my firm belief is, that if he were allowed to rise from the grave, & behold what is now progressing, & learn the various disparaging criticism of his verse,—he would merely shrug his ghostly shoulders, and indulge in a half humorous, half sardonic smile! By the way, how immeasurably absurd are these discussions ab't *first* & *second class Poets*, (ie), carried on as they are, with the plain deduction that a "2nd *class Poet*" is a *Nobody*, & *his* fame not worth a second's consideration!! Now, the true question with every person of sense is, whether such & such a Writer, has fairly established his claim to be viewed as *a Poet at all*; and as soon as we determine that he really *is a Poet*, let us in bare justice, treat him with respect; for assuredly (whatever his precise artistic rank), he *merits* respect!

But *Critics*, now-a-days, seem to me for the most part, a precious set of Donkeys, with boundless powers of *self-assurance*, and unlimited capacity for . . . *braying*!!

My *own* most exquisite enjoyment derived from the visits of the Muse, has always been in the act of *conception*, followed by swift *execution*. When the period of *correction* came, the duty of *labor limae*, I shrank from, and detested it! To the very *last*, I shall *hate* this *duty*! still a *duty* it unquestionably is.

En passant, you allude to the variety of Literature, and literary aspirations; and refer to the Book of "*Ecclesiastes*" which you had been reading aloud to Co*l* Preston.

Of course, in *one* sense, all mortal aims[,] purposes, ambitions, are but *vanity*; still I *do* think that to dwell too long & constantly upon this phase of truth, produces morbid & evil results.

Better contend against difficulties to the final gasp, than bewail an evil fortune, & the sorrows of life eternally! Better fall, man-like, in full armor, fronting the foe, than "make moan," however musically under the drooping willows!

As for *Solomon*, I doubt whether he ought rightfully to be called the "*wisest of mankind* ." Much of his youth & manhood, was spent in selfish worldliness, the "pomp & circumstance" of *Court & Field*; a magnificent *Sensualist*, he exhausted all sources of earthly enjoyment; and then, with *racked nerves*, and ruined energies, began to lament the uselessness of a career, which, (considering all his reputed wisdom)—he surely ought to have estimated *aright*, at a much earlier day.

Upon my soul! his lamentations appear to me to have quite as much of *latent* regret in them, as of true philosophy.

Had Solomon's youth & opportunities been miraculously restored, would he have still harped upon the mournful string of of [*sic*] "*vanitas vanitatum*"?

In *certain moods* one responds to the key-note of the Preacher's teaching, but such moods are not our wholesomest or highest.

I am quite sure of *that*!

Even among the mountains, it appears that this unusual season has afflicted you with *heat*, & all its disagreeable consequences.

We read in the papers of multitudes dying of sun-stroke North, East & West, but such is the equable nature of *our* Climate, that really, we cannot pretend to have *suffered*; altho the thermometer ranged a little *higher* than common for several days last week.

Perhaps, this general heat may be caused by the approach of some unknown Comet to the Sun?

Astronomers cannot *always* predict the advent of these mysterious visitants!

Do you recall Sir Isaac Newton's comments upon the Comet of 1682—3? Had that enormous body fallen upon the sun, (as it very nearly *did*), *Newton* believed that the destruction of all the Planets must inevitably have ensued! Perhaps our Earth may be in some such dangerous position now? O! think, only think of the possibility of *all* of us dying, or being translated together, amid the crash of worlds, and the elements "melting with fervent heat!" There is something terribly fascinating in the idea! No *parting*, slow and painful, from those we love, but a common death, or a translation together!

But really, I must curb my fantastic fancy! Some *additional verses*, lately composed, I enclose for your examination.[3]

They are simple eno', explaining themselves. Cut & slash them, to your heart's content! I shall only thank you for using the dissecting knife of Criticism in the most uncompromising fashion.

Minna has just been reading me your *exquisite* poem "*Comforted*," which is quite worthy of Tennyson. I like it even *better* than I *did* when the piece first attracted my notice.

Involuntarily, I have *copied* your idea concerning the little children & tender women who have passed th*ro* the "Valley of the Shadow," *unterrified.*

Yes! this poem of yours is indeed most *pathetically beautiful*![4]

To Mrs. Preston (continued from July 26)   MS Duke

"*Copse Hill*" *Monday* [July] 29th 1878

Dear Friend;

I was compelled thr*o* certain warning pains, combined with the excessive *heat* to stop writing at the point, reached in my Friday's letter.

On the afternoon of the 27th your sweet note, pencilled on the back of my verses reached me. I am glad that you liked the poems.

As to the *false rhymes "austere"* & "*share*," I let them go *deliberately*, because I prefer a doubtful, or even "false rhyme" *now & then*(!) to the substitution of a *fuller line*, to avoid it!

And in this *special* case, I found the line I tried to put in with *perfect* rhyme, vastly inferior to the original.

Minna will write you *as soon as she* can command a moment's leisure.

I thank you for the *many affectionate* thoughts you bestow upon me. When sick, *next to Minna, I turn to you*!

I enjoyed your "book notices" from the "*So Review*"—very keenly; but *indeed*, you do yourself a *great injustice* in *not attaching* your name to them. You say "by the way it seems unreasonable that the thing of

Criticism should go so wholly unrewarded," & you ask my own experience in this matter, & my plan of reviewing books!—Like *yourself* I have *very seldom* recd any remuneration in money for "book notices"; & also, like yourself, I give away a great many of the vols after criticizing. My plan, however, has *not* been to notice *every work* sent, but only the best & ablest of the collection.

Reviewing *does not* pay simply because the Public are by no means interested in it.

I review *only* in order to procure books which I could not *purchase.*

At the beginning I stipulated for all the magazines (for which I wrote) to be sent me; promising to give them *occasional notices.*

So, they *are all mailed me free*!

In *Jan & July*, I notice the *prominent* ones. Surely you ought to ask Mrs Harris to send you her monthly.[5] She seems so grateful to you, that I'm sure she would gladly do this.

In fact you have a *right* to the work, for an indefinite period.

I have heard nothing from Mrs Dodge, since I sent her my honest opinion of Grant.

That epistle was mailed to the address you gave me in London.

She had a fashion letter in the last "Andrews' Bazar" from Paris.[6]

Prof. Harrison's book I have not seen, but know it must be good since you indorse it.[7]

Let me hope that the Bridal Party arrived safely. My congratulations to them!

At last, we are beginning to feel the full force of this torrid spell, and I must conclude.

All here rejoice at the news of your improved health.

Faithfully Yrs
Paul H. Hayne

1. *Harper's Monthly*, LII (December, 1875), 24. Later collected in *MOL* and *PCE*, 205–206. The final stanza reads in part:

> That states may rise, and states may set,
>   With age earth's tottering pillars bow,
> But hearts like ours can ne'er forget,
>   And though we know not *where*, nor *how*,
> Our conscious love shall blossom yet,
>   A thousand years from now!

2. William Cullen Bryant died June 12, 1878, at the age of eighty-three.

3. One of the poems referred to (indeed, Hayne may have only *one* poem in mind) is "The Inevitable Calm," *Youth's Companion*, LI (November 21, 1878), 402 (collected in *PCE*, 242). Hayne mentions this poem in a letter to Mrs. Preston of October 22, 1878.

4. Since this letter was continued on July 29, there is no signature, and I have not assigned a new number despite the renewed salutation and changed date.

5. Mrs. Cicero W. Harris edited the *South Atlantic* (1877–1882), a monthly published in Wilmington, North Carolina, to which both Hayne and Mrs. Preston contributed.

6. Mrs. Mary B. Dodge wrote a column for the Cincinnati women's magazine, *Andrews' Bazar*, and was a mutual friend of Mrs. Preston's and Hayne's. See Letter 37, n. 1.

7. James A. Harrison (1848–1911), a friend of Mrs. Preston's who taught at Washington and Lee at this time and subsequently at the University of Virginia where he became editor of the Virginia Edition of Poe (17 vols., 1902), had just published *Greek Vignettes: A Sail in the Greek Seas, Summer of 1877* (Boston, 1878).

57

To Mrs. Elizabeth Oakes Smith [1]   MS Duke

February 26*th* 1879.:

My Dear M*rs* Smith;—

Your warm & generous words have touched my wife & self *profoundly!*, and most *heartily* we thank you for them.

Your *Sonnet* I read *with pleasure*, as a poem full of thought tersely, & eloquently expressed.

Let me tell you as a strange co-incidence, that *years on years* ago, the very Thought about Annihilation after death, which you embody, came to me, and now forms part of an early piece of my own.

> "Oh! *rather* would *the spirit bear the yoke*
> *Of torture*, than pass out to *Nothingness!*"

constitute the lines referred to. And indeed, I hold the same opinion still.

The *Pines* to me are very dear; & I am glad that *you* too, so truly appreciate them. *That* was a striking remark of Gen*l* Robert E. Lee's which you quote: So, you knew *personally* our grand old Hero!

By the way, a strange feeling, mysterious feeling comes over me, when I think that I am writing to *one* who was closely acquainted with *Edgar Poe*; who had often doubtless conversed with him upon topics of immortal moment, and listened to *that* wonderful eloquence which has been described as "*supramortal*"!!! The *effect* of Poe's genius upon my mind & spirit, has always been peculiar, and nearly inexplicable!—It appears to me that in some of his Prose disquisitions, e.g. the " *Collo-quy of Monos & Una,*" & "*The Conversation of Eiros & Charm-ion,*"—especially the *latter*—, he has infused an ethereality of senti-ment, and evinced, if I may so express myself, a *naked spirituality,* which thrills one thro and *through!*—With the *solitary* exception of *Nathaniel Hawthorne,* he was the greatest *Genius* America has yet pro-duced; and in *massive profundity* of *intellect,* and vivid powers of anal-ysis, he excelled Hawthorne. *What* a man, and *what* a *fate!* . . . Is it marvellous that during his sad life-career, he should have been, *often,* embittered, & *sour?* Conscious of transcendent faculties, & accom-plishments, he beheld the "small fry" of Letters, *everywhere* buzzing into notoriety, and receiving golden awards, while *he—(the Titan)—* was bound down to the rock of Poverty & Pain, with not *one,* but a hundred *Vultures* tugging at his vitals!—But how gloriously the "whirl-igig of Time has brought about his revenges!" *Poe's* fame unquestion-ably stands higher, at present, *in Europe* than the fame of any *other* American whatsoever!! Have you any slight relic of him you could spare me?—a scrap of his writing, his autograph—*anything?*—

Once, I owned a considerable quantity of his "*MSS,*"—pages from "*Marginalia,*" and his critique on Mrs Osgood—; given me by *the late John R. Thompson of Richmond* but when the *civilized Tecumseh passed* on his way thro Columbia S.C. in 1865—, those incalculable "*MSS,*" with many other *souvenirs,* & relics, not to be replaced, per-ished in the fire which destroyed the *Bank* &c!—[2]

I regret to observe, as you do, that a "good deal of the old hostility to the South *is* reviving," but you'll be glad to learn that "*The Stricken South to the North*" has called forth many letters of warmest apprecia-tive sympathy: (for instance) from Mr *Longfellow, Whittier, Gen Mc-Clellan,* & other distinguished Northerners; together with an exceed-ingly feeling communication from our *Minister* to England the Ho*n John Welsh*;—he (Mr W) courteously mailed me several No*s* of the "*London Anglo-American*" in which the verses had been re-published.

I send you a copy of the "*Benner Poem*" which you had not seen. Mrs Benner wrote me *touchingly* about it; saying that she had "learned to love the South."

O! if the *Politicians* would only let us alone!

Frankly, I often despair of this Country.!! Indeed I begin to distrust *all Republics.*

That doctrine that *"all men are born free & equal," however interpreted*, cannot stand the analysis of Reason, nor the weight of universal Experience. And as for our *poor South*, she has lost, or is *losing* her ancient *virtues, courtesy, sensitive honor, chivalric* consideration, and in their place, what do we see?—

Sordid grasping after riches, *Yankee* keenness,[3] and a low order of *manners*, & I fear *morals* also! Then the *subserviency* which is frequently displayed by men in high places!

I am sick of it.
Ever Most Truly
Paul H. Hayne

1. Mrs. Smith (1806–1893), the wife of Seba Smith, the friend of Poe, and an author for forty years at this date, had written a sympathetic letter on the "Condition of the South" for the New York *World* that Hayne had commented on in a letter to her of February 1. He had also apparently sent her a copy of his "South Carolina to the States of the North," for she remarked on February 5 that she had read "your impassioned poem with great interest." She had also been "moved" by Hayne's "The Pine's Mystery" in *Baldwin's Monthly* for February, 1879. In a letter of February 10, Hayne called her attention to two poems stressing reconciliation—"The Stricken South to the North" and "Hiram Benner"—both of which had appeared in the New York *Sun* (October 6, 1878, and November 14, 1878, respectively; "The Stricken South" was dedicated to O. W. Holmes). Mrs. Smith promptly replied on February 16 that her letter in the *World* was written "from a simple conviction" that the South "was little understood by the people of the North, and was also, most cruelly misrepresented. I wrote from a sense of justice," she added, "hardly expecting it would find permanent lodgement in any Northern mind, but from the letters I receive, and from some abuse that I received from a Boston Journal, I find it has done the people some good; and now, my dear Sir, it has brought me a beautiful recognition from the warm heart of a Poet, I am most abundantly rewarded."

2. For John R. Thompson, see Letter 37. Hayne frequently refers to General Sherman in this way.

3. If Hayne knew about Mrs. Smith's own Yankee background, he certainly forgot about it in this instance.

58

To Margaret J. Preston   MS Duke

December 5*th* 1879

My Dearest of Friends;

Truly, I was touched, (& *how deeply*!) by your affectionate letter of the 30*th* Nov, recd last ev*ng*.

I cannot delay replying; especially as I have some information to give about my Northern tour, & the persons of distinction I encountered last summer.

With *Whittier* we stayed, for the *better* part of a week, (of course at his *express* invitation), in his home, or rather one of his homes, near *Danvers Mass*, called "*Oak Knoll*." A *lovely place* it is, *not* the property of the Poet, but of certain cousins of his;—the *Misses Johnstone* [*sic*];—middle-aged ladies, who treat their distinguished relative with *marked* consideration, declaring that all they have is absolutely & always at his service!—[1]

During the first portion of our visit *Whittier* was evidently quite unwell, suffering from his greatest physical foe—*Neuralgia*; but subsequently the pains left him, and we had the pleasure of beholding him at his *best*.

A simple, straightforward, earnest, & loving man, with profound depths in his nature; one who has suffered too, (I *think*), thro *the affections*.

By many little signs & tokens, I came to this conclusion;—& my belief is, that despite the unvarying kindness of his kinswomen, he feels his old age to be lonely & unsatisfactory, for the lack of *still nearer* ties.

He became, towards the end of our stay, *thoroughly* "at home" with us,—my *wife* & I! Indeed, the "little woman" was so transparently a favorite, that the two would settle near the chimney-corner in *W's sanctum sanctorum*, and discuss every conceivable topic; particularly the *South*, new & old; *negro-slavery*, & *negro-freedom*; *Beecher*, Mrs Stowe, and &c &c &c &c &c !!—

My "winsome Marrow" was just as frank & outspoken as she well could be; and the *Poet* showed a really fine temper, and disposition to learn the truth about Southern matters.

That he has *qualified materially* many of his old opinions, was evident; and I'm assured that the "Eyes of his understanding" were further opened in regard to the *Ethiopian*, & matters appertaining thereto, before that shrewd little Consort of mine allowed him to escape her!! Seriously, he is by no means as "*dour & desperate*," in upholding his peculiar Ideas, as I once believed he would be. We left "*Oak Knoll*" with the pleasantest impression of all its inmates; and the conviction that in the *Poet* himself we have henceforth, a *true, sympathising friend*!—

Thence, we went to *Lynn* (Mass), and were the guests of Mr Charles A Coffin & his wife (who would take *no* refusal). They are exceedingly *rich*, and of Quaker extraction.[2] Mr C——— was *as tender of me as a Brother*; & we were treated with *princely hospitality*! During the week we remained there, the Carriage was placed at our disposal *every day*; & we visited 14 (!!) different Towns in the neighborhood; old *Marblehead* among the others.

Next we journeyed to *Boston*, where we staid about 5 days;— *Longfellow* & Dr O. W. Holmes were *delighted* to see me; the *latter* had just reached Boston, and he told me that Mrs Hayne was the only person in the City he would call upon at *that* time, since his lectures had just begun. He paid us a visit of a *full hour*, & took me to his *first* Lecture, with which I was *charmed*. He was ripe with humor, & *bon homme* [*sic*]; *Dr. Holmes*, in fact, all *over*!!

(*En passant*, my *poor mother* is very feeble, & so Minna has a great deal on her hands at present; but *she* will tell you of our *Longfellow* visit hereafter).[3]

We passed an Ev*n*g with *Edwin P. Whipple*, but my old friend is so changed, it saddened me to *meet* him. All his ancient enthusiasm is gone; & he seems gloomy and despondent.

John J. Piatt was passing thro the City, & called *twice* in one day to see me.[4]

He is unaffected & warm hearted.

Aldrich was not in town; but *Boyle O'Reilley* [*sic*] was *enthusiastic* in his meeting with me;—*a splendid* Irishman, truly!

Under his guidance I "dropped in" upon Dr Joyce, author of "*Deirdré*," & "*Blanid.*"[5]

We found this Celtic Aësculapius, & unquestionable Genius, in his office, *shirt-sleeved* red-faced, moist of eye & lip,—(looking precisely like a roaring, good-natured Sailor "half seas over")—a steaming jorum of Punch on the table, (set jauntily between the skull of a *Mexican Murderer*, and a copy of "*Thomas a Kempis*"!!!), the Doctor engaged in a loud discussion with a Roman Catholic Professor upon the *moral character*(!) *of one of the Phariohs* [*sic*] (!!).

After squeezing my hand nearly to a jelly, Joyce seized upon a copy of "*Blanid*," still dewy from the virgin embraces of the Press—; and presented it to me with an affectionate flourish, after writing my name on the fly leaf as "*Paul Heyne*" &c.

"You have put an *e* where there ought to be an *a*" said I.

"O! to be sure," exclaimed our pleasant Irishman, brimming over with *blarney*; "but *don't* ye see the connection of *ideas*? you've got the soul of *Heine, me boy*, (sure, you look like a lad, for all your gray

hairs!), and so, I'm not certain of the *Capsus pennae at all, at all!*"
Which was a clever way eno' of escaping from the fact that he did not
know how my name was spelt "*at all, at all!*"

"*Blanid*" does not equal "*Deirdré,*" tho full, I think, of *very fine
passages*, &c; *it cannot*, of course, for one moment, be compared with
"*The Light of Asia*"!! This epic of *Arnold's*, I regard as a really *great
work*![6] Years ago, circumstances led me to study the wonderful religion
of *Gautama*; and so I came to the production in question, with a some-
what prepared mind. How suggestive the work is,—and how full of a
solemn power.

I am sincerely sorry to hear of Col Preston's sickness & hope the
cold weather will frighten away the horrible maliaria [*sic*]; also, *how I
regret to hear* that *you* are not stronger! and wish, (*oh! how I do wish!*)
that you could have accompanied us last summer!

Thanks, a *thousand thanks* for your wish to send me your little
"*Brunette*" (the mare). Gladly indeed would I accept the *gift*, were it
not *that just now at least, I am too poor. We are not farming, you
know.*[7]

Were it not for a *small legacy* from one of my aunts, we never could
have dreamed of travelling; & the said money is exhausted.[8]

Nevertheless, something may turn up, in which case if I am still
living & *Brunette* likewise, why, the horse, & the Poet may make ac-
quaintance after all!—

With cordial regards to your Husband, & love to yourself,

I am as Ever

Paul. H. Hayne.

1. The Haynes—the poet and his wife—returned from their "Northern tour" in late
October. Hayne had been advised by his brother-in-law, Dr. Middleton Michel, to make
the trip for his health. The "*Misses* Johnstone" are the daughters of Col. Edmund
Johnson.

2. Charles A. Coffin (1844–1926), a successful manufacturer of shoes and leather
who later became president of General Electric. After Hayne's death, Mrs. Coffin wrote
Mrs. Hayne on August 4, 1886: "Most vividly did your visit . . . come before us, and we
recalled . . . dear Col. Hayne's courteous manner & charming simplicity, how he rose
from weakness, to be stronger mentally, & how his brilliancy of thought and language
constantly surprised us. We have ever felt it a blessing to have known him, and numbered
him among our choicest friends."

3. Emily M. Hayne died a week later on December 12, 1879. Though the date of
December 9 is frequently cited (*CHL*, 480, for example), Hayne's letter to Middleton
Michel, December 12, 1879, gives the correct time.

4. John J. Piatt (1835–1917) was a poet, journalist, and longtime friend of Howells

who had corresponded with Hayne in 1878 and 1879 about southern poets and poems to be included in his anthology, *The Union of American Poetry and Art* (1880).

5. Thomas Bailey Aldrich (1836–1907), the well-known poet and fictionist who would in 1881 succeed Howells as editor of the *Atlantic*, had corresponded occasionally with Hayne since the 1850s; John Boyle O'Reilly (1844–1890), Irish-born poet who at the time edited the Boston *Pilot*, soon became another friendly correspondent; and Robert D. Joyce (1836–1883), another Irish immigrant in Boston, published *Deirdré* in 1876 and *Blanid* in 1879.

6. *The Light of Asia* (1879), a poem in blank verse about the Buddha and his philosophy by Sir Edwin Arnold (1832–1904), is a work that Hayne continued to allude to approvingly throughout his career.

7. When Mrs. Preston heard that Hayne's physician had prescribed horseback riding as one means of dealing with his "nervous prostration," she offered her own mare to him. Hayne later agreed to accept "Brunette," but could not find a way to have her shipped to Copse Hill. Fortunately, he was soon able to buy a horse. See Letter 59.

8. Mary A. Hayne, one of Hayne's father's sisters, died in 1875 and left Hayne a legacy of a thousand dollars, which he received in May, 1876. See the McCrady Family Papers, South Caroliniana Library.

59

To Margaret J. Preston   MS Duke

"Copse Hill," March 14th 1880

My Dear Mrs Preston;

I must answer your last long, welcome letter to Minna; your letter of the *6th* in*st* rec*d* the day before yesterday. How warm, disinterested, and beautiful, a thing is friendship like yours!

Here I find you rejoicing with me, because I have secured a Pony,— as, sincerely, as if some great good luck had visited you, or your *own* household!—[1]

Yes! it *is* in sooth, an unspeakable comfort to have *four sound legs* upon which to rely instead of only *two* rather shaky ones!— Besides, I am a born *Nomad*, a sort of *Arab* by nature, & temperament; and to scour the great wood-lands, or gallop along the solitary bye-roads [*sic*] is to me a "joy forever!"—Do you think there will be any *horses* in *Heaven?*—*not* by any means, of the breed of the "pale stud" of Revelation,—but lovely, ethereal Creatures, somewhat after the style of *Pegasus, winged* perhaps, and capable of *flights* sublime, and unimaginable?—

Upon my faith! I hope so!—

As for my gallant little Gray, my *"Maggie,"* I never speak to her, without thinking somehow of *you*;—Burns' *"emphasis"* *"Meg,"* I'll none of—, the associations being *uncanny*. (By the way, *what* a *wonderful* poem is *"Tam O'Shanter"*!! —'Tis *almost* worthy of *Chaucer*; & beyond *this*, praise cannot go—with *me*!—I read the legend with ever new relish & delight).

I am glad to hear you are "somewhat better," but the troubles you describe must nevertheless, be *exceedingly* severe. I *don't* like to figure you with a chronic *sore-throat*, and (acmé of distresses!)—deaf!—

But then, in my *way*, I'm not much better off—For 6 weeks, nay, "by our Lady!" for two diurnal months, I've been enacting—, how unwillingly!—the *rôle* of Edgar Poe's hero—, the Gentleman who "lost his breath."[2]

True, I did not, like *him*, lose this invaluable article in a quarrel with my wife; nor *literally* speaking, can it, (the *Breath*!) be said to have absconded;—but weary & protracted are its periods of absence; and once or twice, the wretched Deserter *seemed* resolved to stay away indefinitely.—But wait until I get your *"Compound Oxygen,"* (for which I've sent), at work.—there'll be due amendment then, I trust![3]

To return to yourself—The "lowness" of ill-health, in your case, is intensified, evidently, by the Colonel's condition.[4] *Old age* is, indeed *the* calamity of calamities; the great irremediable evil!—If it be correct, as *the Master* tells us,

> "[that] there was never yet philosopher
> "That could endure the *toothache* patiently,
> "However they have writ the style of Gods
> "And made a 'push!' at Chance & Sufferance"—[5]

how *could* it be expected of the *Old*, with a thousand pains, perhaps, added to "the *toothache*," *not* to groan, moan and *ease* themselves a trifle, by lamentation?—Indeed *suffering at all times must express itself*. Look at *Job*, and David; both manly persons, (& still in the prime of life—) & by nature the reverse of lachrymose; yet, did *they* keep silence under their manifold afflictions of mind & body. I wot not! On the contrary, lustier outcries than theirs it would be difficult to imagine! And we *sympathise* with them; a "fellow-feeling," if but of *anticipated* troubles—"makes us wondrous kind."

I am beyond measure disgusted by what you say of the manner in which the Mag*n Editors dare* to treat *your* contributions!!—But let me observe, that I too, have had, and *continue* to have the same sort of difficulties often. The trouble is, that a lady *cannot push her articles* like a *man.*

Do you know, that I have had a Poem (*possibly one of my very best*) refused by 4, 5, even 6! Editors, *one after the other,* and yet *finally accepted,* & *handsomely paid* for at the *seventh,* or it might be, the *eleventh* trial!—Such experiences are *common* with me—.

Long ago I made up my mind to regard all *Editors* as merely "go-betweens," *agents* of the Publishers they served; and to regard the offering of *MSS* in a purely *business light.* And indeed *it really is so,* as any candid Editor is sure to acknowledge!—On *one* point, however, may I not presume to advise you?—*Never,* except in *unusual* cases—, *give any of these People your compositions.* They will at once *take advantage of your generosity*; and expect *always* to receive your articles upon the same terms, or *no*—terms!—Oh! I *know* them! A scurvy set of self-seeking Shylocks!—Trust them (I refer to the *generality of course*), rather *de haut en bas,* or at least, in a *purely business way,* and 'twill be the better for them, and—you!—Many poems in your *best style,* we have seen recently. "*Eugenié*" (e.g) in "Baldwin";—"*Europa's Sale*" (you so kindly sent us, by the way), and yesterday, in "*S.S. Times,*" "*The Wine Vaults of Bergenstein.*"[6]

Surely, *Baldwin* paid for your beautiful piece, and also the "*Times*"? That legend of the "*Wine Vaults*" is told with your own peculiar *inimitable* grace! a grace & spirit singularly characteristic.

As for "*Europa's Sale*" not merely is it a fine *poem* artistically; but it contains so many elements of *popularity,* the "*MS*" *should have brought you a* handsome *sum. What meanness* in a paper like "*The Ev: Post,*" to take *such* a production without the shadow of an *honorarium*!!

But they are *all* alike.

The article by Mrs Kingsley's daughter must have given you no end of annoyance. For myself, I *hate* to receive these commissions, they entail so much that is disagreeable; and *often*—when one has been unsuccessful in negotiating for a friend, an acquaintance, the ill-success is visited upon one's own innocent shoulders!![7]

There is old *Martin F. Tupper*; who (after sending me some most mellifluous epistles), at length despatched to me from England a voluminous article or series of articles *about America, already printed,* mark you!!—, which he requested me to have published in some first-class American periodical, for a *first-class price,* and illustrated (ye Gods!) by his own *likeness*!!

Doggedly I set to work, (knowing perfectly well what the result must be!)—and after mailing *T*'s articles to every possible, and impossible *Editor*, of course I was *forced* to inform him of its *universal* rejection!—

Consequence! the sudden & complete subsidence of the flow of *MFT*'s pleasant epistolary periods, and (*probably*), the conviction on *his* part, that I was, and *am* a *perfidious wretch*; a *non*-appreciator of "*Prov: Philosophy*," and its august author! Ah well! human nature is weak enough;—and we must not be hard upon our erring brethren of the quill.—

I enclose my only copy of "*Snow Messengers* ," which please *return* when you have read it.[8]

'Tis taken from the Poems I am arranging for Co*l* James.

I am now revising *some* of my earlier verses, and also War pieces, since Co*l* James is thoroughly in earnest about his contemplated (complete) Edition.[9]

Two months ago, he was *unanimously called* to the Presidency of the chief Texas college, (viz) "*The Agricultural & Mechanical College of Texas*" "*at College Station*" Brazos Co (Texas).

He writes me that he will have to go North to visit their Institutions of Learning, but will come *to us first*. So I must have all my Poems ready. He will see Publishers, & take along his *sub: list* ("*not* so large," he says, "as *it ought* to be"), & find if he can arrange for producing the work. And now, with *best love* from my wife, and *earnest regards* to Col. Preston,

I am as Ever Faithfully Yr's—
Paul H Hayne.

1. Since Hayne's letter of December 4, 1879 (no. 58), one of his new friends from New England, Rowland G. Hazard (1801–1888), another wealthy manufacturer, had sent him a gift in the form of a check that allowed him to purchase a "Kentucky pony," the "Maggie" referred to later in the letter.

2. "Loss of Breath," under the title of "A Decided Loss," had been published in the Philadelphia *Saturday Courier*, November 10, 1832, and subsequently expanded and included in "Tales of the Folio Club" and published separately in the *Southern Literary Messenger* for September, 1835. See Mabbott (ed.), *Collected Works of Edgar Allan Poe*, Vol. II, *Tales and Sketches* (1978), 51–52.

3. Mrs. Preston had seen an ad on "compound oxygen" and called it to Hayne's attention. He ordered some and received it by April 2, 1880. In a letter to Mrs. Preston of this date he informs her that he is trying the oxygen, but since "only a few inhalations have been made," he cannot report yet on the "effect."

4. Colonel Preston, it should be remembered, was nine years older than Mrs. Preston.

5. *Much Ado About Nothing*, V, i, 35–38.

6. Of these pieces, Mrs. Preston collected only the last in *Colonial Ballads, Sonnets and Other Verse* (1887), 146–49.

7. Hayne, of course, had himself been commissioning his friends for years to sell various poems and prose pieces to the magazines. A little more than a year before this letter was written Hayne had "expressed" the manuscript of a new collection of his poems to Moses Coit Tyler (1835–1900), a former member of the editorial staff of the *Christian Union* and a good friend, to offer to various publishers in New York. See *CHL*, 377. Of course, for writers located in the "pine barrens" as Hayne was, there was often little else but to rely on friends who were in the literary centers or going to them for a period of time.

8. "The Snow-Messengers," *Harper's Monthly*, LX (March, 1880), 590. The poem is a tribute to Longfellow and Whittier based upon Hayne's recent visits with them.

9. John G. James (1844–1930), a native of Virginia who had migrated to Texas after the war, had in January, 1878, suggested to Hayne that a complete edition of his poems be sold by subscription and that he (James) be allowed to supervise the publishing operation so that all profits would accrue to the poet. When this project failed, James managed to convince D. Lothrop and Company, a Boston firm, that the project (already subscribed to by more than two hundred prominent literary men, politicians, military leaders, and others) would be worth undertaking. See Letter 60 for the acceptance of the manuscript by Lothrop. See also *CHL*, 425–99 *passim* and *PHH*, 27.

60

To Margaret J. Preston   MS Duke

"Copse Hill," January 8*th* 1881

My Dear Friend;

Some days ago, my wife wrote you a P.C., from my sick room, which she sent with a *book*, our joint New Year's remembrance. This work ("*Taylor's Pastorals*"), hardly presents that gifted Poet at his highest, & best; but it is nevertheless a significant & characteristic performance;—& I thought it might interest you.

You'll be glad to hear, I feel sure, that I have escaped from my chamber, (to the narrow walls whereof, I was confined for 10 dismal days of sleet, snow, ice, & howling wind). *Such* weather we have not had in these latitudes since 1835;—the innermost Genius of Arctic realms having visited us, with his deadly breath, & his grasp of cruel invincibility! *His*! or *her?*—*That* Genius may be a *woman* you know! Mysogonists [*sic*] would certainly pronounce her of the sex feminine,— her moods have been so various, (*they* would say, the *Infidels*!) & yet, always implacable!—The good news about my *Poems*, conveyed to you by Minna—, has had a good deal to do with my rallying, & *at least, temporary* triumph over the feebleness of disease. *What* a tremendous power do these *minds* of ours exercise over the body! I scarcely know *where* the *limit* of that power may be found.

'Tis difficult for me to *realize fully*, even now, the truly extraordinary good fortune which has at *last*, at *last*, crowned my efforts, as an author. Not merely is *Lothrop* publishing my *Complete Poetical Works* (the title sounds absurdly grandiose, I acknowledge, & reminds one of Cha*s* Lamb's outburst on the subject of modern *Littérateurs*, & their fragile insignificance, as compared with such voluminous *old* fellows as *Burton*, in philosophy, Jeremy Taylor in Theology, & Richardson in prose fiction!); but the enterprising Boston Book-producer has also undertaken a vol of *lyrics for Children*, (to be *illustrated*), concerning a proper title for which the whole Hayne family at "Copse Hill"—(whose "name," however, "is *not* legion")—, have been for some days, vainly racking their brains, and exhausting their vocabulary & . . . patience!—

"Ah!" sighed my wife, if "Mr*s* Preston were only here, with her genius for nomenclature, we would be soon relieved from our difficulty!"

Precisely *when* the two books, one a big "*seventy-four*," & the other a jolly-boat bobbing in its wake—, are to make their appearance before a long-suffering Public, I cannot tell; but 'tis eno' to know they are on the "stocks," & must, in due season, be launched.[1]

As you may imagine—I have been, (until the last "*MSS*" were despatched—,) exceedingly busy correcting, altering, adapting, & fitting up, generally, these verses, in order that they may pass a critical muster;—a somewhat humiliating task since *continually* eye & taste were offended by artistic shortcomings. Of my "*Youthful Poems*" about one half were summarily discarded; & *such work* as I had with the others(!!)—you'll pardon my egotism, *won't* you?—[2]

For *yourself, dear & kind friend*, we (*my wife & I*), must heartily *congratulate* you upon the *number* & *unusual* excellence of your recent poems;—your name of late, has constantly appeared in the N*o* periodicals, & papers, especially the religious journals. Without attempting to particularize, I still cannot refrain from mentioning the poem in the last "*S.S. Times*," about the coming of Christ to the individual soul;—the summons to open the gate &c &c;—it is *very beautiful & impressive.* And I perceive from an advertisement upon the cover of "W*[ide]*

Awake," that a *"ringing Ballad"* of yours, will appear in the Feb. issue of that *capital* monthly.

Apropos, Willie has just composed a *full* & *satisfactory* notice of "WA," in which your forthcoming *"Roman Boy"* is especially referred to. Said notice will appear in a prominent Augusta daily.

By the way, we were all *delighted* too, with your *"Vision"* in the *"S. Atlantic."* The conception of the *"Old Year"* bearing the *"New Year"* in his arms is peculiarly fine, & striking. Why is it that this Idea suggests to me a stanza from the old Ballad of "Sir Patrick Spence [*sic*]"?—

> "Late late yestreen, I saw the New Moon
> With the old Moon in her arme"—

A mere similarity of *position,* as it were, or of *phraseology?*

As I write, the Heavens are cold, and of an iron-grey consistency of dullness, and funereal gloom. The Thermometer too, is falling, and all things point to a renewal of the unexampled severity of temperature which afflicted us less than a week ago. Oh! how I *detest* such weather!! Every nerve of body & soul *rebels* against it!! My *flesh* seems tightened from head to heel; until I'm like a *human Drum,* dry, rigid, & yet horribly susceptible to the *slightest* alien touch!— *You* sympathise with me, I am sure.

Which leads me to inquire how your own health is at present?— Has the terrible winter brought back, or intensified your *neuralgia?*— and how are the Eyes?—

These be no *idle* questions! We love you dearly; and desire to learn everything associated with your welfare.

But I am still in a double sense, "under the weather," and thus, *"tho* the *spirit* is willing, the *flesh* is *weak!"*

Consequently, I must pause scribbling.

With best wishes to *Col Preston,* & *earnest love* from all to *yourself,*

Believe me
Always Faithfully &c
Paul H Hayne. &c[3]

---

1. *Poems* (Complete Edition) appeared in October, 1882. The volume of lyrics for children did not materialize; consequently, some of these pieces were included in the Complete Edition.

2. Unfortunately for Hayne's subsequent reputation, he did not cut, prune, and eliminate enough, and his place on Parnassus is still based upon a collection that, though

it is by no means complete, is actually far too full of work that should have been discarded for aesthetic reasons.

    3. In a note on the envelope enclosing this letter, Hayne wrote: "Have just read your *fine Sonnet* to Longfellow."

61

To Maurice Thompson   MS So. Car.

April *2nd* 1881

My Dear Thompson;

I am *so glad* to hear from you again!! You are a warm-hearted good fellow, if ever a warm-hearted man lived on Earth! About the letter to Gen*l* Wallace, (addressed to your care), I am considerably troubled, since it contained an acknowledgment of a courtesy on his part, (the mailing to me of his "*Fair God*"), and also a species of *resumé* of my convictions of the character & merit of that book.[1] But of course, the P. Office *alone* is to blame.

By the way, *did your wife* receive my note thanking her for the *exquisite* present, she had sent me?—*What* an *artist* she is!—

I am touched by the kind, cordial terms in which you allude to *Lothrop's* "complete edition" of my Poems. To secure the artistic sympathy *of one such man & poet, my friend*, as you are, is worth—*ah! how* much!! The "edition" progresses *slowly*, but surely; "*festina lente*" having evidently been adopted as my Publisher's motto!—and an *excellent* motto it is! Bitter is always mingled with the sweet, however. I can hardly tell you how *disgusted* I was in re-perusing and correcting my *earlier* performances! Yet, some of them I *had* to retain (!!) Certain minds develope *gradually*;—*mine* emphatically, was one of these,—the *deuce* take it!—and thus, the least said of my *Juvenile verses*, the better. D——n them! (a *superfluous* exclamation I *know*!)

Your confidence, of course, about the *Novel* is *sacred*.[2] But, I rejoice to learn of such a work being in progress. After all, a really successful *novel* is of more *practical* service to its author than any number of *poems*, however meritorious. Nevertheless, neither you nor I, are likely to depreciate the *latter*!—

Play-writing seems to be the rage in N York just now! Our friend, *Edgar Fawcett*, made a *second* "hit" recently in his "*Sixes & Sevens*," at the "*Bijou*." By Apollo! *what* a versatile, clever fellow he is!—

Were you not surprised to hear that *Howells* had left "*the Atlan-*

tic"?—³ As for *Aldrich*, (his successor) he seems to me the most brilliant *Littérateur* of *his years*, perhaps, in N England;—but whether a sparkling & able *Contributor* to a mag*n*, is *sure* to make a satisfactory *Editor*, remains (in *his* case) to be proved!—*Entre nous*, I am doubtful as to Aldrich's possession of *that* broad, *comprehensive literary taste*, which recognizes excellence in *all departments of art*, & which is more *essential* to a first-class Editor than any other quality, or *combination* of qualities, whatsoever!

If a poem, (for example) were offered to Aldrich for "*The Atlantic*," which was eminently noble in spirit, tone, conception, and (general) intellectual & imaginative grasp—, I verily believe he would refuse it, if, at the same time, it fell short of his *own* exalted & fastidious *standard* as to form, & expression. A single *doubtful* rhyme, or awkward alliteration would hide from him the splendor of a *chef d'oeuvre* of genius, just as a withered leaf held close to one's eye, conceals the brilliance of the sun! An exquisite worker is *Aldrich*, but I'm afraid he is like that artist who had so long carved upon cherry-stones, that the grand outlines of *Angelo's* frescoes only seemed to him a colossal *blur*! I may be all abroad, of course, all wrong.⁴

Apropos of "*the Atlantic*." I saw some very characteristic & beautiful verses of yours in the last number (but one), "*Before Dawn*." This piece is perfect as a *poem*, & equally perfect as a *picture*. Little if at all inferior is the companion piece in "*Lippincott*," "*At Night*." Well! when your collected lyrics appear in "*Songs of Fair Weather*" here is one man bound to welcome them *heartfully*. (By the way, in the May or June n*o* of "*Harper*" you'll see a poem of mine called "*The dead Child & the Mocking Bird*" which I think Mrs Thompson may like. At least I *hope* so!)

Write me, when you can.

I am *very lonely*; sick *always* in *body*, & sometimes, in *mind*; & therefore, a true friend's letter is valued—you know not *how* much.

Faithfully
Paul H. Hayne

P.S. Do tell Gen*l* Wallace that I hope this letter of mine (above mentioned), will find him, as *my previous one* did,—which (he said), "chased him from place to place." I am anxious he should know I *appreciated* & *acknowledged* his kindness in sending me "*The Fair God*."

---

1. Gen. Lewis Wallace (1827–1905), the author of *The Fair God* (1873) and *Ben Hur* (1880), had lived in Crawfordsville, Indiana, and was a good friend of Thompson's.

In 1881 he completed a term as governor of New Mexico just before he was appointed U.S. minister to Turkey.

2. Thompson had informed Hayne that he was writing a novel for J. R. Osgood's Round Robin Series; thus the reason for the confidence about what would shortly become *A Tallahassee Girl* (1882), the basis for a short-lived quarrel between the two friends.

3. Hayne expressed himself forthrightly about Howells as editor in a letter to Mrs. Preston of March 13, 1881: "No Editor ever managed to render himself more obnoxious to the highest & best literary circles than W. D. H.; by his superciliousness, his narrow critical range, (which *he* deemed unlimited); & what may be called a fastidious literary *foppery*, almost without parallel!"

4. At the same time Hayne was expressing a similar opinion to Mrs. Preston in a letter of April 14, 1881: "From the beginning, I felt doubtful of Aldrich's *Editorial* gifts; & *now*, I absolutely *know* that he *must fail in the end.* Many brilliant nos. will appear under his guidance; but if in 2 or 3 years' time, the Public fail to discover that '*The Atlantic*' represents not American, nor even N. England literature, but merely the idiosyncrasies of Mr Thos Bailey Aldrich himself—, I shall deem the Public a greater ass, than even Aristophanes deemed the *óe polloi* of his day!—" This outburst follows Aldrich's rejection of Mrs. Preston's "admirable 'Keats' Sonnet.'"

62

To F. S. Saltus[1]   MS Duke

September 19th 1881

My Dear Saltus;

You are verily a Correspondent after my own heart!, *one of the few*, the *very* few Correspondents *of this sort*, left to console my *old age*;—for *per Hercle*! there's no denying it! I *am* getting on in life, & shall soon present a *most venerable appearance*; I only pray the beneficent Lord to *preserve* my *front teeth*; caring little about a wrinkled complexion; or gray hair, or stooping shoulders!!

By the way, when I referred in my last communication to the number & variety of your literary productions (within a given time, & that of the *briefest,*) I only meant to warn you seriously against *over exertion of the brain*!

As Holmes (O. W) once said to me, "*imaginative* work takes a *great deal* out of a man!"—Indeed 'tis a kind of intellectual *venery*! Remember *that*!!

You are perfectly correct in what you say of the *true originality* in poetry. The fact is, my own remarks concerning the *New, the Novel,* &c, were merely intended to show that *this newness*, so often aimed at by modern writers, was frequently but a *superficial, trivial thing*; falsely confounded with originality; & the frantic endeavors often which, led to unlucky results.

Essentially, au fond, we perfectly agree with each other.

Your "*Russian Idyl*" will probably reach me by this evng's mail; & 'tis hardly needful to say with what real, unaffected *interest* I look forward to its perusal.

Aldrich's reason for refusing it, seems to me (*entre nous*), *absolutely silly*;—a palpable self-stultification on his part, & (in *one sense*), an *insult* to you!

An Editor who while refusing a contribution, declares he *can find no fault with it*; in fact *doesn't* know why *he objects or refuses*, must have been a *very drunk* Editor, at the time of his penning such a note; or—presumes that he is addressing somebody "*non compos*"(!!)

Of course, as *A——* knows you are a *scholar & man* of *perfectly sane* genius; we'll take the more charitable horn of the dilemma, & conclude that he was—*very drunk indeed*!![2]

I have myself been working "prodigiously," (as Dominie Sampson would say), during the last 3 or 4 weeks.[3]—*One* narrative piece of 2 or 300 lines upon "Kate Shelly," the Western heroine—;[4] a number of lyrics, & lastly, a rather elaborate production, (composed by request) for the great "*International Cotton Exposition*," which opens in Atlanta Ga. on the 5*th* Oct.[5]

All these will reach you in due season.

When you see my song for the Yorktown affair,—your first exclamation will doubtless be, "how could Hayne have condescended to write so commonplace a lyric?"—

Well! my friend! I *deliberately* composed these special verses for *popular approval*,—*nothing* more.

What sort of music *Mosenthal* has married them to, I cannot imagine. If the *music fails*, then look out for a miserable *fiasco*![6]

—It rejoiced me *truly* to learn that *Fawcett's* last novel had been republished in England, & translated in Germany!—[7] *True* success this; & *true trans-Atlantic* fame sure to follow."—

Did you ever hear or read of any thing so pitiful & pathetic as the *long agony* of the Pres*dt*?[8] —My God!!! how his *Doctors* have tortured him!!—One of the Physicians, (*Bliss*), I am convinced is a Charlatan "of the first water." At all events, he is a *Blackguard*, as his conduct to Garfield's old family Physician, (Dr Baxter) clearly proved. Somebody should kick Dr *Bliss*, & make him for the nonce, Dr *Misery* (!!)

If I *wasn't* such an *impecunious* Sinner, I would certainly visit NYork, during the "Indian Summer," were it only to *see, & embrace you*, but Poverty is a Tyrant indeed!!

My *best remembrances* to our good friends, to Haven, Lancaster, Moran, & all of them.[9] —And please, *dear Saltus*, never forget to give my *earnest regards* to your *Father*. I hope he *is well. Write soon*,

Ever affectionately   *Paul H Hayne.*

[P.S.] Did you get my yesterday's note with a Poem?

[P.P.S.] Don't show this letter to Fawcett, because he already (I fancy) thinks me prejudiced against Aldrich, &c

1. Saltus (1849–1889), poet, journalist, and music critic, was introduced to Hayne by Fawcett via correspondence. Saltus, like Fawcett, was a bit of a Bohemian, but lived in New York and was aware of all the latest currents in literature, music, and culture in general. He initiated a correspondence with Hayne in December, 1878.

2. For other comments on Aldrich as editor, see Letter 61.

3. Dominie Sampson appears in Sir Walter Scott's *Guy Mannering* (1815).

4. "Kate Shelly" is based upon the heroic actions of its namesake in preventing a train from crossing a washed-out bridge in Utah. Though published in 1881, the poem was not collected in *PCE* (1882).

5. "The Return of Peace" was completed in time to be read at the International Cotton Exposition, but it occasioned a disagreement with the committee that commissioned it. For an account of this affair, see *PHH*, 127–28. The poem was published in the Atlanta *Constitution*, October 6, 1881, and is collected in *PCE*, 300–304.

6. The "Yorktown Centennial Lyric" was commissioned by Congress and was set to music by Henry Mosenthal. See also *PHH*, 128–29. The poem was published in the Norfolk *Landmark* and the Richmond *Dispatch* and in the Report of the Yorktown Centennial Commission. It was collected in *PCE* , 304–305.

7. Edgar Fawcett's *A Gentleman of Leisure* appeared in Boston in 1881, in London in 1881, and in Hamburg in 1882.

8. President Garfield was shot on July 2, 1881, but he did not die until September 19.

9. All are writers and friends of Saltus who were introduced by him to Hayne via correspondence. All contributed to a short-lived New York periodical called *Evolution* and were sometimes referred to in Hayne-Saltus correspondence as "the *Evolution* lads."

63

To O. W. Holmes   MS Duke

October 19th 1881.:

My Dear Doctor;—

It is a long period since I have written you;—but *silence of this sort* does *not* betoken indifference;—

On the contrary, I cannot tell you how often & how affectionately I have thought of you, & of our last pleasant interview in Boston, about *two* years ago.

A *Solitary writer*, like myself, separated by the *hardest* of *States*, from all his (artistic) fellow-workmen, remembers in a *peculiar* manner, those of his own "guild," whom he *has* had the exceptional good luck to meet, & to personally fraternize with!—

Your individuality, *in especial*, could *not* fail to impress me; for a *many-sided* genius affects one like a prism; keenly, *brightly, dazzlingly*! This is by no means *flattery*; but a mere bald statement of *fact*.

How many important & stirring events have occurred *recently*!!

Of the *President's* death, & its consequences, no *mortal* man has *yet* been enabled *fully* to judge.[1]

Assuredly, *good* has come out of *evil*;—*charity* has been born of *murder* (*so to speak*), when we consider the *wonderfully* ameliorating effect upon party jealousies, & *sectional* hatreds, which followed that fatal shot of *Geteau's* [*sic*]!—That "touch of Nature which makes the whole world akin"—[2] was perhaps *never* so *practically* illustrated before!—

The Spell of *Sympathy* has in this *case*, shamed the power of *all* the *wands* of *all* the *Wizards*, that ever dealt in "glamour" from "the old *Man* of the *Moon*—& *air*," to *Michael Scott*, of eerie fame & blood-freezing capabilities![3]

—*Apropos*, I enclose a Poem, some stanzas of which represent the *genuine* sentiment of *the South* in relation to *Garfield*, & his horrible "taking off"![4] Meanwhile, the Nation is becoming more homogeneous than before, thro the action of yet other influences;—(e.g) this grand "Yorktown Centennial."

I had the honor of writing the Ode, or Lyric, for this occasion; and even as I now address you, here, in the remote back woods of Georgia;—the huge Choir of 300, or 500, voices may be trolling the song—by the banks of *that York*, which *one* hundred years since, echoed the thunder of Artillery, & resounded to the charges of Cavalry, & Infantry!

But "*basta*," enough for the present.

With my wife's *best* remembrances,

    believe me, *dear Doctor*,

        Always Faithfully &

           Affectionately,

        Paul H. Hayne.

P.S. By the way, when I can procure a *correct* copy of this Yorktown Song, I'll mail it to you;—since it has *already* been *mutilated* by the press, North & South, to a *fearful extent*.(!!)[5] Please, *Doctor, write* me *when possible.* I do long to hear from you *once more!*—

1. James A. Garfield had died on September 19 after having been shot on July 2 by Charles J. Guiteau, a disappointed office seeker.

2. *Troilus and Cressida*, III, iii, 175.

3. Michael Scott (1175?–1234?), a Scottish astrologer at the court of Emperor Frederick II, later attained fame as a magician and is mentioned in Sir Walter Scott's *Lay of the Last Minstrel* (1805).

4. Presumably "On the Death of President Garfield," *Harper's Weekly*, XXV (October 1, 1881), 670. Holmes's reply to Hayne of November 1, 1881, touches the same theme Hayne develops in his letter and poem: "Perhaps he could not have done us as much good by living as he has done by dying. 'God works in a mysterious way,' as Cowper's hymn says, and while all Christendom was praying for Garfield's recovery, it may be that wiser counsel decided that it was best that he should teach the sad but long remembered lesson of martyrdom."

5. Hayne's lyric on Yorktown, according to Mrs. Preston, had been published in a Norfolk newspaper in July, three months before the official ceremonies were to take place; in fact, the date of Hayne's letter to Holmes is one of the dates of the centennial celebration. The poem appeared in the *Official Programme of the Yorktown Centennial Celebration* (Washington, D.C., 1881).

64

To Margaret J. Preston   MS Duke

October 24th 1881

Dear Friend;—

It is a rather odd co-incidence that your affectionate letter of the 17*th* (rec*d* two days ago), should bear the *same* date with my *last letter to you*, which it evidently *crossed* on its way hither! Meanwhile, my *wife's* last epistle to you (mailed *before* mine), must somehow have *miscarried*; a very provoking circumstance!—

You speak of seeing my "name *everywhere*, as Poet Laureate for this, that, & the other great national, patriotic, or industrial occasion" &c &c. Well! the present year has been peculiarly distinguished by "occasions" of the sort;—and *I*—it appears—, have had the honor—*wholly unsolicited surely*—of being called upon to write verses therefor!—

Apropos, I enclose my "*Atlanta Exposition* Poem" duly corrected.[1]

The tribute on *Garfield*'s death I had sent you, in the communication of the 17*th*, mentioned above.

I am glad that your Northern acquaintance thinks it "noble."

Is "my *mind triumphing* over the *body?*" you ask, "or *over burdening* it?"

There are seasons when I *must work*;—when the thoughts & imaginations *demand* utterance; & tho a *terrible* depression ensues;—it cannot be helped. "The *night cometh*, when no man *can work!*"[2]

It pleased me to learn that "one of your household had gone to the *Yorktown* Centennial."

I'll now be able to hear how the whole affair culminated; & of *course*, I am naturally anxious as to whether *Mosenthal*'s music *fitted* my lyric. If *not*, the *Song* was doubtless a *fiasco!*

As for *newspaper*-accounts, they are marvellously, *miraculously unsatisfactory*; & then, how unreliable too!

Before quitting the subject of *myself*, I would say, that the same *strange, uncanny oppression* of the chest; compounded of a feeling of hollowness, & half-asthmatic difficulty of breathing, which tormented me last winter & the winter previous,—has *returned*; & thus, my *physical* prospects are *not* of the *brightest*; but I trust that *God* may help me to endure my suffering; and make all things right in the *End!*—

Now, about yourself!

The "*Litany of Pain*," is one of the *truest, sweetest,* most *pathetic* pieces, you have ever penned. It appeals *directly* to all gentle hearts, & may not be read without "the touch of tears!" That the "*NYork Independent*" should have retained *such* a performance for "two years," shows what the Edt's *artistic* taste is worth.

How overrun you must be by company at nearly all seasons (!!) How little leisure seems to remain for aësthetic culture, & aësthetic labors!! And yet, you shame *many* persons, (freed from *your* cares), by the *opulence* & variety of your productions.

You refer (by the way) to *Prof Harrison* among your guests. Ah! *he* is a brilliant fellow,—a genuine scholar, I take it, and a *very* able & suggestive writer.[3]

A *comparatively* young man also, isn't he?—

Yes! Dr Holland has gone!—and Gilder, I perceive, assumes his place as Editor of "*Scribner*"?[4] Of the *latter*, I know little; & of the *former* I can only say "*God rest his soul, he's dead!*"

Once, I liked him as a *personal* Correspondent, & as an Editor likewise; but some time previous to his decease, he turned so *violently* & unreasonably against the South; & displayed a temper at once so *bitter,* & *narrowly* mean, that I could no longer respect the man. Yet, *disease* perhaps was responsible for *this.* May I venture to enquire *who* it was on *"The Century" staff* that refused even to do you *justice?* From the terms you employ, both Minna & I think you must allude to *Dr. Bledsoe's daughter, Mrs. Herrick*!?—

In *that* case, *Madame H,* is a feminine "chip of the old block,"— for a greater *scamp* than Bledsoe, (despite his black coat, & pretentious *divinity*) I *never* have encountered. The *cool rascality* with which he treated me, on one occasion, I can't forget.[5]

I remember what *you* did for *Bledsoe's* "Review." A *pleasant* (!) reward has been granted you, forsooth!

You say "my *complete* [edition] *lingers.*"

Mr. Lothrop's letter to me (of Oct 9*th*), after 6 months of silence), was *copied,* & *sent* you either in *my* communication or *Minna's.*[6]

He *seems* to regret *very much* the delay; but says, it is "owing to Mr Allen's *tedious illness;*" (*Allen* had the whole charge of vol)—He is no longer with them; & they *hope to get your friend, Mr Arthur Gilman,* to *assume Allen's place,* & *carry my vol safe thro the press.*

I earnestly trust they *may succeed* in procuring G's *help*; & for myself, I must be *patient.*

My *presentiment* is, that I *shall never see this Book.*

Nous Verrons!

Minna's *best love*; & with a *devout* hope that your guests may soon depart, & leave you in peace,

I am

Ever Faithfully
& affectionately Yr's
Paul H Hayne.

P.S. Minna begs if you ever visit Lee's or Jackson's grave, that you'll send us some flowers, or leaves, or grass, therefrom.

1. In response to an official request of the appropriate committee, Hayne had prepared an "appropriate ode" to celebrate the centennial of the Battle of King's Mountain for October 7, 1880. The Yorktown poem had been composed at the behest of a congressional committee for October 19, 1881, and "The Return to Peace" had been commissioned by the director general of the International Cotton Exposition in Atlanta for October 5, 1881. See Letter 62.

2. John 9:4.

3. James A. Harrison (1848–1911) was a member of the faculty of Washington and Lee at this time. See Letter 56, n. 7.

4. J. G. Holland died on October 12, 1881 and was succeeded as editor of *Scribner's Monthly* (the magazine had already been sold and was scheduled to become the *Century* the very month Holland died) by Richard Watson Gilder (1844–1909).

5. Sophia Bledsoe Herrick (1837–1919) was Albert Taylor Bledsoe's daughter and a member of the *Century* editorial staff, but it was not she who had refused to do Mrs. Preston justice. Hayne never forgave Bledsoe (1809–1877) for failing to pay him for his contributions to the *Southern Review*.

6. Daniel Lothrop was the owner of the publishing firm in Boston that brought out the Complete Edition of Hayne's *Poems* in 1882. F. H. Allen had been supervising the publication of the volume and was indeed succeeded on his departure by Arthur Gilman (1837–1909), historian, editor, and later the first regent of Radcliffe College.

65

To E. L. Didier[1]   MS Duke

Nov. 29th 1881

My Dear Mr. Didier:—

Your P.C. has been recd., & I will endeavor with my wife's help, to give you what is needed. I can write but little today, having had two attacks of Hemorrhage recently.

The 2nd (second) "Series of Poets' Homes" (D. Lothrop & Co. Publishers, Boston), would have given you all such details as you desire, I think.[2]

Besides "Russell's Maga," whereof I was editor for 2 years,[3] let me say that long before I began to edit, on the 21st May 1852, "The Southern Lit Gazette," (a weekly paper, published in Charleston, S.C.) in connection with W. C. Richards. This paper was amalgamated in 1853 with "the Weekly News," which about a twelvemonth after failed.

From the fall of "Weekly News," until I assumed the conduct of "Russell's" (in 1857), I did a great deal of miscellaneous literary work, & wrote poems for the "Lit Messenger," besides penning many editorials, & articles, sometimes political, for the daily journals.

At close of war (in 1865) I became one of the editors of the "Constitutionalist" of Augusta, Ga.; but broke down after 6 or 8 months work upon it.

In 1866–7, Henry Pollard of the "Southern Opinion," Richmond, (a weekly in part political, but with distinct literary features), offered a prize of $100 for the best Poem connected with the late war. My poem upon "The Confederates in the Field" won the prize. Mr. Pollard then requested me to assume part editorship of his paper, for which I wrote (during about 2 yrs.) all the criticisms of books, a few of the editorials (political), and the "war reminiscences."

But Pollard neglecting to pay me (except by promissory "notes," which proved ultimately worthless) I retired from all connection with "the Opinion," a short time before the death of its Proprietor, Mr. Pollard, who was shot down in the streets of Richmond, by a young man named *Grant* , whose sister's name, he had too freely introduced in an editorial article.[4]

During these years—(i.e.) about 1867–8—you may remember that I wrote not infrequently for the "Balt. Southern Society"—; and shortly after, became a "book reviewer," & a compiler of "War Reminiscences" for the "Banner of the South," (issued in Augusta, Ga.) and long under the (chief) editorial management of Father Ryan.

Since that period, I have done an enormous amount of miscellaneous work, (book reviewing &c) for half a dozen different journals—have contributed poems to "Appletons' Journal," "So. Magazine," (under Hand Browne), "Lippincott's"—"Galaxy"—"Harper's," "Scribner's," "the Atlantic," "Scott's Maga," "South Atlantic" &c &c. Have also written (prose) stories, sketches, essays &c, (for "Appletons' Journal" chiefly). Biographical sketches of Hugh S. Legaré, and Robert Y. Hayne (originally published in Prof. Bledsoe's "So. Review," Balt.) — afterwards in pamphlet form (about the year '71)—, in Charleston.[5] The Harpers have had in their possession a "Memoir of W. Gilmore Simms" (which I wrote by request), for years;—they will publish it, they say, at some future time.[6] No prose writings of mine have been collected in book form. "Advertisement," Coll. Ed. says "the work will be gotten up in *best* style similar to the 'Library Edition' of Whittier & Longfellow."

AUTOBIOGRAPHY

. . . . . . On the 20th May 1852, immediately after graduating at the Bar, I married Miss Mary Middleton Michel, only daughter of Dr. Wm. Michel of Charleston S.C.

My wife's grandfather was Genl. De Michel of the French Army; & her father was educated in Chartres (France), graduated in the "Medical

College" (Paris), & was the youngest Surgen [*sic*] in Napoleon's army. Dr. Michel was wounded on the field of Leipsig [*sic*], in the discharge of his duties. In 1854 Napoleon 3rd presented him (through the French Consul, Charleston), with a Medal in recognition of his "services, under fire, on the field."

On the "distaff side" of the house, my wife is descended from Simon Fraser (Lord Lovat), who was executed for treason on "Tower Hill" March 30th 1747. His estates having been confiscated to the crown, his direct descendant fled to America;—it is interesting to know, that my wife's grandfather (Richard Fraser) gave its name to Beaufort S.C., after his Castle of Beaufort in Scotland.

(Sketch completed by Mrs. H., Mr. H. not feeling strong enough) In 1876 my husband first suffered with hemorrhage—for a year and a half the longest interval between the attacks was three weeks—a year of relief followed—Then again Mr. Hayne was called upon to endure a like exhausting ordeal for a year, with brief points of reprieve, covering from one to three weeks. Since 1879, the attacks of hemorrhage have been less frequent; but during the cold weather my husband is much troubled with shortness of breath—He bears bravely & sweetly this severe taxing of his strength; & great is the surprise of his brother singers that he accomplishes so much "fine work" under the circumstances. The "Yorktown Centennial Lyric" (which has proved so popular), was composed just after one of the hemorrhages. He was quite unwell too when he composed the "International Cotton Exposition Ode." Mr. Hayne is a rapid writer generally—his conception is rapid I mean—but of latter years he has proved himself a careful artist as well. My husband's Library—consisting of over two thousand vols. accumulated for the most part by his labors as a book-reviewer—ar [*sic*] evidence of his mode of writing—on the fly-leaf of many of these works you will find (written in pencil), a verse or two—sometimes an entire poem. When in better health he walked a great deal while reading, and so wrote when an idea struck him, most conveniently upon the book in hand. This habit still continues. Mr. Hayne never sits to write either for the press or to correspondents unless strength fails him.

His mare (Maggy), to whom he is much attached, a gentle creature who will follow him like a dog—& neighs at the sound of his voice, is both comfort & health, or I should rather say, *life* to the Poet. For under

God, this generous gift of a distinguished Northern writer, has certainly prolonged my dear husband's life.[7] Whenever the day is favorable he takes a ride of several hours with gun and dog. For he is a devoted hunter of small game. By the way, his Uncle General Robert Y. Hayne taught him to shoot at the age of 7 or 8—& told his mother that he "never saw a braver little boy with gun or horse." At school and college Mr. Hayne always received the prizes for elocution and oratory. He is a graceful beautiful speaker, & if he had possessed the strength of voice would have made a name for himself in this direction. He wrote verse when he was about nine—& was devoted to "Robinson Crusoe"— "The Arabian Nights" & "The Swiss Family of [*sic*] Robinson"—His mother told me that he would read the former book aloud, over and over again, to her—never seeming to weary of it. I think he continues to do so at least once a year. He was fond, as a youth, of very solid reading too—and for Sir Walter Scott he has the most tender and loving admiration, reading him when he can enjoy nothing else in prose— except Charles Reade's "Cloister and Hearth"—Froissart—Sir Thomas Browne, & Burton's "Anatomy of Melancholy." Mr. Hayne lost his mother two years ago, and his family consist only of his son, "Will," & his wife—We lead a quiet existence, away from Society—in a small rough cottage 16½ miles from Augusta on the Georgia R.R. with 18 acres of uncultivated land attached—The Cottage is on the top of a hill, at the foot of which lies R.R. track —Our home looks inviting only in the spring & early summer months, for then the front garden is full of flowers, the back garden of vegetables—& the porches covered with vines of jasmine, woodbine, & Japan [clover]. Occasionally the silence is broken in upon by some visitor—either a personal or literary friend, or some one to interview, or sketch Copse Hill. But we are never lonely, for all the American Magazines, & many English & Scotch—together with a large number of important and interesting books reach my husband through the kind courtesy of the Publishers, although he had been unable these three or four past years to review either magazines or books. Letters from all parts of this country and from distinguished English authors, enliven us by their kind words of friendly cheer & appreciative criticism.

Mr Hayne comes of English ancestry on the paternal side. [His father was] A gallant young officer, promoted to a Lieutenancy, some years previous to his decease, for his signal bravery in a "cutting out expedition" against Pirates on the coast of Africa. My mother was of

English & Scotch blood.[8] Her father, a Presbyterian minister of talent & great worth, dying (when she was but a child), she did not trace her descent clearly on the Scotch side; but on the maternal, she is of fine English extraction.

I enclose only what Mr. Whipple wrote of "Legends and Lyrics"—with a few words from B. Taylor—It will not do for me to quote such criticism as is contained in private letters of distinguished writers in this country & a few in England—Victor Hugo (as I see by a Paris Correspondent's letter to the "Buffalo Express"), made particular inquiries as to my husband's literary & personal career, some of whose poems the old French genius so esteemed that he selected them for his portfolio.[9] It is enough to say that some good critics prefer Mr. Hayne's narrative verse—some his lyrics—& others his sonnets. The two finest narrative poems—"The Wife of Brittany" & "Daphles"—have won very high praise. True[,] *one* critic, (Mr. Howells of the Atlantic in his review of "Legends & Lyrics") accused Mr. Hayne of echoing W. Morris—but the former poem was written in the year 63 or 64, before Morris was known in this country; or my husband had ever heard of him. "Daphles" was written in 1869, & Mr. Hayne was correcting the proof for "Legends & Lyrics" while reading Mr. Morris' "Jason."

Very Respectfully
Mary M. Hayne

1. Didier, it will be remembered, was one of the editors of *Southern Society* in the late 1860s. Hayne's purpose in this letter is to provide information for a sketch to appear in the *American* (III [January 21, 1882], 231–33). Hayne had also met Didier in Baltimore on his trip north in 1873.

2. This collection of essays contains "Poets' Homes. No. XXIII—Paul H. Hayne" (originally published in *Wide Awake*, VIII [April, 1879], 256–61), an essay by Charles F. Richardson (1851–1913), a member of the editorial staffs of the *Christian Union* and the *Independent* in the 1870s, where he came to know Hayne by correspondence and eventually to meet him in 1879.

3. Hayne actually edited *Russell's* for most of its three-year span of publication (1857–1860). See *PHH*, 19.

4. Henry Rives Pollard (1833–1868) and his brother, Edward A. (1831–1872), founded the *Southern Opinion* in Richmond in 1867, and Hayne served as literary editor from 1867 to 1869.

5. These sketches were brought out again in Charleston in 1878, the proceeds going to the Simms Memorial and the Confederate home for the widows of veterans.

6. This memoir never was published. Hayne wrote other sketches and discussions of Simms for *Appletons' Journal*, IV (July 30, 1870), 136–40; *Southern Bivouac*, n.s., I (October, 1885), 257–68; and *Youth's Companion*, LIX (January 21, 1886), 19–20. Moreover, Hayne reviewed and discussed Simms's poems and fiction in the *Southern Literary Gazette, Russell's*, and in various newspapers.

7. Rowland G. Hazard. See Letter 59, n. 1.

8. Hayne apparently was at this point dictating to Mrs. Hayne, and she forgot to change the pronoun.

9. The letter in the *Express* was reprinted in various newspapers, including the Chicago *Times*, from which Maurice Thompson clipped the article and mailed it to Hayne in a letter of October 20, 1881.

66

To F. S. Saltus   MS Duke

Jan 13 *th* 1882

Dear Saltus;—

Haven't heard a single word from you for "a *month* of *Sundays*," (as the Sailors express it).

When last you wrote, your face & feet were addressed toward classic *Yonkers*, & you were consequently bent upon an "*outing*," which let me hope proved, in every possible sense, *satisfactory*?—

Doubtless,—(since you are in bone, sinew, blood, brain, & spirit a genuine *City*-man), you must have returned to *Gotham* long 'ere this; & I figure you as immersed in business;—with piles on piles of "*Orders*," placed upon a groaning table; and the impatient messengers of the "*Press*," (comic, & sentimental), waiting along the *stairs*, & bombarding the doors of your apartment in "No 23, Waverly Place" (!!)

Well! *my dear boy*, when you have dismissed these exacting fellows; when all things are arranged peacefully once more; and you can enjoy your "*otium cum dig*"[1] &c, at your favorite *Beer* Saloon, —(the aspect whereof I clearly remember), & when the *mornings* (!) yield you rest, & the *nights* satisfaction, (because of honest work, carefully & successfully achieved)—, *then* oh! my young *Apollo*! remember your "*ancient* friend," among the Georgia Pines,—and—"an' it please you," make *some* "sign" (!!)

Seriously, I *am very anxious* to hear from you. Tell me everything of moment, concerning yourself—such as your *literary plans*, for the season; what you have recently done; & what you *hope* to do.

Nothing which interests *you*, *Saltus*, can be foreign to *my* regard. *Recollect* that . . . *always* (!!). Give me an inkling, too, as to your *health*.

For myself, I progress much as *usual*; *chronically* sick; but seldom *absolutely hors de combat*. Of work I've had eno', & *more* than enough.

Did you chance to read in *"Harper's Weekly"* my *"Union of the Gray & Blue"*?[2]

Its success has been remarkable.

The papers tell me of the arrival of *Oscar Wilde* in NY (!!) What an absurd fuss they are making about this sprig of 3*rd* or 4*th* rate English, or rather *Irish* nobility;—since of course it is not his very questionable *verses*,— but merely his *birth*, (or *blood*), and his *affectations* which procure the fellow notice. Bah! . . . it is *disgusting*! Why not import a *Gorilla*, or *anthropöid* ape, paint his tail "pea-green," and ask him to all the receptions? With a little ingenious training, he may even be enabled to "lecture on *Aësthetics*"![3]

By the way, *Walt Whitman* & *Oscar Wilde* ought to be made acquainted. *What* a lovely & congenial couple (!!)

Imagine *Walt* (after a dozen cocktails!), proclaiming himself, *with* the most astounding of his "barbaric yawps," a "Cosmos," & his fastidious *vis à vis* a mere inditer of "Sonnets to *Matilda's* eyebrow," "*too, too* frantic";—and further imagine the aggravated *Oscar* pitching into *Walt*, with all the energy of his *6 feet 3*, of long tho "weedy" humanity (!!)

Dear me! would *not that* be *"luminous, lively & legitimate,"*—to borrow "apt alliteration's *artful aid?*"

By the way *my friend* , from *time to time*, last year, I begged you to procure for me, (& you *did* procure) *certain books*,—which let me hope that *I duly paid you for*. Glance over your *memoranda*, & tell me whether we are in mercantile phrase, *"square." Don't forget*!!

Apropos; tell me where I can procure some of *Zola's* novels (translated)? —Perhaps you can mail me just *one* of them, (the most characteristic in your *opinion*), with *price*, which I'll *immediately* return.

Write soon, just *as soon as practicable*. Best love to your *honored father*. I can *never forget* him.

Yesterday I wrote at some length to *Fawcett*, tho he owes me a letter; but I hate conventionalities.

Best remembrances from my *wife*, who often (how often!) talks of you affectionately.

Ever your cordial &
faithful friend,
P H Hayne.

My best remembrances to Lancaster, from whom I would like to hear! (he owes me a letter), & to *all the Evolution lads*.[4]

1. "Otium cum dignitate"—leisure with dignity.

2. *Harper's Weekly*, XXV (November 12, 1881), 762.

3. Throughout the period of Wilde's visit to America Hayne made similar comments about him in letters to other correspondents—Fawcett, for example. For Wilde's experience in America, see H. Montgomery Hyde, *Oscar Wilde: A Biography* (New York: Farrar, Straus and Giroux, 1975), 56–91.

4. See Letter 62, n. 9.

67

To O. W. Holmes   MS Duke

January 31st 1882

My Dear Doctor;—

To think that 3 months (!) should have passed since the reception of your last cordial letter (!!)—Upon my word!, I could *hardly* believe my own eyes, when just now I remarked the date of your Epistle, Nov 1st 1881.—

But, tho by no means, so pressed to the wall by work, as yourself, I have still been *exceedingly busy*; as much engaged by literary toils, indeed, as my chronic ill health would allow.

For *two years* & upward, disease in me has taken a singular form; evidently puzzling to the Physicians I have consulted.—Upon a certain windy afternoon in the winter of 1880, (while I was laboring under nervous & mental depression, because of the recent death of my venerable mother), I returned home to be assailed by a peculiar species of *shortness of breath, & constriction across the chest*, which nearly drove *me wild* at times, & lasted almost uninterrupted, (tho often *modified in violence*), till the advent of *summer*. Then, it (comparatively) passed off; but with the advent of winter (*1881*) again troubled me. I bore it better than *at first*, for *what* may we, poor mortals, not become, *measurably*, accustomed to? Again in summer I improved; & even when our present *winter* came, everybody observed that my attacks of *brevity of breath* &c were much milder,—"few and far between."

But alack! during *the past week*, I have been *twice* assaulted by my old Enemy, in a manner which shows that he has been "sleeping, not dead!"

Now, just imagine *your own breath—incarnated* (so to speak), in the shape of a malicious *little Fiend*, a small *Devil*, *sticking* sometimes in your *throat*, but more frequently in the upper portion of the *Chest*;— & refusing—for perhaps an hour or more—to perform its proper functions! Results!—constant oppression, & a sort of *nervous irritability* which makes it utterly *impossible* for one to remain quiet. I have had to leap out of bed, under this terrible physical annoyance, and pace up & down the chamber half distracted. Can it be nervous *asthma,* nervous *dyspepsia,* or *what?*[1]

My *old & kind Friend!* pardon thus much of *Egotism* (The Doctors say *my lungs* are perfectly sound)—.

I was glad to hear of your recent literary & scientific employments; & of your success in accomplishing them. It shows how vigorous you still must be *au fond.*

"*The Memorial His: of Boston,*" (to which you have contributed, I venture to say beforehand, the most *valuable* & *brilliant* Chapters)—; will doubtless prove a work of solid, & monumental importance.[2]

Apropos of Pres: Garfield's death, you say;—"I hope that the Era of *good feeling* is at last *inaugurated!*"[3]—Little doubt of this (*me judice*), if the *Politicians* will only allow things to take their natural course.

In this connection, I enclose for your perusal two poems of my own, "*A Plea for the Gray,*" and "*The Union of Blue & Gray,*" which no man in America will comprehend more fully & clearly than yourself. Instead of being *contradictions,* one piece is the *complement* of the *other.*[4]

About the *Boston Literati;*—many are "growing old" you remark; & necessarily the *social* communion of former days has become less *frequent.*

Yes! . . I had heard of the "*failure* of Emerson's Memory"—on sundry points—; & concerning Longfellow's illness, I endeavored to express my sympathy in the "*Sonnet*" published in "*C. Union.*"[5] From Whittier it is my privilege to hear (like yourself) "Now & then"—*always* affectionately;—but nothing has reached me *directly* from him since the 28*th* of last September. By the way, did you not like his ballad in a recent no of "*The Atlantic*"?[6] —It struck me as being singularly picturesque;— in his best ballad style.—

I wonder whether I may venture to ask you a question, touching your literary plans?—Have you indeed written your *last novel?*—So *original, & altogether noble* are those two books "*Elsie Venner,*" & "*The Guardian Angel ,*" that I am unreasonable eno' to wish (*how ardently!*) that you would give the world one more "*chef d'oeuvre*" of imaginative fiction. But, I presume *this* is out of the question now?—[7]

You—with your high artistic conscientiousness, might fear, *in regard to an elaborate work—however unreasonably—*; the reproach of those lines which haunted W. Scott's later time;—"*Superfluous* lags the *veteran* on the stage!"[8] But as for your not *writing Poetry*(!) any more, because you are *Seventy & a trifle over, my friend, I defy you!—you can't help it!—*

"*The Iron Gate,*" a production of but 2 years since, is as *fresh, strong, suggestive,* & beautiful a poem as perhaps you *ever* wrote![9] No: the "*divine afflatus*" will hardly leave you, until a more *physical "afflatus"* has spent its latest force!

You once told me that you did not regularly read the papers;—therefore, I send lady [*sic*] *Hardy's* account of her visit to you; thinking it *just possible* that you might have failed to meet it.[10]

My wife begs me to send her *best* remembrances, & pray *My Dear Doctor*

believe me as Ever
Most affectionately Yr's
Paul H. Hayne

P.S. When you have completely finished with them, do return me the printed poems enclosed.

1. In his reply of February 7 Holmes described several possible remedies for Hayne's "asthmatic troubles," but he refused to prescribe because these "so-called 'asthmas'" are not "all alike."

2. Justin Winsor (ed.), *The Memorial History of Boston* (4 vols., 1880–81).

3. Hayne is quoting here and subsequently—especially about Emerson, Whittier, and Longfellow—from Holmes's letter of November 1, 1881.

4. "A Plea for the Gray" was published in the Mobile *Register* in late October or early November, 1881. "The Union of the Blue & Gray" appeared in *Harper's Weekly* (see Letter 66, n. 2).

5. *Christian Union*, XXV (January 5, 1882).

6. Presumably "The Bay of Seven Islands," XLIX (February, 1882), 145–49.

7. Hayne sincerely admired both novels. See Letter 25, n. 2.

8. Samuel Johnson, "Vanity of Human Wishes," line 308.

9. "The Iron Gate" appeared in the Boston *Daily Advertiser*, December 4, 1879, and was collected in *The Iron Gate, and Other Poems* (1880).

10. Lady Mary Duffus Hardy (1825?–1891), a British novelist who would soon write about her travels in the United States in *Through Cities and Prairie Lands* (1882)

and *Down South* (1883), had visited Holmes in Beverly. He informed Hayne on February 7, 1882, that he already had a copy of Lady Hardy's "'Couleur de rose' account of her visit."

68

To J. G. Whittier   MS Duke

"Copse Hill," Geo March 31st 1882
 # address me Box 275 Augusta Geo
March 31st 1882

Dear Friend,

I write to ask how you are? The effect of the news of Longfellow's death has been such upon me, that I know only too well what it must be upon you![1]

God have mercy upon us all! ! It seems as if, day by day, the horizon were contracting, & the inevitable end comes nearer.

You I see were present, at our friend's funeral. How did he depart?

Was he in pain? —or did the last sleep come upon him quietly with the *thorn* of death blunted by a soft unconsciousness?—[2]

The last letter I recd from Longfellow was dated 1st Jan, 1882 (my own birthday), and acknowledged in his usual sweet cordial manner, some verses I had addressed to him;—in all probability the last of the kind he ever recd, so, at least, as to be enabled to read, understand, & comment upon.[3]

After all, however, his life was so rounded, complete, & exceptionally fortunate (from dawn to evening)—, that we *ought* to suppress our own *grief*, as far as human weakness may, and following the emancipated soul, picture it crowned, & happy among the Immortals![4]

I wonder oh! my friend! if even as blatant an Infidel as the man named *Robt Ingersoll could* stand by *Longfellow's grave*, and say *"all dust & ashes*!!"[5] His individuality, his spirit, (*so termed*), every thing which constituted *the Man*, sleeps here clod-like & *brute-like* forevermore; the *very expressions* carry with them their own refutation.

We are becoming somewhat uneasy & anxious concerning yourself, *not* having heard *directly* from you for a considerable period.

I know you recd my letter near Xmas (because of Phoebe's acknowledgment of the book), & I've written you *once* since, but (as remarked) heard *nothing*. This makes me fear that you have been too *unwell* to write? My wife & I think so often & lovingly of you, (that if your health precludes correspondence) do ask one of the ladies to inform us about your condition. A kiss for my little favorite *Phoebe*, & *warmest regards* to Mrs *Woodman* & the *Misses Johnsons*, from *both* of us.[6]

May Heaven console & beautify your age, & lead you at length to "*where beyond these voices there is peace.*"[7]

Always Faithfully & affectionately

Yrs. *Paul* H. Hayne.

1. Longfellow died in Cambridge on March 24, 1882.
2. Whittier was not able to see Longfellow during his last illness. See Letter 69.
3. Presumably "To Longfellow. (On Hearing He Was Ill)." Collected in *PCE*, 308. See Letter 67, n. 5.
4. Hayne incorporates this idea and some of this language in "Longfellow Dead," *Baldwin's Monthly*, XXIV (May, 1882), 5. Collected in *PCE*, 312.
5. Robert Ingersoll (1833–1899), lawyer and lecturer, was the best known American agnostic of his time.
6. Mrs. Abby Woodman and the Misses Johnson were the daughters of Col. Edmund Johnson and cousins of Whittier's. Phoebe Woodman was the adopted daughter of Abby Woodman. See *CHL*, 113. Hayne and his wife had met all these people and visited them for five days in 1879.
7. *Idylls of the King. Guinevere*, line 692.

69

To Margaret J. Preston   MS Duke

April 11*th* 1882

My Dear Friend;

I *mailed* you a P.C. *yesterday*, expressing our joy at the sight of *your* handwriting, & acknowledging your sweet poem sent to Minna.— When alas! a *2nd* copy of the same verses, with an *Easter Card* upon which was written "*no better!! so dare not write!*" arrived; and *saddened us inexpressibly*!

Believe me, *you* are daily in our thoughts & hearts; & we were encouraged to hope (thro your husband's letter), that at *least* there would be an *amelioration* of your serious trouble. We cannot *bear* to reflect upon your suffering; & pray that *ease* & *sight* may be restored to you in God's good time! Patience! and hope![1]

Please ask your son *Herbert*, if he is with you—, or your *brother*, to drop us a P.C. *every week* stating *how* you are.

My wife sends her *dear love*.

Taking up "the Lit World" last ev*ng*, I came across your *Sonnet* upon Longfellow's Death; and read it aloud to Minna.

We think it *exceedingly beautiful*; most delicate in conception, & true in feeling.

By the way, I had myself composed a couple of Sonnets upon the same melancholy theme; & by an odd coincidence, certain lines embody the very *same* thought, which you express.

Observe:

> . . . Aye! it is well! crush back your selfish tears,—
> For, from the half veiled face of *Earthly* spring,
> Hath he not risen on heaven-aspiring wing,
> To reach the spring-tide of the Eternal years?
> With life full-orbed, *he stands amid his peers,*
> *The grand Immortals! a fair, mild-eyed king,*
> *Flushing* to *hear their potent welcomes ring*
> Round the vast circle of those luminous spheres:

The *italicised* lines convey your *exact* thought; & yet these pieces were composed in different places, at different times; without the possibility of any intercommunication.[2]

Upon my soul! I'm proud to think of this co-incidence . . . for my *own sake*!

What an unparallelled outburst of feeling, the civilized world over—, has followed the decease of our sweet & noble Poet!! Let *Politicians*, & so called *practical* men everywhere,—the poor fools who prate of the wisdom & self-sufficiency of the "Gradgrind" stock—, look at *these* manifestations of grief & sympathy, for one, who was a *Poet*, "pure & simple," & henceforth, "hide their diminished heads!"[3]

A *class* can only be fairly judged by the performances & influence of its *highest* exemplars; & *thus* judged, the *Poet class* ought to stand high to day.

I rec*d* a letter from the dear old Quaker Poet *Whittier*, in which he says—"Ever since our *great Poet* fell asleep, I have wanted to write thee;—but I have had scarcely courage, or strength for the effort."

Thro Mrs James T. Fields, he had heard of *Longfellow's* wish to see him. Consequently he went to Cambridge, as soon as possible, on the

Sunday of Longfellow's last week. But he could only see the *daughter*, (Annie L), because her father had been taken suddenly ill the night previous.[4]

It seems a bitter grief to *Whittier* that never *in life* could he look upon his *brother* Poet's face again.

In his own words he adds, "During the *last two* days of *L's* life, he slept much & appeared quiet. And so he passed out, as from *one* lower chamber to one higher. Ah me! but the world seems less for his leaving!, and a feeling of great loneliness oppresses me! The shadow of the Eternal World is falling over me!"

We must all comprehend this.

God bless you, my friend!

I *would* write more; but am anything but well just now.

Most Affectionately Yrs,
Paul. H. Hayne.

1. Mrs. Preston's eyes had given her trouble for many years, but at this stage of her life her physicians advised her not to read or write. During the last ten years of her life she was almost blind.

2. The sestet of "Ultima Thule. H. W. L." (collected in *Colonial Ballads*, 1887, p. 10) reads:

> And he has laid his travel-garb aside;
>   And forth to meet him come the mystic band
> Whom he has dreamed of, worshipped, loved so long—
>   The veiled Immortals, who, with holy pride
> Of exultation, take him by the hand
>   And lead him to the inner shrine of Song.

For Hayne's poem, see Letter 68, n. 4. Since the rapid deterioration of Mrs. Preston's eyesight, the two poets had seldom exchanged manuscripts of poems for criticism.

3. Gradgrind appears in Dickens' *Hard Times* (1854). The quotation is from *Paradise Lost*, IV, 35.

4. See Letter 68, n. 2. Whittier's letter had been written on April 6, 1882.

70

To Maurice Thompson MS So. Car.

April 28*th* 1882

My Dear Friend;

A day or two since, your letter (to *Willie*) arrived; my boy being in Charleston, I *opened* this communication, knowing there would be something in it about the man *Quigley* &c. Your news concerning him, was *precisely* what I had anticipated!

I—, or rather my *wife*—, read your "Card" to *Q*—, and he has perforce, made up his mind to seek work nearer home.

And now, my *dear fellow*, a few words in reference to "*the Tallahassee Girl.*"[1]

Is it needful to observe *how* delighted we are to hear of the signal success of your book?—I really don't think that even your (comparatively) ordinary acquaintances, if good hearted, could hail *your* successes without a certain feeling of sympathy; *what* then, must be the feelings of your *genuine & intimate friends*?

Firstly, apropos of this novel, I do *not object*, (as you seem half disposed to think I might), to the *political position* assumed in it. On the contrary all things considered, it seems to me *fair enough.* You have taken (as the Roman Philosopher recommends), the *medium* course, the *juste mil* which if the safest, is also often the most *truthful. Neither* Section is likely to quarrel with your views. *Certainly* not the North, nor do I *think* the South.

Artistically, what pleases us, (ie my wife & I), *especially*, in "*The Tallahassee Girl*" is the poetical & graphic word-painting of landscapes, and *localities.* The quaint, quiet, out-of-the world old Town, and its environs, so picturesque peculiar & romantic, are made, (under the glamour of your touch), vividly present to the "mind's eye";—& thus, scenes *not* actually visited, nevertheless appear *subjectively before us*; now & then, with startling effect.[2]

The same combination of realism & imagination, which made your last article in "*Lippincott*" (e.g) such pleasant reading, appears repeatedly in this work.[3]

Don't be vexed with me, if I frankly say that in *construction & characterization* I cannot think the novel equals the delicate, *vraisemblance* of its descriptions of what Painters would call "still-life." Parts of the story strike me as a trifle abrupt; the Chapters (to use a Carpenter's phrase) not being compactly "*dove-tailed.*"

And the *characterization* is too *sketchy* in certain cases (lacking the needful elaboration of detail, & completeness of coloring)—, while in *others*, (*me judice*), there is some inconsistency, if not contradiction.

Look at *Vance* for instance. Granting all its proverbial power to *jealousy* when fully aroused, I cannot conceive how such a Gentleman, so courteous, self-respectful, moderate, & delicate-minded as at first depicted, *could*, in a moment, (for next to no (logical) *reason* at all)—, descend to the level of a petulant, passionate child—; ask of his supposed Rival's friend the rude, *parvenu* question as to Willard's gentility, & after subjecting himself to the treatment of a naughty schoolboy,— swallow *finally*, with Quaker meekness, what really *amounted* to personal chastisement, & become his Northern Chastiser's very humble, obliged, & obedient servant, accepting *political* favors from him in the most matter of fact way.

The somewhat melo-dramatic device of the Telegram (as to the father's illness), which abruptly stops this quarrel, & the subsequent death of Vance [*sic*] Son may be supposed to have cooled the young man's blood, & brought him to reflection; but nothing, absolutely nothing could have induced a Southerner of his birth, breeding, and *ante-bellum* proclivities, to accept *favors*, (legislative or social) from *Cauthorne*, after that scene in the Hotel room!

He would have thought, that if his question concerning Willard was unjustifiable, still *Cauthorne*, (recognizing his abnormal excitement), need not have *taunted* him as he certainly did; thro throwing not oil, but fuel on the flame.

After all, *however, the true gist* of the matter is *this*. A So aristocrat like *Vance* would never have appealed to Cauthorne at all. Once convinced,—whether rightly or wrongly—that another man was trifling (or taking *liberties with*) with [*sic*] his Sweetheart, he would have sought one of his old Comrades, as Second, demanded an explanation of Willard, & (were that refused), challenged him in due form. As matters are represented in the story Vance violates every tradition of his "order."

Again, as to the old "*Judge*." How wretchedly he is made to appear in that final interview with Willard (!!) Vascillation [*sic*], greed, and subserviency, rule him by turns. Now, we were hardly prepared for such a moral *denouement* as this!

Very charming is the young heroine in her beauty, innocence, & sweet amiability.

But, my dear boy, I find her *vague*; A lovely, but undeveloped *child*, who when Willard makes love to her, acts with a certain *hoydenish placidity*, (if the terms are not contradictory)—, and altogether impresses me as a very pretty, *naive*, picturesque Creature, but mentally, a trifle insipid.

True, she *does* exhibit some interest in the glimpses of a higher world of art, & Culture vouchsafed her by the two Northern admirers,—but it seems hardly sufficient to make her, (in any *intellectual* sense) markedly attractive.

She's *dumb* too, when she should have spoken to the purpose;—& lives in an odd mist of uncertainty, or at all events, gives one that impression.

Basta! eno' of fault finding. Your negro *patois* & negro scenes are *capitally perfect.* But beyond doubt, the most suggestive, and really dramatic scene in the book—a scene of *great force & pathos*, occurs in Chapter XX—, headed *"Thou art the Man."*

The whole of this interview, between *Cauthorne*, and the crippled Confederate, impresses one deeply; it is thrilling, and full too of a "reserve of power."

—*Surely* there *are noble* elements in this work, which abundantly account for its success;—a success *let me repeat*, which is *most gratifying to us all here.*

As for my candor upon what (*mistakenly* perhaps) *appears* to me its faults—, am I not paying you the *highest* compliment by such frankness?

—To a *mere* acquaintance, one might be *conventional, & reticent*, if not actually insincere—, but to a *Friend & Brother*; one should open both *heart & mind.* [4]

—Your dear *little wife must not* erase my name from her good books, because I have written thus.

Nay! I am *sure she won't*:—She'll comprehend the *purity of my motives.*

We anticipate with eagerness the advent of your *Poems.* They are *sure* to bring you permanent, & unshadowed fame. You are a *Poet-born*; no sweeter, stronger *Lyrist*, has the Country produced.

Some of your (*hunting*) poems, for example, if I may use that term—, are simply *wonderful, wonderful* in the blending of a passionate feeling for Nature at large:—and a minute, careful, *vraisemblance*, as to special phases.

All hail to *"Songs of Fair Weather!"* [5]

My own *"complete Edition"* will appear about the same time, since *the Lothrops* say they "want to issue it for the early 'Fall Trade.'"

So, we shall appear before the Public—as it were—together. Delightful!!

Excuse pencil!

I am *chronically* sick; & find pen & ink wearisome.

Best remembrances from my wife to Mrs. *Thompson & yourself.*
God bless you!

Write often!

Faithfully & affectionately

Paul H Hayne.

P.S. Now, that you know my views, would you not like me to compose a notice of "*The Tallahassee Girl*,"—*making my objections* but a *foil* to just commendation of its excellencies? And shall I put my name to the article, or not?[6]

1. *A Tallahassee Girl* appeared anonymously in March, 1882, in the Round Robin Series of James R. Osgood and Company, Boston.

2. According to Otis B. Wheeler, some of the reviews of the novel also make this point (see *The Literary Career of Maurice Thompson*, 133).

3. Thompson's "last article" in *Lippincott's Monthly* was "Grand Traverse Bay," XXVIII (October, 1881), 321–33.

4. Thompson's response came promptly. On May 1 he defended himself against Hayne's "strictures" and attacked Hayne's views as being politically motivated and not based upon literary principles. Hayne responded to this challenge on May 8 with a long justification of his consideration of the novel. Thompson, having cooled off, wrote on May 10 that he was "sorry" and added that if he had given Hayne a "pang," he would "never forgive" himself. On May 12 he wrote again in this vein and at length: "In a moment of temporary resentment I wrote things which no doubt seemed to mean more than I intended. . . . But all this is trash. . . . I am a wolf to have snarled at you. . . . The truth is I had laid great store by having you thoroughly like my book. I should have liked your praise more than that of many a professional critic who had praised it." Even here Thompson couldn't avoid putting his foot in his mouth: Hayne had been reviewing books, including fiction, for thirty years. As Wheeler has pointed out in another connection, Thompson "could not accept criticism and would go to any length to justify himself when criticized" (*The Literary Career of Maurice Thompson*, 137). Nevertheless, the quarrel was patched up, and the two friends continued to correspond, though not quite on the same basis. For an account of this argument, see Moore, "The Old South and the New: Paul Hamilton Hayne and Maurice Thompson," 115–18.

5. *Songs of Fair Weather* actually did not appear until 1883, but Hayne never received a review copy from either author or publisher and, as a consequence, did not review a book he had anticipated with favor and pleasure for several years before its appearance.

6. In his letter of May 1 Thompson informed Hayne that an unfavorable review would hurt the critic more than the author or book. Though Thompson eventually modified this position, Hayne apparently never published a review of the book.

71

To F. S. Saltus   MS Duke

Wed—24th May 1882

Dear Saltus;

I could not help laughing at your emphatically expressed disgust of "*the Plow*" as a subject for verse. Yet, I wish that I were as sure of certain things in Heaven & Earth, as I am that you are radically wrong in this matter. If my poem, called "*The King of the Plow*" is indeed a failure, a mechanical piece of composition &c, I (*the Singer*), am to blame;—& by no means the *topic*, which *could be* superbly treated. *Apropos*, it is a mistake of the younger Poets of our generation, (especially for "*aësthetes*"), to rather disdain all homely themes. They ridicule Wordsworth for his "archaism" & simplicity, and are continually talking like the immortal "Gandish" in "*Penndennis*" [*sic*] of "'igh 'eart!'"—[1] Now, the older I grow, the more assured I become, that a Poet, while working in due measure for *Art*, & its Etherialities [*sic*], ought likewise to walk, at times, about the common paths of men;—finding nothing "vulgar or unclean," which is capable *au fond*, of being elevated by feeling, fancy or imagination, to the poetical *status*.

To command an audience, "select tho few," is a *fine* thing; but to touch the great *heart* of Humanity, or even wholesomely to stir & stimulate its *brain*, [is] more desirable still.[2]

You refer to *Zola's* last novel as absolute "*trash*." The English Reviews seem to agree with you.

By the way, procure the "*NY Eclectic*" (for June), and read *Lang's* critique upon *Zola's* works *en masse*—(copied from "*Fortnightly*")—.

Concerning its justice or injustice I cannot speak; but at least I found it exceedingly entertaining. The French Critic M. Sarcey referring to *Zola's* play "Thérèse Raquin" observes:—"*Moi*! *je suis malade*! *Ce Zola me rend positivement Malade*!"[3]

He must be living on his *past* reputation!—*Entre nous* is he *drinking* to any great extent?—That would explain *everything*.

Your sketch of the "Duel," (principals ———, ———), is *capital*; & so are the other sketches, particularly the "trumpet scene." But how does ——— like this sort of thing?—Of course, I presume he understands, & laughs as heartily as anybody else?—[4]

I am provoked to hear, (& so is my wife), of the cool rejection of your "*Gibraltar*." It is a singularly spirited lyric; and would have graced

"*The* ———," far better than some verses I've seen therein, during the last twelvemonth.[5]

Then, to have your Longfellow tribute (lovely as it is), returned from Cal!! Upon my soul! you are *most* patient.

You inquire whether *Marston* is *blind*?[6] Aye, poor fellow, he has been blind since his 4th year; and in addition to this crowning misfortune, affliction after affliction, like huge black waves of the sea, have [*sic*] rolled over his youth & manhood, until now he stands, desolate, forlorn, bereaved in every way; and yet if sad, wonderfully *brave* and steadfast! My heart bleeds for him.

—'Tis marvellous, (all things considered), what he has accomplished!—

And so you anticipate dining with Oscar Wilde, & Miller &c? Be sure to report *fully* for my benefit. I am an "outside Barbarian," & yearn to learn something of the "*utter*, most *utter*," of *aesthetic* civilizations, & divine "*dilettantisms*."

Did you notice in *Stedman's* article upon Lowell, ("*Century*") his significant, & stinging allusion to O. W. under the ingenious application of certain passages from "*Hamlet*"?[7]

It was at once the *neatest*, & most sarcastic reference I have seen for many a long day.

But perhaps you'll find *Wilde* personally clever & agreeable. In one sense he has unquestionably made an enormous Donkey of himself, and (in fact, acted the public *rôle* of a degraded mountebank), but for all that the fellow has brilliant talents, & may prove a charming diner-*out*, or *in*!

Nous Verrons!!

You desire to know for some mysterious reason (which all my ingenuity *can't* fathom) how long it is since I read Dumas' "*Three Musketeers*"—& whether I read this work *translated*, or *in* the *original* ?—

It must be *16 or 17 years* since I *first* perused Dumas' *masterpiece*; but between *1864—5* and [the present] period I've re-perused it several times, but *always* in "*translations*." Wherefore this query? Expound, oh! Daniel!—

Thompson's poem in "*Century*" is capital; just one of those wonderful realistic pieces, (yet touched also by a delicious dreamy fancy), for which he has a special genius. He is steadily rising in the world of Letters.[8]

Be sure to carry out your design of reading "*Ben-Hur*" in the Country.

Three scenes in that work stand out, to my memory, in boldest relief—

1*st* a sea-fight (*Roman* & *Pirate* Galleys engaged)

2*nd* Chariot-race in the Circus of Antioch—

3*rd* Scene, by moonlight, near the steps of *Ben Hur's* ancestral home in *Jerusalem*, the blended horror & pathos of which thrills one to the soul.

Of the *denouement* I speak not; because I want *your* opinion of that, unbiassed in one way; or the other.

Here I am reminded to ask whether you have read Kingsley's "*Hypatia*," Melville's "*Sarchedon*," & Mrs. Hunt's "*Wards of Plotinus*"?—[9]

All remarkable productions, "*Hypatia*" especially.

I am waiting, as patiently as I can, the arrival of those promised "Choruses" from "*Bel-char-uzzur*," the "*Market Song*" beyond all—[10]

True, my Sonnets ("Decline of Faith") have *not* appeared, *according* to *Editorial* promise, in June No of "Century." Crowded out perhaps! Since the "proof sheets" were furnished me 7 or 8 weeks ago, I *suppose* they'll appear soon. I *warn* you to expect little from them. Excepting the *idea* of 1*st* Sonnet, they are *didactic*, & perhaps *dull*.[11]

Your account interested me much of your good Father's "*decorations*," "orders" &c.

Many must be invaluable.

As for *Bernadotte*, yes! he *was* a *scoundrel*.[12]

Tho myself—of *English* descent (on both sides the house), and tho my reverence for the English race, & Literature is unbounded; I look upon *Napoleon* as simply a phenomenal genius; and regard his St Helena imprisonment, as a *shameful Crime*, & a *meanness*, which must ever stain the *English* escutcheon.

But basta! must close here.

Willie has returned & sends you his best regards. My wife's remembrances.

Always affectionately
Paul H. Hayne

1. Gandish appears in *The Newcomes*, not in *Pendennis*, though of course Pendennis purportedly tells the story of the former novel.

2. Touching the "great heart of Humanity" is an important theme of Hayne's late poetry, one he discusses in his prose and sounds frequently in his poems. "The King of the Plow" was printed in *Home and Farm* for May 1, 1882, and collected in *PCE*, 311. Hayne's comments on the poem are in reply to Saltus' remarks in a letter of May 18 on its mechanical qualities and his conclusion that Hayne was "by no means as enthusiastic over your subject as you make people think you were." Within a week, according to one of

Hayne's correspondents, the poem was reprinted in five Massachusetts newspapers, and Whittier wrote on June 6 that it was "admirable & timely. It will be," he added, "worth more to the country North & South, than all the political speeches which will be made in both sections for a twelve month to come."

3. Hayne is quoting from Andrew Lang's "Emile Zola," *Eclectic*, n.s., XXXV (June, 1882), 826.

4. The "Duel" is apparently a satire on two of Saltus' friends, one of whom may be Edgar Fawcett. Hayne has deliberately left the blank spaces open.

5. The name of the journal is not legible.

6. Hayne had been corresponding with Philip Bourke Marston (1850–1887) since 1879. See Letter 119.

7. XXIV (May, 1882), 97–111. According to Stedman, "affectation and self-seeking in art, as elsewhere, are detestable. . . . It makes no difference whether the affectation be one of virility or of refinement; the self-seeking is apt to be that of the author or artist who devotes one day in the month to work, and all the rest to advertising it. You may see his outward type in the water-fly Osric, of whom Hamlet says that ''tis a vice to know him.'".

8. "In the Haunts of Bream and Bass," XXIV (June, 1882), 210–11.

9. Charles Kingsley, *Hypatia* (1853); G. J. Whyte-Melville, *Sarchedon* (1871); and Mrs. John Hunt, *Wards of Plotinus* (1880).

10. Saltus at this time was working on, among other things, a series of poetic plays on Biblical topics, of which Bel-shar-uzzur was one.

11. "The Decline of Faith," *Century*, XXV (January, 1883), 458.

12. Jean-Baptiste-Jules Bernadotte (1763–1846) was the son of a French attorney who became one of Napoleon's marshals, but when elected heir to the throne of Sweden by its Diet, he turned against the French and eventually became King Charles XIV in 1818.

72

To Elizabeth Oakes Smith[1]   MS Duke

"Copse Hill" Georgia, 19th June 1882

My Dear & Honored Lady;

I felt *exceedingly gratified* by the reception of your thoughtful & truly cordial letter of the *7th* inst. Your "sympathy" in my *chronic* ill health, & the (comparative) *poverty* which the Civil War brought upon me & mine, I *appreciate*, you may be sure. The *more* so, perhaps, because from the *latter* of these evils, *you*, as I *regretfully* understand, suffer also.

How hard for those, past the meridian of life, to be *forced* to endure all kinds of privations; especially if the sufferer be a woman! However, *your* spirit is a brave one, and doubtless now, from the trials and turmoil of Time, you are looking calmly, and confidently forward to the ameliorations of that mysterious Future, where, "Beyond these voices there is *peace*!"[2]

You refer naturally to your deprivation of society; sympathetic society I mean. With *me* there is *next* to no *society* whatever: But then, I *don't* miss it, as alas! *you must*; for my *wife* is friend, companion, helper, sympathiser, soother, and amanuensis! One capable of adorning any society, but an "Angel of the Hearth" besides!

So *my* compensation for many losses is complete. How *dare* I complain?

The *present* year, (as you observe) has indeed, been a year of bereavement, in the number & magnitude of its victims claimed by Death!

Longfellow's decease came deeply & sharply home to me;—for I *loved* that gentle noble spirit; and had *good reason* to love him. Of *Emerson*, (*personally*), I knew but little; tho his *works*, of course, had long made me familiar with his peculiar genius.

His "*contemptuous*" allusions to *Edgar Poe* were probably inevitable; *less* the result, however, of any difference of *intellectual* temperament & endowments; than of a very *natural* bitterness on *Emerson's* part touching *Poe's* analysis of the N England metaphysical school, the *niaiserie* of the "*Dial*" contributors &c &c.

Briefly, *E's* "contempt" of *Poe* had its roots primarily, in Poe's very decided *antecedent* "contempt" of *him*; (ie) of his philosophy in some of its "*Kantian*," or *Moonshine* phases! And doubtless, this feeling was *intensified* by the *enormous* spread of Poe's fame in recent years.

There have been recently some spasmodic attempts on the part of *Henry James Jr*, & his "*claqueurs*," to ridicule & depreciate *Poe*; but a man whose works have been translated into the languages of *most* civilized & artistic Peoples, & have passed into the blood & bone of the general Literature of the world, is safe from the blows of *Lilliput!*, and its snortings of vaporous fume!!

By the way, I was re-reading yesterday Poe's notice *of your vol of Poems* published in the year 1840, (of which I spoke in a former letter), & this *time*, I was more particularly struck by his *last* series of quotations from "*The Sinless Child*." What an exquisite delicacy of perception was *his*!— His imaginative vision penetrated to the *core* of poetical merit & meaning!—[3]

Once—in *ante bellum* times—, I owned some invaluable "*MSS*" of *Poe's*, given me by my friend *Jno R Thompson Ed* of the *Richmond "Lit Messenger*," some verses of the "*Bells*," *fragments* of "*Eureka*," & "*the Rationale of Verse*," & about six pages of the critique upon *Mrs. Osgood*; but alack! when the *gentle* Generalissimo, *Tecumseh* (!) *Sherman*, passed thro Columbia S.C.—, disembowelling the Banks, & all places of *fancied* security in his *Ghengis Khan* march to the sea, (your pardon! but I consider *Sherman* as an utter Barbarian), these *valuables* disappeared, together with my family "silver," which I had left in the vaults for security![4]

If you *have a line of Poe's* which you could spare me, how thankful I would be (!!)

Your *Sonnet*, I have not only *read*, but carefully *analyzed.*

It seems to me *a very thoughtful,* and suggestive performance. Especially I like the slow gathering up of the metrical waves, & their concentration in the billowy *roll* of the last 3 or 4 lines!—

My wife begs me to *send you* her *best,* & most *loving remembrances*; & please believe me

Most Faithfully & Cordially Yrs
Paul H Hayne:
 # PO Box 275, Augusta Geo.

PS. Write me when you can. I'll always feel *glad & honored* to hear from you. We hope you have *perfectly recovered* from your *late illness.*

My wife cut the enclosed slip from this morning's paper, & as you have always taken so kindly an interest in *her husband's* work, she sends it to you.

I *never* see *Potter's* Magn but must procure the no with your Emerson paper.

1. See Letter 57.

2. For this last line of *Guinevere,* see Letter 68, n. 7.

3. Poe's review of Mrs. Smith's *Poetical Writings* (1840) appeared in *Godey's Lady's Book* for December, 1845, and is collected in James A. Harrison (ed.), *The Complete Works of Edgar Allan Poe* (17 vols.; Virginia Edition, 1902), XIII, 78–93.

4. Compare this list and account with those in Letter 57.

73

To Margaret J. Preston   MS Duke

"Copse Hill" Georgia
Oct 9th 1882.

My Beloved Friend;

Your *letter* to my son, *Willie,* was *eagerly* read by our entire household;—& in *some* degree, it relieved our *great anxiety* on your account, for we *began* to fear that you must have been ill!

Still, it is a sad thing to learn that your *eyes* are *essentially* no better;—while the *added* intelligence of your young nephew's *death*, is indeed most melancholy news.

How many trials of this *crucial* sort, seem to have visited your family of recent years!! Yes!—as you say, "*death is* terrible," often "terrible" to the *one* taken, but *more frequently*, to the *survivors*!

Yet ought we to school ourselves, (as far as practicable), *not* to succumb to its horrors!—

Yesterday, I chanced to take up Tennyson's poem called, "*Gareth & Lynette*," and was especially struck by the *denouement* of that narrative, which represents the "*Knight of Death*," with his awful helmet, & churchyard paraphernalia, advancing against the youthful champion, who in half desperation, strikes many a "doughty blow," till "Death's" sable casque rolls off, revealing the innocent & blooming face of a *little child*!!

Here is a beautiful *allegory*, with possibly a profound *truth underneath*!

Ah! my friend! *how* we *have* missed your delightful Correspondence during the last weary 8 or 10 months!

Of *course*, we appreciate *fully* the *reason* which would make it *suicidal* in you to *attempt* writing often; but *henceforth*, (DV) we shall *write to you*, as usual, in the old times, whether you are able to *reply or not*;—thinking that we may interest you occasionally.

Your late Poems in "*the Independent*" we have read with *true* pleasure—viz "*Anice & Cummin*," &[1]

Before, I told you (did I *not?*) of the rare satisfaction I had derived from those *art-pieces* of yours in "*W. Awake*"?

You have a *special* genius for that kind of work! My dear friend, the half dramatic, & *half lyrical*, which is so effective in a *master hand*.

"*Copse Hill*" *Saturday 21st 1882*

I stopped writing upon the *9th inst*, somewhat abruptly, as you perceive, because just then, an unbound copy of my "Complete Edition" reached me from *the Lothrops*; and I have devoted my days since to a minute examination of the text, hoping that all Errata might be prepared in due season for insertion in the back part of the vol.

A most *exacting* task it was, as you may imagine, when I tell you that the Book (a *large* duodecimo) numbers nearly 400(!!) double-columned pages![2]

But alack! my labors have been (for the present at least) in vain, much to my chagrin, because there are more typographical errors than I at all relish, & besides certain very provoking *omissions*! hard to comprehend! Chief among *these*, (which really distressed both my wife & self) was the omission *of your* "Dedication" to "*The Mountain of Lovers*," and Minna's to "*Legends & Lyrics*." *They*, (the Publishers) undertook to class *both books* under the general title of "*Legends & Lyrics*," & the *Sonnet* addressed to yourself—, instead of having the correct *initials* "*To MJP*," has "*MIP*" (!!) & one *important monosyllable left out besides* (!!)

These omissions are simply unaccountable; since I sent them *clear copies* of both the vols mentioned, *with as clear* directions. Not a *solitary proof sheet*, could I see, the *Lothrops* saying it would be inconvenient to send them *so far*; & declaring moreover their own *proof readers* to be *experts* (!!) *Surely* they ought to have mailed me an *unstitched copy*, so that "*Errata*" could be furnished where needed. Again, I had asked them to close the *main*, (or adult's vo*l*) with "In Harbor" preceded by "*The Pole of Death*," which they have *not* done. "*Old Geoffrey's Relic*," *one* of my *best children's* poems, *should* have completed the entire vol. *Mrs Pratt* had that piece in hand *more than 8* (!!) *months ago*, with the *understanding* that she should publish it in "*W Awake*," in time for its subsequent insertion in my Book; & now I learn it is not to appear until *January*!

Why they omitted that *exquisite* illustration of "Motes" is a mystery.

Now, that I've done *with fault*-finding, let me tell you what a *really beautiful* vol (upon the whole) it is. The Lothrops may well be proud of its typographical execution, (notwithstanding errors); for the paper is of the heaviest, richest kind, the type quite large enough, & borders broad.

There are no less than 61 Illustrations, including *the fine* steel *portrait*; & the "vignettes" are exceedingly dainty & delicate. Of *course*, as is the case with *all* Illustrated Poems, *some* few engravings fail to give *any idea* of the poem;—in this instance, notably "*Fire Pictures*," "*PreExistence*," "*Widderin's Ride* [Race]," one upon "*The Wife of Brittany*," the illustration of "*The Vengeance of Diana*," & "Hopes & Memories"!

The *Nature Poems*, (as a rule) are *finely* illustrated.

Here & there we find an *Idealization* (in heads) which is striking, (viz) of "*A Plea for the Gray*," and the *head* suggested by "*Allan Herbert*," *a dramatic* sketch —also, the picture of "*Memory*" in the *Simms'* Ode &c.

You'll like I think the illustration of "*Nellie in Prison.*" The artist Miss *McDermott* sent me the original sketch, (wonderfully fine), which I have framed.

O! my friend! if your eyes were only strong eno' to examine them! The thought that they are not, takes away *much of our pleasure*!

We trust in God they may yet be restored!—

You kindly ask after all of us. My wife is in her usual health, but not strong. For myself I *manage* to keep up; but am a great sufferer, from *sharp pains*, and attacks (tho moderate ones) of *hemorrhage.* Our son, Willie, has recently developed a very delicate *vein* of fancy. He *deeply appreciates your letter*, tho still silent. When composing, he seems to find *letter-writing* difficult.

Our *united love* to the Colonel

as always *Most affectionately* Yours
Paul H. Hayne

1. Hayne failed to complete this sentence.
2. The Complete Edition actually contains 386 pages.

74

To Joel Chandler Harris   MS Duke

"Copse Hill"
Georgia Railroad
Feb. 1st, 1883.

My *dear Mr. Harris,*

I must have seemed to you unmindful of your request as to my opinion of your sketch in the Xmas "Harper."[1]

The truth is, I was in the midst of an elaborate piece of work, when your note reached me, and the Muse, (most *imperative* of womankind) would not have her rights encroached upon!

The *Harpers* (old, old friends of mine) sent me this Xmas issue, & I read your article at *once with interest.*

The type of Georgia "Cracker" 1. as described by you I *have* met *once* or *twice,* since my residence in the State; 2. I think your characterization *undoubtedly accurate.*

My immediate neighborhood is peopled by the other & lower type of "Cracker" so perfectly drawn by *Betsy Hamilton.*[2]

As usual, your success with the *negro* is unapproachable.

I look forward with peculiar interest to the perusal of the more elaborate work upon which the journals say you are now engaged.

> Believe me Cordially yrs.
> Paul H. Hayne.

1. "Mingo: A Sketch of Life in Middle Georgia," *Harper's Christmas Pictures and Papers* [1882], 24–25.

2. Pen name of Idora McClellan Moore (1843–1929), Alabama-born author of southern character sketches published in the Atlanta *Constitution*.

75

To Margaret J. Preston   MS Duke

"Copse Hill," Geo, Feb 27*th* 1883

My Dear Friend,

We have returned home after a 10 days visit to Savannah;—where we had *really* a most delightful time.[1]

We were the guests of that *illustrious Georgian,* Gen*l Henry R Jackson,* & were charmed with his *wife* & *himself.*

I enclose you a copy of the "*sesqui-Centennial Ode,*" which was *superbly delivered* by the *General!*—This poem seems to have entered into his very soul.

You'll be glad to learn, (despite your *detestation* of "*Odes*" generally), that mine proved a great success. *Would* that I had leisure & strength to inform you of *all* the appreciation I recd, *so grateful to my spirit, because it came from my own People!*

Why, they could not have paid me *greater honor,* had I been *Tennyson*(!!)

The *practical liberality* of the "Committee" will actually enable me to buy a *buggy* , if "*Maggie*" only consents to draw in harness; in which case my little "*winsome Marrow*" will have the opportunity of riding abroad with me!

Do *not* think, *dear friend,* because I have begun with *ourselves,*—that *for one moment* we have ceased to be anxious concerning *your* Eyes, & also your *general* health.

Please get your *niece* to drop a P.C., so that we may hear, as soon as *practicable, how you are.*

I would write more *at length,* but am much *fatigued.*

Minna sends her *dearest love*, &
Believe me *now* as *Ever*,

Most affectionately Yours,
Paul H. Hayne.

PS When *you have entirely finished* with the *copy* of "Ode," *will* you kindly *return it*? I have *no other copy*!

1. Hayne had been asked in December, 1882, to write the ode in honor of the 150th anniversary of the founding of the colony of Georgia. Since his health was poor, he declined. He was thereupon asked to reconsider by Charles Colcock Jones, Jr., an old friend and kinsman who represented the official authorities, and Governor Alexander H. Stephens. He consented, composed the poem, and with Mrs. Hayne attended the ceremonies in Savannah as guests of the sesquicentennial commission in the home of Gen. Henry R. Jackson (1820–1898), U.S. minister to Austria before the war and to Mexico afterwards and a poet himself. The ode appeared in the Savannah *Morning News*, February 13, 1883, and in the Atlanta *Constitution* on the same date. Hayne received an honorarium of five hundred dollars, the largest sum he ever received for any literary work.

76

To Maurice Thompson[1]   MS So. Car.

(*Excuse Pencil*)
"*Copse Hill*" Geo—
Saturday Night—
March 17*th* 1883—

My Dear Friend;—

Your *affectionate* note of the 15*th* has just arrived; & let me *assure* you that I *deeply* appreciate its kindness, and thoughtful consideration. But, I clearly perceive from its term, that my *special* letter to you of the 12*th* March—, must have miscarried; or at all events, it had not reached you upon the 15*th* inst, as it *ought* to have done (!!)—*Too bad* (!!)—I *so* wished you to be *immediately* apprized of my *earnest* & *grateful* recognition of the *noble* work you had accomplished in my behalf, in your "*Times*" "*Criticisms*."[2] In this (*probably*) last *letter*, of mine, I emphatically dwelt upon the fact that you have *demonstrated* your firm friendship for me, (a *friendship*, never clouded but *once*; & *now only* the *brighter* for a *transient* Shade's) by *making the time*,— *forcing* it, (so to speak), out of a most exacting Profession, in which to compose an article equally *elaborate*, and suggestive; & fraught with *conclusions*, as to my poetry, which cause me to humbly hope that I have not written in *vain*!—

Briefly, you have been *very generous, my friend*, in your literary commendation; & I am never likely to *forget* it! *never*!!

As for the "*Lit World*," and their "*minor Poet*"—well,—the notice was courteously *designed*, at least;—& some would tell you rated me too highly, despite "the *minor*" key!—[3]

The term you employ in allusion to my *Savannah* "*Ode*," gave me a *thrill* of pleasure. You'll be glad to hear, that its success has been *extra-ordinary*. A *practical* proof rests in the fact that the "*Sesqui-Centennial*" Committee *volunteered* to pay me, (*for I charged nothing*), the sum of $500—for this performance!

"*Basta*"! enough of *egotism*. It is a *matter of congratulation that* you have another novel in press, and likewise your vo*l* of *Poems*.—How I long to welcome them *both*!

Your *descriptive* lyric poetry is glorious, so full of out door beauty & sunshine & healthful power;—no infernal *metaphysics, psychology*, or morbid questioning of fate, & God,—but a gush of grateful *Song*, or *such* word-painting, as necessarily *must* take the artist soul *every-where*!—

Then, your *classic* vein seems to me, singularly marked & pure.

"*Diana*" I read with an ever new *interest*.

All this you know already; for how often have I said it?—yet somehow, I *can't* help saying the same thing over again!

Do you correspond with *Fawcett* now, or *Stedman*?—The *latter* tells me his *Emerson* article will appear in the next "*Century*"; *look* out for a superb analytical production.

Fawcett's later letters to me have been (*entre nous*), chiefly occupied with gushing praises of O. *Wilde*, and *Mr Henry James*;—altho it would appear that the *latter* had rather snubbed him! (This in strict confidence).

Following James' lead, Fawcett, published some months ago, a rather absurd article against *Edgar Poe's* poetry,—in the course of which he characterized "*The Raven*" as abominable *twaddle*; "*The Bells*" as *brazen bosh*; and (in a word) echoed Mr James' *dictum* to the effect that admiration *of Poe* was *per se* a sign of low, crude, miserably uncultured *taste*![4]

Unfortunate Tennyson!! *Beötian* [sic] *Swinburne*!

Stupid *Baudelaire*!!

You are right to say that *will-power* can *measurably* control disease & chronic ill health. Certainly your *most* illustrious example of this, was *Alex H. Stephens*!! *Shall* I ever cease to remember my conversations with him during our fraternization in Savannah?

Ah! the grand old man (!!) I have written an "*In Memoriam*" upon him, which will appear in "*The Home & Farm*."[5]

Mrs Thompson's cordial letter reached my wife some days ago; & will be answered as soon as *practicable, be assured*. Give your *dear* little "winsome Marrow" our *united love*—

En passant, I only found out recently the name of the author of this quaint phrase, "*winsome Marrow*." It is the old Scotch Lyrist, *Hamilton*,[6] & he begins[7]

1. This is one of only two incomplete letters in this edition, but since it contains important literary content, it is being included.

2. Thompson had reviewed the Complete Edition in the Chicago *Sunday Times*, March 4, 1883, and ranked Hayne "among the foremost living American poets," but in his letter of March 15, he had warned Hayne that his "Southern hereditament [*sic*]—the cramping limitations of an unfortunate sectional bias which is rooted in disaster, has, in certain ways, hurt your flight, which otherwise would be a mighty one." And in a postscript, he added: "You must not permit yourself to become *sectional* or *local*, nor must you be *pars temporis acti*. Look ahead!"

3. XIV (March 10, 1883), 74. The reviewer, after acknowledging the "delicate suggestiveness" of Hayne's nature poems and the "concentration of masterly force" in the sonnets, assigns him an "honourable place among the minor poets of America."

4. Hayne apparently is referring to James's comment that an enthusiasm for Poe's poetry is "the mark of a decidedly primitive stage of reflection" ("Charles Baudelaire," *Nation*, XXII [April 27, 1876], 279–81). For Fawcett's opinion of Poe, see "Antipodes," *Fantasy and Passion* (1878), 182–83.

5. Stephens died March 4, 1883, in Atlanta after his return from the sesquicentennial celebration in Savannah. "Alexander Hamilton Stephens: In Memoriam" appeared in *Home and Farm*, April 1, 1883.

6. Hayne frequently refers to his wife as his "winsome Marrow," a phrase from "The Braes of Yarrow" (1724–1732), a poem by William Hamilton (1704–1754).

7. The rest of the manuscript is lost.

77

To Andrew Adgate Lipscomb[1]   MS Duke

"Copse Hill" Geo Feb 7*th* 1884

My Dear Sir;

Your letter of the 25th ul*t* gave me, I *assure* you, a *heart-felt* satisfaction. I am indeed proud & happy to have rec*d such* a communication from one whom to *know*, is to *honor*.

Thanks for the poems, so full of grace, & *earnest* feeling & also for the discourses upon the "Virgin Mother," & upon "Christian heroism." *Both* the sermons I read aloud to my dear wife, and she agrees with me in thinking them worthy the genius of Fred Robinson himself![2]

Original in *conception*; & written with a scholarly elegance & force very unusual now-a-days; characterized by profound sentiment, & a vivid imagination, they are in my view essentially *prose-poems*; quite as much so as Macaulay's description of the Trial of W. Hastings, Milton's pamphlet "on the liberty of Unlicensed Printing," De Quincey's "Vision of Sudden Death," or even Sir Thos Browne's "*chef d'oeuvre*," that magnificent treatise concerning vanity of human aspirations, particularly the desire for posthumous renown which you doubtless remember under the title (quaintly pedantic) of "Hydriotaphia," or "Urn Burial." There is a *rhythm* in exalted prose, which causes it to approximate *poetry proper*, in a very marked manner. Thus, passage after passage in your discourses could readily be turned into verse; & even as it stands, the *effect* often of the style, is to create in the reader that sort of *lofty pleasure* which results from the charm of *harmony*.

Such a *Style* is a befitting Embodiment of *Thought*, at once *virile*, and tender.

Briefly, these compositions have *deeply interested* and *charmed* me; and I clearly see in them the broad-minded Christian, the reflective Philosopher, and the man of poetic sensibility.

For the pleasure & instruction derived from your productions, I venture, *en rivanche*, to enclose you my own *last* poem, one of a series upon various phases of agriculture, which I am writing, from time to time, for the Louisville "*Farm & Home*," at the Proprietor's *request*.[3]

Perhaps you may like it.

It grieves me to learn that your useful, noble, and most distinguished career has been, *measurably*, interrupted by chronic ill-health. *Few* persons, probably, could sympathise with you more keenly than *I* do! For I too suffer, and have long suffered from the languor, the exhaustion, the discouragement, the terrible "*tedium vitae*" of *protracted* disease. Ah! these *bodies* of ours, *how* they weigh down the ethereal spirit!!

Soon, however, we may hope for freedom.

To be able to live nearer God, in some one of His "many mansions," freed from physical infirmities, with the *soul sinless* & untrammelled forever & forever—, can Imagination conceive a loftier Heaven?

I would be *more* than pleased to hear from you, at your convenience; & meanwhile, *my wife* joins me in sincere regards, & wishes for your recovery.

Always *Faithfully* Yours,
Paul H. Hayne

1. Andrew Adgate Lipscomb (1816–1890), prominent Methodist minister and chancellor of the University of Georgia (1860–1874), had written Hayne on January 25, 1884, that he had been meaning to write for so long that he had felt he was "committing a fraud" upon his heart if he didn't write. Thus begins one of the two most meaningful correspondences of the last two and a half years of Hayne's life.

2. Hayne obviously means Frederick W. Robertson (1816–1853), a British clergyman whose influential sermons were published in five series, *Sermons Preached at Trinity Chapel, Brighton* (1855–90).

3. "Seed Visions" appeared in *Home and Farm*, February 1, 1884.

78

To A. A. Lipscomb   MS Duke

Copse Hill Geo
April 6th 1884

My Dear Mr Lipscomb;

Many thanks for your letter of the 28 ul*t*, as usual full of instruction, & suggestive matter. I *appreciate* your writing me, the *more*, because I am well aware of your literary engagements, & those, like "the London Commentary," of a peculiarly exacting sort, and also of your suffering state of health.[1]

Indeed I must beg, *my dear friend*, to hold no ceremony with me. When opportunity & strength permit, I'll always *rejoice* to hear from you, but upon no account would I have you painfully exert yourself.

Of *ceremony* between us there must positively be *none*!

I am gratified by your asking me to accept the Milton Poem.[2] Of course I shall retain this copy thankfully. And so I chanced upon the very passages which you yourself like? Well! author & reader were in sympathy, this time, you perceive.

You kindly allude again to the "*Smith Poem*."[3] That it should "grow" thus "upon you," is surely a good sign. As for my "Collected Poems," I cannot but feel that I have *not* labored in vain, when a man of *your* scholarship, native power, and perfect sincerity, has found it possible to write *such things* of my verses!!

To revert to *Milton*, there were some points I failed to touch upon in my last.

Apart from the extraordinary & really pitiable nature of his *domestic* relations, one pauses bewildered before the tremendous latitude of opinion he allowed himself to express upon the most *vital* affairs connected with religion.

He defends *polygamy* upon *moral grounds*(!), only doubting its *expediency*; and as for his reputed *Calvinism*, Heaven help Milton had Calvin himself somewhat earlier, got hold of him. Why, he *plainly* leans toward the heresy of *Servetus*, & in the *homöousios*, & *homoiousios* controversy, took the latter ground.[4] How he regarded the sanctity of the marriage tie may be imagined when he tried his best to persuade the beautiful & virtuous Miss Davis to marry him, while his *own* lawful wife was a few miles away in the Country. Had the young lady only hearkened, what a spectacle would have been presented to Puritan England! Fortunately she did *not*!

About Milton's *Eve*! Did he really behold the *first woman*? Miss Brontë, in her noble novel called "*Shirley*," says "no!"

The heroine of that book remarks; "*Milton* was *great*; but was he *good*? His *brain* was right; how was his *heart*? He saw heaven, he looked down into hell; He saw Satan & Sin his daughter, & Death their horrible offspring. Angels serried before him [in] their battalions; the long line of adamantine shields flashed back upon his blind Eyeballs the unutterable splendor of heaven. Devils gathered their legions in his sight; their dim, discrowned, & tarnished armies passed rank & file before him. Milton tried to see the first woman; *he saw her not*!

"It was his *Cook* he saw; making custards, preparing a cold collation, preserves, & "dulcet creams," puzzled "what choice to choose for delicacy best," bound to satisfy all tastes, "upheld with kindliest charge!"

There's too much truth in this.

But oh! he *was* truly inspired by some *Titan Muse* at his best & grandest! His verse then becomes like the thunder echoed among a thousand hills; like the roll of many waters, like the Trumpet almost of the archangel!

And *what* sublime energy he showed during those darkened years; what "grit," manhood, resolution, gigantic Purpose! No Hypocrite was Milton; he always acted according to *Conviction*, however wrong his *conviction* might be!

An *inspired Poet* of the first order (!!)—A *loveable man*! no!—

How thoroughly right you are about *Shakspeare*! *Our* age *does* merit applause for its appreciation of *him*. Did he *wholly appreciate* himself?

I doubt it!!

Of course, he knew how *lofty* his position was above his contemporaries. *He* could *smile* at Ben Jonson's *lordly* contempt concerning his possession of "*little Latin & less Greek*"; he could look down with immeasurable scorn upon such a hound as *Greene* &c &c, but did he know the *real measure* of *earthly immortality* within him?

(*Apropos*, I *hate* that term "immortality," as applied to any work of man's device, even if the meaning be *confined* to our poor little *planet*—! Still, we *must* employ it *now & then*!)

I figure Shakspeare to myself a perfectly unpretentious man! a prosperous *burgher* of *Stratford*, liking to sit in the sunshine;—& converse pleasantly with all passers by. His grand capacious soul took in all Humanity. Not the veriest beggar or scoundrel was beneath his notice, nay, his sympathy.[5]

How he *revels* in the absurdities of some of his characters; & how, now & then, the profoundest pathos is eliminated (if I may thus express it), from the humors of even fools & blackguards!

Recall I pray you, Scene III, Act II of King Henry V*th*.[6] Pistol, Dame Quickly, Nym, Bardolph, & Boy are present. When Pistol announces the death of *Falstaff*, in his usual Bombastic vein, but with evident deep feeling *au fond*, what does poor Bardolph say?

With passionate earnestness he exclaims;—"'Would I were with him, wheresom'er he is, Either in *Heaven or in Hell*!" Now, could devotion go further than this?—Then, observe how the half-grotesque, yet genuine pathos of the scene, is modified, or contrasted, (so to speak) by what follows a little after!

The imp-like, mischievous little rascal of a Boy asks, "Do you not remember 'a (Falstaff) saw a flea stick upon *Bardolph's nose*; & 'a *said it was a black soul burning in hell-fire?*" And Bardolph's irresistible answer, "Well! the *fuel* is gone that maintained *that fire*! that's all the riches I got in his service!"

Do you know that in all my reading of Shakspearean criticism, (& I've read a good deal in that line), I never have encountered anything *finer & truer* than your paragraph about him, running thus; "Shakspeare had no nationality, and could have had none, if he was to be Shakspeare! His *nature* was the *solvent of all the races*, and his Genius sprung from the decomposition into the form of the race. Evidently, he dates beyond the *Tower of Babel.*"[7]

Noble this! very noble!—A Criticism of complex suggestiveness in 45 words!—

I am pleased & encouraged that you liked my "*Quatrain*" upon "*Faith.*" I have done a number of these things lately; and when they are published, must send you copies.

Here are one or two rather crude ones needing the *labor limaë*, but still comprehensible.

Have you not often in life met the following personage?

> His soul, an unfilled outline problematical,
> Deems *love* a blood-boil; *Art* a monstrous sham;
> Blind to all thoughts divine, all dreams ecstatical,
> He moves, a human—*parallelogram!*—

I'm not at all sure of the Image here. Perhaps it is grotesquely absurd. 'Tis the spirit *baldly outlined*, with just no filling in whatever I wanted to indicate.

This quatrain, however, you may like better.

> *Malice.*
> What now! you deem that fiend of Malice dead?—
> *Medusa* died!, & yet her severed head,
> Brave Perseus bore o'er Lybian dune & dell,
> Shed blood-drops, changed to scorpions where they fell!—[8]

Surely, I can comprehend how sad your task must have been—I mean the composition of the epitaph for the monument of *Yancey, your old friend*. I have heard a vast deal of Yancey's extraordinary talents; indeed some pronounce him a man of exalted genius; a Statesman of the "first-water," & one who *ought* to have been President of these "U-States"! I would like to learn your own view of him as *man, & statesman!*[9]

Ah! *what* a thing it is to be old (!!), to stand upon a narrow "strait of land," between the receding Past, & the hazy, mysterious Future!! to feel— "*abiit ad Plures*"—[10] that one by one, our friends have joined the majority; & that we, like poor Sir Bedivere, in that magnificent conclusion of Tennyson's "*Passing of Arthur*," have left, at all events, our *Earthly best* behind us; & henceforth must

> "go forth companionless,
> While the days darken round us & the years,
> *Among new men, strange faces, other minds!*—[11]

Very beautiful are the *religious* consolations of old age, as so subtly &
eloquently presented in your own treatise on the subject; but alas!, there
is *another side* to the picture, the *wholly human side,* which is full of
sadness.

Your reference to my beloved & honored uncle, Genl R Y Hayne,
profoundly interests me.

I recall his noble face, when I myself was a Child, a little fellow of 8
or 9, whom he *taught to shoot*; and had he only lived, I would have
found in him a *Father!* (my *own* Father died, when I was a *mere infant*):
Only think! you heard him in the grandest of congressional debates, the
controversy on "*Foote's Resolutions* [*sic*]!"[12]

Apropos, I prepared some years ago, a brief biographical sketch
of him, which—after appearing like the Life of Legaré, in Bledsoe's
"*Quar: Review*," was re-published in *pamphlet form.*[13]

I am about to write to Charleston to see if I cannot procure a copy
for you.

It is a very unambitious article; but therein, I have tried to show, by
a *careful analysis*, (simplified from McDuffie's masterly Eulogy), of the
entire scope of the *Constitutional* reasoning, that *Webster*, despite his
brilliant ironics, his sarcasm, wit, and *bold* amplitude of *assertion*,—
fails to prove his *main point*, against the constitutionality of "*States'
Rights*";—that he avoids *cunningly* many a damaging fact; is sophisti-
cal, & now & then, full of "*Buncome*" [*sic*] where he coolly, (eg) tells us
that the bones of *New England's* soldiers are scattered all over the *So.
States*, (referring to the old Revolution), when if one is to believe Wash-
ington's testimony, there will hardly be a "Corporal's Guard" of these
precious dead Yankee heroes *South* of the Potomac to answer the Trum-
pet of Resurrection!!

My wife returns her heart-felt thanks for the vol you so thought-
fully sent her "*Lessons from the Life of St Peter.*" Need it be said, that
she, & I too, will preserve this book carefully. As yet we have had no
chance of reading it, but upon next Sunday we look forward to the
great pleasure of doing so.

Mrs Hayne also sends you a Sonnet to myself by the poor blind
English Poet, *Marston*;[14] thinking it might interest you.

Some trifles of my own are included.

I cannot wonder at your rather disliking *Spring*; despite her beauty.
She brings certain influences with her, which work upon an Invalid's
system disastrously; and how—when the physical man is out of gear,
can we appreciate nature's loveliness?

Do you think that a person suffering from rheumatism, neuralgia, or dispepsia [*sic*], (granting the possibility of such a condition *there*), would enjoy even the beatitudes of Paradise? I trow not!

Well! I must conclude.

With my wife's *affectionate regards*, believe me
 Always *most sincerely* & *Cordially*

Y'r friend,
Paul H Hayne.

1. Concerning the "London Commentary," Lipscomb had written Hayne on February 12 that he was "engaged on the Pulpit Commentary (Kegan Paul, Trench & Co., Publishers, London), and my work is on St. Matthew's Gospel."

2. Lipscomb's "Milton poem" appeared in *Harper's New Monthly*, XX (May, 1860), 771–78.

3. At the request of the Class of 1883 at Smith College, Hayne wrote a poem to be read at commencement exercises June 20. Hayne was not able to be present, but the poem was read by John Wesley Churchill, Andover Theological Seminary, and published in the Hampshire County *Journal*, Northampton, June 23, and shortly thereafter in pamphlet form. "The period is now at hand," Hayne had written Lipscomb on March 2, 1884, "when Woman is destined to fulfill her *true* mission. What that mission is by our modern lights, I have myself *tried* to outline" in this poem. And the mission for the female of the eighties is to take advantage of the loosening of the "chains of custom" without asserting "equality with man" or revolting "against the eternal plan" or refusing to be wife and mother; and to roam with a "free, unburdened Mind" through the realms of Science and Art.

4. Michael Servetus (1511–1553), physician, scholar, and religious reformer whose views on the Trinity and other theological matters led him to be condemned for heresy by the Roman Catholics in Vienna and subsequently by Calvin and the civil authorities in Geneva, where he was burned at the stake in 1553.

The *homoousios* and *homoiousios* controversy is based on different interpretations of Christ's relation to God. Those who supported the former view held that Christ was coeternal with God the Father and of the same essential being, whereas those who accepted the latter view maintained that Christ as Son was subordinate to the Father and of similar substance rather than of the same essential substance. See Kenneth Scott Latourette, *A History of Christianity* (New York: Harper, 1953), 152.

5. Hayne had held this view of Shakespeare since 1873 and in all probability before. See his newspaper article on "Shakespeare's Funeral," a play published anonymously in *Blackwood's* for April, 1873. The clipping of Hayne's article in the Hayne Papers, Duke, has no date and is not identified as to source.

6. Hayne frequently cites this scene as an example of Shakespeare's capacity to deal with absurdity and pathos at the same time. See Letter 24, and n. 3 under it.

7. Lipscomb's letter of March 28, 1884, contains this passage, but there is more that deserves to be quoted. The comment begins: "No author is growing in the world like Shakespeare, and one thinks better of the age for this revival of the true spirit of admiration. I do not dream that we ever shall fathom him and I am quite as sure he was as great a mystery to himself as to us. Milton was English through and through—indeed a typical John Bull—yea, the most thoroughly so of all the types of the John Bull that expired in 1688." The rest of the passage, with the addition of one or two commas and capitals, is as Hayne quotes it.

8. Two of the three quatrains mentioned were printed and collected by Mrs. Hayne and William Hamilton Hayne for a proposed final edition of Hayne's poems —"The Last Poems of Paul Hamilton Hayne"—that never appeared. The title of "Faith" was changed to "Faith in Conflict," though the printed text chosen for "Last Poems" gives no indication of place of publication or date. The second quatrain may not have ever been polished to the poet's satisfaction, for there is no evidence of publication and it was not selected for inclusion in "Last Poems." "Malice" appeared in the *Atlantic Monthly*, LIV (November, 1884), 648.

9. Lipscomb had lived in Montgomery, Alabama, before the war and had known William Lowndes Yancey (1814–1863) very well. A member of the Alabama legislature and of the U.S. House of Representatives for one term, Yancey subsequently devoted himself to states' rights and eventually became a fervent secessionist who was recognized as a leading spokesman for southern rights.

10. He has gone to the majority.

11. Hayne has changed two words to fit the context of his passage.

12. Lipscomb remarked in a letter of March 28 that as a boy he had "heard your uncle, Senator Hayne, speak on the Foote Resolutions, and his appearance and manner made such an impression" that he retained "it vividly to this hour."

13. Hayne's sketch of Robert Y. Hayne appeared in the *Southern Review* for October, 1870; it was expanded and published in Charleston as a pamphlet in 1878. A copy of the pamphlet was eventually sent to Lipscomb.

14. Marston's "To Paul Hamilton Hayne" was collected in *Wind-Voices* (1883) and subsequently in *Collected Poems* (1892).

79

To William Hayes Ward[1]   MS Duke

Address me—Grovetown at Grovetown, Columbia Co Georgia
June 22nd 1884.

My Dear Doctor;

It is *many* years since I have contributed to "The Independent"; but now I wish to "give you the refusal" at least, of a poem with which I have taken much trouble; the enclosed piece upon *Charles Reade.*—

At first I designed sending the "MS" to my friendly Correspondent, Wilkie Collins, who would have it published in a prominent English periodical; but really it seems to me that something adequate in regard to Chas Reade's genius ought to appear in America.[2]

If you *accept* my poem, please let me know *immediately*; if rejected, you will at once return "MS" & thus oblige

Your old acquaintance & well wisher
Paul H Hayne.

P.S. I would not hurry you, but 'tis important that verses of this sort should be disposed of promptly.[3]

In the event of *acceptance*, we can readily agree, I am sure, as *to price.*

Only tell me what you are willing to give. Since the issue of my "Complete Poems" by the *Lothrops* two years ago, I *have (frankly)* been able to command much *higher* prices than formerly.[4]

Have no more stamps by me; but if you have to return "MS" will *remit Postage.* Hayne

1. Dr. William Hayes Ward (1835–1916), clergyman and editor, was a member of the staff of the *Independent* from 1868 through 1913 and was editor of the weekly from 1896 through 1913.

2. "Charles Reade: In Memoriam" appeared in the *Independent* for July 17, 1884. Both Wilkie Collins and Richard D. Blackmore were interested in seeing the poem published in England, but the journals approached refused to print a poem already published. See Collins' letter of July 16, 1884, and Blackmore's of October 3, 1884.

3. Charles Reade had died on April 11, 1884.

4. Hayne received twenty-five dollars for the poem.

80

To Margaret J. Preston   MS Duke

"Copse Hill," 26th Sep 1884.

My Beloved Friend,

I wrote to your son, & discovered from him that you would probably be home about the 1st Oct. So, I send you this letter of affectionate *greeting*; & also, of response, *grateful* response—, to your 3 *interesting*, & *invaluable* communications, written *abroad*, under circumstances of difficulty, (as to your eyes), & natural, *engrossing* excitement amid new scenes & personages, which, your time being *limited*, would have prevented *most* people from writing at all!

How closely & *eagerly* we followed, (my wife & I), your course of travel, & how deeply we sympathised with the delight which this glorious *"outing"* has given you![1]

Ah! to have been with you, *especially* during the English & Scotch tours!! At *Abbottsford* what a *keen pride* must have been yours, to recognize your *"Coat of Arms!!"* For *myself*, I'm more & more convinced of the advantages of *"high descent,"* I mean of good, wholesome, untainted *blood* derived from honorable ancestors!

The *levelling* tendencies, the *mobocratic craze* of our Time, simply revolt me! Look at their *results* in almost *universal* corruption of morals & manners.

As for the "*Vox Populi Vox Dei*" theory; here is my conception of its philosophy:—

> *Once*, on a Donkey Heaven's miraculous choice
> Wise Speech bestowed beyond the brute-born masses;
> *Now*, God imparts *His* wisdom's potent voice,
> *Not* to *one* Balaam's Ass—but—countless *asses*![2]

Many thanks! my *thoughtful friend*, for the beautiful little photographs you sent us. They are all so *clearly* cut; but beyond question the loveliest are those which represent the *Chateau de Chillon*, & *The Falls of the Rhine*. In the *former*, one seems to view infinite depths below the surface of the water; the appearance of which suggests to me the waves of "*Lake Winnipesaugee*" [*sic*], in N. Hampshire, a sort of inverted Heaven so lucid, and unruffled for fathom upon fathom, as to be marvellous!

In "*The Falls of the Rhine*" 'tis curious to see the Steam-Cars with their modern & unheroic associations, passing beneath the old & "castled crags"!

You have now, innumerable scenes, & circumstances stored up in memory, have you not? Most of them *doubtless*, agreeable, & some *sublime*!

Yet for a period, I fear that under the peculiar conditions surrounding you, there *must* occur a *re-action* from all the excitement of travel. And then, the contrast between Europe, & European capitals & culture, and our American provincial towns!

By the way, is not *Lexington* a rather dull little place?—Somehow, (apart from the University) I have rec$d$ the idea,—*possibly* a *false* one—, that a certain decorous uniformity of life pervades the place; and that its *general* culture is not particularly brilliant.

In *one* of your letters from abroad, (the 1st I think,) you mentioned some injury to the *optic nerve of one of your eyes*, which, however, it was thought you would recover from!

Unable to decipher the *special* words which alluded to this *hurt*,—will you not tell us now what was the matter? Likewise, inform us of the *present condition* of your *eyes*, & your *general* health?

I wish that it were possible to speak hopefully of my own *case*. But the summer has been hard upon me; and the autumn thus far *harder* still.

Mine old Enemy, *shortness* of *breath*, the result, in part of many colds—, but *yet more, I feel assured,* of a general *nervous decline*—, has greatly tormented me; "My wound is *deep*, I fain would *sleep*!" &c[3]

Sick I have been, & *am*; but not *idle*. During a *few* months, I have composed,—2 or 3 long poems, and a number of lyrics, not to speak of scores of carefully finished *Quatrains*.

An "*In Memoriam*" upon Chas Reade, published in the "*NY Independent*," and sent afterwards to England has gained me credit among those whose good opinion is worth a vast deal to me. R D Blackmore, (author of "*Lorna Doone*," & *me judice*, the most *original* & *vigorous* of living British novelists,) says the "*In Memoriam*" is "*powerful*"—, & that he was sorely tempted to send it on to "*Blackwood*"; only he hesitated about doing so without my *consent*!!

Wilkie Collins, likewise, delighted with this piece, has *actually* sent it to *Messrs Chatto & Windus*, (*Reade's* publishers), for reproduction in some form.[4]

I must not omit telling you that when your melancholy letter, detailing your Md illness, & the consequent breaking up—as *you then supposed*—of all your plans of foreign travel—, reached me, I *immediately* & *sympathetically* replied; and your son *acknowledged* the receipt *of my* letter (as you had left).[5]

I hope that Col *Preston's* health has improved? Please remember us to him, & accept *for yourself* a *great deal of love* from both of us, also earnest remembrances from our *son*. Would, *dear friend*, that I could write more; but I am *feeble* & must close,

Ever affectionately & loyally
Paul H Hayne.

1. Mrs. Preston had been on the verge of leaving for Europe when she encountered some "lobster salad," as she wrote Hayne on June 7, 1884, and was forced to "abandon" her "plan." Upon recovering from the bout with the "hated Yankee crustacean" (as Hayne described "the little beast of Nantucket" in a letter of June 15), she and her party resumed their trip and voyage and stayed until early October. Two of the letters Hayne mentions as having received while she was abroad may now be found in part in Allan, *The Life and Letters of Margaret Junkin Preston*, 308–12.

2. Hayne also copied this "epigram" for other correspondents during this period. See, for example, Letter 81. In "Ante-Bellum Charleston," Hayne attributes this quatrain to Emile St. Quentin Laboucher, Marquis of Brittany (*Southern Bivouac*, n.s., I [October, 1885], 261). This is his own translation.

3. "The Battle of Otterbourne," stanza LVII. The last half of the line reads: "I am fayn to sleep."

4. See Letter 79, n. 2. *Blackwood's* declined to print the poem because it had already been published. Chatto & Windus refused for the same reason.

5. Hayne had written on June 15, 1884.

81

To J. G. Whittier   MS Duke

"Copse Hill" Geo
Oct 26th 1884

Yours of the 10*th* in*st, My very Dear Friend,* reached me a few days ago; and I need hardly say how glad we, (my wife & I), were to receive it!

It seems to me, from the tone of this communication, that you are in better health & spirits than usual; at all events the *physical* depression of the summer heat, has left you.

I can well imagine how lovely your autumn woods now are! The variety of foliage, & its remarkable richness at *"Oak Knoll"*: I could not fail to observe, when we were with you in 1879. Indeed, your Northern forests far excel ours, (*ours* in *this particular latitude*, I mean) in complexity and *splendor* of tint! But our *skies* are *unrivalled.*[1]

You allude to *Holmes*. Yes, he *"is active* as ever;" & really, I wouldn't be surprised if he continued to work, & *work well,* up to his *one hundredth year*!!

The vitality of the man is *marvellous. Everybody* nationally, is on the *"qui vive"* to read his Life of *Emerson.*[2] The *only* thing—, *entre nous*—which I fear, in reference to *that* Biography is this;—(*viz*), that *Holmes* should have allowed his *personal* friendship, & *cordial relations* with the Philosopher to influence over much his critical decisions.

He is just the man to fall under such a temptation.

The power & interest of his work is "a foregone conclusion."

Your *"Birchbrook Mill"* in the last *"Atlantic"* is a *very* characteristic poem; so *simple*, yet *strong*. The *suggestiveness of it,* one recognizes *immediately*—

For example, in the stanza;—

> "They dare not pause to hear the grind
>   Of Shadowy stone on stone,—
> The plashing of the water-wheel,
>   *Where wheel there now is none!"*

& still finer,—

> What nameless honor of the past
>   Broods here forever more?
> *What ghost his unforgiven sin*
>   *Is grinding o'er & o'er?"*

Adjustment (in the *Oct "Andover Review"*), strikes me as being full of *subtle* meaning.

I *try* to hope with you that all the *agnosticism* & *Phyronnism* [*sic*] of our age may finally be "*overruled for good*,"—but ah! *my friend*, 'tis hard to *credit* it!

I'm afraid that instead of *an angel* "troubling the Fountain," 'tis a *Demon*.[3] Heaven grant I may be wrong!

My son (who will always cherish your kind words in his behalf), has requested me to enclose a little piece of his,—accompanied by his loving regards—which may interest you.

His health has been, from a period far back, very *precarious*; and unfortunately this has prevented him from *roughing* it thro the world, as otherwise (for he's *a manly* fellow), he certainly would have done.

It is gratifying in the extreme, & I may add *most encouraging*, to receive such criticisms as yours upon "*Midsummer*."[4]

This poem belongs to a series, which treat [*sic*] of farm life & labor. Published in "the *Louisville Home & Farm*," they have proved quite popular.

My wife sends you her *warmest love*, & begs—as I do—, to be always kindly remembered to your cousins.—Good news I consider it of *Phoebe*, that she has developed into a fine Horsewoman.[5] *Our* love to her!

What a disgusting Presidential Canvas is now progressing!! Ah: my friend! depend upon it our Fathers made a grave error, when they so arranged Constitutional matters, as to force an election for the chief Magistrate every *four years*! The period is too short.

And only remark what fearful illustrations we are daily having of the stupidity or corruption of the masses!

Apropos, the following epigram, penned in a rather bitter humor, may amuse you, concerning the Principle "*Vox Populi Vox Dei*." *Once*, on a Donkey Heaven's miraculous choice / Wise speech bestowed beyond the brute-born masses; / *Now*, God imparts *His* wisdom's potent voice, / Not to *one* Balaam's ass, but countless—asses![6] That "*epigram*" would have cost me my head at *one* epoch, & in a certain Country—eh? I *do* wish that we *could* come & see you once more, or that you could come & see us! But *alas*!—God be with you, my honored & beloved friend!—I have a profoundly tender feeling for you in my heart of hearts. And the same is true of my *wife*.

Always affectionately & faithfully   Paul H Hayne[7]

Did you chance to see my *"In Memoriam"* upon Chas Reade in "Independent"?

    1. At this point in the manuscript, Hayne apparently stopped momentarily and resumed writing on a new page.

    2. Holmes's *Ralph Waldo Emerson* was published in the American Men of Letters series late in 1884.

    3. *Taming of the Shrew*, V, ii, 142–43.

    4. "Thy 'Mid-Summer,'" Whittier had written on October 6, "is full of delicious poetry—passages that Marvell might have written."

    5. For the "cousins" and Phoebe Woodman, see Letter 68, n. 6.

    6. Quoted in Letter 80.

    7. The last page of the manuscript has Hayne's name in Whittier's hand.

82

To A. A. Lipscomb   MS Duke

"Copse Hill," Geo
14th Nov 1884

My Dear Friend;

All your *invaluable* letters have safely come; but before I reply in *detail* to them, let me thank you for copies both of the "Macon Review," & the "NY *Methodist* Quarterly." The *former's* article on the *Sonnet* is a clever, and careful *resumé* of an exceedingly interesting topic;—but *what am I* to say of *your* "Hamlet treatise," or "study" in the *latter*? To *my* mind, it *must stand* in the very *front rank* of "Hamlet" criticism, and analysis. From beginning to end, one is borne along, upon the tides of a discussion so absorbing, so suggestive, so wonderfully lucid even in the abstruse parts,—that one cannot fail to be equally instructed & charmed.

Coleridge, Lamb, Hazlitt, in England, Hudson, Grant White, & Whipple in America,[1] have written many noble things upon Shakspear's [sic] *"chef d'oeuvre,"* but *nothing superior* to *your* searching observations, your *minute* examination of motives, character, temperament, controlling causes of action, or of non-action in the Hero of this great Drama!

You have made *some points*, in fact, unrecognized & untouched upon, (so far as I know), by any previous *Shaksperean* [sic] critic, the Germans not excepted.

For example, the *very key-note* of *Hamlet's nature, & his destiny,* is struck, when you remark that his extreme *temperamental sensitive-ness* is *wholly dissociated from sensuousness*!, & nothing *could* be finer than your illustrations of Hamlet's *introspective* soul, his indifference to even legitimate forms of sensuous enjoyment; the enormous unconscious Egoism of the man, leading him to make of his spirit, a Scenic edifice, for the display of "*a drama of Nerves &c*"!

I am glad too, that while you exhibit Hamlet as subjected to "an overmastering hysteria," you show with equal clearness, that he was *not insane*!!

This essay is one to be studied again & yet again,—the fruit of subtlest meditation, of a long acquaintance with the inner workings of the great dramatic *master*'s mind & mode of imaginative labor, & of a learning as profound, as the philosophy is true!

I congratulate you upon *such* an achievement; so *grand*, & *noble* a specimen of the metaphysical, & analytical, in what may justly be called *creative Criticism.*[2]

Of your *poems* so kindly enclosed, I like "*The Hell of Inhumanity*" *best*, because it seems to me *strongest*, & most *pungent* in thought & imagery.

"*Mysterious Tears*" is a *Sonnet*, the controlling mood of which I perfectly comprehend. By the way, *must I not* return these "*MSS*," they are so carefully & beautifully done? *Tell me*!

"*To a Mystic*" I, of course, enclose, because you ask me to "tell you how to better it &c"—(Here, I put down my pen to read over these lines to "a *mystic*") & I find that certain *strong phrases* in "*The Hell of Inhumanity*" (like "*maw of money-lust*" &c) had unjustly made me express a preference for that piece; when in fact, I *now* perceive that the "*Mystic*" is *far superior; fine as the first is*. As to *verbal criticism*, I see but a *word* in the 3rd stanza, 2nd line which may be amended, (viz) "*ordained*," ("*ordained* aid" &c). The rhythm, as that line now stands, requires too great a stress upon the *middle* syllable. Is it so?

You are doubtless a great sufferer physically. I find you diverting your mind by rising from bed on a sleepless night, (when tormented by a bowel complaint), and "sketching out" the plan of poems &c! What an amount of *will power*, this must require!

Never could I understand how Sir W. Scott composed many Chapters of "*Ivanhoe*," while suffering from some abdominal disturbance! In *my* case, the *stomach* if out of order, simply *paralyzes* the *Brain*. *Other pangs & agonies* I can endure, & work, but the Stomach! . . . *no! no!*

"What do I think *of Edwin Arnold's* poem on the Cholera?" Well, I have not seen it!—But, I don't wonder at its great *force*, as you describe it.

Arnold is a genius of marked imagination & *vim*. His "*Light of Asia*" is *magnificent*.[3]

I'm glad that my "poor *Babes* in the Wood"[4] have found more favor in your sight; but *dear friend*, please never *talk* of "*presumption*" on your part, in regard to *any conceivable criticism* wherewith you may honor me, past, present, or future.

"*Presumption!*" say rather, a *most kindly condescension*!

I am but a Poet, *a minor Poet*, if a *true one*;—*you* are a *vast deal* more; *one* of the subtlest, *deepest, philosophical* Thinkers of our *Time*.

And what do I not owe you in the way of most heartfelt *commendation*, & all the encouragement which comes from praise & appreciation of the finest quality? Here you are *kindly* stimulating me again, about the *Reade* "*In Memoriam*."[5]

It is simply *delightful* to find you dwelling thus upon the piece, with which I certainly took much trouble. And you have indicated *precisely* its peculiarities. These however, *not belonging*, (of necessity), to the realm of the higher imagination, must vivify the poem only so long as the Public *continue* to recognize the genius, and admire the character-drawing of the *novelist*, whose works I have passed by in flashing review. See! the vast difference then, between this "*In Memoriam*," and my nature-poem, called "*Unveiled*," (in "*complete* Edition")—In "*Unveiled*," I gained, *me judice*, my highest water mark!, for I do think, at least I *hope*, that therein, (to borrow your own exquisite phraseology) "the two ideals of the *spirit* & the *sense* have come *together* like the dust of the Paradise in Adam's body, & the breath of God."[6]

I perfectly comprehend the dreamy mood in which you read your "*Copse Hill*" Quatrains, as I may term them, in print.

Like yourself, much that I write, passes from my memory.

Apropos, you lay me under obligation after obligation; for *could* I fail to be touched by your "*Hidden Light*"? with all its tenderness & affectionate cordiality? And there is a mist in my eyes, while I peruse such lines as these:

"If I had any higher Earthly happiness, than writing *to you*, and I am foolish enough," (no! say *good enough*!) "to add, *for* you, in order that I may think & work *with you*, I should *not write* so often!)"[7]

Aye! these be "*comfortable* words," as old *Bunyan* hath it! They are to me as balm to wounds, as sweet breezes in a Tropic noon, as the shadow of palms in a desert land!

Like yourself, & I fancy everybody else, South, I felt confident for 24 hours of Blaine's election. But *"laus Deo!"* he has evidently been *beaten*; and the *"Independent Republicans"* having joined the Democrats, I really *don't* believe the *Fraud* of 1876, can be repeated![8]

Had the Democrats *won by themselves,* we should have been subjected to precisely the same infamy.

While firmly convinced of *Blaine's* triumph, I composed the following *impromptu.*

> O! what a monstrous deed this day is done!,
> Defying reason, past all sane belief,
> The sacred seat of glorious Washington,
> Free to this mouthing Cheat, this arrogant Thief!
>
> God! 'ere he takes it, while with conquering pace
> He nears the dais, let Thy thunders roll!
> Smite Fraud incarnate, blast his Judas face,
> Defend the land, & purge the Capitol!

My wife rec*d* a very affectionate letter from *Marston* a few days ago. She had told him of your message, & in reply he says:

"Many thanks for sending me the charming reference to your far-off friend from Chancellor Lipscomb. Will you kindly tell him, when you next write to him, or see him, *what pleasure* it gave me?" Poor fellow, he is the *warmest-hearted* of men, no less than the most *afflicted.*

And now, *dear & honored Friend, au revoir!*

Best love, & wishes from all at *"Copse Hill."*

Ever Cordially & affectionately,
Paul H Hayne.

1. Henry N. Hudson (1814–1886) published *Lectures on Shakespeare* (2 vols., 1848) and *Shakespeare: His Life, Art, and Characters* (2 vols., 1872), and he served as editor of the Harvard Edition of Shakespeare, (20 vols., 1880–81). Richard Grant White (1821–1885) wrote *Shakespeare's Scholar* (1854) and edited *The Works of William Shakespeare* (12 vols., 1857–66). E. P. Whipple (1819–1886), Hayne's old friend, had discussed Shakespeare in *Literature in the Age of Elizabeth* (1869) and elsewhere.

2. Hayne's appreciation of Lipscomb's essay on *Hamlet* (*Methodist Quarterly Review,* LXV [October, 1884], 665–78) led the critic to respond on November 18:

> I am delighted that you like the Hamlet article. I had given it up in despair, for it was written months ago, and found by the new editor of the Review when he came into office this summer, and he was pleased to publish it. I can truthfully claim it to be original as I had not even a suggestion of the line of argument from any outward source whatever. In opposition to some of our recent critics,—most of them Physi-

cians,—who explain Hamlet on the theory of madness, I try to show that his very eccentricities (Hysteria at the bottom of all), saved him from Insanity. I am greatly comforted by your estimate of the essay.

3. Hayne had admired Arnold (1832–1904) since his *Light of Asia* had appeared in 1879. Arnold's "Cholera in Italy" appeared in the *Independent* for October 30, 1884. In a letter dated merely November, 1884, Lipscomb characterizes the poem as "vivid, ghastly vivid."

4. "The Babes in the Woods," *Independent*, XXXVII (May 14, 1885), 638.

5. For the Reade lyric, see Letter 79.

6. "Unveiled," dedicated to William Cullen Bryant, appeared in *Scribner's Monthly* (January, 1878). Lipscomb replied on November 18 that he found the ode "uppermost among all your poems as to the individuation of Nature's power over the spiritual senses and the entire subserviency of sense-impressions to the higher subjectiveness. It is," he continued, "a very subtle and profound reading of Nature's meaning as the counterpart of the soul."

7. Lipscomb had visited the Haynes at Copse Hill in September and subsequently wrote "Hidden Light" and other poems and articles about his friendship with Hayne. The poem—dated November, 1884—was enclosed with a letter dated November, 1884. No day is given.

8. James G. Blaine, the Republican candidate for president in 1884, was defeated by Grover Cleveland, the Democratic candidate.

83

To Margaret J. Preston   MS Duke

"Copse Hill" Geo
Nov: 19th 1884

My Dear Friend;—

Firstly, I must *cordially* thank you for a copy of *"Shakespeariana,"* containing your *Sonnet* upon "Jessica." I have read & *re*-read it, & to *my* mind, it seems as sweet as Lorenzo's kisses upon the lips of his sweetheart! The lines are full of melody; they flow along mellifluously towards a golden close.[1]

After your *wonderful* holiday, I can imagine the feeling with which your footsteps pressed once more their *"native heath"*! It must have been a *complex* sentiment;—joy no doubt at a safe return home, but modified too, by a certain sadness, the conviction that you had *perhaps* left "fairy-land" forever!

Verily, a fairy-land to you, with your vivid imagination, high art culture, and deep poetic instincts, must the great European realm have proved! The glowing radiant fashion in which you describe the wonders you beheld, shows this, clearly enough.

Age! what a store of memories shall always illuminate your mind hereafter! When days are dark, and nights mournful; when the prosaic Present weighs upon your moods, and the nerves become, (in Mrs. Carlyle's favorite phraseology), "fretted to fiddlestrings," you will re-call the magnificence of the Alps & view again in reverent quietude, "*Mount Blanc*," "so suggestive of 'the Great White Throne;'" or you will pause (in fancy) by crystal *Leman*, muse in "*Père la chaise*,"—and crossing the Channel, roam thro quaint, antique *Edinboro'*,— wander near "Dryburgh," or explore the Stony streets of our modern "Babylon the Great,"—*London*, the miraculous & unrivalled.

What a privilege to have one's memory thus marvellously furnished (!!) You "declined," it seems, "all Society while abroad," being "unwilling to dress so often &c &c." You will not even "hunt up the *Kingsleys*, tho with a *pressing invitation* to visit them!"

Frankly, *dear friend*, don't you think Mrs. Kingsley will profoundly regret this;—and oh! how *very very sorry* we feel that you failed to see Miss *Ingelow*, & *above all, Philip Bourke Marston*, altho you were near *Euston* Square.[2]

He would have been *overjoyed* to meet you, I know.

But, it can't be helped now.

My *son* feels truly complimented by what you have written of his notice (in "*The American*") of your Poems, months ago.

Yes! thus far his literary career *has* been fortunate, & encouraging.

Willie possesses a peculiar delicacy of fancy, & I think a rather *original vein of thought* now & then. Your own *boys* I rejoice to observe, are progressing. All success to Dr. George when he settles in Balt. and may your *Herbert*, when *his* path is chosen, succeed gloriously likewise!—

Willie has asked me to enclose a *Song* of his published in "*The Manhattan*," which he hopes you will like.

In the same magazine was published a poem of my own, called "*The Mocking Birds*;"[3]—I have but a single copy, or I would mail it to you.

I am *sure* you'll be glad to learn that it delighted *Swinburne*, Marston, Jno Burroughs, & many *others*.

Apropos, I don't send you my Poems as *once* I did, knowing that you have not been able even to read the verses in the "complete Edition;" because *my poor, dear friend*, of your failing eyesight. Ah: how I miss *your old luminous* criticisms (!!)

To return to *Marston*, (from whom I had a charming letter, last evng), he writes me, (*Sep: 15th*) thus; "*what* you tell me of your friend

Mrs. Preston, troubles me; as I admire *so* much of her poetry; and always remember, *very tenderly*, the *beautiful* Sonnet, she wrote to me."

Now , you perceive that Marston *would* have given you the warmest of welcomes, and *highly* prized your visit.

My *wife* sends a great deal of *love*, and hopes you recd a letter from her, mailed before your departure for *Europe*; not of course, that she expected you to answer it.

But the mails are bad, & she wanted you to know that she *had* written.

And now, *beloved Friend, au revoir*!

God be with you & yours (!!) With *best* remembrances to the Colonel,

Ever affectionately
Paul H. Hayne

1. Mrs. Preston's "Sit, Jessica" is collected in *Colonial Ballads, Sonnets and Other Verse* (1887), 2.

2. Hayne is quoting and paraphrasing from a letter of October 20 (Allan, *The Life and Letters of Margaret Junkin Preston*, 312–13). The Kingsleys referred to are Mrs. Charles Kingsley and her daughter—Kingsley himself had died in 1875. Mrs. Preston had corresponded with the Kingsleys for many years. Mrs. Preston's poem in memory of Kingsley is collected in *Cartoons* (1875), 192–94. Jean Ingelow (1820–1897), British poet and novelist, had corresponded with Mrs. Preston since the early 1870s. Marston, of course, was Hayne's friend, though Mrs. Preston had been mentioned in Hayne's letters, and Marston had invited her (in a letter to Hayne) to visit him when she came to London. Marston lived at 190 Euston Square. On November 9, 1884, she wrote Hayne for Marston's address so that she could explain her failure to visit him (Allan, *The Life and Letters of Margaret Junkin Preston*, 313).

3. "The Mocking-Birds," *Manhattan*, IV (September, 1884), 331–32.

84

To A. A. Lipscomb   MS Duke

"Copse Hill" Geo
Dec 3rd 1884

My Dear Friend,

Your letters are indeed a great benefaction; I may go further, & say they have assumed the importance to us here of an *Institution*! Could you see *how* they are welcomed, you would acknowledge that the above is no mere idle compliment, or vague figure of speech.

Yours of the 27th ul*t*. was *delightful*, in *all* but one particular. I *don't* like to hear of these frequent "bleedings at the bowels;"—they must prove terribly debilitating, and—equally exhaustive of body and mind.

How *can* you keep up your intellectual energies as you evidently do?

Then, the present season is so trying to Invalids!! *Yesterday*, the peculiar gray cloudiness of the atmosphere, and a penetrating chilliness, foreboded *Snow*, but it never came & this morning tho cold—is "clear as a bell"!

It is very encouraging to have your lucid & marvellous criticisms upon my *verse*. They *not* only *stimulate*, but *instruct*;—I value them immensely, & shall preserve them for my son & his children, if he ever marries.

About the little shoe poem; I had composed it months on months ago; and thought it rather inferior. So (often *it had* been *rejected* by—I know not how many Yankee juvenile periodicals—), I tossed the "*MS*" into my waste-box, & by *merest* accident, coming across it the other day, took heart of grace to offer it to "The *Independent*." Much to my surprise the Editor not only *accepted*, but seemed to especially fancy the piece; & *now* it actually promises to become popular to a *marked* degree.[1]

By the way, I could write a curious essay concerning rejected "MS" poems. Some of the ablest, & finally most popular of my verses, have gone the round of the periodical Editors, only to be coolly refused.

You in your special department have *sometimes* had a similar experience; but not *often* I am sure.

In your next tell me of the *political* essays lately written, & offered for publication. Are they to appear, & *where*?

And now, I want your advice touching two versions of the same Idea.

—The *first* is called—"*The Renegade*"; (indeed both versions come under that title), & is thus embodied in a Quatrain—

> —Some mighty Cause he feigned to work for lost,
>   His spurious fervor feels a killing frost—;
> —Past blindness mourned, his "*mea Culpa*" cried—
> —This Stentor of War—Shouts on victory's side!

I have amplified the Conception *thus*;

> —A glorious Cause! true: but the Cause lies dead!
> —Most like an outstretched Titan, gaunt & pale,
> —With awful, sightless eyes, and shattered mail,
>   Lax limbs supine, & Earth-recumbent head;

O! kingly form, no more disquietude!
While faithful thousands thy dark doom bewail,—
—*One* traitorous knave hath only tongue to rail,
And mock the vows his own false lips had said:

How *once* he feigned: Yea, flattered, fawned, and lied,
For gifts that gleamed, in that frank, labored hand:—
Now, for spirit blessing, his dead Lord is banned;—
Past blindness mourned, his "*mea culpa*" cried,
—Blithely he joins the conqueror's proud command,
And Stentor-Judas—Shouts on . . . Victory's side![2]

My wife thinks the Quatrain better, that the Sonnet is *diluted*, &
weakens the general effect.

What do you *think*?

I *earnestly* trust that your next letter will contain far better news of
your health.

With love, & best wishes from our household,

> *Ever affectionately* yrs
> *Paul H. Hayne.*

Yes: I receive "The Independent" regularly. Did Willie's note reach you?

1. "Praying for Shoes. A Boy's Thanksgiving," *Independent*, XXXVI (November 27,
1884), 1531.
2. For a slightly later version of the sonnet, see Letter 85. The final version, called
"The Renegade. Suggested by a 'Painting of Kaulbach's' in Munich," appeared in the *In-
dependent*, XXXVII (January 22, 1885), 97.

85

To Margaret J. Preston   MS Duke

> *"Copse Hill,"* Geo
> *Dec 16th 1884*

My Dear Friend;

I truly appreciate, (as indeed we *all do*) your cordial letter of the
11*th*.

It is most encouraging to me, most gratifying, to have you speak as
you do, of the two poems, *"Literary Immortality,"* & *"The Mocking-
Birds."*[1]

You know well in *what* esteem I hold *your* opinion upon *art*, espe-
cially upon poetry.

Apropos of this topic, I must tell you how *delighted* we have been with your exquisite piece (published in "*The Sunday School Times*" of Phil*a*) called "*Her Promise.*"

Since my perusal of Wordsworth's immortal ballad, "*We are Seven,*" I don't think that I have encountered any poem of its order, more beautiful & touching than this.

It exemplifies that golden simplicity of both fancy, & execution which it appears to me is becoming somewhat rare in modern verse. Yes, you are to be congratulated upon a performance so altogether lovely.

One would think that its pathos, sweetness, and religious trust, might touch even the "*dry-as dust*" spirit which hangs about the shelves of college libraries, & lead your very large-minded, & enlightened neighbors to suspect, that perhaps they have among them a more important personage, than "the *little* woman who stays at home, & has— *dyspepsia*!"

You inquire after my health. Well, of late it has been better, I think, than for some time past.

Every day I ride out in my buggy, the "Bonny Brown Hand"[2] by my side, along the Country roads, lined by our beloved pine woods, which however, (I regret to say), are becoming too rapidly thinned by the axes of people who despise the Picturesque in about the same proportion that they *adore* the *Tar*, or *Lumber* which may be rated by dollars & cents![3]

You are recommended to live "out of doors," you say, as much as practicable. Doubtless you will do so; but alack! the season is upon us, when among your mountains, I presume, it would be out of the question for any but strong men to brave the winds & snows.

Just a moment ago, my son, (who had been looking over some old published poems &c;) came upon your Sonnet—penned long ago, to *Dante Gabriel Rossetti*. A wonderfully fine thing it is, with a conclusion full of force & harmony.

I have one precious letter (did I ever tell you?) from Rossetti, written only *5 weeks* before his comparatively sudden death? A warmhearted man, & a magnificent artist! I have a note from *Browning* too; but none can compare with some lines from *Tennyson*.[4]

We wish you a pleasant *Xmas*, & New Yeartide! When I write (as D.V. I *often* shall), do *not* think it needful to reply *ceremoniously*, nor in any other way. You must *not exert your* eyes, & *pain* them, as I fear you have done *before*.

Have you been struck—I *have*, by the manner in which certain representatives of the so-called "*New South*" are now in the habit of answering for their *elders*? (e.g.):—Mr Cable is pleased to remark in his last novel, that *everybody South* now "*execrates* the idea of slavery" (or *words to that effect*—) & altogether undertakes to be spokesman, the miserable little *ci-devant* Clerk & Parvenu, a *thorough Yankee in blood*, wherever, by *accident*, he was born—for this entire section of Country, touching past political beliefs & principles, of which he knows evidently *next* to nothing (!!)[5] Yes, & *scores* of young men are following his lead; & men also, by no means young—old Confederates, quite willing to defile the Graves of their Fathers. Here is a Sonnet which explains itself—;

The Renegade

A glorious Cause! . . . true! . . . but the Cause lies dead,
Most like an outstretched Titan, gaunt & pale—,
With awful, sightless eyes, & shattered mail,—
Lax limbs supine, & earth-recumbent head:
O! kingly form, no more disquieted;—
While loyal thousands His dark doom bewail,—
One traitorous Knave hath only tongue to rail,
And mock the vows his own false lips had said;—
How *once* he feigned, yea, flattered, fawned & lied,
From gifts that shone in that frank, liberal hand;
Now, for spent blessing, his dead Lord is banned:—
Past blindness mourned his "*mea culpa*" cried,—
Blithely he joins the Conqueror's proud "command"—
And—Stentor-Judas—, shouts on . . . *victory's side.*[6]

Well, "*basta*"! "*basta*"!

Ever Most Faithfully & affectionately,
Paul H. Hayne

1. In sending "Literary Immortality" to Mrs. Preston on December 6, Hayne had described it as a "rather gloomy poem, but surely *true*." For "The Mocking-Birds," see Letter 83, n. 3.

2. Hayne often refers to Mrs. Hayne in this way. "The Bonny Brown Hand," a lyric about Mrs. Hayne appeared in *Appletons' Journal*, II (November 20, 1869), 433, and was collected in *LL* and *PCE*, 106–107.

3. Hayne remarks on the depletion of the pine forests often and always makes the same point.

4. Dante Gabriel Rossetti (1828–1882) died on April 9, 1882. He wrote Hayne in March (no day is given in the typed copy at Duke) in answer to a letter from Hayne. Browning wrote Hayne on December 16, 1883, in response to an inquiry about the Complete Edition of Hayne's poems. He had not received the copy sent him by Hayne on October 12. Tennyson had written Hayne April 15, 1884, thanking him for a copy of the Complete Edition and for a copy of his "Lines on Tennyson," a short lyric that chastises those who criticized Tennyson for accepting a peerage. Hayne had also enclosed a copy of the poem in a letter of February 29, 1884, to Lipscomb. The last stanza reads:

> Free is the modest offspring!—*he* as free
> To condescend toward the gift they bring;—
> No Sodom's apple is a Lord's degree,
> To foul the lips of him—our Poet-King!

5. Hayne apparently alludes to the passage of *Dr. Sevier* (1884; the novel had completed its serial run in the *Century* for October, 1884) in which the Union "cause" is acknowledged as "just. Lo, now, since nigh twenty-five years have passed, we of the South can say it!" Hayne's opinion of Cable is freely expressed in his letters of 1885–1886 to Charles Gayarré. See below.

6. See Letter 84.

86

To Charles E. A. Gayarré [1]   MS Duke

Copse Hill Geo
Jan 18th 1885

My Dear & Honored Sir:—

A few days ago my attention was called to a paragraph in the Augusta "*Chronicle and Constitutionalist*" to the effect, that you were preparing for "*The Times Democrat*" of N. Orleans, "a series of articles in reply to Mr Cable's miscegenation screed in '*the Century.*'" [2] I hailed this announcement with *delight*; for I have *long* been familiar with your reputation as a profound Thinker & Historian, a vivid, logical Reasoner, a brilliant Scholar, and *last* but not *least, one of the truest* of old School Southern gentlemen. I felt therefore how safe the Cause of the South, or any portion of the South would be in your hands; and eager to read your articles, I at once wrote to the Proprietors of "*T.D*" requesting them to mail copies to me.

Last eveng by an odd co-incidence I chanced to receive the "Democrat" with the *first* of your essays, & this I read aloud to my wife. [3] We were *both* particularly impressed by the lucid power, the calmly (& most *properly*) superior authority of tone & information, the effective sarcasm, and conclusive argumentation of the whole performance;— and now we impatiently await the appearance of article number *two*.

It is right, it is *imperative* that a man of your exalted social, & intellectual position, should thus vindicate the character of his People, against attacks from men who are far more dangerous than any *aliens* could possibly be, *because such persons* are *aliens* in *heart, soul,* affection, & principle, while pretending to be "to the manner born."

Mr James Randall (from whose "Chronicle" article I have already quote*d*) proceeds in the same editorial to observe:[4]

"Judge Gayarré is indeed the proper person to expose & confound Cable, & he will perform the task in an incomparable way.

"It is one of the sarcasms of Fate that a novel like his '*Fernando De Lemos,*' a masterpiece of fact & fancy, should *not* be as popular as the mendacious jargon of Cable!"

I have unluckily *never* had the pleasure of reading this work.

Will you kindly tell me *where* I can procure a *copy?*[5]

And now please believe me,

> *my dear Sir,*

>> Most Respectfully, and Cordially Yours,
>> Paul H. Hayne
>> PO Box 275 Augusta Georgia

1. Gayarré (1805–1895), the historian from Louisiana and a member of several distinguished French and Spanish families, had served his state as legislator, judge, and writer. Hayne had mentioned him on occasion in his correspondence but presumably had never written him before. Part of this letter has been printed by Charles Anderson in "Charles Gayarré and Paul Hayne: The Last Literary Cavaliers," in David K. Jackson (ed.), *American Studies in Honor of William Kenneth Boyd* (Durham: Duke University Press, 1940), 226.

2. The "paragraph" in the *Chronicle and Constitutionalist* appeared in the issue of January 15, 1885. Cable's "miscegenation screed" is a reference to "The Freedman's Case in Equity," *Century,* XXIX (January, 1885), 409–18.

3. Gayarré's first article appeared on January 11 in the Sunday edition, and the second came out a week later on January 18.

4. James Ryder Randall (1839–1908), the author of "Maryland, My Maryland" and editor of the Augusta paper, held views of Cable similar to those of Hayne and Gayarré.

5. *Fernando de Lemos* (1872) was out of print. Gayarré wrote on January 23 to say that he himself did not even have a "single" copy. "It was," he added, "a great success as to reputation, but not financially."

87

To Margaret J. Preston   MS Duke

> *"Copse Hill," 22nd Jan 1885*

My Dear Friend;

Many thanks for your several remembrances to us at Xmas. We enjoyed the *Ruskin* Book, & *Willie* begged me to thank you also, (just before he left home for Montgomery—) for your kind thought of him.

It was so like you to mark the Taylor poem re-published in "*The London Lit World.*"[1]

We enjoy the reading of—these papers.

Then again I have to thank you for "The *Home Journal,*" with your *particularly beautiful* Sonnet "*Attar of Roses.*"

And *now* in behalf of my *wife, son* & *self*, please accept every loving wish for your happiness & good health during the year just opened.

I *do* trust that your eye sight is none the *worse*.

Please pardon my use of the pencil, as I am quite sick *again*, just recovering slowly from 3 attacks of *Throat hemorrhage*; the *1st* on the 28*th* Dec;—which prevented our going to Atlanta,—where large preparations had been made to celebrate my birthday. First, a dinner was to have been given us, (to which the guests were already invited—). The Art & Literary Club had prepared an entertainment, & there were to be social parties given during the period of our stay—[2]

On my birthday—(among other presents,) was a Sonnet to me, from *Philip Marston*, which Minna will copy for you. *En passant*, in his last letter, he says, "when you write *Mrs. Preston* next, please give her a scolding for not calling at *Euston Square*, where so many Americans come, in whom I am *not* interested. There is something *ghastly* in your *dear* friend being so near me, & not calling."[3]

I also heard from Miss Jean Ingelowe [*sic*] (on my birthday)—. She says, "I dare predict that your 'memorial' upon *Chas Reade* will be a favorite among your poems."[4]

She likes the *structure* of the piece—and "it appears to me," she adds, "a new thought to produce the *characters* of an author's writing in a *kind* of *pageant.*"

"I am (Miss Ingelowe further observes) altho you have naturally not heard it, *writing another* book. I suppose my Publisher will print it. But he will not have a fortnight's possession of it,—for it is sure to be *pirated* in *many forms*. I *shall*, of course, have no *pecuniary* reward; and not the pleasure of coming out in a pretty *lasting* form. It is not really worth any one's while to spend so much time over *my* books, at least in the first year—, they being sure to be taken at once (a *sentence* I don't comprehend). I'm thinking to spend the *whole* winter at home in *London*; if I go away for three or four months in the year it breaks up our family circle so much.

"If all is well, my next book (*another vol of poems*) will come out next spring. These poems are very various in length & style. I *hope* they may be liked; but it is always a doubtful experiment to let a good many years go by, & *then* come forward again &c!" What a *modest* woman our Lincolnshire Poetess is!—With all her genius she seems to have the simplicity of a *frank hearted* child! And her kindliness of nature is manifested by abundant charities to the London poor! Let me revert here to your Sonnet, "*Attar of Roses*"—It has for me a *peculiar* charm. *What is* this charm? Well! I think it consists of a certain blending, in this *exceedingly* artistic piece, of a noble *rhythmical* "rounding," (which in the *last* line, reminds one of the swell of a wave as it breaks upon the beach), with the richest sensuous color, & suggestion.

"*Attared my thousand roses into one!*" lingers on the ear, dying gradually away, like the echo of the billow which exhausts itself along a shore, unscourged by any wind!—[5]

Did you chance to read in a recent number of the "*the Century*," the article by Mr. Geo. Cable, upon what he styles *the Freedman's Case in Equity?*

This *infamous* essay, in which a *Yankee* of *much* cleverness, (who because he chanced to *be born* at the South, calls himself a Southerner), undertakes to arraign the whole South for brutal maltreatment of the Freedman,—and in *effect, advocates miscegenation,*—has been answered superbly by Judge *Chas. Gayarré* of *New Orleans*, who handles Cable "without gloves," shows his utter *ignorance* of the People (Creoles) of whom he slanderously wrote, in the *first* instance, and *supreme incapacity*, in the *second* place, to treat of so *momentous* a topic as the relations of the *two* Races (negro & white), at the South. Judge Gayarré, among other things, comments upon the imperative need of true statesmanlike logic, calm judgment, supreme, impartial reasoning in a question, the puzzling details of which might well bring any but a fanatical, one-sided arrogant Iconoclast to pause, & really *think* before he speaks. The harm that fellow *Cable* has done to the South cannot be estimated. He encourages *Renegadism* of every kind, and has evidently a large following among members of what I believe is called "*the New South.*"[6]

But I must conclude.

The weather here is *dreadful. Sleet, wind,* and a penetrating dampness which goes into one's very bones!—Were it not for the rich, resinous reserves of our fat *light-wood,* what *could* we do?

Best love from my *"winsome Marrow,"*—Kindest remembrances to the *Colonel,* & to your *sons,* & Believe me, as Always

Faithfully & affectionately,
Paul H Hayne.

1. It is not clear whether the poem in the *Literary World* is Mrs. Preston's "Prince Deucalion," collected in *Colonial Ballads* (1887) or Hayne's "To Bayard Taylor Beyond Us," collected in *PCE,* 320–21.

2. The plans and preparations had been arranged largely by two friends and admirers, Charles W. Hubner (1835–1929), journalist, editor, and poet, and I. W. Avery, secretary to Governor Alexander H. Stephens, lawyer, and soon-to-be editor of the Atlanta *Evening Capitol.*

3. Hayne had previously remarked on Mrs. Preston's failure to visit Marston in Letter 83.

4. Jean Ingleow was also a friend of Mrs. Preston's. See Letter 83, n. 2.

5. "Attar of Roses" is collected in *Colonial Ballads* (1887), 11.

6. See also Letter 86 and subsequent letters for more castigation of Cable.

88

To Charles Gayarré   MS Duke

"*Copse Hill,*" *Jan. 27th 1885*

My Dear Sir:

Your most courteous & interesting letter of the 23*rd* inst. reached us last evng, & its perusal gave us (I mean my wife & self), the greatest pleasure.[1]

Mr*s* Hayne read your communication aloud, & when she came to the sentence in which you express your "gratification that Mrs. H had favored with a smile of approbation the aged knight who has ventured to couch his lance against so vigorous an adversary as the standard bearer of Africa," she exclaimed, "oh! *this* is old time courtesy which is fast departing from our So land! Do remember me cordially to 'the ancient knight,' & tell him I hope that many years may be added to his useful, & illustrious life!"

Touching your *second* article to the "*Times Democrat,*" as far back as the 17th Jan, I wrote to the Editors requesting that this 2nd article should be mailed me when it appeared; and later on I sent an *original* poem "To the New South."[2]

To neither communication have they made *any* response; & therefore, I have failed to see the conclusion of your reply to Mr. Cable.

Could you kindly have it sent to me? *Apropos*, I mail you "*the Lit World of Boston*," (recd this morning).

You *might wish to reply* in the same Journal. (At *your leisure*, would you kindly return "*The World*," as I keep numbers of this weekly filed).

I have read with peculiar sympathy all you have so kindly told me as to your productions.—*Verily*, there *is* "*luck*" in these matters. A strange element of *chance does* enter into Literature & literary fame. All History shows *this*.

An author with certain popular *qualities*, of vast *comparative* inferiority as to genius & art,—may not only outstrip his superior, in temporary *repute*, but sometimes be *permanently* elevated to a place greatly *beyond* his deserts! I am *very* glad you mentioned the names of the Publishers of your "*Aubert Dubayet*" so that I can now procure that work.[3] I *don't* wonder, of course, at your "sending the fellow who offered you *$10,000 per annum* for degrading your endowments & manhood, to 'Jericho'"!! If you had sent him to the *Devil*, I think it would have been, like *Uncle Toby's* oath, forgiven you!!

I cannot exaggerate the feeling of pride & pleasure with which I correspond with a *time-honored Southerner* like yourself.

All the most-sacred memories & associations of the *Past* come over me as I write. *How can* we,—you & I—and all persons of the *old regime* fail to regard with contempt the flippancy and irreverence of too many of our "younger South" *brethren*? *Brethren* alas! only in name. Here is a Sonnet which explains itself.

The Renegade
A glorious Cause! true! but the Cause lies dead!
Most like an outstretched Titan, gaunt & pale,
With awful sightless eyes, and shattered mail,
Lax limbs supine & earth-recumbent—head:
O kingly form! no more disquieted,
While loyal thousands thy dark doom bewail,
One traitorous knave hath only tongue to rail
And mock the vows his own false lips had said:
How *once* he feigned, yea! flattered, fawned & lied,
For gifts that shone in that frank liberal hand
Now for spent blessing his dead Lord is banned,—
Past blindness mourned,—his *mêa culpa* cried,—
Blithely he joins the Conqueror's proud command,
And Stentor-Judas, shouts *on victory's* side![4]

I wish that I could write you more at length; but I am a *great physical sufferer.*

Only believe that I shall *feel inexpressibly honored & gratified*, if you can find time to correspond *sometimes* with

Yours most Faithfully &
Reverently
Paul H Hayne.

PO Box 275 Augusta Geo.

1. Much of Gayarré's letter of January 23 is printed in Anderson, "Charles Gayarré and Paul Hayne," 226–27. "Commendation bestowed on me," he observed, "derives its value from the source whence it comes. The clear and sparkling stream that flows from the mountain top has always been the most pleasant to my eye."

2. Hayne received the "2nd part of the . . . reply to Cable" from Gayarré himself and read it to Mrs. Hayne. See Letter 89. The poem appeared in the *Times-Democrat* in March, 1885, and later in *Dixie*, I (September, 1885), 51. The poem itself is reprinted in John A. Carter, "Paul Hayne's Sonnet 'To the New South,'" *Georgia Historical Quarterly*, XLVIII (June, 1964), 193–95.

3. *Aubert Dubayet* (1882), another novel, is a "complement," according to Gayarré, to *Fernando de Lemos.*

4. This text of the sonnet should be compared with that in Letter 85.

89

To Charles Gayarré　　　　　　　　　　　　　　　　MS Duke

"Copse Hill," Geo Feb. 4th 1885

My Dear Sir,

I recd (and was proud & glad to receive) your interesting letter of the 30th ult. with enclosure. The 2nd part of the Cable article, or rather the reply to Cable, I read aloud to my wife last night, and had you been present, I think you would have been satisfied with the style of its reception. It is in *every* particular, equal to the *first*—equal in logic, acumen, illustration, cool contemptuous irony, and a species of flashing sarcasm that withers where it strikes.

The deep, quiet scorn, with which you, (a Gentleman & Scholar of the *ancien régime*) cannot but regard this presumptuous *parvenu*, who dares dictate to the *South*, who upon the strength of certain lying fictions, talks in "*King Cambyses' vein* to us," declaring that we *must do* this, & that, according to *his Sovereign* pleasure,—is apparent in every paragraph, & is (*me judice*) *just* the tone, the *proper* tone to take.

One thing only I regret, *viz*, that your masterly answer did not appear in the columns of "*The Century*," so that it might have had a circulation equal to that of the slanderous "screed" of your Adversary.

Possibly had you sent it there the mag*n* which seems inclined to put this fellow Cable, after the fashion adopted towards clever *Monkeys* in zoological gardens, would have refused it; still the chance was worth trying,—& such a refusal might have been *utilized* as affording proof of the *animus* against us![1]

This Country is verily in a miserable condition. I *don't* believe that these Yankees will ever feel otherwise than intense hatred towards the South—We are essentially different People, and why in the mysterious providence of God, we were allowed to be conquered by them is to me the puzzle of puzzles.

My very *faith* is *sometimes* shaken by it, & I think of Napoleon's or *some* Conqueror's aphorism about "Providence being always on the side of the *heaviest artillery*!"[2]

Rather jubilant *at first* upon hearing of Cleveland's election, I am cooling off sadly. The Democratic triumph, (after all, won "by the skin of their teeth," as "Job" says), will prove but a *slight* transient drag upon the downward wheel of Republicanism, or I prefer to say, "*Mobocracy*"!

"*Licence, they* mean, when they cry . . . liberty!"

As a slight sign of the times, a straw showing which way the corrupted tide is flowing please, *My Dear Judge*, glance over the printed paragraph (from some Phila journal), enclosed.

The *Blaine Campaign* for 1888, has already begun you perceive.

By the way, the longer I live, the less do I believe in what are called "free Governments," at all events, Governments of the *People*.

Here is my honest conception of *Vox Populi vox Dei.*

> *Once*, on a donkey heaven's miraculous choice
> Wise speech bestowed beyond the brute born masses;
> *Now, is* it heaven that gives such potent voice
> Not to *one* Balaam's ass, but countless . . . asses?[3]

I never dreamed that the article in "*The Literary World*" had been penned by *Cable*, or need I say that I would not have mailed it to you. "The *black man & Brother*" is not merely admitted into Yankee journals, however; even N*o* hotels are opening their doors to his odorous & odious presence.[4]

The "*NY 5th Avenue Hotel*," (for mere political purposes of course,—that Hotel being the head-quarters of *Republican Committees*, &c) allows any number of negroes to sit at its tables, to sleep in its choice rooms, to perfume the atmosphere *anywhere*, and *everywhere*! And in this den of corruption & Sans Culottism, it is reported that Pres. Elect Cleveland, designs to stay, as a Boarder, for 10 *days en route to Washington*!

Comment is superfluous!

In your 2nd Cable article, you quote a verse from "one Thompson," who like Mr C——, regards the "Idol" of *Slavery* with *abhorrence*!! Said Thompson (whom I know personally & who is unquestionably a man of brilliant talent) proclaims himself a Southerner *par excellence*;—one who *fought for the South & loves the South, and* of course only wants to purge & purify her—, Well! it is a curious fact, that turning over the pages of "The Cambridge Book of '*Prayer & Song*,'" I come upon this *statement. "—Thompson Maurice—Born, Fairfield Indiana, Sep 9th 1844.*"[5]

When "Aubert Dubayet" comes, I shall read it with avidity, if possible (ie, if my throat allows, for I suffer from *hemorrhages*), I shall read it to my wife; and then tell you "frankly," as you do me the *great honor* to request, "what I think of it." I have a conviction that the work will prove of special *interest*.

You may remember that about 2 years ago, Mrs. Harriet Beecher Stowe, ("Bitcher Spew," as my friend across the seas, *Charles Algernon Swinburne* calls her), celebrated her 70th birthday, by inviting various persons North & South to burn incense upon the altar of her enormous vanity!—or at least her Publisher did it for her. *Cable*, (as you remark in effect), promptly responded. He absolutely *gushed* over her "*Uncle Tom*," & drivelled about his love, reverence & admiration of N. England.[6]

Some other persons of mark, at the South, (shameful to say!), threw themselves "upon the marrow bones of their souls," before this wretched old woman!—

It may amuse you to read certain verses I composed on that occasion, *not published* of course—& for obvious reasons never to be published. I enclose them![7] You say, towards the close of your letter "that you will always be happy to hear from me, whenever I am disposed to write &c!" I am *sure this* inclination will come upon me *often*.

Indeed, I cannot exaggerate my satisfaction at having formed your acquaintance as a Correspondent,—even at the 11th hour! We of the "*Old South*," have need, *God* knows, to stand by each other *staunchly*. The *new Generation* hardly comprehends us. May not *each of us* say with "King Arthur's last knight, *Sir Bedivere*,

> "and I go forth companionless,
> And the days darken round me, & the years,
> Among new men, strange faces, other minds."[8]

My *wife* joins me in the *best regards*. As before intimated, she keenly *appreciates*—profoundly admires your articles on Cable.

Ah! our women of the *grand old Confederacy*, how much truer they h*ave been*, and *are, than the men*! May God preserve you, honored old Southerner, *sans peur et sans reproche*, & believe me,

Faithfully Yours,
Paul H *Hayne.*
P.O. Box 275, *Augusta Geo.*

[At top of page 1 of this letter:]

Under the *first* feelings of triumph of G. Cleveland's election I wrote a poem (in view of his inauguration) of a *hopeful* kind. It may appear North; but I *feel gloomy* now.[9]

1. Henry W. Grady (1850–1889), editor of the Atlanta *Constitution*, was asked to prepare a reply to Cable and his "In Plain Black and White" came out in the *Century* for April, 1885, but Hayne and Mrs. Hayne characterized it as "logically defective on several points." See Letter 94.

2. This statement has been expressed in several ways, but it may ultimately derive from Voltaire: "On dit que Dieu est toujours pour les gros bataillons." *Lettres*, to Le Riche, February 6, 1770.

3. This quatrain has previously been quoted in Letters 80 and 81.

4. Hayne has apparently misunderstood Gayarré's observation in the letter of January 30. Gayarré did not say that Cable had written the article in *Literary World*, "The New Orleans of George Cable," XVI (January 24, 1885), 29–30.

5. Thompson had indeed been born in Indiana, but he had relatives in Georgia, lived there as a boy and young man, and served in the Confederate army for three years.

6. Swinburne in a letter to Hayne of May 2, 1877, referred to Mrs. Stowe as Mrs. Bitcher Spew—the letter is printed in Lang (ed.), "Swinburne and American Literature," 345. Hayne is referring to Cable's letter of June 9, 1882, which declined an invitation to the party Hayne mentions and which was printed in the Boston *Evening Transcript* for June 15. In it he said: "To be in New England would be enough for me. I was there once,—a year ago,—and it seemed as though I never had been home till then. . . . I can only send you, Blessings on the day when Harriet Beecher Stowe was born." See Jay B. Hubbell, *The South in American Literature, 1607–1900* (Durham: Duke University Press, 1954), 811.

7. Since the verses enclosed with this letter have been removed, Anderson, in

"Charles Gayarré and Paul Hayne" (p. 233), has conjectured that Hayne has reference to "A Character," a poem he included in the Complete Edition, 248–85. There is no further evidence to adduce at this time, so the conjecture of 1940 still serves as well in 1982.

8. *The Passing of Arthur*, lines 404–406.

9. "Columbia" appeared in *Harper's Weekly* for March 7, 1885.

90

To Margaret J. Preston   MS Duke

Excuse Pencil!   *"Copse Hill,"* Geo
Thursday, Feb 24th 1885

My Very Dear Friend;—

Your affectionate, & *thrice* welcome letter to my wife came this ev*ng*, and I must answer it immediately.

How glad we are that the quotations from Marston's communication so deeply interested you—And I am glad also that you sent them to the literary lady you mention, who in turn has transmitted them to George *Cary Eggleston.*[1]

I am anxious that the true genius of my poor blind *friend*, one of the *noblest*, and warmest-hearted of mankind—should be known everywhere in *America*. I cannot adequately convey to you the impression of tenderness & sweetness, & large-souled geniality, which *two years'* steady correspondence with *Marston* has produced;—with a *will* of *iron* he combines the gentleness of a girl![2] We rejoice to learn that you are about to test the *Type-Writer*; but on the other hand, it *shocks* us to have you speak of the return of that *deafness* you mentioned some years ago.[3] God in his mercy grant that *this* affliction may be spared you!!

I can't help saying again how we wish that you were near enough to enjoy *all* our *English* letters.

Have just had a *charming* & characteristic letter from Wilkie Collins, a most *affectionate* one too; & often I hear from Rich. D. Blackmore, the author of *"Lorna Doone,"* a noble Christian Gentleman; and in my opinion, the *grandest-novelist* at present in *Britain.*

Collins, tells me he has begun a new novel;—and oh;, I musn't forget—to mention that Miss *Ingelow*, (in a recent epistle), informs me that she will have a new vo*l* of verse out next spring.

(By the way, I told you that (*did I not?*) in my last letter)—[4]

I wrote a few rhymes upon Tennyson's acceptance of the *Peerage* &

rec*d* a *courteous* acknowledgment from him. The piece has lately come out in "*Home Chimes*," a London Mag*z recently* started by *F. W. Robinson*, the distinguished *Novelist*—[5]

You ask if I don't "envy" sometimes the "*London Literati*," and the aesthetic atmosphere in which they dwell? *Yes, I do*, but then, the thought occurs to me, that the *great God* knows what is *best* for his *children* and that you may be *right* in believing I am better off—well! just *where* I chance to be!

Many thanks for your fine *sonnet* upon "*Cripplegate Church*;" which has affected me deeply; and in another way, your *Randolph poem* has been greatly enjoyed.

Nothing short of death, I *truly* think will *ever* destroy your *exquisite poetical* genius;—& verily Death, when one reflects, will *not* have the power to do *that!*

"*Emigravit*"!—as once you said of a great German artist;[6] the *power* will only be transferred above!!

It has been my fortune during the last *two* years to form the *acquaintance* of one of the *most extraordinary* men, in America; (viz) ex-Chancellor A. A. Lipscomb of Athens G*a.*

About 68 old [*sic*], he has *twice* honored me with a *visit*, and I sincerely wish you could have been here, to listen to his eloquent, suggestive, powerful talk!—[7]

Odd to say, while the Yankee *Publishers* know comparatively little of his enormous scholarship, & wonderful original genius, the *London Publishers* are *better informed.*

Kegan & Paul are now printing certain essays of his.

Did you ever meet with his work, called "*The Forty Days*"?—A marvellous performance, worthy of the subtle Englishman, the Rev. *F. W. Robinson*!![8]

I presume *Harper* sends you his publications;—at all events, you see his "*Weekly*," & "*Monthly*"—

Please glance over the "Weekly" for the 4th March. I shall have a lyric therein upon the *Presidential Inauguration*, which I would like you to read.[9] It embodies my *first ardent hopes*, when the news of the Democratic triumph came! But alas! those hopes are *sadly* modified *now!*

I *begin* to despair of this Republic.

No *one* man, (were he a Titan), can turn back the tide of ruin & corruption!

Write when you can, oh, my friend.
Your letters are very *precious* to *us.*
With the *tenderest love* from my Minna,—

Ever affectionately yours,
Paul H Hayne.

1. George Cary Eggleston (1839–1911), a native of Indiana whose family had migrated from Virginia, had fought with the Confederate army and had written *A Rebel's Recollections* (1874). For a decade Eggleston had served as literary editor of the New York *Evening Post* and from 1884 to 1889 he was editor-in-chief of the New York *Commercial Advertiser.* For Marston, see Letter 87.

2. Hayne had actually been corresponding with Marston since 1879; he presumably means that the correspondence had been steadier in the past two years.

3. Mrs. Preston had been having difficulty with her eyes for years, and now she was also having to deal with approaching deafness. Eventually she became almost blind *and* deaf. The reference to the typewriter, by the way, suggests that Mrs. Preston was coming a bit late to this useful addition to the writer's tools of the trade, for Marston had begun to use it in 1881.

4. See Letter 87.

5. The text of "Lines on Tennyson" is included in Hayne's letter of February 29, 1884, to Lipscomb (not included here, but see Letter 85, n. 4). F. W. Robinson, the editor, by the way, should not be confused with F. W. Robertson, the clergyman. Hayne often writes *Robinson* when he means *Robertson* (see n. 8 below). On June 12, 1884, Robinson had written Hayne that he would be pleased to print "Lines on Tennyson" in *Home Chimes,* but that he could not pay for verse. Since Hayne had been "free-listed" with the magazine since April 15, 1884, he apparently gave the poem to Robinson gratis.

6. "Emigravit" (collected in *Cartoons* [1875], 56–58), is a lyric celebrating Albrecht Dürer, of whom it was said that he was "not dead, / only gone hence."

7. Lipscomb visited the Haynes in September, 1884, and February, 1885. He saw them for the last time in Augusta in March, 1886. Actually the correspondence had begun with Lipscomb's letter of January 25, 1884.

8. *Studies in the Forty Days Between Christ's Resurrection and Ascension* (1884). *Robinson* is a slip of the pen for *Robertson.* The F. W. Robinson mentioned should, of course, be F. W. *Robertson.*

9. "Columbia." See Letter 89, n. 9.

91

To A. A. Lipscomb   MS Duke

"Copse Hill," Geo
Tuesday 3rd March 1885

My Beloved Friend,

This morning I sent you a P.C. acknowledging the reception of your delightful letter of the 27th ult, & also the reception of a copy of *the "Wesleyan Christian Advocate"* with your *incomparable* article upon *"Copse Hill."* [1] *Again,* oh! best & gentlest of Friends, allow me to express my deep, *heart-felt* gratification at such a paper as this.

In point of style, of critical analysis, of a profound conception of the true uses of Poetry it is worthy the columns of the ablest periodical in the world. And verily, had I ever failed to gain recognition as a Poet *elsewhere, such appreciation* as yours would be equally a consolation & delight.

You have given to both my *"Mary Unwin"* [2] & myself, one of the keenest & purest delights our lives *have ever* experienced.

Yes, we missed you, (I cannot say how much) after your departure. [3] Every now & then I would turn round, as if to address you, & there occurred a sort of mental & moral blank, when I encountered instead of your venerable & beaming countenance, only the *empty* air!

About the *cutting* down of literary prices this year, it would seem as if *authors* are merely called upon to share the consequence of a *general depression* in business. [4] *Why* this (ie) the "general depression" is, I cannot tell.

That you think I am "growing in power & popularity" is pleasant eno' to hear.

As regards our Countrymen of the South, I believe this to be absolutely *true—,* I mean as to the *"popularity."*

Thank heaven for the same.—You are correct in what you say of the *costliness* of my "Complete Edition." [5]

But that the *Lothrops* will be persuaded to issue another & cheaper edition I much doubt. Nous *verrons,* however! [6] I hope that your own very modest wishes as to an *income* [are] sufficient to remove *anxiety;* and likewise in reference to *literary* occupations may be granted.

Entre nous, I would *not* be surprised altho I can't say positively— if you recd some special offers to become Contributor to certain No periodicals of repute.

You "look for my complete success in the Gordon poem." Alas & alas! I have by no means reached the Standard of excellence at which I aimed. Far from it! There are imperfections, artistic blunders, commonplaces of thought & phrase, I'm afraid. But this lyric came hot from the *heart.* It is enclosed for your examination & *candid criticism.* *"Give it fits"* (as the boys say), if it deserves such treatment. [7]

I am profoundly despondent at times touching my verses.

O! God! how the *fair ideal* recedes & recedes!! To grasp its *fiery skirts* may be possible; but to clasp *Itself* 'tis of all human efforts the vainest, & there is the torture of *Tantalus* in this!!

Concerning *Gordon*, as *man & hero*, you are perfectly *right*. I did not mean to affirm that he was a "*reproduction*" of England's "*ancient times*" in any other respect than a certain *straight-forward mediaëval fervor of simplicity.*

That he was "*ready* to die" is unquestionable; *ready!* nay—! he was *anxious to die*, as many passages in his Correspondence show.

How could it have been *otherwise?* Here was a man struggling, fighting, *agonizing* to perform, too *often*, the *Impossible*; because his *Duty* had him in the direction of attempting the amelioration of Barbarians, who comprehended him not; and the establishment of an *authority* which crumbled to the dust, so soon as he was forced to turn his back!!

But his majestic *Christian example* must remain *forever!*—

I am glad you have lately had the opportunity of meeting with the *true* Philanthropist, & generous gentleman Mr. George Seney.[8]

He is worthy of *all* respect & *gratitude.*

I have been able, *thus* far, to see only a few extracts from Daniel's *Oration* upon *Washington*; but those are very fine. Daniel has unquestionable genius; & originality.[9]

One image of his (the image wherein he speaks of the "*mirror of admiration*" in which we view Washington, being broken into fragments, & *every fragment* nevertheless, *presenting a perfect* character &c) is magnificent.

Yesterday a very agreeable letter reached me from *Hamilton W. Mabie* of the "*C. Union*," a perfect gentleman & truly vigorous writer.[10] What a contrast to that *old dog Beecher*; [?][11] hypocrite, who once dominated the same journal!

With renewed love & thanks from my wife for *all your* generous kindness to her *Husband*, I *am Ever Faithfully* and affectionately yours,

Paul H Hayne.

(P.S.) I think that I failed to thank you for your *generous words* in the Macon paper as to myself & the poem called "*Unfaith*."[12]

My heart is overflowing in view of all these lovely things, coming not only from your *head*, but from your noble *heart*.

[At the top of page 1 of this letter:]

Hardly worth while sending a MS copy of the Gordon piece, since I hope 'twill soon appear in "*Independent*."

1. The *Advocate* was published in Macon, and the article appeared in late February, according to Lipscomb's letter of February 27. The paper with "my humble tribute . . . the offering of my heart" has "just come." "Every word," he added, "is out of my soul." On the anniversary of his first letter to Hayne, Lipscomb had written on January 24, 1885: "You have revived my interest in life. You have been a lesson and an inspiration to my heart, and I am the stronger intellectually and the better spiritually, because of the year's close fellowship with you."

2. Lipscomb frequently referred to Mrs. Hayne as "Mary Unwin," a salute to her character based upon William Cowper's Mary Unwin, the subject of his touching poem, "To Mary" (1793).

3. Lipscomb had visited Copse Hill from February 12 through 16. He wrote Hayne upon his return to Athens on February 17: "Thanks to kind Heaven for that visit—thanks for the gloomy weather that shut us in-doors so closely—thanks for all we shared together through five days of unremitted blessing to my heart! The visit is technically over, but it can never be over to me."

4. Hayne had written Lipscomb on February 24 that "one of the very best of my Editorial friends" (R. W. Knott, editor of the *Home and Farm*) had written that 1885 would "be a miserably poor time, especially for poetry! Our own moderate income," Hayne added, "is sure therefore to be sadly cut down."

5. The price of the regular cloth binding was four dollars; there were, of course, other, more expensive bindings, with the most expensive being morocco for ten dollars.

6. Hayne had already written Daniel Lothrop about a cheaper edition, and Lothrop had replied on June 25, 1884, that the sale "has been quite limited" and postponed consideration of another edition until the sale improved.

7. Hayne had mentioned in his letter to Lipscomb of February 24 that he was "trying to complete a lyric upon the *death of* [Chinese] *Gordon*. The *general Idea* is clear eno before me, but how shall I clothe it in proper *rhythmical flesh* & *blood*!!" Charles George Gordon (1833–1885) died at Khartum January 26, 1885. The poem appeared in the *Independent*, as Hayne announced to Lipscomb in a letter of March 9, 1885, that it had "just been published."

8. George I. Seney (1826–1893), New York banker, art collector, and philanthropist, contributed to the support of Lucy Cobb Institute, a school for girls in Athens, Georgia.

9. John W. Daniel (1842–1910), U.S. senator from Virginia, delivered an oration at the dedication of the Washington Monument in February, 1885.

10. Mabie (1845–1916) was a member of the editorial staff of the *Christian Union*, a periodical Henry Ward Beecher (1813–1887), brother of Harriet Beecher Stowe and well-known preacher, had established in 1870 and edited until 1881.

11. Left blank in the manuscript.

12. "Unfaith" had also appeared in the *Wesleyan Christian Advocate*, Macon, Georgia, in early March. The poem had first appeared in the *Andover Review* for January, 1885.

92

To A. A. Lipscomb   MS Duke

"Copse Hill" March 16th 1885
(*Night*!)

My Dear Friend,

You are surely a wonder to me; a wonder of goodness, no less than genius. Verily I have never encountered in my life of 55 years before, nor do I expect to encounter again, *such* a *friend*, as you have shown *yourself* to be!

I hope someday to prove my gratitude & appreciation practically.

Both your letter & P.C. received. We grieve to hear of your sickness—especially of the bad cold being complicated with "fever"—

Take care of yourself. Do *not* work *too* strenuously. Here you are, on my account, despatching copies of the Letter, (the *great Letter* I call it), all over the Country, and actually composing additional notices of "Copse Hill,"—for I feel tolerably sure that beautiful article in the Richmond paper, is by your hand, & yours only.[1]

Impromptu, or not, your *sonnet* is very successful.

I *don't* say this, *because* the piece was written to me; but because I really & honestly so consider it.[2]

Would like to see your lecture on LEL.—Years on years ago, I remember reading her verses; but finding the sad life she led, & its melancholy *denouement* more interesting than her poetry; which seemed to me deficient in *backbone*;— As a *writer* don't you think her about as dead now,—as—well—as

> "dead as the bullrushes round little Moses
> On the old banks of the Nile"?

The interest in her fate, so full of pathos & a species of mystery buoyed up—so to speak—her verses for a season, but I doubt if they can be said to have entered into the permanent warp & woof of English Literature. Poor girl! She was but a girl after all!—What a destiny was *hers*![3]

You refer to the manner in which Editors have discouraged you. Inexpressibly provoking! but my *friend*, not only are two-thirds of them no detectors of real merit; but as Middlemen, or Agents, acting for the interest of Publishers, they continually fix their eyes upon mere marketable, or popular qualities in the articles considered.[4]

Another thing!— The depression in trade & general business, has assailed Literature. Did I tell you?, a portion, (one half or two thirds)—

of my own poor literary income is to be cut off during the present year by a radical change in the policy of the "*H & Farm*" which paid me far better than any other journal *whatsoever*.

They have suddenly & unexpectedly so reduced their prices, that I cannot continue writing for them at all.[5] It seems hard.—

But "*che sera sera!*"—

Tuesday Mch 17th 1885

Thus far I had written in pencil last night. Now, let me resume, my letter;—and congratulate you with *all* my soul (*of course Mary Unwin* joins in this congratulation) upon the 3rd edition of "*the Forty Days.*"[6]

A *signal triumph this*! That a work of the profound philosophical, & metaphysical nature of the "*Forty Days*," should have run up to a 3rd Edition in a few months, should indeed encourage you *beyond measure*.

A delightful circumstance that, of the letters from a "French gentleman in the interior of France!"

Did he write you in his own language or ours? Very seldom can his Countrymen command the English tongue.

Tell me all about him & his communication if you don't mind.

The interview between Messrs Cable & Grady in *Atlanta* has an exceedingly "fishy" appearance! I cannot say I like it. But Traitors & Renegades, whom God confound!—must each "dree his weird" someday.[7]

Dante places them in the lowest & hottest portions of his "*Inferno;*"—and—rightly!

I am *so* very glad that you continue to like "Gordon" so well! It was a "burst," but unluckily there are serious typographical errors in the piece as published by "Independent," (*partly my own* fault).

Twice the Printer makes me responsible for bad grammar, and "hero" is repeated where I feel sure I must have written "*soldier*" &c &c[8]

However, when the lyric is re-published, you shall receive a *correct* copy.

"*Eric Mackay*" is a *trump*! not merely a true poet, but a true *Artist*. Three lines in his "Gordon" verses beginning

> "*And above the roar of the*
> *sixth Cascade* &c &c"

are *superb*! They ring in my ears![9]

That *"Impromptu"* I scribbled off for you, when you were here *won't* do. *Burn* it, and substitute the following.

These stanzas I would at *once* have published, but for *one* imperative *reason*: Of late you have written so much that is cordial, affectionate, & wonderfully beautiful in reference to "Copse Hill" & its inmates, that the appearance *just now* of my piece would assuredly provoke from the *charitable world* most unkindly comment.

People would say sneeringly, "behold! a *mutual admiration society*!" not comprehending the profound *sincerity* of the tie, intellectual & spiritual between us. Therefore, I *merely* send the poem to *you*, for your portfolio; *intending, of course, to publish it at the expiration of a judicious period of time. Am I not right?*[10] Mary Unwin says, that *in her heart* she composed this poem too, only *couldn't give it utterance.*

Think *last week* of my receiving a most cordial letter from Philip James Bailey, author of "*Festus*." A reply to a brief note I had written him. The "old man eloquent" was much pleased with my sincere tribute to his *genius*; & *what a genius*!![11]

Let us hope that the improvement in your cold, mentioned in the last part of your communication has progressed.

Best love from my wife.

Remembrances to your daughter.

Ever affectionately,
Paul H Hayne.

1. Lipscomb's letter about Copse Hill had appeared in the *Wesleyan Christian Advocate*, Macon, Georgia. See Letter 91, n. 1. A similar letter was published in the *Advocate* of Richmond, Virginia, and another in Nashville, Tennessee. See Lipscomb's letter of March 7, 1885, to Hayne.

2. Hayne had received Lipscomb's "tender, eloquent & *profoundly appreciated Sonnet*" on March 9. Lipscomb had characterized it as "thoroughly impromptu" in his letter of March 12 and noted also that it had appeared in the Nashville *Advocate*.

3. Lipscomb had lectured on Letitia Elizabeth Landon (1802–1836), poet and novelist, at Lucy Cobb Institute. She was well known for her novel, *Ethel Churchill* (1837).

4. Nor could Hayne forget, as he wrote Lipscomb on March 9, that "Yankee periodicals are *crowded with* contributors from England & the No. & No. Western States of America." The consequence is, he concludes: "The poor Southerner stands at the foot of the authorial class, unless he chances to be a *clever* & *unscrupulous Renegade*; *then*, he will not find it, 'a *long* cry to Loch Awe,' as the Highlanders used to say." In *Rob Roy*, Scott gives this as a "far cry to Lochow."

5. See Letter 91, n. 4.

6. *Studies in the Forty Days* had appeared in 1884. Hayne had mentioned the work in Letter 90, to Mrs. Preston, and see n. 8 under it.

7. Hayne uses this phrase to mean "fulfill his destiny."

8. See Letter 91, n. 7.

9. Eric Mackay (1851–1898), a British poet, had also written a poem on Gordon.

10. The "stanzas" are presumably the poem later called "The Guest." The lyric was subsequently subtitled "(To A. A. L.)" and published in the *Sunday School Times*, Philadelphia, XXVII (December 19, 1885), 803.

11. Bailey (1816–1902), a friend of Marston, published and revised *Festus*, a version of the Faust legend, over a period of fifty years—1839 to 1889.

93

To A. A. Lipscomb   MS Duke

"*Copse Hill*" (Thursday night 11 o'clock)
Mch 26th 1885

My Dear Friend,

Your letter of the 24th (as *ever most welcome*), has arrived. Many thanks! Only we both feel rather anxious as to your health. You were "barely able to leave your Bed," at the period of writing, & complained of unusual chilliness, despite warm clothes & good fires! Well! I don't wonder. March under the *best* conditions is a very *disagreeable* month, & under the *worst*, (such as have accompanied her this season), is intolerable—almost!—

I must hunt up a quatrain which I composed last year comparing March to *Petruchio's* "Kate," & contrasting the vixenish Creature with that lovely "Cordelia," April; you will like it—I *think*! That is a striking expression of yours (viz) "that every *man* has his *own climate*," & in a sense is perfectly true; but there can be no doubt that the "individuality," or peculiar temperament which *makes* the "said Climate," is in *its* turn curiously influenced by the more prosaic atmospheric conditions of the *material* world.

I stand amazed by the ingenuity, the complex & varied ingenuity of your suggestions in regard to the Japonica Quatrain.[1] They'll help me beyond question, to make the expression perfect.

Concerning those two pieces, "The *Welcome*" & "*Easter*," your criticisms are *thoroughly correct,* unless indeed they err on the side of leniency.

I don't think there is a spark of "genius" in either; and I would not dream of putting them into a volume. Both were written to *order* and "Pegasus in Harness," is *not* much better off, than "Pegasus in *pound*" !! Yet, *occasionally* these "*order*" *Poems,* may rise into the true Parnassian atmosphere, when the topic is thoroughly congenial. At this moment I am engaged upon a lyric of this sort, of which more *anon*. It is *inexpressibly pleasing* to hear of your daughter Mr*s* Frank Lipscomb, being so "enthusiastic" over my "complete Edition;" especially over such pieces as have a martial or dramatic tone! *Many* of these, (if I may confess the truth), are my own favorites, having been written *con amore* certainly!

Odd to say, the older I grow the more decidedly do I find my Muse turning toward topics, *purely lyrical*, battle themes,—subjects that stir the blood, & thrill the nerves, & make one feel like a Captain suddenly called upon to accomplish some deed of "*derring do*"!—Meanwhile, the more grave-mannered Muse of philosophical & moral ideas, for the *time* retires! Perhaps tis a *last flash* of youth in the pan!, or the flaring up of its expiring candle?

How can we thank you for your thoughtfulness in sending copies of the beautiful sonnet, (addressed to myself), copies so neatly printed upon separate *sheets*? Be assured, they will *always* be *deeply* prized.

Friday Morning

At 12 last night I stopped writing and gazed long into the embers of the dying fire, "revolving many memories." And the grand "Confederate Past" came before me; and I could see our armies under Lee & Jackson advancing from victory to victory, until (fatal day!) "Stonewall," (our *Napoleon* in genius, our *Cromwell* in singleness of purpose), fell;—and then, the slow, but *inevitable* End!

And my *heart* was very full, and my brain *aflame*; in a fit condition to round off, & complete a certain *lyric*, you shall receive in due season.[2]

En passant, let me return for a moment to your gifted *daughter in law*, "*your* Mary,"[3] as you so tenderly & pathetically call her & suggest her perusal of my poem on page 309 of "Complete Edition," entitled "A Plea for the Gray." Also I'd like her to read "*Cambyses & the Macrobian Bow*" (p. 116) & "A Feudal Picture" (p. 150).

If the *gifted women of* the land, especially of *the South*, begin to like my poetry, there'll be some chance of the verses surviving.

Their influence is subtle & pervading. They rule not *merely* "the Camp, the Court, the Grove," as Scott says, or sings, but often the highest realms of *art*.

The weather here continues most dreary. As I write, we hear the drip, *drip, drip* of the continuous Rain & the landscape is really funereal!

One might fancy passing slowly & sadly among the misty shadows of the desolate trees, a troop of ghosts, such as haunted the shores of *Acheron*, or wandered by the black Lethean river!

My "*Lady Mary*," (*again I thank thee* for *that* phrase!) has, with her usual infallible perseverance & skill discovered the quatrain about March & April to which I alluded.

Here it is,

> *Contrast!*
> The blustering March is like Petruchio's Kate,
> A stormy vixen, loud and passionate,—
> But April, our sweet Perdita, uprears
> A face half glimpsed 'twixt sunshine, & soft tears!

We would like to have heard your little grand daughter (Blanche) render "Major *Jones' Courtship*." The editorial comments of "*The Telegraph & Messenger*," on your *exquisite* article about "*Copse Hill*," "touched us to the quick." *Is* the gentleman who wrote it—Mr. Hanson—on the staff of the journal? Will you please give me his Christian name &c, in order that I many send my acknowledgments?[4]

My wife *will carefully* "keep" the paper for you, as desired.

Shall *I not, after all, in due time*, accept Mr. Hanson's suggestion, & *publish* the song which I have sung "of the gray hairs & white soul of our venerable Christian Rhetorician & scholar!"

Upon deep consideration it is my earnest wish to do so, & *was* my intention *unless* you *prefer it otherwise.*

You'll be absolutely candid about the matter my friend. Tell your daughter *Mrs. Green*, we vastly enjoyed her *incomparable oranges.*[5]

With warm regards to her, & love to yourself.—Always affectionately
> *Paul H Hayne.*

[On the side of the last page of this letter:] *Harper* is bringing out now, a very fine Dictionary which will serve in the place of Roget's *Thesaurus. Many thanks*, all the *same*!![6]

---

1. Hayne had sent a draft of the Japonica quatrain in a letter of March 19. Lipscomb had suggested a number of possible changes in his next letter.

2. This is the first mention of "Broken Battalions," a poem later sent to a fair in Baltimore in support of a Confederate charity.

3. Mary Rutherford Lipscomb, the wife of Lipscomb's dead son Frank, lived with him and taught elocution at Lucy Cobb Institute.

4. Harry Stillwell Edwards actually wrote the article, as Lipscomb acknowledged later in a letter of April 6.

5. Mrs. Ella Lipscomb Green had sent the Haynes a box of fruit on March 15.

6. On March 24 Lipscomb had offered to send Hayne a copy of *Roget's Thesaurus*.

94

To Charles Gayarré   MS Duke

"Copse Hill," April 1st 1885

My Dear Judge Gayarré;

I heard with pleasure of your having lectured recently in NOrleans, upon Cable's "Grandissimes," & doubtless, you scored this *Parvenu*, & colossal liar, as deeply in the Lecture as you did in your *"Times-Democrat"* paper![1]

How I wish, by the way, that you had met, & annihilated him in the columns of *"The Century"*!

Grady's reply therein, my wife has read, & pronounces *able*; but logically defective on several points; *"ah"* she observed, "the *Judge* would have made no such damaging concessions; nor "so failed here & there, in his argumentative fence."[2]

"The *School for Politics*," I read aloud to Mrs. Hayne, & we were both profoundly interested.

It is a satire surely as *brilliant*, as *true*.

The humbug & hypocrisy of American *Politics & Politicians* were never more clearly exposed.

Let me hope that you have *secured*, or may be *about* to secure the *Naval* office in NOrleans to which you previously referred.[3]

Enclosed I send a lyric upon the great & good "Gordon" for your *perusal*.[4]

And with *best* wishes, & regards from my wife, believe me

Most Faithfully and Cordially,
Paul H Hayne.
PO Box 275 Augusta Geo

1. For Gayarré's response to Cable's "The Freedman's Case in Equity," see his exchange of letters with Hayne above, beginning with Letter 86. Gayarré lectured on *The Grandissimes* (1880) in the hall of the Union Française on March 22, 1885. His view of the author of the novel hadn't changed. He "is as deprived of all moral sense as the crocodile." See Arlin Turner, *George W. Cable* (Durham: Duke University Press, 1956), 203.

2. Grady's "In Plain Black and White" is cited above in Letter 89, n. 1.

3. Gayarré did not receive the appointment to the naval office.

4. For the poem on Gordon, see Letter 91, n. 7.

95

To Charles Gayarré   MS Duke

"Copse Hill," 14th April 1885

My Dear Judge Gayarré;—

I am *touched* by the kindly interest of your letter (of April 11th) as to my health; my thanks for your cordiality & friendship.

But, how disappointing it is to learn that two, *at least*, of my communications failed to reach you!

The *first* of these referred to *"Aubert Dubayet"*; I mean to the completion, the full *denouement* of that work.[1] I told you, therein, how greatly we—my wife & self—*admired* the *entire* production; but that if ever there was a noble *concentration* of forces towards a brilliant dramatic end, made singularly effective, and vigorous, such a concentration would be found in this masterpiece of blended imagination & History.

In particular I must compliment you upon the manner in which you have, as by lightning flashes, revealed the prominent mental & moral features of your chief *"dramatis personae."*

In the *second* of my lost letters, I conveyed my thanks for *"The School of Politics;"* a brochure as brilliant, as it is *philosophical!*[2] Assuredly *you* comprehend, as very few do now-a-days, the peculiar *Genius*, (*Heaven save* the *Mark!*), which moves our political Puppets, & causes them to dance, & *attitudinize* to the *immortal* tune of *"Yankee Doodle!"*

Apropos, I remarked in the communication mentioned, how sorry I was, that being only a *secluded* scholar & writer, I had myself no *shadow* of *political influence*; that *if* such had been granted me, how *cheerfully*, nay *proudly* I would [sic] exerted it all, on behalf of the gifted Gentleman, the venerable Author, the noble *representative* Southerner, who, should—in his honored old age—, have been placed (by acclamation) in *one of the highest* offices under Government, instead of being denied a comparatively *humble* one!![3]

Well, Judge, *cui bono*? Why be discomposed? Can we make a "purse out of a sow's ear"?—

Can we convert the dirty *"frieze"* of Thos. Jefferson's *"all men are born* free & equal" (his vile *"Sans Culottism"*—) into veritable "cloth of gold"? A thousand times over, are you right in observing, that if Geo. Washington were now living, "he could not be appointed a Turnkey to jailbirds"!

I cannot exaggerate our delight at the superb success of your lectures against that *parvenu Cable*! The fame of them is singing thro the land. Even so blatant a Republican journal as the *Phila* weekly "American" is compelled by the nature & force of your reported argument, sustained by *invincible* historical illustrations, to *virtually* desert the Cable banner, and confess he is wrong!! When this lecture is published in English, you will, I am sure, *not forget* your kind promise to mail me a copy?[4]

A word here, concerning Cable's article about "*The Freedman's Case in Equity.*" *You ought* to have been selected to answer him in "*The Century*"; instead of so superficial a writer as this man *Henry Grady*. I read carefully eno' half of Grady's reply, and then put it down *disgusted*. When he concedes so much to the North as this, (viz) that they were *perfectly justified* in *abolishing Slavery*, & that we ought better to be grateful for the same—, I cry, *halte la*!![5]

On other points, he shows himself wretchedly superficial. For instance, this dreadful problem touching the Negro, & his relations to the whites of the South, M*r* G. dismisses after a somewhat airy & *insouciant* fashion!

He *actually* maintains that the *Negro* has no desire whatever towards social communion & *amalgamation*; that the Inferior Race desires to keep itself apart from the Whites &c; of course, a mere solecism!

Mr. James, of Texas, is one of the dearest friends I have on Earth, altho personally we have never met. My "Complete Edition" of Poems was dedicated to him.[6]

His article upon yourself, your works &c, we read with *deepest* interest. He is one of the *noblest* & most unselfish of men.

How *glad* I am that the Gordon lyric pleased you. It has had quite a success.[7]

The "*Inauguration poem*" appeared in Harper's weekly of the 4th or *8th* March.[8]

My "*winsome Marrow*" (to borrow that beautiful expression of old Randolph, the ancient Scottish poet)[9] reciprocates your kindly & cordial expressions & unites with me in best *possible wishes* to you, & "*her* whose life is dearer to you than your own!"

Believe me, *Now & Always*

Most Cordially, (& May I not dare to add?) affectionately

Your *friend & admirer,*

Paul H. Hayne

P.S. My son, Willie, was delighted with the visit he paid you.

1. Gayarré had expressed pleasure on January 30, 1885, after learning that Hayne had ordered a copy of *Aubert Dubayet* (1882). Hayne's reference to "the full denouement of that work" indicates that he remembers that *Dubayet* is a "sort of sequel" to *Fernando de Lemos* (1872).

2. *The School for Politics* (1854), an "opuscule" according to Gayarré, had been sent to Hayne on February 17.

3. Gayarré's application for the "naval office of New Orleans" had not been successful.

4. Gayarré also delivered the lecture as "The Creoles of History and Mr. Cable's Creoles" (it was originally given in French), and when it appeared as a pamphlet, sent a copy to Hayne on April 17.

5. Hayne had made these points earlier. See Letter 94.

6. John G. James (1844–1930), a native of Virginia, was superintendent of Texas Military Institute from 1868 to 1879 and thereupon president of Texas A & M College until 1883, when he founded a bank and became its president. He was largely responsible for the publication of Hayne's *Poems* (Complete Edition).

7. "The Gordon poem," a paean to Chinese Gordon, had appeared in the *Independent* for March 12, 1885.

8. "Columbia" had been published in *Harper's Weekly* for March 7, 1885.

9. This expression is erroneously ascribed by Hayne to Randolph on several occasions. It appears in William Hamilton's *Braes of Yarrow* (see Letter 97, n. 3).

96

To Charles Gayarré   MS Duke

"Copse Hill" Geo.
April 29th 1885

My Dear Judge Gayarré,—and if you'll permit me to add—*my dear & honored Friend*—

Your note of the 24th is before me, with the printed letter enclosed.

It is pre-eminently right & proper that your communication to the President,—so *noble* & dignified in tone,—*should* be "noticed" by *all* the Southern journals, of any real influence, or character.

The position taken in this communication touching the claims of So *literary men,* cannot for a moment be *logically* questioned.[1]

I shall write *immediately* to *Jas. R. Randall* of the *Augusta "C & Constitutionalist,"* & from my knowledge of his expressed admiration of your genius, character, & productions, I feel assured that he will comment judiciously upon your letter, and its purpose.[2]

Meanwhile, we sympathise—my wife & I—, you know not how deeply—with your feelings in reference to the trials of public lecturing;[3] but already your brilliant exposition of facts; your vindication of the truth of history; your complete subversion of the views, & exposure of the renegade meanness of the great advocate of the *"bonnêt rouge,"* nay, the *"bonnêt noir,"* in La, must prove some consolation for the pain of contending against old habits, & running counter to old associations.

Briefly, you have accomplished a vast *deal of good. Pray think of this*!

The copy of your lecture, delivered upon the 25*th ult* (in pamphlet form), we shall *eagerly* look for. We—of the *"old South"* must stand by each other. There is a horde of *mongrels*, already abroad in considerable numbers, who *would*—if they *could*—degrade alike our traditions & our manhood.

Concerning *"Columbia,"* I'm glad that you liked certain lines,—but really, I must confess that the poem was conceived & executed in a moment of natural, but rather unphilosophical enthusiasm. After 20 years I saw the *"old Democracy"* up again; & failed in my excitement to reflect that *this very Party* could no longer be what *once it was*; that indeed *Mercutio*'s cry, "a plague on *all your Parties*," befits, with *some justification*, of course, *all* the divisions of American political Power.[4]

Not merely is there "something rotten in Denmark," but this *rottenness* is becoming a "rank offence, & smells to heaven!"[5]

But I must close, *my dear Judge*, with my *wife*'s best remembrances, & *good* wishes, believe me *Always*

Cordially & Faithfully *yrs*,
Paul H Hayne.

PO Box 275, Augusta Georgia

1. As a "Southern man of letters," Gayarré had written President Cleveland on March 4 applying for the "Naval office in New Orleans." See Letter 95.

2. Randall's comment in the Augusta *Chronicle and Constitutionalist* was forwarded to Gayarré with Hayne's letter of May 8, 1885. See Letter 97.

3. Gayarré had pointed out in his letter of April 24 that "such exhibitions of my person in public are exceedingly distasteful to me and entirely foreign to my habits." As the nephew of Robert Y. Hayne, as the editor of *Russell's Magazine*, and as a spokesman for the Confederacy and representative poet of the South, Hayne had lectured on many occasions, but he seldom enjoyed the strain on his throat and lungs. In the 1880s he refused invitations to lecture or read his poems, even those prepared for public occasions such as the centennials of the Battle of King's Mountain or the incorporation of the city of Charleston or the sesquicentennial of the establishment of the colony of Georgia.

4. For "Columbia," see Letter 95, n. 8. Mercutio's characterization of Romeo and Tybalt, of course, is "a plague o' both your houses" (*Romeo and Juliet*, III, i, 103–104).

5. *Hamlet*, I, iv, 90, and III, iii, 36.

97

To Charles Gayarré   MS Duke

"Copse Hill," May 8th 1885

My Dear & Honored Friend;—

Yesterday, I sent you a P.C., acknowledging your very *kind* & touching letter to my wife; and this morning, I mailed you ("by register"), a copy of my *"Complete Poetical Works," a joint offering of love and respect* from *Mrs*. Hayne & myself, which we trust may please you.[1]

As unfortunately I was *not* allowed a correction of my *proof sheets*, (the Publishers *assuring me, however*, that they had secured a first-class set of proof Readers), a *vast* number of errors occurred. I had *"Errata"* prepared in *Augusta*, for literary *friends*, & *one* of these my wife has pasted at the end of the *vol*. The *Lothropes* [*sic*] having undertaken this publication *measurably* at their own risk, I could not dispute their will.

Mrs Hayne begs me to observe that she would reply to your deeply valued communication, but is *fearful* of intruding upon your time. She would have liked much to have been with *Mrs. Gayarré*, listening to Dr. Palmer, for whom we both entertain a *warm* admiration.[2]

How nobly, beautifully, tenderly, you write—to borrow a quaint expression of the old Scotch lyrist, Randolph—of your *"winsome* Marrow!"[3] The *very words* you employ in reference to *her*, I *could use* touching the character, *&* conduct, & life-long devotion of my own incomparable *wife*; *but for whom* I should, *long long ago, "abiit ad plures,"* have gone to join the *Majority*!

Apropos, when you read my book, I beg you to glance over the pieces, entitled *"The Bonny Brown Hand," "An Anniversary," "From the Woods,"* & *"Love's Autumn."* Let me go a trifle farther, and even have the boldness of asking you to *read them aloud* to *Mrs. Gayarré*.[4]

The mention you make of your *intimacy* with *Gilmore Simms*, is only *another*, & a powerful *link* of affectionate sympathy between us. He was old eno' to be my father, but there was no reserve in our association. For 20 years I knew him, as perhaps few others *did*; loved the man for his many *frank, manly* qualities; made every conceivable allowance for patent faults of manner, & stood by him to the *last*. (In the *Poems*, p. 315, you'll find my *Simms "In Memoriam."* I can add nothing *now* to that tribute which came *"ab imo pectore,"*[5] as *you* will at once perceive.)

By the way I have learned with intolerable disgust that some Yankee firm—*Houghton & Mifflin perhaps*, have chosen *Cable* (!) as Simms' *Biographer*,—upon the *"lucus a non lucendo"* principle, of course, which they have systematically followed *throughout*, so far as *Southern Celebrities* are *concerned*![6] Remark, how a *German*, in this connection, was made the *Biographer* of *Calhoun*!—an able man, I am told; but *how* could such *an* [sic] one by any *possibility*, possess that species of *"rapport"* with the subject of his work, that subtle sympathy, & comprehension, which are far more needful to a really vital *"Life,"* than any sum of mere outside facts. Moreover, *this* German, (if I have been correctly informed), is *par excellence* a *"Consolidationist"* &c &c.[7]

Enclosed, you will find, a paragraph from Randall's pen, in *the* Augusta *"Chron; & Con,"* touching your letter to *the President*, about which I had *specially written* to him.[8]

I *regret* that he did not say *more*, & say it very emphatically. However, his article, such as it is, has been copied in *"The Wilmington* [N.C.] *Star,"* & may go the rounds of the *Press*.

I am delighted to hear of the speedy publication of your *"Lecture upon the Creoles of La,"* & shall welcome my copy with enthusiasm. In *French*, let me confess that I cannot begin to do it justice; because my knowledge of *that* language is so imperfect; as regards delicacies of *expression*.[9]

Your plea concerning the honors due to *literary* men in any *civilized* Country, cannot be disputed;—but under the present *regime*, and indeed, under any Republican *regime—Litterateurs* are never likely to have their *deserts*.

Cleveland, whatever his virtues, is evidently a *mere Politician*; a bullheaded, determined fellow in his way, & perhaps as things go, nowadays, moderately honest;—but possessed neither of special refinement, nor *special* culture.[10]

The *only Poet* he condescends to read, I understand, is *Walt Whitman*, and his favorite *novelist* is *"Sylvanus Cobb!"*[11]

—*Basta!* surely "the d——d *literary fellows*" need not trust in *him*.

With my wife's earnest regards to *Mrs. Gayarré* & yourself; (& I beg you to remember me likewise *most sincerely* to the former),

Always *Faithfully*, and
Cordially,
Paul H. Hayne
PO Box 275 Augusta Geo.

1. In return Gayarré sent his *Philip II* (1866) and on May 13 observed: "On this occasion you will find that I am a thorough Greek" (one who allows himself to "be surpassed in generosity"), for, "in return for the refulgent gold of poetry, I send you the coarse and valueless iron of prose." Gayarré's comments on individual poems begin to appear in his letter of May 29.

2. Benjamin Morgan Palmer (1818–1902), one of the best-known Presbyterian ministers of his time, had been born in Charleston and preached there before he went to New Orleans in 1856. The Haynes had known him for many years.

3. Hayne has erred again. See Letter 95, n. 9.

4. All of these poems are addressed to Mary Hayne.

5. From the depths of my heart.

6. George W. Cable was indeed announced by Houghton, Mifflin as the author of a forthcoming volume on Simms in the American Men of Letters series; Charles Dudley Warner, the editor of the series, had asked Cable to write the book in the fall of 1881. See Turner, *George W. Cable*, 116. Cable collected materials on Simms—see Letter 105—but William Peterfield Trent, instead, wrote the book, which appeared in 1892. For Gayarré's trenchant comment, see his letter of May 29, 1885.

7. Hermann von Holst (1841–1904) took a Ph.D. at Heidelberg in 1865 and came to the United States in 1867. His *John C. Calhoun* (1882) appeared in Houghton, Mifflin's American Statesmen series while he was teaching at Freiburg.

8. See Letter 96, n. 2.

9. Gayarré's pamphlet in English was delayed, for he had stated on April 17 that he was sending the French text in "this day's mail." The text in English arrived on May 18.

10. For Gayarré's letter to Cleveland, see Letter 96, n. 1. Cleveland, of course, was a Democrat.

11. Cobb (1821–1887) was a popular writer of dime novels and fiction for such periodicals as the *New York Ledger*.

98

To Charles Gayarré   MS Duke

"Copse Hill," May 17th 1885

My Honored Judge, and dear friend;

Yours of the 13*th* just recd, is a most pathetic letter. Let me refer, in the *first* place, to your allusions to *Mrs. Gayarré*. Verily, my heart is *touched* & *warmed*, by what you tell me of her, & I think there was a mist in my own bonny little wife's eyes, when I read of your Baucis, & her devotion to her illustrious husband;[1]—such a "mist," (to use Tennyson's words in "*Enid*"), such a "*mist*"—

> "as made the heart of Eden green
> *Before the useful trouble of the Rain!*"[2]

Ah! *my friend*, you have been fortunate, *thrice* fortunate in a "helpmate" so tender, so unselfish, so altogether womanly, & sweet, & noble. If fortune frowns, old comrades turn coldly away, griefs, disappointments, tribulations, pressing more closely, morn after morn, more darkly night after night, *still* ah! still, there is precious consolation left; & you can say, as I once did, in the blackest hour of my existence,

> o'er shattered wrecks of fate,
> The relics of a happier time & state,
>   *My nobler life*
> Shines on unquenched; oh! deathless love *that lies*
> In the clear midnight of those passionate eyes;
>   Joy waneth, fortune flies,—
> What then? thou still art here, soul of *my soul, my Wife!*[3]

The welcome you give to my book is delightfully cordial. And to hear of *Mrs. Gayarré's* liking the verses, and "loving" the author on their account, *is* well!—more than charming. It is full of encouragement, and moral *stimulus*.

One point in your letter I must "join issue with;" that Homeric illustration of yours touching the *Greek* gifts! Now, the invaluable work, (*Philip II*), you have so *thoughtfully* sent me—a work long desired—, is *not* as compared with the "*gold* of poetry," "useless *iron.*"[4] On the contrary, I am *sure*, from all the testimony of scholars & historians, that it may be described in the language of the Old Chronicler applied to a certain sword presented by Francis of France to Bayard:—

"A blade of trenchant *steel*, bright as any mirrour, so inlaide, & ingrained with gold & silver, and jewels, that whiles it did looke like the sun, & [it] dazzled the eyes of beholders."

A literary task now before me, accomplished, & how gladly shall I peruse your History!

Bancroft's Preface I have already examined.[5] It is good *eno* perhaps, and yet, (*I may err,*) but yet it makes *somehow* upon my mind the impression of an "*ex Cathedra*" "screed," with just a *soupçon* of the pedagogue tone about some sentences. *He* need not speak of *your* "*over* ornamentation,*" for now & then his *own* style is absolutely *cumbrous* from superfluity of "phrases, & similes."

I presume now that you are poor he no longer condescends to address you.

My wife sends a few buds & ivy leaves to Mrs. Gayarré;—the full-blown roses are exquisite, but would crumble; & the *buds* can be *pressed* & preserved.

With affectionate regards from us both to yourself & dear wife,

Ever your *faithful friend,*
Paul H. Hayne

1. In his letter of May 13, Gayarré had referred to his wife and himself as Baucis and Philemon and had noted that Mrs. Gayarré loved Hayne because he was her husband's friend.

2. The passage from *Geraint and Enid* reads: "But o'er her meek eyes came a happy mist / Like that which kept the heart of Eden green / Before the useful trouble of the rain" (lines 768–70).

3. "From the Woods," one of the poems addressed to his wife (see Letter 97, n. 4), was written during the early days at Copse Hill and published in *Lippincott's* for May, 1868.

4. See Letter 97, n. 1.

5. George Bancroft (1800–1891), the author of a *History of the United States* (10 vols., 1834–74), had written an "introductory letter" to Gayarré's *Philip II of Spain* (1866). The subsequent reference to Bancroft's failure to "address" Gayarré is based upon Gayarré's comment to Hayne on April 17 that Bancroft had not answered Gayarré's request for support in his application for the naval office in New Orleans.

99

To Charles Gayarré   MS Duke

"Copse Hill" May 19th 1885

My Dear Friend;

I recd. last evng. your kind note with a copy of *the Lecture* on *"The Creoles of History & the Creoles of Romance,"*[1] and immediately I *made* the needful time to read it aloud to my wife & son, & a very intelligent young man now staying with us.

It is *amazing*, the *self-control*, & *coolness* you display in discussing a question which must have made your blood *boil*; the *reserve of power* everywhere apparent; the *un*-heated analytical skill wherewith you dissect Cable's mendacious *dicta*, and finally *annihilate* him upon every point of *history*, and *ethnology*.

Your People,—the Creoles *en masse*, should show their gratitude in the most *substantial* way; but alas! there is precious little of *that* commodity to be found now!

An old man is ever said to be *"laudator temporis acti"*[2] &c, yet surely one is right in pronouncing this Time *sordid* & *selfish*. In the "young South," so-called, I observe a growing tendency towards contempt for the *Past*, & a *truckling spirit*, so far as *Yankee* ideas, & *Yankee prejudices* are concerned. One thing is *certain*! If miscegenation does not occur, amalgamation of *North & South*, in b*lood*, brain, purpose, aims, *social* affinity,—everything is *inevitable*!

Aye! the "Saints" have conquered. Are they not already entering upon the possession of their *"Canaan?"* You and I are "old fogies."

So be it! At least, we will die, as we have lived—*gentlemen*!

Again, I congratulate you upon your powerful "*Lecture*." There is some satisfaction in lashing a Hound, or rather a *mongrel Cur*, altho the cowardly *beast* no doubt may be expected to sneak after his Chastiser, and bite his heel, if a safe chance should occur!

Ever Faithfully & Cordially,
Paul H. Hayne

1. This is the title Gayarré gave to the English text of the lecture. The title to the French text was "The Creoles of History and Mr. Cable's Creoles." See Letter 95, n. 4.

2. A praiser of time past (Horace, *Ars Poetica*, 173).

100

To A. A. Lipscomb MS Duke

May 24th 1885

My *Very Dear Friend*;

When I looked upon the date of your last letter (the 12th May), this morning, I could scarcely believe my eyes! But, in fact, the time has passed thus unconsciously almost, because I have had 3 literary tasks on hand, an elaborate prose paper for Knott's new mag*n*; a long narrative Child's poem for "*Wide Awake*," the Boston juvenile monthly, and finally during the 48 hours just ended, a versified "*In Memoriam*" in reference to V. Hugo.[1]

Still sick, I have tried, you perceive, to cure physical ills by mental work; *not* successfully, I admit; but nevertheless one *can thus* temporarily forget, & to a certain extent modify the pains of the body. Only *intellectual* work *mustn't* be *overdone*!, as *frankly*, I think *you are overdoing* it.

The "supplementary Chapters" to the "Forty Days," involved by necessity, an elaboration of thought, metaphysical, philosophical, psychical, which must prove terribly trying to the brain, & thence to the *nerves*.[2] Beware! my Friend! Allow no publisher to urge you unduly on. The consequences in your present condition of health may prove serious.

Evidently, this extraordinary Spring has treated you as badly as it has treated me, and indeed others in our neighborhood.

Liver & bowel afflictions are said to be common. At "*Copse Hill*" everybody has been *hors de combat*;—even my wonderfully energetic "Lady Mary" had to partially succumb, & take to *Calomel* last evening, & magnesia this morning.

There's some adverse influence in the atmosphere. God grant that it may not be the *avant Courier* of the *Cholera*, concerning which Physicians are prophecying fearful things,—declaring that it is sure to cross the Ocean, and visit America *soon*!

V. Hugo has passed away, at the age of 84!! *What* a life his has been! So full of *outward* adventure, & vicissitude, no less than of potent *inward* experiences. The impulse (as before remarked) coming strongly upon me, I composed his "In Memoriam," the night before last.[3]

We *all* were pleased to hear of your son's approaching marriage to so "excellent a young lady, so agreeable a person, charming to all your family."

He has our *best* wishes for his future.

Accept the *united love* of our small household. Whether I write, or fail to write, *always my beloved & honored friend*, understand that my *heart* is with you! There must be no *ceremony* between us. When your time is occupied, & your health is feeble, do *not dream* of exerting yourself, as my Correspondent.

You are ever with me *in spirit*.

I am reading a very remarkable work (in the intervals of composition), by Judge Gayarré of N. Orleans; (viz a History of Philip *2nd* of Spain).

Anything of the sort more dramatic, picturesque, & vigorous, cannot be found,—so far as my experience goes in the English language! The account of *Philip's death* actually made me sick at the *stomach of my* soul (& *the physical stomach too*). I had to put the book down, seek the Garden, and inhale the scent of the Bay blossoms, and roses! Otherwise, there would have been an *upheaval*!! "*Lady Mary*" *& my son* unite in love to you. Our cordial remembrances to your *daughter*, & *daughter in law*, & likewise to your son when *you* next see him.

Ever affectionately yours,
Paul H. Hayne

1. The paper for "Knott's new magazine," the *Southern Bivouac*, is presumably "Confederate War-Songs" (June, 1885); the long juvenile for *Wide Awake* is probably "The Story of an Ambuscade" (February, 1888); and the poem on Victor Hugo appeared in the *Independent* for June 11, 1885.

2. Lipscomb had written on May 12 that he had agreed to write a "series of articles, 'Essays Supplementary to the Forty Days' [his book—*Studies in the Forty Days*— appeared in 1884] for the Nashville *Wesleyan Advocate*," but that he had found it a "burden."

3. A few years earlier Maurice Thompson wrote Hayne on October 10, 1881, that he had seen an article quoting a source in the Buffalo *Express* which mentioned Hayne as

one of the American poets Hugo admired. On October 20 Thompson sent a clipping of this article from the Chicago *Times*. Subsequently, other papers quoted from the same source. On November 5, for example, Hayne received a clipping from a New Orleans newspaper.

101

To Charles Gayarré   MS Duke

"Copse Hill," July 7th 1885

My Dear, & Honored Friend;

Your affectionate letter to my wife reached us last eve*ng*.[1] I cannot postpone a response to your kind solicitude concerning my health. It is very much in *status quo* now; which means that th*o* feeble en*o*, I am permitted to *labor*.

What a benefaction!! Oh! *my friend*! discovered at the 11*th* hour, yet perhaps, the *dearer* on that account; one can bear all the ills of our mysterious existence, so long as the Imagination & the *Heart* survive—

And I am *sure* that you feel with me, that we *Knights of the Quill* would desire like the Chivalric knights of Old, rather to *fall in armor*, the bright steel of honest work,—than plunge into the "pool of Helas," or rather be *consigned* thereto, after having endured—as the Northmen need contemptuously to express it—a "*Cow's* death!"

It *is*, as you observe, "a *miserable* condition to be compelled to write for Bread;" & *more* or less, I suppose that "we of the South have been forced into this intellectual "gustapeno," since the war; and have had to pay a heavy price for the—"heaven save the mark:"—the *Privilege*!!

Yet even *thus*, "cabbined, cribbed, confined," the genuine Artist is true to himself, & his vocation!

His humblest "literary *Calicos*" may be threaded with gold!, & from the "Inkstand of the Devil," *may magically* come some glittering drops, drawn from the very hearts' blood of Apollo!

You are only too right in your estimation of the horrors of *Poverty*, especially in old age.

It afflicts us to learn that you have failed to obtain *any* position under the City or Federal Government, *you*, who have a right to d*emand* some honorable office.

And *then* to think of your being unable to leave the *City* during this heated term, with your wife!!

Alas! what can *Poverty* do, but offer sympathy to *Poverty*!!?—a *barren* offer indeed!

And to make matters *worse*, I see that you *also* are laboring under the curse *par excellence* of your age, & So Country—, the curse of *servile* insubordination, & impudence! In the face of emancipated Ethiopia, & all its terrible evils, present, & to come,—I am amazed to hear men who *haven't* the excuse of being *Idiots, prating* about the glories of "*negro* freedom," & "a' t*hat* & a' *that*" *pestilent stuff*!! Our *women*, the most *refined ladies in the land* are verily the "*slaves*" now!—while a horde of brazen ebony wenches, or nondescripts of *mixed* blood makes the world hideous with their impertinent grimaces, and monkey-like affectations!!'

Meanwhile our *wise* Southern legislators in many States oppress the whites with iniquitous taxes to furnish emancipated *Congo* with "*free education*," embracing the highest "aesthetic branches!!"

The only comfort is, (as you remark), that the said *Education* may have the same effect upon the *Negro*, which *rum* had upon the *Indian*!

Your *noble "Philip the 2nd"* I am reading aloud; to the delectation & delight of our small household circle.[2]

It is, indeed, a *great* book; picturesque as *Macaulay* at his *best*, and, it appears to *me*—with a *suggestive depth* of philosophical acumen, which Macaulay but seldom *displays*.

No *novel* or professed *romance*, was ever more brilliantly interesting! The "*dramatis personae*" live, more, are *vital* creations. And, as I think that I told you before, your analysis of the genius & character of *Philip*, is *masterly*.

The man's placid *self confidence* in the very face of death, after his demoniac life, can really be explained, *only* upon *your hypothesis*, (viz) that *he believed himself conscientious throughout*; *that* monstrous fallacy concerning "the divine *rights of Kings*," having in *his* case been exaggerated to an extent, which resulted in a sort of *cold devilish self-exaltation*;—a monstrous *Egotism*, stamped with the *fiend's* own mark!!

Before beginning to read your history *aloud*, I had perused it to the close of *Chapter V*; and then, deliberately turning back, *I reperused the whole* down to the same point.

Now, I have completed "*Chapter VI*;" and more & more as I progress, does the power of your magnificent production impress me!! With all my *soul* do I hope that *another* edition may be called for, &c.

For *myself*, I am just now *engaged* upon a series of articles (*prose*) upon "*Ante Bellum Charleston & some of its Celebrities;*" *Simms' life & genius* will be treated of in *article no.* 2.[3] The magz[s] containing them, shall be mailed to your address—

And now, *my kind friend*, with love from my *wife* to *yours*, & *every* wish for the breaking of a *brighter, clearer morning*, even *this* "*side the veil,*"   Believe me,

> *Most Cordially, & Faithfully Yours,*
> *Paul H. Hayne.*

1. Gayarré's letter to Mrs. Hayne was dated July 1, 1885.

2. *Philip II of Spain* (1866) is a historical account of Philip's life and reign. Gayarré had sent Hayne a copy on May 13, 1885. For Hayne's comment, see Letter 100.

3. "Ante-Bellum Charleston," *Southern Bivouac*, n.s., I (September, 1885), 193–202; (October, 1885), 257–68; and (November, 1885), 327–36. Simms, indeed, is discussed in the second installment. Though Hayne points out in the third part of the series that he has "attempted nothing more than a fragmentary account of 'Ante-Bellum Charleston,' and her society, illustrated by biographical sketches of a few of her wise and great men" (p. 335), these three essays are among the best he ever wrote.

102

To Charles Gayarré   MS Duke

> "Copse Hill," Geo.
> *Aug 9th 1885*

My Dear, my *very Dear Friend*;

How am I adequately to thank you for the superb present of your *His*: of Louisiana in 4 vols just rec*d*?—[1] I'll read this History aloud to my little family circle, & expect as *much* information, & pleasure from it, as we derived from a perusal of your great history of Philip II.

This morning we had a visit from Mrs. Crawford, who tells us that she had the satisfaction of hearing you deliver your Lecture "upon the Creoles of history & the Creoles of Romance;" & of being personally introduced to you.

She expresses herself as being charmed with the Creole ladies & gentlemen with whom she became acquainted.

By the way, I hear (thro Mrs. C——) that you received several calls from *Charles Dudley Warner.*

Entre nous, what impression did he make upon you?

Knowing him merely as an *author*, I have *never* met, or had any correspondence with him.[2]

Have you seen the *beginning* of Joaquin Miller's poem, called "*The Sword of the South*," in "*Literary Life*," & *did* you chance to read the *note* accompanying it?[3] This poem has *some* strong lines, tho very rude in construction;—but Miller is assuredly a man who does not pander to public taste, & who seems warm-hearted & true.

Observing that this is the 3rd Edition of your "History," let me hope it is bringing you in some *substantial profit*?[4]

I have been so *nauseated* by all this fulsome, & wretched adulation of—*me judice*—a rather commonplace man (Grant); especially on the part of the South, that I could not forbear from composing the enclosed rhymes, which may amuse you.[5]

Our *united* love, *Dear friend*, to Mrs Gayarré, & yourself; & believe me,

Always affectionately y*rs*,
Paul H. Hayne

P.S. am writing an article on Simms now. *Soon as possible*, I shall do myself the *honor, & pleasure* of composing something abt Louisiana's *great* historian.[6]

1. Gayarré's *History of Louisiana* had just appeared in a third edition.

2. Gayarré had met Warner (1829–1900), but knew him only "superficially." Nevertheless, Gayarré offered his opinion in a letter of August 30. Warner "appeared to me to be a man of polished manners and cultivated mind, tinged, however, with the peculiar *je ne sais quoi* that belongs to his latitude—that latent, innate consciousness of superiority assumed in the days of antiquity by the *gens togata*."

3. The *Literary Life* was published in Chicago and "The Sword of the South" appeared serially in the late summer and fall of 1885. Gayarré in his letter of August 30 found the "fearlessness of nobility" in the preface to Miller's poem.

4. On August 30 Gayarré wrote that only five hundred copies of the third edition had been published and that his royalty was 10 percent. Since the plates of the *History* had cost $2,500, Gayarré did not expect to make any money.

5. U. S. Grant had died on July 23, and Hayne had been incensed by the "late nauseous cant and greasy hypocrisy over [his] death." (Hayne to Lipscomb, August 19, 1885). The "rhymes" Hayne enclosed are no longer included with this letter or the one below to Mrs. Preston (Letter 103).

6. For the article on Simms, see Letter 101, n. 3. Hayne's three-part essay on Gayarré appeared in the *Bivouac* for June, July, and August, 1886.

103

To Margaret J. Preston   MS Duke

"Copse Hill" Geo
August 10*th* 1885

My Dear Friend;

My last letter crossed in the mail your cordial communication of the 13th inst July, and *now* your welcome letter of the 22*nd* is before me.

Being up to my eyes in literary work, (I mean work which has been *engaged*, & must be completed soon), I am sure you'll pardon me for confining myself *chiefly* to the replies to your practical questions.[1]

1*st* Would a Publisher be willing to "receive & print from *pasted slips*, as readily as from '*Ms*'"?

Certainly: (in sending a copy of my own book half of it consisted of these same "*printed slips*").

2*nd* Is it needful to separate, & paste "the verses as I would wish them to appear on the printed page?"

Not needful!

3*rd* "Could I paste a slip, printed in *small type*, such as I would wish in a Book to occupy *three pages*—could I crowd it all on *one* page?"

Certainly! again:

4*th* Would it do for pasted slips, type-writer copies, *and manuscript copies, all* to be put together, in the *same book*, that is, the one "submitted to the Publisher & Printer?"

—Once more, *emphatically Yes*!

All a Printer—working under the Publisher, desires in this world, is a "*clear copy*" of whatever sort, & such a "copy" he is bound, according to the motto of his craft, "to *follow*, even if it *leads him out of the window*!"

You "blush" you say "in *talking so much about yourself*."

Well! You couldn't please us *better*, than by this same sort of "*egotism*," (as you call it).

Everything concerning you, & *your interests*, must ever deeply & warmly engage *our* attention.

Have you been able to *survive* this *deluge* of national, & *especially Southern* fulsomeness, in regard to the death of the most extraordinary Humbug of all time, Grant!

The enclosed verses express my own ("old fogy") notions on the subject.[2]

Pardon so brief & inefficient a "scribblement" in reply to your charming, & affectionate letters. I'll do better hereafter.

But, you see, (as intimated *before*) that if not "up to the chin in the *Pierian flood*," at all events, I have a literary load upon my back, which like poor "*Pilgrim's*," *must* be dropped, or got rid of *speedily* in *some* fashion.

Best love from all at "*Copse Hill.*"

& Believe me,

> *My very dear Friend,*
> Ever most *Cordially*, and *affectionately*,
> *Paul H. Hayne.*

1. Mrs. Preston was considering the publication of another volume of poems, one which eventually became *Colonial Ballads, Sonnets and Other Verse* (1887).

2. Letter 102, n. 5.

104

To Charles Gayarré   MS Duke

"Copse Hill" Geo.
Sep. 17th 1885

My Dear & Honored Friend;

Do not think it, I pray you, strange that your two *last* interesting letters should have remained thus long unacknowledged.[1]

I have been overwhelmed by necessary work; and ever I am quite sick. Last *night* such an attack of a most *unwanted* abdominal sort came upon me, that I suffered miserably, & am now much enfeebled & hardly capable of thinking, or writing consecutively.

But I *must thank you* for your cordial communications, (to be *fully answered* when *strength* returns), & for the *Suggestive "Test of Love,"*[2] which you ought to have heard me reading aloud to my little *family*, to the particular delectation of my wife,—who says you are one of the very few persons of your sex, (*& mine*) who comprehend *women* & comprehend *love*.

More of this anon.

Meanwhile, I mail you the first copy which has reached me,—a species of final revise—, of the Simms article. Read it *mon ami*, with some indulgence. Penned for a popular mag*z*, & designed to win the popular ear, I have introduced some trivial matter, (anecdotes &c), which otherwise would have been excluded.[3]

One more paper will complete my "*Ante-Bellum Charleston*" essays, and then with what *real, unaffected* joy, (DV!)—*God only granting me* the power, shall I take up my pen on *your* behalf;—

That striking pamphlet of yours which you *enclosed*, in reply to "*The N.O. Courier*" in 1854, will help me much.[4]

Send me at *once* also, *any* other *memoranda, relating to your family life, and literary career*. I wish to do you *full* justice.

As for Cable's "Silent South," I know nothing of it, except what my wife reports, who having perused the article carefully *agrees with* you *thoroughly*, as to its contradictions, illogicality, hypocritical professions of *devotion to the South*; & general involved "twaddle."[5]

The fellow has shown his *cloven foot* so plainly that even our once rather subservient People seem disgusted with him.

Again, I *beseech you* to pardon this *brief* scrawl. Have mercy, & drop me a consoling line; so that I may at least know that you understand my position, & are not *hurt* by my comparatively long silence.

Ever affectionately,
Paul H. Hayne.

1. Letters dated August 30 and September 3, 1885.

2. "The Test of Love" was a "bagatelle" accepted by the New Orleans *Times-Democrat* but never published because Gayarré would not make a change ordered by the editor. Gayarré enclosed it with this letter and presented it to Mrs. Hayne.

3. The essay on Simms appeared in the *Bivouac* for October, 1885. On September 22 Gayarré commented on the "biography of Simms." "It is very good indeed. Some passages have touched me deeply. . . . I perused it solus cum solo; it was half past eleven when I finished it, and after I went to bed the impression it had produced still lingered in my dreaming mind during the night."

4. The pamphlet was a reply to the *Courier's* attack on Gayarré's *School for Politics*. See his observations in a letter of August 30 to Hayne.

5. "The Silent South" appeared in the *Century* for September, 1885. On September 3 Gayarré characterized it as "very long, very flat, full of contradictions, misrepresentations and obscurities. In style and matter," he continued, "it is not worthy of a decently intellectual brain. . . . This pigmy author of the 'Grandissimes' seems to me afflicted with a mental disease which a physician would not hesitate to characterize as being 'diarrhea of words and a constipation of ideas.'"

105

To Charles Gayarré   MS Duke

"Copse Hill"
25th Sep. 1885

My kind, dear, & Honored Friend;

I must reply at *once* to your valued letter of the 22nd inst. Thanks, *firstly* for your generous solicitude concerning my *health*. Yes, it is chronically bad; and has been so for upwards of 20 years. Troubles of the digestion, of the lungs, of the nerves, it has been God's will that I should endure; and were it not that there is a mysterious sort of *resilient* power in my constitution, I am sure that long ago death would have claimed me. *In confidence,* (for *Heaven's* sake my friend, do not even hint at this in your reply, for my wife's sake), in *confidence,* I feel assured *Octogenarian,* as you are, that I shall precede you to the other world.[1] *Only* because of the grief of my *beloved* ones, *do I care.* But basta! who can tell the Future?

Thanks, warm thanks, for your commendation of the Simms paper.[2]

Alas! '*tis* the merest sketch; I had no *room,* no proper *room* wherein to spread myself; "*Cabbined, cribbed, confined, was I!*"

Apropos, I was *horrified,* & *immeasurably disgusted* by reading in the Publication list of forthcoming works from the firm of *Houghton & Mifflin,* the following,

In Preparation.
"Life of W. G. Simms by Geo Cable."

I must write to Simms' daughter at *once*; for I know, that some year or two ago, she withdrew her *memoranda* & *material,* (which *supposing* Cable to be a *gentleman & Southerner,* she had been induced to loan him), informing him at the same time, that she protested against his writing anything in reference to her *Father's religious & political* views; but that if *he* (Cable) *did write on these topics,* she claimed the right of seeing what he had composed, previous to its *publication.* And now, I am confident that the *infernal scoundrel,*—(altho his Biography *may* still *be* in *embryo,* since it comes *low upon the list*—I mean of announced Books), designs to *ignore Mrs* Roach's charge; and will produce a "*Life*" for the *Yankee Market, a book to sell!*

Good God! that our old friend's biography should fall into such hands! It seems the *very irony* of *Fate*![3]

But one thing is certain. If *Cable does* wrong Simms' memory in any way I can take hold of—"*by the Eternal*," (as *old Jackson* used to say)—I will *break every bone* in his (intellectual) carcass. *Nous Verrons*!

Your *pardon* my friend! I know this is rather unbecoming language; but my veins are still full of *red blood*. I *can't* help it.

I was up until 12 or 1 o'clock last night reading & re-reading your "Address to the People of Louisiana," in 1854. Many political pamphlets have I studied from *Bolingbroke* to *Burke*, & from *Burke* to *Gladstone*, but *never one more powerful & convincing than this of yours. It is a magnificent argument, magnificently put*!! Our *united* love to *Mrs Gayarré* & yourself. The poor little rose petals *enclosed* are for your dear & good *wife*, whom may God *bless* & *protect*.

I'll soon be (*after a rest*), upon the article referring to your *literary achievements*.

Ever affec*t* & *Faithfully*,
  Paul H. Hayne.
D——n *Cable*! *Positively*! I'm compelled *to say* it!

 1. Hayne died July 6, 1886; Gayarré on February 11, 1895.
 2. See Letter 104, n. 3.
 3. Hayne kept in touch with Mrs. Augusta Simms Roach, and her growing reluctance to cooperate with Cable on his biography of her father presumably was a factor in Cable's subsequent decision to drop the project. In any event, William Peterfield Trent (by 1890) had assumed the assignment, and the book came out in 1892. Ironically, Trent's "reconstructed" view of the Old South and his opinion that slavery had a deleterious effect on southern literature produced a book not unlike one that Cable himself might have written. See also Letter 97, and n. 6 under it.

106

To Charles Colcock Jones, Jr.[1]   MS Duke

"Copse Hill" Geo.
Sep. 29th 1885

My Dear Friend & Kinsman;

I was surprised to find among my letters one of yours dated as far back as May 22*nd* & marked, (oh ye Gods of Procrastination! "*unacknowledged!*"). Pray extend to me your pardon!—You referred therein most kindly to my poem called "*The Broken Battalions*," and truly I am proud to think that the little poem "delighted you." How I wish that I could have procured a neat copy to send you; but the edition was so limited.[2]

And now, a word as to your recently published articles upon Green[e], Pulaski, & R. H. Wilde.[3] They are eminently instructive & interesting.

It is melancholy indeed touching *Wilde*, that his grave should be so neglected—and really it seems as if in his "Summer Rose" he had prophesied his own fate! Yet not so! Even if his mortal resting place should be forgotten—*one* sad simple strain which goes straight to the heart of Humanity, will long preserve his name. *All* his speeches are forgotten, his forensic ability is but a tradition, his political cause as lost as some desert wind which blew over *Saharan*—ten thousand years ago, yet awakening an echo in innumerable souls, we listen to his pathetic refrain of "*My life is like a Summer rose*" &c.

Technically the Song has serious faults, and Marsh's dictum to the effect that in the blending of *Sound* & sense, that line before the last is unrivalled in English verse, strikes me as *absurd*—I would undertake during a single morning & in Tennyson's verses *alone*, to match it over & over again; but what matter? the *sentiment* of the *little* lyric is so embodied that the very commonplaceness of it is endowed with *perpetuity*.

There isn't a particle of creative imagination in it (such as one sees for example, in *Swinburne's* masterly lyrics, like "The Garden of Proserpine,") nor a scintilla of *originality*; yet for one person that Swinburne's *chef d'öeuvre* has gratified & thrilled, Wilde's has gratified & thrilled hundreds! Everybody can comprehend the homely lines and they appeal to a universal instinct.

By the way, have you seen "The Louisville Bivouac"?

Let me know, for if not, copies shall be sent to you.

It would gratify me to have you read three "*leaders*" of mine on "Ante Bellum Charleston;" which have had some popular success they tell me. At least they might amuse you in *parts*—while other parts are sad enough, God knows!—[4]

I write of the "*old South*," as one of that *ancien regime*; as a man who while disposed in every fair way to welcome, & say "God Speed!" to the "*New South*" sternly refuses to encourage the miserable *icono-*

clasm of such creatures as *Cable* (e.g. & his entire hypocritical, & servile *"following"*!).

Best regards from all *here*, to you & yours.

> And believe me as ever
> *Faithfully & Cordially*
> *Your kinsman,*
> *Paul H. Hayne.*

1. Jones (1831–1893), a member of a prominent Georgia family, former mayor of Savannah, author of several books of Georgia history, was collaterally related to Hayne by marriage (his wife was a cousin of Mrs. Hayne's), as well as through Hayne's own family, and had recited Hayne's commissioned "ode" at the centennial celebration of the Battle of King's Mountain in 1880.

2. Mrs. Hayne wrote Charles Gayarré on June 10, 1885, that "the edition of 500 sold as fast as the little book could be tied with ribbon." Since the proceeds of the sale went to the relief of Confederate veterans, few copies were available for complimentary distribution.

3. Nathanael Greene (1742–1786), revolutionary war general who removed to Georgia after the war and died near Savannah; Casimir Pulaski (1748–1779), Polish patriot who joined the Continental army as a cavalry leader and was mortally wounded during the siege of Savannah; and Richard Henry Wilde (1789–1847), another immigrant to Georgia, served in Congress, wrote poetry, and eventually moved to New Orleans and became professor of constitutional law at the University of Louisiana. He is remembered chiefly, even now, for the lyric, "My Life Is Like the Summer Rose."

4. See Letter 101, n. 3.

107

To A. A. Lipscomb

MS Duke

> *"Copse Hill" Geo*
> *Oct 1st 1885*
> *Excuse Pencil*

My Dear Friend;—

I was delighted at the coming last evening of your letter of the 27th *inst.* Despite those *abdominal* troubles whereof you speak, it seems to me that your spirits are at least, a trifle better. Am I right?—

It is well; nay, a *mercy of mercies*, my friend, that while the *body* (alas! our *poor* bodies), gives you so much *trouble*, the mind is *imperially* clear, & active;—

From the *beginning* I recognized those "Recluse" letters in "*The Capitol*," as yours & nobody else's!! Who in broad America, but *you* could have penned them? They have your *mark*, your *signet*, your un-mistakable "*mental crest*" stamped upon every *line*, & word.[1]

Col. Avery's *compliment* in his editorial columns is fully merited.[2] Indeed, neither Addison nor Irving, if the truth must be told—could have written these particular treatises. Neither of them possessed a particle, the merest *soupçon* of *subtlety* in the high, or rather the *deep* metaphysical sense, and without such *subtlety, first-class critical* & I'm even disposed to think first-class descriptive writing is impossible. Look at Addison's review of Milton. Fine, *very* fine in *its* way, I grant you; but it views Milton from *without*, rather than *within*!

Compare it with similar critiques by *Henry Giles* & *Whipple* in *this* Country, and by De Quinc[e]y in G. Britain!—[3]

How much there is in a name!!

I have struggled for years to get *rid* of what may be termed *conventional reverence*; (i.e.), the disposition to maintain that *everything* composed by a *very illustrious* author, *must have merit*. The fact is that even *Shakspere* [*sic*] not only "*nods*" sometimes,—(to use the outworn comparison, applied to Homer); but goes "*fast asleep.*"

Ben Jonson was right in saying there are *thousands of his lines* which he *ought* to have "*blotted.*" If this is true of Shakspere *à fortiori*, how incontrovertible it *must* be of *inferior* authors, however distinguished!!

How am I adequately to thank you, *my friend*, for what you have said of *me* in these "Recluse" papers?—

You are continually doing me favors of this kind, so spontaneously, simply, and cordially, that I feel like a *Bankrupt*, who can never repay your considerate kindness!!

What you said about the Reade "*In Memoriam*" &c &c in "*The Capitol*" my wife has carefully & proudly cut out to preserve in her most precious "*archives*;" but unluckily, that number of "*The Capitol*," which contains your remarks about M*rs* Preston's "*Ode*," and my Tennyson Sonnet, was *lost* by my son Willie in coming from the Station; but I'll send for *another* copy.[4]

It is encouraging indeed to find that you like my poem to Tennyson, now, that you have seen it in *print*, and can judge it fairly. "*Lady Mary*" by no means considers it among my best "*Sonnets*," yet, I am strong in *your* support, and may acknowledge that I have all along had a "*sneaking* partiality*" for these verses.

Our united love to you, & to all at "Wee Willie Cottage." [5]

Ever affectionately yrs,
Paul H. Hayne.

Have just rec*d* & read your truly admirable article on the Rev. Mr. Jones. Read it *after sealing this letter.* [6]

1. Lipscomb had been contributing letters on various topics, signed "Recluse," to religious journals, but this apparently is the first one contributed to a newspaper for general circulation.

2. Isaac W. Avery (1837–1897), politician, historian, and journalist, was editor of the newspaper from July, 1885, until July, 1886. Avery was a friend to Lipscomb and Hayne.

3. Henry Giles (1809–1882) was a clergyman and essayist who wrote on Shakespeare but whose collections of essays and lectures do not include a piece on Milton. E. P. Whipple, it will be remembered, was a well-known American critic and an old friend of Hayne's. If he wrote on Milton, he did not publish the work in book form. Thomas De Quincey's essay on Milton (1838) is mainly a biographical study and is seldom mentioned as one of the author's major essays.

4. The poem on Charles Reade had appeared in the *Independent* for July 17, 1884. Lipscomb had liked the poem the first time he read it. On July 24, 1884, he had received a copy from Hayne and immediately responded: "I am brimful of the Poem. It is your genius in its best estate, most charmingly melodious, and altogether new in opening of resources which have been latent hitherto. . . . The Poem absorbs me. . . . In sustained continuity without the least monotony, you have done nothing, I think, that discloses so much nature in so much art." In a series of "Recluse articles" entitled "An Invalid's Summer," Lipscomb discusses Hayne's "A Life Behind"—a sonnet to Tennyson—that had appeared recently in the *Independent* (September 24, 1885) and Margaret J. Preston's "Ode" in honor of the celebration of the centennial of Washington and Lee University. Lipscomb comments on these poems in his letter of September 28, 1885, and Hayne criticizes Mrs. Preston's lyric in Letter 109. Hayne also discusses the lyric in the *Critic* for October 3, 1885.

5. Part of this letter may be lost, though the final greeting given here is included on stationery different from that used for the remainder of the letter.

6. This statement appears on the back of the envelope and is dated October 3, 1885.

108

To Charles Gayarré   MS Duke

Excuse Pencil!
"Copse Hill," Geo.
Oct. 8th 1885.

My Beloved & Honored Friend;—

I congratulate myself *often* & *heartily* upon the fair Chance which brought me the inestimable privilege, *first* of your acquaintance, & af-

terward of your friendship, & affection. More & more as our corre-
spondence proceeds, do I perceive that upon numberless *important
questions* we thoroughly sympathise. *God* has given me your compan-
ionship (mental & moral), to supply the dreary void made in my spirit
by the decease of trusty & beloved comrades of the Past.

If you *are an* octogenarian, your soul is *young*, your *intellect* bright
as ever.

Thanks for your pamphlets, *all* of *value* & interest!![1] Now, I have
before me (*laus Deo!*) abundant material for the article on yourself to
which I recently alluded.

Would to Heaven that I could command a large *Quarterly*, so that
no "cabbined, cribbed & confined" feeling should be mine, *apropos* of
this *Biography of you* & half-critical *resume* of your various & brilliant
literary labors!

Ah well! I'll make the very best of my opportunity, limited as it may
be. Meanwhile, I have clearly discovered *one thing*. *No* man (unless a
shallow Charlatan), could pretend to notice, even in a *comparatively*
summary way, such various, learned, & profound works as yours, *with-
out deep, honest study of them.* Every chance I am now seizing to mas-
ter your "*His: of Louisiana;*"—& a *thorough* re-perusal of "*Aubert
Dubayet,*" & *other* productions I find *absolutely needful.* My *own
mind* is by no means a *quick* one;— I *must pore over & over again*
really thoughtful, & suggestive books; or the fullness of their merit I
may not grasp. Nevertheless, early *next* year,—(remember, I'm compos-
ing for a *monthly* not *weekly* periodical)—it is my hope to have this
paper, *so close to my heart, ready.*[2]

At all events, depend upon me when I say that I shall write of you
almost as I would write of my *own father*; & that if "festina lente" may
seem my motto, 'twill be because I aim at something like excellence in
the accomplishment of a task, which is likewise a privilege, and *pleasure*.

About comparing your pamphlet "*on the State of Parties in La*" to
the writings of *Burke* &c &c!!, I *don't* recede *an inch* from what I af-
firmed: *My Friend!* this world is ripe with *Humbug*; and often literary
men are (critically), the biggest conceivable Cowards; they dare not
wage war against *convention.*[3] "What!"—one of these Conventionalists
would exclaim; "*do* you say Judge *Gayarré* (or any living author for
that matter) has penned anything equal to "Edmund Burke's Style"?—
in answering "*yes*"! I picture the poor timid craven creature, falling
back into a *syncope*!!

Why can't we judge an *intellectual,* or *Art*-performance upon its *own* merits, and if these are so *high* as to justify us, fearlessly declare that they occupy, or *should* occupy a position—with some *chef d'öeuvre* of the *Masters?* And on the other hand, *why* do we always praise the productions of these acknowledged Masters, even when they fall palpably *below* the height of excellence? There are poems *for example,* penned by Byron & Burns which would hardly be accepted *now* for the second class periodicals; and yet the Critics are ecstatic over them!

A really independent Critic is a *"rara avis"* indeed!

Speaking of Poetry, have you seen Miller's *"Sword of the South,"* which is appearing, by installments—in the Chicago *"Literary Life"*?[4]

Artistically faulty, it is *nevertheless* full of warm striking passages, and we of the South should *never forget* him for his noble generosity, his high sense of justice. *"Justissimus et servantissimus aequi"* as Virgil says of—(*who* was it?) *Ripheus*?[5]

A prose-note to one of his *stanzas* alludes to *Tecumseh Sherman* in terms so scathing that it made my very soul leap to read it. Yes! *a man, every inch a man*!

We are having lively *October* weather, altho I dread the advent of *Winter,* my worst Enemy *now.*

Just a moment or two ago I went into the Garden, & plucked some roses the petals of which sweeten this letter, as you beautifully remarked of my former epistle—with the *"fragrance* of *friendship."* These petals are again for *Mrs. Gayarré,* whom we often & tenderly think of &c.

My wife speaks of her continually, and wishes that she were near eno' to see her. My wife is equally anxious to see *you,* she declares, & to shake your knightly & loyal hand!

With our united love to you *both,* ever my friend,

Cordially & devotedly,
Paul H. Hayne

P.S. The Simms sketch is having an exceptional success.[6] My wife says *never think* that *she can blame you* for *drawing upon my time &* attention. It *delights* her to see me writing to you.

---

1. Gayarré had sent three pamphlets on September 22, including "particularly" an "Address to the People of Louisiana on the State of Parties" (1854), and forwarded four more on October 2.

2. The articles appeared in the *Southern Bivouac* for June, July, and August, 1886, the last installment after Hayne's death on July 6, 1886.

3. Hayne had drawn this comparison in Letter 105. The point he makes about comparing present writers with those of the past, of course, is an old one, but it suggests that

Hayne was not always the "old fogy" he sometimes claimed to be. Hayne had made this point before. See, for example, Letter 107.

4. Hayne had already discussed "The Sword of the South" in a letter to Gayarré (see Letter 102, and n. 3 under it).

5. The full passage in the *Aeneid*, II, 426–27 reads: "Cadit et Ripheus, justissimus unus / qui fuit in Teucris et servantissimus aequi." In his rendering of the epic (1954), Rolfe Humphries translates these lines: "Ripheus fell, a man / most just of all the Trojans, most fair-minded."

6. See Letter 104, n. 3.

109

To Margaret J. Preston   MS Duke

"Copse Hill," Geo
Oct. 11th 1885

My Dear Friend;—

I am glad to learn from yours of the *6th* ins*t* that the article in "the Critic" pleased you.[1] I wish that I could have made it more elaborate; but these No journals seem chary of accepting contributions of almost *any* sort from Southern sources. *Brief* at least we are *expected* to make them!

You would like to know *exactly* in what "points you failed," *me judice*, (and remember my judgment may be *utterly erroneous*), "as to a *technique*."

These "*points*" are trivial enough, and I should *not* have even hinted at their existence but but [*sic*] for *one reason*. As your name is so closely associated with my life-work—, the *"Complete Edition of my Poems,"* and as Will had written a notice of your "Centennial" for "the *Boston Lit World*," to which he *appended his name*—, I thought that my article would have more effect *for just a little fault finding*.

Don't you think so too?—I observe that the *"Literary World"* has published Will's notice as *an Editorial, without his name, therefore*.

My son wrote you a letter, which as you do not mention it, I fear failed to reach *Lexington*. He expressed the *great* pleasure it gave him to serve you at any time, & in any *manner*!

In your letter to my wife you *mentioned that Prof. Harrison* thought my criticism *"sharp"* on his "Spiridion." "*Sharp!*," why I tried desperately to make it as *soft* as possible. He is a great *scholar*, & a picturesque writer of prose;—but his poetry baffles me. It has a very confusing effect, like that one experiences when examining a *kaleidoscope*![2]

And *now* about those "*points*" in your "Ode."!³

They are,—let me repeat—the *merest trifles*; & any reference to them may appear *hyper* criticism.

1st upon page 2nd.

> "And ere that April day was done
> Was fired the shot whose startling sound
> Went-*echoing all the world around*
> The battle-shot of Lexington!"

Do you recall *mon ami*, Emerson's "*Hymn sung at the Celebration near the Concord monument, April 19th 1836*"?—The concluding lines of the first quatrain, run thus:—

> "Here once the embattled Farmers stood
> *And fired the shot heard round the world.*"

Your lines repeat Emerson's idea, only as the expression is *direct*, on *his part*, (see the line *italicised*), & is an *inversion* on yours, for example,

> —"the shot
> Went echoing *all the world around*" &c,

Why, the idea is rather *weakened*; and is besides un-original; borrowed *unconsciously*, in fact, as thoughts *must* sometimes be; I care not *who* is the author, & how greatly gifted!

2*nd*—page 13—;

> "Pale students did not ask
> In that unworn, & younger day
> To have the edge of their appointed task
> By such attrition worn away,
> As ball, and hop & "German" furnish *when*
> The temples ache with intellectual *pain* &c"

"*When*" & "*pain*" can hardly be called rhymes; and somehow, making every allowance for the contrast designed, there is, to my mind, a certain flatness in the passage; a "*je ne sais quoi*," hard to *define*, but *felt*!

Page 20th

On this page you quote literally the words which *Lee* addressed to his troops after the *surrender*. There *is* beyond doubt a *homely pathos & power in them*; but they are *not effective*, when put into *metrical form*. Read over these lines yourself, and tell me if, *in this one case*, I am not right?—

—Trifles all!!

It *delights* me to hear of the fact that you have "recd such multitudes of letters, containing the *highest praise*" of your Poem—; the *Ode deserves* it;—& nobody *could* be *more* pleased than I am by such commendation!

Thanks, dear Friend, for your remarks, touching some of my *own* recent verses. God has spared my life far beyond the period when when [*sic*] I supposed that "my soul would be required of me," & of course, I have tried to work honestly on & on!

How odd it is that sometimes pieces which cost us *next* to nothing in conception, & *composition*, are the very pieces which finally prove most *popular*!!

E.G. my little poem called "*This too shall pass away*," a mere hasty rendering into rhyme of *Solomon*'s famous saying, has gone the rounds of the press, *North, South, East & West*;—while really thoughtful poems fall "*still born*"![4]

Best love from *all here*. Your name is verily a "household *word*" at "*Copse Hill*;" & every letter you send us, a *benefaction*.

Cordially & affectionately,
Paul H. Hayne.

P.S. *Entre nous*, Prof. Harrison has (unintentionally) placed me in a very embarrassing position. He sent me a copy of his extraordinary poem, "Spiridion," & wanted to know, whether I thought he should proceed up the slopes of Parnassus?

Dear me! *What could* I say? Probably, I've made an enemy for life. Alas!—[5]

1. Hayne had briefly discussed Mrs. Preston's "Ode" in the *Critic*, n.s., IV (October 3, 1885), 162–63.

2. James A. Harrison, it will be remembered, was on the faculty of Washington and Lee and was a friend of Mrs. Preston's. His *Spiridion*, a poem of twenty pages, was privately printed in Lynchburg, Virginia.

3. See Letter 107, n. 4.

4. "'This Too Shall Pass Away,'" *Sunday-School Times*, XXVII (August 29, 1885), 547.

5. There is no evidence that Harrison took Hayne's criticism personally.

110

To Charles Gayarré   MS Duke

"*Copse Hill*,"
19th Oct. 1885

Your most affectionate note, *My very Dear & Honored Friend*,— your note I mean of the 13*th* inst. reached me late last evening. The first thing I did this morning was to write to Mr Knott, (Editor of the "Bivouac") telling him of your willingness to contribute to his mag*z* your important narrative of an interview with *Seward*.[1] I am much mistaken if Mr. Knott does not soon solicit you to send your article on. He pays per printed page precisely what "Harpers" magz does, (viz) $5.00.

"*The Review*" so kindly sent, has also arrived.[2] Of course, I will eagerly read your paper, upon the occurrence of the very first opportunity. Just *now* I am profoundly studying your "*His: of Louisiana*," & re-perusing your pamphlet upon "*The Creoles of Romance*, & *the Creoles of History*,"[3] taking *notes*, as I go along; in a word, arranging my material for a sketch of your life & writings. *Apropos*, I have requested Knott to allow me *more* space than usual, for this paper in his monthly; —have indeed, proposed 2 articles instead of *one*.[4] I *do* hope he may consent; since the more I learn of your genius, & works, the more important I consider them. Of course as (before intimated) I must take time for such an article.—And now, altho I hate to trouble you *thus*, there is one *more* favor, in connection with this matter, I must ask.

In my last, I spoke of the expediency of introducing as much *color*, *local*, and *general* into my sketch of you as practicable; and suggested the furnishing of a few anecdotes of your *personal* career, & of the distinguished men you have met, in Europe & America;—now, can you give me a list of your works—(not including the political pamphlets) in the precise *order* of their publication, with the dates of *first* issues of them, and also tell me precisely *where* & *when* each was composed. True! I have most of your Production, thanks to your great kindness— but a clear list from your own hand, fulfilling the conditions specified— would aid me *materially*.

And anything anecdotical about your early *student life* in especial, & your *French* experiences (to hark back for a moment), would be a benefaction.

Am I annoying you? I hope not.

Do *not hurry*; there is plenty of time.

Concerning your likeness!! It must stand at head of article, & the question is, shall I send to Engravers the likeness at present in my possession, or would you like to furnish me with another?—These Engravers take months sometimes to do their work, so let us on this one *point* be *expeditious*. Consult Mrs *Gayarré*. By her decision we must abide.

Ever affectionately & Loyally
Paul H. Hayne.

My hand is so much *eased* by using a Pencil, that you will excuse its informality, I hope?

1. Richard W. Knott was also editor of *Home and Farm*, a Louisville biweekly owned by the firm that published the *Southern Bivouac*, and he had corresponded with Hayne for several years and actively sought his contributions. Knott did indeed solicit Gayarré's article on Seward and published it subsequently in February, 1886. See Letter 111.

2. Gayarré had sent Hayne copies of the *North American Review* with his essay on "The Southern Question" (November and December, 1877).

3. The title is "The Creoles of History and the Creoles of Romance." See Letter 99.

4. The piece on Gayarré was eventually published in three parts—June, July, and August, 1886.

111

To Richard W. Knott   MS Duke

Oct. 24th 1885

My Dear M*r* Knott;

Yours of the 20*th* duly received.

I am *heartily* glad that you have written to Judge *Gayarré*, concerning his *Seward* article, a *perfectly original* article, as I understand.—[1] *Now*, concerning the paper which I purpose giving you upon the life & literary claims of *Gayarré*, be assured that I shall not introduce a *single needless word*. I thoroughly agree with you in thinking "that biographical sketches lose a large part of their interest, when they become continued stories."

But you are *equally* correct in declaring that "where it is impossible to *do justice* to any subject in a certain (*limited*) space, it is better to make *two* papers of it"—With Gayarré, however, I may yet succeed with *one*. May! but 'tis *doubtful*.[2]

And be *assured* of *this*;—if the 2*nd* article must "*par nécessité de roi*" be composed, I'll endeavor to be as *sprightly* as *practicable*.

I enclose the *maps* concerning "*Fort Wagner*"—The "MS" of essay itself shall reach you, (D.V.!) about the 20 or 25*th* of next November.[3]

I am rejoiced to learn of "*The Bivouac's*" success.[4]

Certain Northern Correspondents have written me about it in warm terms of commendation.

I really begin to think that *success* is before you.

Ever Faithfully
PHH.

1. Richard W. Knott (1849–1917), editor of the *Southern Bivouac*, published Gayarré's article in February, 1886. See Letter 110, n. 1.

2. As stated in Letter 110, n. 4, three installments were eventually needed.

3. "The Defense of Fort Wagner" appeared in March, 1886.

4. Either Hayne or Knott is too optimistic about the magazine's situation, for as late as the following March Knott observed to Hayne that the circulation at the end of the first year of publication would be fifteen thousand when twenty-five thousand was needed to make a profit.

112

To Margaret J. Preston   MS Duke

"*Copse Hill*,"
29th Oct. 1885:

My Very Dear Friend;

Your long interesting, cordial letter of the 24th has been rec*d* & truly appreciated by us here.

As for the few points discussed in your noble "Ode," what trifles they are, after all! You know why I mentioned them. Yes, I am familiar with Stedman's "*Century*" articles upon the American Poets. They fall far short in excellence of his "*Victorian*" vo*l*! The *latter* contains beyond doubt, some of the subtlest criticism in our language.[1] Indeed, no man *could* estimate the critical genius of the author more highly than I do! But (*entre nous*) Stedman lacks *moral courage*; and in dealing with the Poets of this Country, he has shown himself utterly incapable of independence and manliness; nor has he in any degree "*the courage of his opinions!*"

Concerning *yourself*, the man really knows that you deserve something *infinitely* beyond his self-stultifying half dozen lines, which would seem to imply that you are only a *clever* echo of Mr*s* Browning;—but Mr*s* Preston is "too closely identified with the old *South*" to make it *judicious* for a popular Yankee (Republican) Critic to commend her!![2]

As for *me*,—I *could* appeal were it worth my while not from "Philip drunk to Philip sober,"—but from Master Edmund in his Conventional *Reviewer's tights* before his packed audience, to Master Edmund writing down his (apparently) *genuine* thoughts of my poetry, *unsolicited*, and with absolute bursts of enthusiasm, *apropos* of "*Unveiled*," & the "Simms Ode"!![3] Well, let it pass; it is characteristic of his whole "guild." "W. Whitman" is a good band for him to play, he supposes!—

Why, he almost confesses that his article on W. W. is penned under *protest*, but there's a *little* clique of Englishmen chiefly, who'll think nothing of *him*, if he does not dance to *their music*,—to follow their lead; nay, if he does not vow, despite his own senses, that a very palpable "Jack" is the "Ace of Hearts" (!!) But a *thousand Stedmans* could not bolster up "*Walt*." Nay! Were *Apollo* to come Earthward, declaring, "*Walt*" a *Poet*, I would know, by the mere fact of such a declaration, that his Godship had been *over-dining*, & *wineing* at the *Olympian* table, and had got into very bad company in consequence.[4]

Did you ever read Peter Bayne's notice of "*Walt*" in "*The* (English) *Contemporary Review*" for April, 1876—7?[5]

Bayne therein discusses the subject thoroughly, and likewise he discusses the arguments of "*Walt's*" principal critical advocates—, Dr Dowden, Mr Buchanan, Rossetti, and *others*. Such a *perfect* "crusher"!!

In this connection, it is worth while reading *Sydney Lanier*'s strictures upon "*Walt*" in his lectures (since published in a vo*l* upon the "*English Novel*"), before the "John Hopkins" University in the winter of 1881—2.[6] Taken as supplementary to *Bayne's* review,—the two completely annihilate Stedman's incincere [*sic*] and tortuous special-pleading. I have seen it *asserted* that *Tennyson* admires "*Walt*," and cordially corresponds with him; *nay*! that he has asked the preposterous old "*Yawper*" to visit him (!!!)

Let us hope for the *Laureate's sake* that this report is *untrue*.

If correct, however, I can only observe, that the lamentable fact would remind me of an old saying, or *proverb*, attributed to a certain Arabian Sage, to the following effect;—

That only let *any man,* (were he *Solomon incarnate, live long enough, and have the opportunity, and once at least, in his career he must enact,—thro the necessity of his being,—the rôle of a fool!!*

Basta!

I stand amazed at the enumeration of Prof. Harrison's achievements! He must be an absolute "Admirable Crichton," in the ways of scholarship![7] As for the *new* wife; if she is *really* devoted to her "*prayer book*," and also never neglects the "*cookery* book," I'm by no means sure that the Professor's chances of happiness are not excellent.

For a woman to believe in God, and in the efficacy of a good cuisine, are anything but contemptible qualities, after all!

As to *my* "*Copse Hill*" housekeeper, ah, *my friend* seldom deal by wholesale in *such* spirits. They come "few and far between," and those to whom they come may *not begin* to deserve their gracious ministrations!

I *am honestly* delighted to learn of your having *all* your later Poems collected and arranged for publication.

"Would it be the least use," you inquire, "to offer them to any Publisher, and do I think an edition of 700 would sell so far as to make it worth while to incur *the* expense?"

About the "selling," *Dear Friend*, I dare *not* say *anything*; for *who among men*, or *angels*—, can gauge, or even *guess at* the varieties of public caprice; but very *sure* I am that you would be merely *doing your genius justice*, by the issuing *of this work*! *God* gave you the *genius, and* would it not be right & wise to place its fruits, in *completeness, & maturity before* the *Public*? One thing tho, needs amending. *Frankly,* you must have more confidence in *yourself*, and your *gifts*.

If a *dozen*, instead of "two *Publishers* in *succession*," declined to undertake my vo*l*, why in your place, I'd only feel the *more* resolved to bring it out! And *Critics* (!!)

A *clever* Critic's help *is* acceptable; and his appreciation consoles & encourages;—but the true point is, *consciousness in one's own soul of having accomplished genuine art-work*!!—

Let *that* grand consciousness exist, and all the Critics on Earth, (and I am tempted to say, in *Gehenna*)—are, or *should* be, as "sounding brass, and tinkling cymbals!"

By *all* means, put forth Poems, in defiance of Publishers, & Critics alike!—

With the *former* (*Shylocks*, one & all)—, make the best terms you *can,* and send the latter—well—to *Jericho*;—where a good many should be told "to tarry until the *beards* of their *understanding be grown*!"[8]

Your articles on "*Oxford,*" & the "*Crypts of Canterbury*," are *intensely* interesting! How much of delightful information, how many stores of fancy, and feeling, and what innumerable charming memories your trip to *Europe* has furnished you with (!!)[9] Meanwhile, your friend here at "*Copse Hill*" sits in his poor cottage, among the Pines, listening now for the 20*th* winter, since Fate exiled him from his Country, & stripped him of everything but the means of base support, wondering no longer whether Destiny will relent, & give him an opportunity, (even at the 11*th* hour), of realizing with one he loves his youthful dream, and visiting the land of his fathers far over the gray Atlantic waves; wondering no longer—, for the *final* decision has been against him,—and his hair grows white, and his hands thinner, & the music in the pines, speaks now of the moaning of sea:—without a shore, billows vast & dark, no *Columbus* ever crossed; with no green, drifting branches from San Salvador to tell of a fair shore at hand![10]

But no! let me think that there is something better on the waves, & thro the darkness, than the verdure & the lights of that lovely Island, which greeted the eyes, & crowned the dream of the *Genoese*;—the Star on the forehead of that wonderful Angel, beheld of S*t* John at Patmos, *&* the name of the Angel is *Faith*; the Faith born of the vision of the things to be, and of the dreams to be fulfilled in the fullness of the days, & of the Glory still waiting unclouded revelation.[11]

The beauty & splendor of the ancient places of the Earth—these after which perhaps I have yearned too deeply, it has not pleased the All-Wise to let me see, & enjoy—but what matter, oh, friend, of mine, what matter, if after the voyage, we *all* must take, I am permitted to pass up the shining shores of the Country, imperishable, and to enter a temple fairer than York, and a tabernacle more majestic than Westminster; there to worship, not amid dead-men's ashes, and fugues of broken music, but *such* light, peace & harmony, as, occasionally, (in the purest moments of lofty but still fleeting spirituality, granted to mortals) has overwhelmed, even while they enchanted us!—

How small, I often think, this earth-life will look to us hereafter!— Its gratification, and disappointment, triumph, and defeat; we may smile half-pityingly over them, & especially over our trifling ambitions, as one, even now & here, remembers, and smiles over his far-off childhood, and its wonderful *pettiness*, so momentous *once*, such heart-breaking trivialities!!—

Oct 31st 1885

My wife, who talks of you *continually, has* gotten *thro* with her "preserving," but company dropping in, and only *one servant*, (think of it)! and she unable to use her eyes after dark—why she finds the days too short to accomplish her manifold duties.

But be *assured* that she will write you as soon as possible. My son hopes that you rec*d* his letter—(not that he expects you to reply—), and he thanks you for the "*Lit Worlds*," mailed from time to time.[12]

To revert to your Poems, I should suppose that *Messers Roberts &*

Bros after publishing 3 *editions* of "*Cartoons*"—for which they were *overpaid*, without doubtless giving you a proper royalty—*ought* to undertake another vo*l* on *their own account.*

Have you consulted them?—

If not, it *is as well to do so*; altho I fear they'll make some glib excuse.[13]

Love from all! Do wrote me *as often as you can.*

> Ever Faithfully & affectionately y*rs.*
> *Paul H. Hayne.*

1. Edmund C. Stedman's articles in the *Century* were included in *Poets of America* (1885). *Victorian Poets* had appeared in 1875.

2. In a letter of January 31, 1878, Stedman had confessed his ignorance about other southern poets, and Mrs. Preston's work is the first to be described in Hayne's answer of February 10, 1878 (*CHL*, 252).

3. Stedman had praised both poems in a letter of January 31, 1878, to which Hayne refers on February 10 (*CHL*, 248).

4. Hayne expressed the same general view of Whitman and his poetry from 1860 until the end of his life. See Moore, "The Literary World Gone Mad: Hayne on Whitman."

5. Peter Bayne (1830–1896), Scottish author and journalist, concentrated his critical attention chiefly on British drama, on British writers such as Carlyle, Tennyson, Ruskin, and on religious topics.

6. *The English Novel and the Principle of Its Development* (1883). Upon discovering *Leaves of Grass* in 1878, however, Lanier had written Whitman rather fulsomely about it on May 5 (Anderson, *et al.* [eds.], *Centennial Edition of the Works of Sidney Lanier*, X, 40).

7. In addition to his poetry and teaching (see Letter 109, n. 2), Harrison was editing textbooks and revising travel books on Greece and Spain.

8. A slight change of 2 Sam. 10:5.

9. Mrs. Preston had visited Europe in the summer of 1884. See Letter 80, and n. 1 under it.

10. Hayne's best opportunity to travel to England had come in 1882 when William A. Courtenay, mayor of Charleston, had offered to pay his way "to and from Liverpool." Hayne's grateful response of November 9 was that his health was "too uncertain to admit of separation from [his] wife" and that he had "no means of defraying expenses" after reaching England (MS So. Car.).

11. This passage anticipates the central theme (especially the fifth stanza) of one of Hayne's last poems, "Face to Face," *Harper's Monthly*, LXXII (May, 1886), 884.

12. Mrs. Preston had been sending copies of the London *Literary World* to various members of the family for years.

13. Mrs. Preston's last collection of poems, *Colonial Ballads, Sonnets and Other Verse*, was published by Houghton, Mifflin in 1887.

113

To A. A. Lipscomb   MS Duke

"Copse Hill," Oct 31st 1885

Truly, my Dear & Venerated Friend, you bankrupt me in the matter of gratitude!

Here again I find you in our friend Avery's "Capitol," referring to me in a beautiful tender, & affectionate way. What have I done, what have I *ever* done, to deserve such love, and commendation as *yours*? Yet, am I not the less, nay perhaps only the *more appreciative*, because (of your free-will; and with no question of the "quid pro quo") you thus honor and strengthen me. I was glad to read the "Harvest Moon" in the "Capitol." As I told you, the *slightly* changed lines make a really great *improvement* in the *tout ensemble* of the poem, rhythmically considered.[1]

Concerning Stedman's "Twilight of the Poets," I probably wrote to you before, did I not? It would have pleased me much more, had he left out *my* name *altogether*. I respect his critical genius, but he lacks independence wofully [*sic*] & *"the courage of his opinions."*

Some time, I'll show you this man's letters to me, touching my poetry,—what he terms my *breadth, creativeness,*—ardor &c, & how my verses must live, when the present school of *cabinet poets*, is forgotten,—and a good deal to the same effect. If I repeat myself here, *forgive me! Basta!*—let it pass!

He devotes, you observe, *pages* of labored *sophistry* to *Mr Walt Whitman*. Why? because he honestly admires Whitman? Not at all;— but because, he wants to conciliate a certain *English* clique. Dr Dowden, Mr Buchanan, &c—&c.[2]

They affirm that Tennyson likes *Whitman*. If so, I should say of the Laureate what *Aglaus*, (a minor Greek lyrist), once said of Apollo. According to Aglaus, the God of Song had been dining & "wineing" *very* imprudently one day, at the Olympian table.

While his ears were buzzing & his eyes dim, a *Boeotian pretender* to the lyre, was brought before him, and *Apollo* in a maudlin humor, (in plain *Greek—"half seas* over") crowned him with a huge bunch of laurel, and vowed that he had eclipsed *Homer*!!

I agree with you; (after a *second* careful perusal), that Eric Mackay's *"Rhapsody of Death,"* altho a *noble* poem *altogether*, has *some* palpable faults.[3]

It delights me to hear that he has dedicated his "forthcoming vol" to Joaquin Miller.

The South should love Joaquin;—he has sacrificed much to his sense of truth & fair play on her behalf. Obscure, and artistically barbarous (*entre nous*)—, as too many portions of his long poem (*"The Sword of the South"*) unquestionably are,—still what nobility of thought, what *high appreciation* of *all* that is purest & noblest in Southern character it shows![4]

My verses in "*Dixie*" you read in "M*s*" long ago. You'll recall them under the title of—"*Libation*." *Apropos*; I enclose a "Sonnet" which may interest you, however commonplace the subject (*Please return it*).

Dr. Farrar's address on classical learning I have not seen, but can well understand it is *all* you describe.

The Doctor is himself a *genuine* scholar, & a man of fine native force. For his talents & attainments my admiration is sincere; but of late I have learned to thoroughly distrust *the Canon*, (morally).

His eulogism upon *Grant* in *Westminster* was *more* than fulsome; it was—*all things considered, blasphemous*! And here he is in *America*, vowing that he will *not* lecture *anywhere, under any* conditions—for less than $300 *a night*(!!)

I'm now convinced that my "epigram" erred *only* in being *too mild*.[5]

He (*Farrar*) has deliberately descended to the lecturing level of "Mark Twain," *Cable, et id omne genus*; his *one* purpose being to make money (!!) I don't believe in *dignitaries* of the *Church of Christ* becoming platform expounders, at so much *per head*!

How different are *your* lectures, my *friend*, at the "Lucy Cobb," and elsewhere!! The young people enjoy an *inestimable* boon, I know in your expositions of *Shakespeare*.[6] Thank Heaven that your *storehouse* escaped burning down! & let us be grateful also in another sense that you have successfully *revised* the "supplementary studies" of "*Forty Days*." You have every reason to be *proud* of the superb success of your great work; and well assured am I that the "supplement" will fulfill your most sanguine hopes.

At D*r* Campbell's suggestion, I am trying for my *asthma* strong coffee, in slight doses however. It seems to have done me *some* good. Soon I will mail you, or rather re-mail you, the little piece to yourself, called "*The Guest*."[7] To escape from nervous misery, I am laboring at prose. By the way, tell me how many numbers of "*The Bivouac*" have reached you? The *last* article on "*Ante-Bellum Charleston*" I want you *particularly to see.*

"*Lady Mary*" sends her *best love* to you, & *all your household.*[8]

God be ever with you.

Affectionately

Paul H. Hayne.

1. Lipscomb had just published another essay in his series for the *Capitol*, "An Invalid's Summer." "Harvest Moon" is one of Lipscomb's poems Hayne had commented on in manuscript.

2. Hayne's comments on Stedman and Whitman should be compared with those he makes to Mrs. Preston in Letter 112.

3. For Eric Mackay (1851–1898), see Letter 92, and n. 9 under it.

4. For Miller and "The Sword of the South," see Letter 102, n. 3.

5. After reading Frederic William Farrar's (1831–1903) "eulogism" on Grant, Hayne wrote a sharp epigram which he sent to Lipscomb and which Lipscomb urged him (to no avail) to hold before he published it (see Lipscomb's letter to Hayne, August 22, 1885). At this time Farrar was archdeacon of Westminster.

6. Lipscomb lectured on Shakespeare twice a week at Lucy Cobb Institute, Athens, Georgia.

7. "The Guest (To A. A. L.)," *Sunday-School Times*, XXVII (December 19, 1885), 803.

8. In his letters to Hayne, Lipscomb, after visiting Copse Hill, began referring to Mrs. Hayne as Mary Unwin. Subsequently, he changed to Lady Mary, an appellation Hayne applauded and adopted.

114

To Charles Gayarré

MS Duke

"*Copse Hill,*" *Nov 26th 1885*

My Dear Friend;

Your long, interesting, pathetic letter of the 18th *inst* came a few days ago, & like everything you send me, was most *welcome*; most *deeply* appreciated.

It is encouraging to learn how much you enjoyed my "Bivouac" paper concerning "Lord John," & the old Russell "emporium" in *Charleston*![1]

Also, I perceive, that you like the "*Sesqui-Centennial* Ode." I am glad and proud of *this*. Yes, I poured out my soul in those concluding lines to *Georgia*. She has *not*, as you *justly* express it,—been a *marâtre* to me, but a *true* "Second Mother," in some respects.[2]

And so, the *rose-plants* arrived safely.

That is excellent news;—and we are *honored*, & *touched* by Mrs Gayarré's having herself put them in the ground, & having called the spot "the Poet's Corner in your *little Westminster*"! It affects me to find you writing so very mournfully of your future. I mean in *this* world, but then I ask myself, how under the conditions,—it *could be* otherwise!

No wonder that you feel often like one in a dark dream or "bewitched," when you reflect *upon* your reputation in *Louisiana*; your long, splendid career of services, *all* for the benefit & aggrandizement of the *State*, rather than your own,—the manner in which these services have been freely confessed by the Public, and then turning to your desolate & impoverished home, in the period of old age, discover no sympathy, no *help anywhere*, your *needs* neglected, while the mere *nebulous, political whims* of *other*, & inferior men are officiously gratified, even *before* they have been expressed!!

(*Vide* that Naval office!)[3]

Seldom in the history of *States*, or Communities, has Ingratitude—*base vile Satanic ingratitude*—been more powerfully exemplified.

Can it be a marvel then that a perfect stranger—a Foreigner passing thro the City of *New Orleans*, should have written & published an article particularly inquiring whether the *Louisianians*, beyond all, "the Creoles" were *an ungrateful Race?*—

Alas! there is no difficulty in answering *that significant* question.

That is a most *touching* & remarkable anecdote you tell me of the effect of your "*Fernando de Lemos*" upon the character, & destiny of an unknown lady!

How strange! that you & I, *as authors* in our different ways, should have had the same exceptional experience.

Many years ago, I published in "*Harper's Magn*, a poem called "*The Lyric of Action*"—to be found now upon page 285 of my "Complete *Poetical Works*."[4]

Imagine my feelings when one day a letter from a Correspondent whose home was *not revealed*, reached me, to the effect that my *Lyric had prevented the writer from committing suicide*!! The *style of the* communication convinced me that *a female* was my correspondent, altho, of course, I may *have* been mistaken!

Neither of us therefore, oh! my *Friend, have lived in vain*; whatever *Destiny* may still have in store!

I rejoice that your *Seward* paper will appear in the *January Bivouac*."[5]

Yes! doubtless as yet this periodical has a small circulation; & 'tis needless to observe how much I would prefer publishing my sketch of your *life & genius* in "*Harper's*" or "*Scribner's*." But *such* periodicals are closed practically to me; & to *all* of the "old South" writers, & why "*kick against the pricks!*"[6]

What you intimate to me, my *Beloved Friend*, in *reference* to your "*private life*"—and the "mysterious Power" which has "presided over *it*," strikes me with a certain sensation of—what the Italians would call, *Maraviglia timor!*[7]

And *one* thing *credit*, & *ever believe in*;—*my sympathy with you is* genuine, & *from* the *depths*.

What you tell me of *Texas*, and your application for a Chair of "*belles Lettres*" therein, *and* the *result* is but one link in a chain of evidence proving the worthlessness (generally) of the South & West in matters of practical education, firstly, and artistic appreciation, secondly.

The Southern author, & scholar has always been between *Scylla, & Charybdis*, the Scylla of Yankee *prejudice, & hatred*; the Charybdis of *Southern indifference*!

Heartily do I agree with you about *Froude*. When long since, I read his Chapter *upon the death* of *Mary of Scotland*,—every drop of blood in my veins rose up indignant, against the man's *demoniac malevolence*, his suppression of facts, and his *exposto* pleading against a poor, persecuted dead *woman*, & her *cause*, as if he were Counsel in the "Old Bailey" against some miserable Creature, whom it was needful to *torture*, hang, & quarter!![8]

I have never been able since to read *Froude* with pleasure, or patience, whatever his topic;—and Heaven knows what a botch he has made of the "*Reminiscences*" of *Carlyle*, whom he styled his *friend*!!

Referring to *history & its lies*; you are as *right as right can be*!

Most histories, I verily believe, ought to be designated as *romances*.

And now, with love from all at "Copse Hill" to you & yours, Ever

Affectionately
Paul H. Hayne.

Your Comedy of "*Dr. Bluff in Russia*," which you bequeathed to my *wife*, she says, *I must tell you*, she will value *very much*. Our son read it aloud to her the other night, & they both enjoyed it, & thought it might make an excellent acting play.[9]

You know what I think of it!

The "Bivouac" is making its way, tho a new *periodical*. Every recent no. with my article has been sold. It is gaining a position everyday.

1. The third part of "Ante-Bellum Charleston" (November, 1885).

2. The apostrophe to Georgia at the end of the "Ode" begins: "Georgia! My Second Mother! . . . / Hast thou not given me bread and balm and wine?" And repeats: "Georgia! My Second Mother; on Thy breast / The saddened exile found a couch of rest—" And concludes: "Thus, brave Protectress! at thy shining feet, / Alas! alas! 'tis only mine to lay / This simple wild-flower wreath of votive song!" The full passage is quoted in Claud B. Green, "Charles Colcock Jones, Jr., and Paul Hamilton Hayne," in Horace Montgomery (ed.), *Georgians in Profile: Historical Essays in Honor of Ellis Merton Coulter* (Athens: University of Georgia Press, 1958), 254–55.

3. For Gayarré's unsuccessful efforts to win the appointment to this office, see Letters 95 and 98, n. 5.

4. "Lyric of Action," *Harper's Monthly*, XLVIII (March, 1874), 586.

5. Gayarré's "W. H. Seward on Reconstruction" actually came out in the February number.

6. In bringing up the subject on November 18, Gayarré admitted that few realized "how difficult it would be to get admission" into these magazines.

7. In a note, Gayarré translates this phrase as "evil eye." He offers some examples of "maraviglia" in his own experience in a letter of December 7, 1885.

8. About James Anthony Froude (1818–1894), the English historian, Gayarré had written on November 18: "What a scandalous tramp he is in the domains of History, particularly in what concerns poor Mary Stuart against whom there never was a little evidence that would be admitted before a Justice of the Peace against a negro, thief or preacher." Hayne apparently has derived "exposto" from *ex post facto*.

9. *Dr. Bluff in Russia; or, The Emperor Nicholas and the American Doctor. A Comedy in Two Acts* (New Orleans, 1865), 49 pages.

115

To A. A. Lipscomb   MS Duke

"Copse Hill" Geo, Dec 23rd 1885

My Very Dear Friend;

When your letter of the 21*st*, (Monday) reached me *last evening*, & after I *had carefully* perused it, let me assure you that I drew a *deep breath of relief & gratitude*!!

Not only have you comprehended—& most *completely* comprehended my design, & feelings in, at *length* publishing this Poem, (*"The Guest"*) inscribed with your *Initials*, but you speak of it as "a precious tribute" which has moved your "*heart* as *it never has* been *moved before!*"[1] *Such* an acknowledgement, in turn "*moves my heart*"—ah! *how profoundly*!! Not vainly have I lived to receive this cordial response.

Your sumptuous Xmas present is in our Cottage; we have opened the box, and "*Lady Mary*" says "*it seems a gift from heaven*," which *indeed it* is because it came from *your generous* heart.

We shall feel that *you* are our *Guest* on *Xmas day*, & will ask God's *richest* blessing upon you & *yours*!

My wife says that "the Crystal wafers" are food fit for a Shakspeare & had you specially consulted our taste, you could not have sent anything *more* welcome.

We shall enjoy the *"dried beef"* (*not* tasted by us for years) very much.[2]

A *Check* from the late Vanderbilt for a Thousand dollars, could not have expressed in *money value* your gift; & *what* then, *shall we* say of the *heart value?*

Apropos of "The Guest," you tenderly observe, "that it links your name with mine, which you prize *above* all incidents of your life," &c. I am going to have the poem re-published in "*The Macon Messenger,*" & "*The Capitol,*" & to make "the link" complete—*if you don't object*—, would it not be best *now* to *give your name in full?*

But remember, *this* you *must* decide, as your own feeling dictates.

Of *course, dear friend*, I'll await your answer before sending the verses on.

God ever bless & keep you!
Cordially & affectionately
Paul H. Hayne.

1. For "The Guest," see Letter 113, n. 7. With the exception of tense, Hayne is quoting Lipscomb exactly. Hayne had sent Lipscomb a manuscript copy of the poem as early as October, for he wrote him on October 22 requesting that the copy be returned. On November 23 Lipscomb remarked concerning the poem: "how dear it is." Apparently Hayne had submitted the poem for publication without discussing his decision with Lipscomb. He is obviously trying to rectify any such oversight in clearing the way (later in this letter) to its republication in the Macon and Atlanta newspapers.

2. In addition to the wafers and dried beef, the box included "Breakfast Bacon" and other "substantial articles." See Lipscomb's letter of December 21.

116

To Margaret J. Preston   MS Duke

Excuse Pencil!

"Copse Hill"
Jan. *6th* 1886.

My Very Dear Friend,

Your last letter rec*d* just before Xmas, has given us *all* the *profoundest* pain! To think that it should have come to this,—a certainty almost of loss of sight on your part!! At all events, a preservation of imperfect sight by the *sacrifice*, as you observe, of everything nearly that interests you![1] It is beyond measure melancholy; nay *terrible*! How you bear it as well as you do, is a mystery. I'm sure such a misfortune would drive me *mad*. Those born blind, or who (like our friend *Marston*) lost their vision when but a few years old, are indeed to be pitied; yet are they vastly better off than the person who in middle age, or *beyond* it, is deprived of the most invaluable & beneficent of all the organs of sense. *Custom* in the case first supposed, must partially ameliorate the evil; but what amelioration *can* there be in a case like your own?

Our hearts are *very very heavy* on your account—dearly honored, & long beloved friend.

We seem, after perusing your letter of the 19th ul*t*, to more fully *realize* your condition. Somehow, hitherto, I have been buoying up myself with the hope that some favorable change would occur, & I am certain that Minna felt measurably in the same way. But now, cher! *cher*! What is to be thought, what hoped for?—

All the Xmastide, I have had you oh! so sadly before me! A hard, strange, miserable world, is ours for millions upon millions! Verily there *is* "*something*" (a vast deal) *in the world amiss*?

Shall it indeed, as the Poet prophesies, "be unriddled by & by"— We *must hope so*, or our last *cable* snaps, and away goes the ship into roaring seas, and the blackness of darkness & despair.

There are periods when human suffering is so brought home to us, thro the sufferings of those we love, that faith grows weak, and one cries out in agony,

> "I falter where I firmly trod,
> And falling with my weight of Cares
> Upon the great world's altar stairs,
> That slope thro darkness up to God,
>
> "I stretch lame hands of faith and grope,
> And gather dust, and chaff, and call
> To what I feel is Lord of all,
> And faintly trust the larger hope."

Pardon me for yielding to these reflections; and *you* too, in such need of consolation!

After all, I will *not abandon* hope on your account. Infinite are the possibilities of life; and even the scientific expert is occasionally mistaken in his prognostications!!

I am proud to learn that my Savannah "Ode" pleased you both, (the Col & yourself) so much.[2]

When you refer to Stedman's "*Dartmouth Ode*"—do you mean his long poem upon *Hawthorne*? Ah yes, Stedman's work upon *American Poets*,—great as its merits are—falls far short of his "Victorian Poets." I *don't* say this, because he has treated me, (as you kindly remark) so *coldly*; but because honestly such is my opinion, a general view which would have remained the same, had the Critic written of Hayne as enthusiastically in Public, as he has written in Private.[3]

You ask if I am fond of *Miss Murfree*? I'm rather ashamed to say that as yet I have not read any of her stories, tho both my *wife* & *son* are enthusiastic about her, considering her a woman of decided *original* genius. As she is *Southern* too, I *must* soon peruse what she has written.[4]

Concerning Miss *Edith Thomas*, I am in no position to speak critically; for *here* again, I am ignorant, at least of the major part of her productions. Only 3 or 4 pieces of hers which I *have read*,—struck me as unquestionably *artistic*, with certain touches of a Keats-like *grace* & art. *Minna* who has read more of this lady's verses does not especially like her.[5]

One sign that I am getting old, may be found in the fact, that I rather shrink now from many if not *most new* books; and am eternally reading & re-reading such works as *W. Scott's*, *Cowper's* &c—*not to* speak of Shakspeare, whom I seem only *beginning* to really appreciate.

To descend from *Scott* to the *artificial* level of the *Jameses* & *Howellses*, with their vapid fashionable society, and the subjective morbid analyses of characters, utterly useless, and dismally boring, is a *fearful* thing!! Yet, thousands read, & admire, or *vow* that they admire the works of these authors!! A quarter of a Century hence, they will probably be as dead as a *door nail*!

Your beautiful Xmas gift to Minna (with remembrances to us all), we *particularly* value; That at *such* a period of personal & bitter trouble, you should thus think of us, is very *pathetic*.

And now, with earnest-remembrances to your Husband & family, & the deepest love & solicitude for Yourself. I am *Always affectionately*

Your friend.

Paul H. Hayne.

1. Mrs. Preston had dictated a letter on December 19, 1885: "He [her oculist] says I have so little eyesight left, (being able to see only with one eye) that to preserve it at all I must abstain from everything. Although I really knew it must come to this, it seems more desperate to have it formally announced to me."

2. The Savannah "Ode," of course, is the lyric Hayne wrote for the sesquicentennial celebration of the founding of Georgia in 1883.

3. Hayne had remarked on both of Stedman's books in Letter 112.

4. Mary N. Murfree (Charles Egbert Craddock, 1850–1922), the well-known author of *In the Tennessee Mountains* (1884) and other dialect stories, is one of the few southern writers of the period Hayne had not been among the first to recognize.

5. Edith Thomas (1854–1925), Ohio-born poet and editor, had published *A New Year's Masque* in 1885. In her dictated letter of December 19, 1885, Mrs. Preston had remarked: "You never told me yet whether you are one of the devotees who worship at the Shrine Sappho, Edith Thomas! I surely am not."

117

To Charles Gayarré   MS Duke

"Copse Hill" Geo Jan 21st 1886

My Very Dear Friend;

At last I have the opportunity of acknowledging, & replying to your 3 valued letters, of Dec 24*th*, Jan 7*th*, and Jan 8*th*. The unparalled [*sic*] cold weather which continued for about a week here, (ie) until the 17*th*, (dating from the 10th of this month), put me nearly *hors de combat*;—I could scarcely hold a pen; & often felt indeed, like an animated Iceberg, endowed with rheumatism![1]

Approaching the fire, one experienced the sensation of being subjected to the toasting process of the Tropics in front, & the freezing force of the North Pole in the rear!

Ex-Chancellor Lipscomb,—(a dear & honored friend) wrote me to the effect, that he couldn't believe such weather Providential, but rather a direct emanation from the malignity of the *Devil*; & I thoroughly agree with him.

Monsieur of the black robes, & Chief on the "opposition" benches, according to Dante's "*Inferno*," deals as often with *Ice* as Fire for purposes of torture!

In addition to the outside cold, I have been cold at heart, I mean, thro the keen touch of *Sorrow*.

A young friend of ours, long known, & long beloved,—(*Maxwell Hill*, the son of a *neighbor*—) *one* of the gentlest & noblest of young men, high-toned, conscientious, gifted,—died last Tuesday, of consumption after a protracted illness.[2]

He was *our* boy's most intimate & beloved companion; & almost like a child of our own.

"*Whom the Gods* love die young" was a favorite saying of the *Greeks*; but the observation, after all, is *morbid*, and unphilosophical.[3]

"The death of any reasonable human being"—*Kingsley* remarks somewhere—, "altho he may be past fourscore," is a damnable solecism;—& how much, yes! "*a portion*," how much more true is it that the decease of *the young*, seems a horrible contradiction, a smiting of Nature in the face!

But *what* know *we* of the *ways of God? Darkness* wraps us round about; we grovel in the low, misty valleys of mortal humiliation.

Some time the sun of the spirit will rise. Secret things shall then be made plain; mysteries be explained.

What you tell me of the newly discovered *manuscript, apropos* of *Joan of Arc*, is *exceedingly* interesting.[4]

So divinely endowed a Creature is not *destined to die*, even in the memories of mankind.

Yes, *Bismark* [*sic*] was correct (in a general sense) when he spoke of the "*reptile Fund*," and associated it with political Editors, & their journals.[5] Nor are *literary* Editors, upon the whole, much better; the Yankee ones especially. They are pretty sure to *cheat* you, (with some few *glorious* exceptions), if only you give them a chance!—

How I wish it had been possible for me to send you a "Pandora's Box," *fifty* times as spacious as the poor little box transmitted about Xmas! *Still*, I comfort myself by thinking of your *egg nog*; & exchange of toasts by the fire side.—[6]

Your *own* Xmas gift to Mr*s* Hayne in the shape of that anecdote of your wife proved *pathetically* acceptable!

Ah! what a *noble, unselfish* woman!! She is worthy of all *honor*; of the *reverence* of *every one* capable of appreciating the *loftiest* sentiments of the soul, not *vaporized in* frothy *language*, but illustrated by practical *action! May* Heaven protect, & rescue her from trouble!!

An anecdote so wonderfully striking, which exemplifies the heroism & self-abnegation of the *best* of our Southern women, during the war, ought not to be lost. Am I at liberty, (*upon my own* responsibility), to relate it in the course of my sketch of your life & works?—[7]

Tell me frankly. The fact of your own political contumacy in refusing the *oath*, might just now, prejudice some persons, (despicable wretches, yet, perhaps influential), against you. *Reflect upon this subject*, and let me know your decision.

Your picture of the visit of Gen*l* Beauregard, & *Judge* Poché, on behalf of a Committee, who desired you to make a speech at the "Exposition," is graphic indeed!! You were right, *my friend*, to be perfectly *candid* in detailing your reasons for a refusal.

My God! how the ears *of those* Gentlemen, *ought* to have burned, & *tingled*, when you quietly detailed the circumstances of your position.[8]

I have written to Mr. *Paul Tulane* (of *course*, in a perfectly independent way, & in no manner *involving you*, as an *applicant*)—urging upon him the creation of a *Professorship in his University, for your* sake; & *the Country's*!

I put the matter strongly before him; & now *nous verrons*!![9]

It rejoices me to learn from Mr. *Knott* himself, (to whom I had *especially* written concerning the odd delay in the appearance of your *Seward paper*) that the article will appear in a few days; (ie) in the February issue of "The Bivouac"; pay will shortly follow, at the rate of $5.00 per page, the *same price* granted by "*Harper*."[10]

Write something else for this monthly, which *is prospering*. The ample & invaluable notes you sent me upon your *life & literary* activity I shall use very much in their present form, which could scarcely be improved.

Previously I had written 12 or 14 pages of biographical matter; but consigned them to the fire, upon the lucky reception of your *own terse*, minute, & admirable narrative. I am going to give your Louisianians "particular hell" because of their conduct towards you.

Remember I alone am responsible for this & deliberately assume the responsibility. If any gentleman of the "Old South," or the "New South," shall feel aggrieved & should demand satisfaction, as a Patriot, etc., he shall receive satisfaction.

I have the neatest & sweetest of smooth bore duelling pistols in good order & I may say without boasting that my "right hand has not yet forgot its cunning."[11]

Our *united* love (my wife's & mine, Willie being absent in Montgomery) to Mrs Gayarré, & yourself.

The thermometer (thank Heaven!) has risen here to 56°, which is an Edenic state of atmospheric affairs, compared with the condition of things last week!!

Write *whenever you can*, and believe *me Always*,

Cordially & affectionately
Paul H Hayne.

23rd Jan 1886

Last evng my *very Dear Friend*, yours of the 18th arrived, & exceedingly sorry we are to hear of your depressed physical condition. But no wonder!

The recent cold was eno' to affect the nerves & strength of the most powerful of mankind. May you soon recover!

In my *own* case altho the arctic spell has passed, its effects are with me still.

Your lady friend's letters may be flattering, sweet as "orange flowers," but where, as you so justly observe, "where is the *orange?*"

I don't like the atmosphere of this epistle. There's a smug satisfaction about it, an affected self consciousness!

A *Giant* among pigmies! Yes! But if the pigmies swarm by thousands, . . . *torment*, & then *starve* the *Titan*, what then?

The devil fly away with such sympathy!!!

By the way, it *does seem* unaccountable, this putting you *nolens, volens* into positions you never dreamed of occupying.

Look at "*The* Gayarré Loan," at the Exposition, for example.

But Editors like Fallstaff [*sic*] lie—*by instinct*!!

Again Ever *Yrs'*
P H H

---

1. In a letter of January 9 to A. A. Lipscomb, Hayne noted that "the thermometer in our library [was at] only 19°" and two days later he wrote Philip Bourke Marston that the temperature was "only 9° above zero." "I doubt," he added, "if such weather has been experienced here for half a century!!"

2. Maxwell Hill was the son of Joseph A. Hill, Hayne's closest friend in the neighborhood.

3. The quotation as given is from Byron, *Don Juan*, Canto IV, stanza 12, though Byron's source may have been Plautus, *Bacchides*, IV, vii.

4. On December 24, 1885, Gayarré had informed Hayne that a "manuscript from one of the contemporaries of the heavenly inspired maid had just been discovered in Rome" and that it confirmed "the miraculous deeds related of her."

5. In his letter of December 24 Gayarré had recounted an anecdote about Bismarck and the "reptile fund," an appropriation of money for the press.

6. Hayne had sent Gayarré some "California brandy" for Christmas.

7. The anecdote about Mrs. Gayarré involves her husband's legal advice to her concerning sixty thousand dollars in promissory notes due her in 1863. In order to "protest" them she had to go to occupied New Orleans from their country home and take the oath of allegiance to the U.S. When she learned that, although her husband thought the oath invalid, he would not, as a matter of honor, put himself in a position to take it, she thereupon refused to go to New Orleans and take the oath herself, and she lost all her money. Gayarré would not allow Hayne to use this anecdote in his articles for the *Southern Bivouac*. See his letter of February 3, 1886.

8. General Beauregard and Judge Poché invited Gayarré to make a speech at the American Exposition in New Orleans on January 8, 1886, but he refused because he had no clothes adequate for the occasion. Subsequently, however, another committee came to him and requested that he preside at a "Creole Day" in February, and, feeling obliged to accept, he wrote Hayne on February 3, 1886, he also had to go into debt "for a pair of unmentionables."

9. Paul Tulane (1801–1887), merchant and philanthropist, donated property whose income made possible Tulane University (1884). Tulane had already offered to help Gayarré with money, but he did not establish a professorship for him.

10. The article did indeed appear in the February issue.

11. Hayne had participated in several duels in 1855 and subsequently. See *CHL*, 12–13, 133, 225, 227, 324–26, and Edd W. Parks, "When Paul Hamilton Hayne Fought a Duel," *Georgia Review*, XI (Spring, 1957), 1–5.

118

To Charles Gayarré   MS Duke

"Copse Hill," 30th Jan 1886

Bravo! My Beloved Friend!

Read this from "the *Wilmington Star*"—Judge Gayarré exposed most mercilessly the ignorance of the Romancer *Cable of Connecticut* in his picture of Creole life & manners.[1] In Dec, "the *Modern Language Association*" met in Boston.

"Among papers read, was one upon the "*French language in Louisiana, & Negro French Dialect.*'"

"The discussion was *very damaging* to the Traitor, *Cable*, & showed him up as *ignorant*, and . . . *worse*!

"The Lecturer was a *Northern* man, but was equal to the demands, & said that Cable's Creole French was 'an absurd, contradictory, & *utterly* impossible jargon.'"

This lecture is soon to be published. . . . *Significant this*, coming from the *particular* quarters whence it has eminated [*sic*]!!²

By the present mail, I send you copy of another sketch of mine in reference to Simms, just issued in "*Youth's Companion.*"³

We—*my wife* & I—were much interested by your remarkable interview with *Seward*, just out in "*Bivouac.*"⁴ *This* paper is invaluable historically.

Let me hope, *dear friend*, that my rather long letter of the 20*th* (I think), has duly reached you? I feel some anxiety touching your *health*, for you write of many aches & pains in your latest communication; & no wonder! This winter has simply been *diabolical*.

Am *slowly*, but I trust *surely*, working on your biography. Oh! *If God* only helps me, *won't* I give a certain class of Ingrates the—well! ... "*particular fits*" about *their conduct to you?* . . . Pardon *brevity*! I am expecting, daily to hear from Mr. Paul Tulane. With love from my wife to Mrs. Gayarré & yourself—Ever affec*t*

PHH.

#Your "brief" exposing Froude—why not send it to "Bivouac"?[5]

1. Hayne contributed regularly to the *Star*, a paper edited by T. B. Kingsbury (1828–1913) from 1876 to 1889.

2. This paper was read by Alcée Fortier, a member of the faculty of the new Tulane University and a friend of Gayarré's, and published in *Transactions of the Modern Language Association of America*, I (1884–85), 96–111.

3. Hayne's sketch of Simms for the *Companion* appeared in the number for January 21, 1886.

4. Gayarré's "remarkable interview with [W. H.] Seward" appeared in the February *Bivouac*. The interview, according to Gayarré, took place in Washington in October, 1866, and the article is a printing of Gayarré's effort immediately afterwards to "put on paper verbatim all [Seward] had said. . . . I have not omitted, changed or modified a single word" (October 25, 1885).

5. Gayarré was of the opinion that Froude had been grossly unfair to Mary, Queen of Scots. See Letter 114, n. 8, and Gayarré to Hayne, November 18, 1885.

119

To Philip Bourke Marston[1]   MS Duke

"*Copse Hill*," Geo 7*th* Feb 1886

My Very Dear Friend:

After 48 or 50 hours of very severe cold, (I told you in my last what an unexampled winter we have had in Georgia, & indeed, this cold seems to have been universal), there is this morning, a slight degree of *relenting* in the atmosphere, proved not only by a rise in the Thermometer, but by some little thawing in my own ice-bound veins, & partly congested *blood*! Then too, glancing out of the window, I detect along the horizon, a certain *vague mistiness*, which I recognize as the *first breath* of *Spring*; the faint and as yet half-graying vapor sent far onward, from her lips, as a sign & prophecy of her own final appearance in bloom & beauty! May *she* come quickly!!

Now, taking up your letter, beginning with the 4*th* of November, (alas! how time flies!) I perceive that you allude to *two* visits of yours during the Autumn: one to *Dover*; the other to *Salisbury*.

The names of *both* these old English towns are very familiar to me.

Touching the first, (Dover), how could it be otherwise to a reader of *Shakspeare*; Salisbury too, has been celebrated in many a fine English poem & romance. One Ballad, the scene of which is chiefly located there,—a *blood & thunder* Ballad, the title whereof I have forgotten, used to affect my childish fancy much as "*Cumnor Hall*" affected *Walter Scott* (the *Scotch Shakspeare* & *Chaucer* combined, I *almost think*). It was the story of a gallant knight, who went to the wars of Palestine, leaving his Betrothed to the care of a younger Brother;—& very tender his mercies proved; for he *seduced* the maiden in the *first place*, & murdered her afterwards!! Her ghost plays an important *rôle* in the story; and a miraculously fluent Ghost it is; for *20 verses* of *8 lines* each, are taken up with a sermon upon the text, "*Thou shalt not kill!*"—Nevertheless, that "Ballad" moved me, as I have seldom been *moved* subsequently.

You tell me that "your best stories have had to knock at many doors before they found admittance." I am not surprised to learn this! *Editors* frequently show themselves *marvellously unappreciative*;—and the *same* may be remarked of the "Readers" for great *Publishing* Firms. Do you recall the fact the "*Ms*" of *Jane Eyre* travelled half over *G. Britain*; coldly rejected by one house after another,—until the sensitive author had nearly *abandoned* hope? Now just imagine *her* as *completely desponding*; and as *burning her work*!!—What a loss to 19*th* Century *Literature*!! Were the truth known, I believe firmly that not a few men & women of genius,—worn out by the carelessness, or the idiocy of Publishers, & their precious "*Readers*," have succumbed to a *bitter fate*; and gone down in despair to the grave!!—

"Demorest's Monthly," is unquestionably a poor *magazine*, in every particular;—and I regret that your "*Bryanstone & his wife*" appeared therein. But how could this have been helped if other & abler periodicals refused the tale?

One *great* difficulty *here*, is the "*The Century*," "Harper's" &c. stick pertinaciously to a few *popular novelists* to the frequent exclusion of *others*. *Howells & James*, for example, appear from *month to month, & year to year* until a *portion* of the Public, at least, feel utterly sick, & exasperated.[2] Then, this fellow *Cable*,—a Yankee who was born & raised in Louisiana by *mistake*, having publicly dangled the poor *Negro* for a "consideration," & worked upon the sympathies of the "Bon-a boo lah Gha," fanatics—*poses* himself—continually, (in "The Century")—, keeping up lies against the *South*—with an undeviating mendacity which amounts after its fashion, to the sublime!

But *my friend*, (mark you!) it is just this *sort of thing now-a-days pays* handsomely in America!

Of course, Cable has *brains*,—very *keen* brains—, and taking advantage of the fact that he *was* born—as I have said—, in N. Orleans, & lived there for years,—he calls himself a *Southerner—tho of Yankee* lineage, and Yankee proclivities, from the top of his *mean head*, to the bottom of his slippery heels, and thus pretends to speak "*ex Cathedra*," and as "one to the *manor* [*sic*] born!"—[3]

The miserable "skunk" pouches $50,000 *per annum*, probably, by his inventions!! The "*indignatio versus facit*," of a Juvenal ought to be launched against such creatures; but "*cui bono?*" they would *grin* a ghostly *grin*, when the thunder bolt of scorn smote them; & then proceed, in some safe corner, to balance their *accounts*!! "No no!"—, as *the "Chevalier Bayard"* used to express it, *apropos* of such *cowardly Traitors*, "there's but *one* way to reach *them*;" and that is "*per argumentum baculinum*" [*sic*];—Observe; he would not even allow them the honor of a back-handed stroke from a *sword scabbard*;—a *stout cane or club* was what *they needed*![4]

Monday, Feb 8th 1886—

Still *warmer* this morning! The *Thermometer* has mounted up to 52°—which really seems a benefaction!!

I took a *good "buggy" ride* along the Country roads (as usual in fair weather) with my wife, proceeding to our Country P. office; and enjoying a little gossip with *acquaintances* & neighbors along the way. Old Dr. Primrose in "the *Vicar of Wakefield*," could scarcely have led a quieter existence than *we* do in this remote part of the world. "*Our only excursions*," said the Doctor, "for 20 years, were from the brown bed to the blue!"—What a picture of *tranquility*!!

This mention of Goldsmith's *chef d'oeuvre*, reminds me naturally of his friend *Johnson*! When indisposed to read anything else *almost*, I resort to "Boswell's Biography," & invariably with benefit of some sort. A little while ago, I glanced over the Chapter relating to "*Irene*," & then procuring the *tragedy perused* some scenes in it. How ineffably dull & stilted!—

How it *could* have run from *9 to 13 nights*, seems unaccountable!! By the way, what a *naïve* confession the bluff, heavy squint-eyed Lexicographer made, when he observed to *Davie Garrick*, "Davie! I must stop visiting your *Green Room*;—I find that the *silk stockings*, & white bosoms of your Actresses excite my *amorous propensities*!"

By Venus & all the graces! Fancy D—— J——, making ponderously & "amorously" up to the *Woffington*, for example, or *Mrs. Pritchard*;—or sprightly *Kitty Clive*!!⁵

He used to "leer" upon pretty women;—when especially *amiable*;—Ye Gods! How they must have scuttled away from the half-blind, & wholly bleary-eyed old Cyclops!!

9th Feb 1886

Still, good spring-like weather;—& still, *that* haze on the horizon of which I spoke yesterday, betokens the gradual approach of the beautiful Goddess of vernal winds & fragrant blossoms.

In this connection, turn for a moment, to page 147 of my "*Complete Works*," & glance at the piece called "*Nature Betrothed & Wedded*." Once, long ago I witnessed in the far South a violent snow storm in *April*!! Here is a quatrain upon the strange phenomenon.

> White, bloodless Passion of this vernal day,
> Thou hast the power Earth's budding grace to slay—,
> Thy weapon a snow tempest fierce & fleet—,
> At once the death-spell and the winding sheet—

I may have *sent* you these lines in a different form, if so, pardon me.

Perhaps you have seen in the papers some account of the sad bereavement which has come upon our *Secretary of State*, Mr. Bayard, in the sudden death *firstly* of his *beautiful* and clever young daughter, & soon after of his *wife*.

Bayard is one of the very few real Statesmen in my opinion, of whom the *U States* can at present boast; a Gentleman too by birth, & education; and a person of equally noble manners & morals. Of the representatives of *Mobocracy*, (*that Tarquin*'s rod which smites down all the lofty & fragrant flowers in the Garden of Society),—the disciples of "the Great Unwashed" the elite of the Gutter, there is not *one* who has *failed* to throw *mud* upon *Bayard*;—instinctively such "*parvenues*" detest our *Aristocrat*—exclaiming with all the venom of little "D[ard]"—(the victim of "odd jobs" in Charles Reade's famous romance of "White Lies")—"the Devil take & singe *him*!," "*aristo va*!"

And yet, before a terrible affliction, the consequences of a direct bolt from Heaven,—the very worst men often grow thoughtful, & perhaps for the *time*, compassionate, and sympathising. This *idea* is at the bottom of the ensuing lines,—suggested by Sec. Bayard's bereavement.

Recompense.
The scythe of Death has cleft his hopes in twain—,
And mowed his field of love, till all seems bare—;

Yet loss reveals an aftermath of gain—,
  Grief holds a *benediction*—unaware!

Of late Distrust & Envy dogged his way;—
  Cold Misconstruction Watched his course apart—,
All sordid Passions stand re-buked today,
  Before the pathos of a breaking heart.

While other hearts are softened by *his* pain—,—
  On Death's dark background Sympathy grows clear
The chaff of loss may hide some golden grain,
  And Grief enfold a blessing unaware!![6]

February 14th 1886

You cannot agree with me as regards *Geo Eliot*, "the woman"— She was *soft hearted* you tell me, & required somebody to lean upon! Granted!! but *why then*, did she not as a matter of *decency*, if nothing more, of mere good taste, choose a less youthful & verdant support, than a fellow who might *have been her own son?*[7]

Certainly, as you observe, she was "*not bound to the corpse* of her dead Past," especially as represented by the memory—a *deuced* un-savory one, I'm afraid, of *Geo Lewes*—, but "*Holy Blue!*" my *friend*, (as the Frenchman says) *why* should she have courted so undignified, & even (in *some* senses) so *disreputable* a Future?—

I don't believe in venerable widows—with the propensities of "*the Tower of Pisa*," reclining upon the *bosoms* of ambitious *youngsters*. You think in living with Lewes she "*took her courage in both hands*," and you rather admire her for doing "*so fine a thing!*"

After all would not the true test of this question, be a *home one* (!!) Could you bear the thought of a *mother or sister* following *such an example?*

What would become of our *domestic* relations, if such a precedent were *generally* accepted?—

Then, look how inconsistent she was!! After professing to ignore the marriage tie; she—as an *ecclesiastical* rite, she is nevertheless mar-ried to *Cross* by the *Episcopal service!!*

Don't think me *bigotted* [*sic*]! The issue is a *practical* one, which would remain the same if *Christianity* had never come into the world!—(*En parenthèse* I have a blessed consciousness that in arguing any question with you, upon which we chance to differ,—that you'll *never miscomprehend*, nor deem me arrogant—for which "*Laus Deo!*")—

Now about the *genius of "Geo Eliot"*!! Most *thoroughly* do I respond to your *admiration*.

I too would reverently have "kissed the hand" of the wonderful *Artist*, who wrote "*The Mill on the Floss*," "*Adam Bede*" &c

And "*Middlemarch*"—her *last* great work! How great it is!! *Only* of *late* days, have I *fully appreciated* the combination it exhibits of *consummate characterization*, (dealing with *many differing* personages) and of the power of *local coloring*.[8] "Dorothea," as you observe is verily "adorable"!! A unique woman, possessed of every feminine grace, with a force of *intellect* added & of keen tho half unconscious *perception* touching the weaknesses & selfishness of others, which results in sympathy, not detraction or disgust!!! *How* hard the poor girl, (she is almost a girl!) tries to make allowances for her Husband;—when she has unavoidably found him out!—*Apropos*, I can't pity *Casaubon* as *you do*!—His "Will,"—with its mean, insulting provisions—, could never have been dreamed of, far less *executed* by any *man* not *unfathomably selfish & vile*!—

It does me good to read *over & over* your eloquent tribute to *Mrs Browning*! "Very curious," your remark "how *her fame seems to have* faded out!"—Yes! only "*seems*"!! Let us recall in this connection, the *fact* that during the reigns of James, the two Charles'—& the 1*st* & 2*nd* George, even *Shakspeare* was almost forgotten;—and everywhere absurdly *depreciated*, when his works came up for discussion!—As in his case, so in Mr*s* Browning's there will, *there must be* a glorious resurrection, a *grand revival*!

Sat—20th Feb 1886

Observe, how slowly this letter progresses! In truth, our winter has, (after some deceitful promises of amendment) come upon us more spitefully than ever.

The terrible cold is nearly killing me. . . . Yesterday, I had a hemorrhage, *from the lungs I fear*; and the effect upon nerves & spirit has been well-nigh *intolerable*!

O! these *bodies* of ours,—and their capacity for *suffering*! I can scarcely hold the pen, & everything seems steeped in gloom & misery. But I shall *fight it out* to the final extremity!

21st February.

A trifle *better* today! The temperature has moderated somewhat; and the horrible *Winds* are less demonically cold and exterminating. Twenty four hours ago, they appeared ready to tear down the Cottage, & blow us all into "smithereens."

Last night, feeling unusually ill & despondent, I took up for amusement a novel which a Western lady—visiting our pine-woods for her health, had loaned me, called *"The Strange Case of Dr. Jekyll, & Mr Hyde"* [1886] by *Louis Stevenson*.

I read some chapters aloud to my wife, who began to shudder, and (since we are very lonely here, especially after dark)—she complained of a "creepy sensation," & proposed a speedy adjournment up stairs, where safely *locked* in our chamber,—I completed the weird narrative! Really, it *is* weird, and managed with singular ingenuity, tho marked by a few artistic blunders—*me judice.*

The *root-conception* or a *portion of it, at least* was evidently derived from *Poe*; Don't you recall his (Poe's) Ligea [*sic*]? If not, reperuse it, and you will see what I mean.[9]

Thursday 25th Feb 1886

Weather moderating still more;—but a thin, drizzling rain has set in; and our woods are enveloped in that species of gray, fluctuating mist, which seems *uncannily* alive; and instinct with unwholesome, malicious vitality! Gloom everywhere!! One might fancy our poor *Mother Earth* at her last gasp; or rather dead already; and here are certain lugubrious *Spirits of Air* winding about her an impalpable pall!

March 4th 1886

Only think of our having had a touch of snow, 3 *days* ago, the unwanted white patches glittering all over the ground next morning!! And now the sky is once more gray, & the *peculiar* "feel of snow" is in the air!

There can be no doubt concerning it! Some Arctic *Sprite*, or rather some malicious Arctic "Aspect" has taken possession of our *South*, for a time, & intends to do us all the harm he possibly can—

Here are two Sonnets, (which I may have sent you in "MSS"—, but perhaps you may like to obtain the printed copy) suggested by our exceptional Season.[10]

I don't like to hear of your 'Sleeplessness'. "Insomnia" is becoming a disease—a *Special disease* of our modern Civilization! The *reason* is obvious:—*Steam*, not content with whirling our *Locomotives* along at 50 or 60 miles an hour—has *taken possession of the blood, brains & marrow* of *Society*;—and every man & *woman* too, must enact the *role* of a *Locomotive*, and be whirled by the *shortest* path, & at the quickest pace to the *Devil*!!

How can people (under *such conditions*) *sleep* comfortably this side of the deep, mysterious sleep of death!—

We sneer at our *"Slow" ancestors*; and prate compassionately of those *"benighted Mediaevals!"*

Well!—they had their faults,—*among* them, the disposition often to split open the skulls of foes,—but how natural they were!—how manly, how vigorous;—how beautifully they *used to snore*, after a hard day's work—; & how independent they were of *"Chloral,"* and *"opium," and "Coca"*!!

Doubtless you are correct in calling *Landor*, like *"olives,"* an *"acquired* taste!" But some *"acquired tastes" stick, don't* they?—and *Landor* is *one of these*!

What a bundle of *contradictions* the man was!! *Au fond*, the *gentlest of the gentle*, he could nevertheless, rave like a *"bull of Bashan,"* and make his disagreeable marks, like an infuriate beast in a *"china shop!"*

March 5th 1886

It is a pleasant & encouraging thing to feel that one's own People appreciate one! Yesterday I rec*d* two evidences of such appreciation which I am tempted to tell you of!!

The *first* came from *Augusta*, where there *has* been for *years* a *"Literary Society"* called after my name;—This "Society" invites me, & my "winsome Marrow," to visit the Town, in order to hear *three* Lectures on *Shakspeare* by my illustrious friend, Dr. *Lipscomb*, ex-Chancellor of the "Vanderbilt University,"—(of whom I previously wrote) and assuredly among the ablest Shakspearean scholars of *the world*!! Coleridge never grasped *Shakspeare's logic of art* more closely & effectively than my aged friend has done![11]

The *second* invitation came from a *Macon* association, asking us to visit them in *April* or May,—when it appears that they are to have a meeting for the purpose of discussing my unworthy self—, or rather my *works*. (By the way, how *Charles Lamb* used to sneer at the notion of moderns speaking of *their* "Works![")])[12]

I have just carefully read—by no means for the *first* time your Sonnet in *"The Youth's Companion,"*—an *Invocation to the New Year*!! It is a *very beautiful, & pathetic* poem;—full of that touching appeal to our sensibilities which only a brute could fail to realize!!

You are marvellously successful in your *Sonnets*. Far more than a fragment of *Rossetti's* mantle has fallen upon *your* shoulders.[13]

Dear me! how I wish, & how my wife wishes, that you could be here with us in *Augusta & Macon*, so that we might introduce you to our *friends, & the Public*! How enthusiastically they would welcome you!—our noble Georgians!! Well you may come here some day!

Heaven grant it!

Saturday March 6th 1886

You refer in your paragraphs of Nov 20th to a copy of "*The Southern Bivouac*," which *Mrs Hayne* mailed to you.

I am now writing *regularly* for that periodical; and (by the way,) I *wish you would send* to me a *brief poem for their* pages. They'll pay at least as well as the "*NY Independent*."

Touching my long narrative poem for "Wide-Awake," I only know it will appear *some time* during *the present year*, but *when* precisely God *only* knoweth!! The illustrations take time.

How repeatedly your work must be interrupted by people calling upon you! All right with *real* friends; but your Conventional fashionable *visitor*,—full of twaddle and "*tempests in a tea pot*"!!—from *such*, good Lord, deliver us!!

Of course I recall the wonderful Chapter in "*Esmond*" which you allude to;—the scene after Cathedral service is indeed pathetic. But somehow, let me acknowledge that there are periods when Esmond's courtship of & final marriage with *Lady Castlewood*, strikes me unpleasantly! The whole affair assumes a bizarre unnatural appearance. To be frantic for years about the *daughter*, & then, to wed the *mother*(!!!)—I don't like it!¹⁴

The "dark, dreary, drizzly day" of 24*th* Nov which you employed in such *constant* work, has been matched by many such amongst us; & I'm afraid that I did not scruple to slip in the other word to complete the alliteration; touching a number of these *dismal* periods!

How did you get thr*o* with your poems "penned to order," for new Juvenile mag*z*? Verily, it *is* a *hard* thing to compose *verses* under such conditions—the *Muse* rebels; she looks sternly in her Poet's eye remarking; "ungrateful wretch!—is it *thus* you *dare* to treat me? Am I expected to rise at your "venial commands and to furnish you with brilliant fancies, or grand imaginations," because, forsooth, some miserable dog of a Publisher desires you—at so much a line—, to fill a page or two of "his probably worthless periodical(!!)?—*What*! I am to be "prostituted to *your* convenience & to his? Irreverent and ungrateful Creature: I say to the mean spirit within your heart, '*Retro Sathanas*!'"

Positively I have heard my own *Muse* addressing me in *these* precise words; & how they terrified me, you may imagine.

Tuesday, March 9th 1886

Last night your long, delightful letter came, with a hundred *details* of your *London* life which be sure were most interesting to us!—Such a "diary" is indeed charming, but we were troubled by that *fall* of yours.[15]

Get the young fellow staying with you, to lock the door of the room at night in order to avoid such another catastrophe and then, the trouble in your eye!! That is another source of anxiety to us!

Your letter rec*d* last evng, & the one to my wife, came *again* in company with communications from my beloved & honored friend *R. D. Blackmore*. A strange co-incidence *is it not?*—

What a tremendously busy existence is yours: I stand amazed before the record of such industry;—of compositions, prose & verse, accomplished under every conceivable disadvantage of physical disability (upon *one* important point), & the exacting claims of a restless society, forever moving like the waters of ocean! How *do* you manage it all?—

But, my dear fellow, *are* you not "burning the candle at both ends?"—Active brain-labor on one side, and as active society & Club life on the other, are enough to injure the strongest nerves, & to impair even *your* constitution which must be powerful! Excuse my *loving* hint; I don't mean to indulge in what the Chinaman would contemptuously call, "*Preacher! Preacher* (!!) [*"*]

I perceive that you are much interested by Howells' last books, "Silas Latham [*sic*]," and "*A Modern Instance.*" Odd! but these are the only productions of his of which I *know nothing*; and you evidently regard *them* as his *best*! Judging him by the other works wherewith I have, I acknowledge H's brilliant talents—[16] The school of fiction to which he at least *partially* belongs—the James school—makes me sick at my moral & mental stomach.[17] I have long known H by correspondence and also personally—tho 12 years have elapsed since I last saw his confoundedly "ugly mug"—His natural conceit has been made towering—of Himalayan height—proportioned by the subservient flattery & the unmeasured devotion of his vassals whose names are doubtless legion. He regards his literary position as unique and *himself* as a critical & artistic Pope! After quite a dubious fashion, he patronizes poor old exploded *Sir Walter Scott*, observing that he supposes!! good God! that he supposes that Scott must have been a man of genius!! And as for *Thackeray* & *Dickens*—both of them—poor devils! are ruthlessly snubbed! But basta! enough![18]

1. Marston (1850–1887), the blind British poet, had been corresponding with Hayne since 1879. See Letter 90, n. 2. His exchange of letters with Hayne is one of the most interesting in the Hayne collection at Duke, but since the letters of both writers are usually quite long—Hayne's letter of January 1–15, 1884, for example, covers forty-three pages of typed copy—they can only be represented in this edition. This letter itself is presumably incomplete (though it covers eighteen triple-spaced typewritten pages), but it is shorter than most letters of this period and yet typical of the correspondence with Marston.

2. Hayne seldom missed an opportunity during this period to criticize the fiction of James and Howells. A recent example may be readily found in the second part of his "Ante-Bellum Charleston," *Southern Bivouac* for October, 1885. See also n. 16 below.

3. Hayne invariably points out that Cable is not a true southerner and that he "lies" about the South for money. Gayarré, of course, holds the same opinion.

4. The Latin expressions may be translated as follows: *per argumentum baculi*—through the argument of a stick; the Juvenalian tag is usually cited as *facit indignatio versus*—indignation makes verses.

5. Peg Woffington, Hannah Pritchard, and Kitty Clive were all well-known actresses of the period.

6. Thomas F. Bayard (1828–1898) was the son and grandson of members of the U.S. Senate, and he served in that body himself before he became secretary of state in 1885. For another version of the poem, see Letter 120, and n. 4 under it. "Recompense" appeared in the *Independent* for February 18, 1886.

7. Mary Anne (Marian) Evans Cross (George Eliot) was born in 1819 and died in 1880. John W. Cross was born in 1840, married George Eliot in 1878, and died in 1924.

8. Yet Hayne had written a friend in 1872 that the book "is infinitely a greater performance than the ablest of mere novels. We have *character painting*, crisp & distinct as Shakspeare's—, & an exhibition of insight into human nature & human motives, startling in its profundity, and searching significance. 'Middlemarch' must take its place at once beside the classics of the English tongue!"

9. Since the tale had only recently appeared, Hayne is surely among the first to point out Stevenson's possible debt to Poe.

10. "Winter Sonnets" appeared in the *Independent* for February 11, 1886.

11. The Hayne Literary Society, sometimes called the Hayne Circle, had been formed as early as 1883 (the first written communication from the society to the poet is dated February 9, 1883). The lectures were delivered in March, and the Haynes were the guests of Lawton B. Evans, superintendent of the public schools in Augusta.

12. The Athenaeum Club of Macon held a reception for "our own Southern poet" on May 20—Hayne selected this date because it was the thirty-fourth anniversary of his marriage. A. J. Battle, president of the club and of Mercer University as well, extended the invitation in a letter of March 2, 1886.

13. Marston and Dante Gabriel Rossetti had been close personal and literary friends until the latter's death in 1882.

14. Hayne had admired *Esmond* since its appearance in 1852, though he had maintained reservations about it similar to those expressed here. The similarity with Hayne's views of the marriage between George Eliot and J. W. Cross should also be noted. Such opinions, by the way, are not merely characteristic of Hayne's late years; they had been expressed from time to time throughout his life.

15. Marston was a "sleep-walker," and on a recent occasion had fallen down the stairs during one of his "dreams."

16. Though Hayne had praised Howells' early fiction, he had been irritated by the way he thought Howells treated him as a contributor to the *Atlantic*, and by the time Howells left the *Atlantic* in 1881 Hayne had little regard for the man or his work. See Moore, "'The Absurdest of Critics': Hayne on Howells." Nor did Hayne care for the "finical" fiction of Henry James. He expressed himself often and consistently on the subject of Howells' and James's fiction during this period. See n. 2 above. Hayne, by the way, was only one of many who did not care for the analytical fiction of James and Howells and who were particularly alarmed by Howells' criticism of the work of Dickens, Thackeray, and Scott as outmoded. As an expression of a similar opinion, see Edmund Gosse's delightful "motto" addressed to Howells in a letter of November 8, 1882:

> Ho! the old school! Thackeray, Dickens!
> Throw them out to feed the chickens.—
> Ho! the new school! James and ———
> Lay the flattery on with trowels.

Gosse (1849–1928), the well-known English poet and critic, was a good friend both to Howells and James, but the point he makes in the quatrain was widely appreciated in the 1880s. For Gosse's letter, see Paul Mattheisen and Michael Millgate (eds.), *Transatlantic Dialogue: Selected American Correspondence of Edmund Gosse* (Austin: University of Texas Press, 1965), 102. Gosse discusses the matter more seriously with Howells in a letter of November 14 (pp. 103–104).

17. At this point five or six words are scratched out in the manuscript and are consequently illegible.

18. The manuscript breaks off here—at least this is all that is available in the file at Duke. It is, of course, possible that only the usual valedictory remarks are missing.

120

To A. A. Lipscomb   MS Duke

Monday night Feb 8th 1886

My Dear & Honored Friend;

Both your letters of the 4*th* duly arrived. My wife thanks you for hers, and I thank you for mine—

How full they are, (*these* precious communications), of *affection*, altho it is evident that you are laboring under great physical weakness, and a consequent *mental* depression.

No wonder! Our *past* winter, (let us hope & pray that it *is* virtually over), was enough to try a physique of iron; *a fortiori* therefore, it was bound to injure *your* constitution & *mine*.

A species of walking *Iceberg*, galvanized by Rheumatism, and permeated by neuralgia,—I proceeded half mechanically to perform my daily duties;—conscious that but a little more of Arctic *diablerie* was needed to finish me altogether!! *How* any man can be such an *ass* as to voluntarily seek the *North Pole*, passes my poor comprehension.

It is *wonderful news*—this of your Augusta Lectures; and (*God willing!*)—you may be *sure* that *we* shall be there to listen to them.[1]

Apropos, a full column of the "*Chronicle*" is occupied this morning, in the revival of what *me judice*, has ever seemed a monstrous heresy, viz—the assertion that *Bacon* was the author of all *Shakspeare's* Plays;—that Shakspeare did not even know how to *spell*, far less write &c &c!—But some wise-*acre* has revamped Miss *Bacon's* essay which appeared in *England* 20 or 30 years ago, and the "Chronicle" Editor has been caught by its specious sophistry.[2]

Of course the evidence of such men (as *Ben Jonson* e.g) who knew Shakspeare *personally*, & have left on record their conclusive testimony as to his *genius*, is very conveniently *ignored*!—By the way, I do wish you *would knock this theory* on the head, (you can do it in five *minutes* time) when you speak in *Augusta*!!—

About your "*Supplementary Studies*," don't conclude they have failed, because of any slowness of sale. The book is a *wonderful continuation*, and will finally assert its power, or I am greatly mistaken.[3]

Am so proud & glad that my recent poems have pleased you. Here is a "*Quatrain*" which holds—*perhaps*, a somewhat original thought, or *fantasy*,—if *thought* be too ambitious a phrase!

Haunted.
What haunts him now?—(behold that anguished face!)
What haggard Horror, or malign *Disgrace*?
His own soul's evil shadow outward cast,—
Limned on the ghastly background of *his Past*!

A Northern friend—himself a *Poet* of genius—declares that this Quatrain "is *Baudelaire*-like; or rather of a quality which reminds one of *Balzac* &c"—But I'm afraid you *won't like it*, because I have observed that the *fantastic* in verse, has but little charm for you. For my *part*, I am carried away by it, sometimes, tho I acknowledge its *dangers*—

Here is another little poem I'd like your *candid opinion* of—*Pitch into me, my friend*, when I *need pitching into*! *Discipline is good for the soul.*

It is called "Recompense," & was suggested by the recent sad bereavement of Sec. *Bayard*, one of the few real *Statesmen* in this Country; & also a Gentleman of culture & experience.

Recompense.
The scythe of Death has cleft his hopes in twain,
And mowed his field of love till all seems bare—;
Yet loss reveals an aftermath of gain,—
Grief holds a benediction unaware.

Of late, Distrust & Envy dogged his way,—
Cold Misconstruction watched his *course apart*—
All sordid Passions stand rebuked *today*,
Before the pathos of a breaking heart!

While *other* hearts are softened by *his* pain,—
On death's dark background *sympathy grows clear*—
The chaff of loss may hide some golden grain—;
And grief enfold a blessing unaware!

Observe! the *change* of the imagery in the 3*rd* line of final stanza, from
"*loss with* its *aftermath* of *gain*," (which occurs in opening verse) to
"*the chaff of loss* &c"—

I made this alteration deliberately upon a certain principle of *Art*!
The question is, was I *right*, or wrong?—Perhaps the *whole* piece is a
failure however? I feel very uncertain. *You* will resolve my doubt in one
way or another.[4]

Our terrible winter set me to thinking of a violent snow-storm,
which I beheld (in Charleston, mark you), years ago, & which actually
occurred in the Spring!! *March*, I think! *Thus* I endeavor to celebrate it.

White bloodless Passion of this vernal day,
Thou hast the power—Earth's budding grace to slay—,
Thy weapon—a Snow-tempest, fierce & fleet—
At once the death-spell, and the *winding sheet*!

The same "*power*" which *kills* the tender, budding beauty of the sea-
son, furnished the "winding sheet." First "beauty" is murdered, then
buried, by the glittering deceitful "snow." But *enough*! Let us hear if
possible, that you are better & stronger. *Love* from *Lady Mary*.

> Commend us to all your family,
> Ever affectionately,
> *Paul H Hayne.*

1. A reference to Lipscomb's forthcoming lectures on Shakespeare for the Hayne
Circle in Augusta. See Letter 119, n. 11. The Haynes did indeed attend the lectures on
March 23, 25, 26, 1886.

2. Delia Bacon's essay had appeared in *Putnam's Monthly* in New York in 1856 and
her *Philosophy of the Plays of Shakespeare Unfolded by Delia Bacon* in 1857. The
"*wise-acre*" referred to is probably Nathaniel Holmes, a Missouri jurist, whose two-

volume work on the theory appeared in a fourth edition in 1886. With regard to Hayne's request, Lipscomb replied on February 22 that he was reluctant to give special notice to the "Bacon Illusion respecting Shakespeare" because he thought the lectures themselves would demonstrate that Shakespeare "is about the most real and veritable person who lived on this planet within the last three hundred years."

3. The *Supplementary Studies* appeared in late November, 1885, and is an addition to Lipscomb's *Studies in the Forty Days* (1884). Lipscomb had been discouraged by the book's reception and observed in his letter of February 4 that "it is a failure up to date."

4. This version of the poem is different in matters of mechanics from the one written to Marston—February 9—in Letter 119. On February 13 Lipscomb offered his view: "But I am not so clear as to the sustained unity and interior force of the 'Recompense.' Can there be any *recompense* for the death of such a wife as Mrs. B.? Can there be any recompense to a bereaved husband by anything—to the *Statesman*? So much for your generic idea. . . . But I am not sure of my criticism. I only suggest further study for you." Lipscomb's comments brought forth from Hayne on February 15 a rather full explanation and defense based upon the "degrees" of recompense and an acknowledgment that the title might be "faulty." As a result of Hayne's discussion of his meaning of *recompense* in the poem—"merely as a partial compensation—the *aftermath*"—Lipscomb took back his criticism on February 22. The poem appeared in the *Independent*, XXXVIII (February 18, 1886), 193.

121

To Richard W. Knott   MS Duke

2nd March 1886

My Dear Friend;

I finished reading the *March* "Bivouac" last night. Let me congratulate you. The Mag*zn.* has steadily improved; & I think the last no perhaps the most valuable of *all*. A *very important* series of articles are there on the great Kentucky Resolutions!! The poetry also is good; especially Harney's ballad. The *conception* too of the piece on Lanier is excellent. Its execution not quite so good. (By the way did you read Lanier's letters in "*The NY Critic*," which I had published with explanations recently?)—They are curious & exceedingly characteristic![1]

This winter has nearly killed me; but (*laus Deo!*), I feel spring in the air! After such arctic *desolation* how, I for one, shall welcome the beautiful Goddess!

But a vast deal of vitality has been taken out of me. Life narrows daily.

Well, as the Spaniard says, "*So que ha, de ser, no pueda faltar!*" The *Inevitable must come to pass*![2]

I only pray for a year or two more, to strike some honest blows for *So Literature* in your gallant little organ.

How is your *own* health?

Good I imagine. Take care of it. A man who is invalided is but half a man; nay; but *nine tenths* of a man like the proverbial *Tailor*!

Ever
PHH

P.S. Did I ask you to *return* Gilchrist's likeness, (ie) if you *cannot use* it?[3] Drop me a line as to *possible time* of appearance of the Gayarré article. I am by no means *impatient*; but the knowledge will help me as to the *2nd* paper.[4]

1. R. T. Durrett's article on the Kentucky Resolutions is the first of a series, the second and third parts of which followed in succeeding numbers. The poem by Will Wallace Harney is "The Light-House Rock. Key West." The "piece" on Lanier is "Hopeset and Sunrise. Suggested by Sidney Lanier's Life and Poems," a poem by Jasper B. Cowdin. Lanier's letters to Hayne appeared in the *Critic* for February 13 and 20, 1886.

2. The quotation actually should read: "Lo que ha de ser, no puede faltar." Hayne's translation of the Spanish is acceptable.

3. Major Robert Gilchrist was an old friend of Hayne's who was a Confederate officer assigned to Fort Wagner and who figures prominently in Hayne's article for the March number of the *Bivouac*, "The Defense of Fort Wagner" (n.s., I, 599–608).

4. The three-part essay on Gayarré began in June and concluded in August, 1886.

122

To Charles Gayarré　　　　　　　　　　　　　　　MS Duke

March 23*rd* 1886.

My Beloved Friend,

Last evng I rec*d* yours of the 19th *inst*, the *third* letter—most affectionate & cordial—which has reached me lately.[1]

Would that I could reply to all these invaluable epistles as they *deserve* to be answered; but alas! I have *been & am very sick*.

All the energies of life, & nerve force, all my once bright spirits, & intellectual interest in art &c, seem failing me. I'm under medical guidance, but the end looks gloomy eno'.

At 56 I am really older than you are at 81!, & shall probably pass over to the "majority" long before you do. *But we shall meet*, I cannot but believe that we shall meet, where "beyond these voices there is peace!"[2] "*Kismet*"! My doom is written, & *sealed*, so far as earth is concerned. What then? Did not my Master Shakspere [*sic*] die at 50 or 53? Lugubrious eh?—Only, I am writing to a dear, *dear* friend! Why, should I not open my *heart*?

Basta! sickness is so apt to make one egotistical.

The result, *thus far*, of your 6 lectures, has not merely disappointed me (in a *pecuniary sense*), but I feel *outraged* on your account. Such ineffable meanness! And even the ladies seem implicated here!![3]

Shame! shame!

Pardon this *miserable* "screed."

If strength serves, I'll write again soon.

The present is just *no answer* at all to your wonderful letters. Have patience with a poor suffering devil, & believe me in this world & the world to come,

> *Forever Your friend,*
> *Paul H Hayne.*

1. Hayne apparently is referring to letters of March 11 and March 15, in addition to the one of March 19 mentioned in this paragraph. Interestingly enough, the date of Hayne's letter, March 23, is actually the date announced for A. A. Lipscomb's first lecture on Shakespeare before the Hayne Circle in Augusta.

2. "Guinevere," *Idylls of the King*, line 692.

3. Gayarré had delivered six lectures on Louisiana history that were free to the public, for which he was to be paid $500 (to be raised by subscription). He observes in his letter of March 19 that he had received $220; subsequently, with the help of Paul Tulane, a total of $500 was achieved, but Gayarré, for reasons he never understood, received only $400 all told. See, for example, his letter to Hayne of April 24, 1886. The reference to the implication of the ladies is to Gayarré's observation that only one of the fifteen "patronesses" attended the last four lectures and that, after the first lecture, the sponsorship of the lectures changed without explanation from that of the ladies to that of Tulane University.

123

To R. W. Knott   MS Duke

Private & Confidential

> *Sunday night,*
> *April 4th 1886*

My Dear Friend;—

I *know* that you will be sorry to hear what I have now to tell you. Yesterday, while writing at my desk, (upon the *Gayarré* article),—I was attacked by a sudden giddiness,—lost my balance,—fell, and must have been unconscious for at least 5 or 6 minutes!

No one, (laus Deo) was present,—and so, *thus far*, I have been enabled to conceal my condition of health from my poor wife;—hoping that matters *may improve*.

Yet, is there small chance of *this*. *Frankly*, I *don't* believe that my life is "worth 3 months *purchase*!; perhaps not 3 weeks!"—[1]

Well,—what would you?—

"Kismet" is written upon all our foreheads.

I'd like to see & *correct* the proof of the 1*st* part of the *Gayarré* article; and be assured that *2nd part shall reach you*, if the *power* is given me to complete *it for June*.[2]

If not, and I *am still here*, it may be completed *later*.

Give me your sympathy, and believe me, *here & hereafter*,

Your sincere, affectionate, *grateful*
Friend—
Paul H Hayne.

Don't mention my attack please when you write.

1. After bouts with hemorrhage or asthma or other illness, Hayne had remarked on occasion in the past that his time was about up. Somehow he had always recovered, but, despite his subsequent intellectual and physical activity—the trip to Macon in May, for instance—this fainting spell did indeed presage the end.

2. Before his final illness in June, Hayne did manage to read proof on all three parts of his essay on Gayarré as statesman and author. See his remark to Gayarré in Letter 124.

124

To Charles Gayarré   MS Duke

"Copse Hill"
Friday April 16th 1886

My Beloved Friend,

I have been re-perusing your last affectionate letter of the 27*th* ult, (to which I was enabled *only* to send a P.C. reply), and it has deeply touched me. If our friendship *was* formed late in life, what then? It is not the less earnest, & precious.

My health continues in a sad state, the whole nervous system appearing in collapse, but 3 days ago, I sent back the proof of 1*st* part of article on "*Charles Gayarré the Statesman*," & today I shall dispatch the 2nd Part upon "*Charles Gayarré the Author*."[1]

I'm afraid that they bear the signs of weakness, one's *physical* often affecting one's mental condition. At least they were composed *con amore*. Upon *one* point—I must explain.

Examining *again*, & with increased attention your "*Fernando de Lemos*," I could not but pronounce it on some points of conception your *most* original work; & yet, (frankly), the *execution* struck me as defective.

There is, as it *seems* to me, a certain lack of harmony, of parts, & occasional diffuseness, which with you is an unwanted, & uncharacteristic fault. Not wishing my review to seem *all rose-color*, I have briefly mentioned these matters, remarking however, that even if I am right, the *superb* general power of the work, not to speak of such episodes as the charming picture of the old Priest of the Pyrenees, and the weird portraiture of Calandro *more* than counterbalance a little hastiness of construction, & composition.[2]

I refer to this *solitary example* of a mild sort of—what shall I term it? *expostulation*(?), so that you may not miscomprehend me, or think that I said one thing in private (in my letters abt "De Lemos"), and now modify or contradict the same in public?—of all *meannesses* the *worst*!!

A *touch* of *adverse* criticism in an article upon the whole enthusiastically favorable, gives the reader a sense of the writer's sincerity; it is the bit of *shade* to a picture which otherwise might be pronounced unnaturally bright.

Am I correct *mon ami*?

What satisfaction it afforded me to pitch into those d——d hounds of the (so-called) Louisiana Democracy touching their infamous conduct to you! The *people* at your request I *let alone*; but the servile, time-serving, ungrateful Politicians! Whew! I bared my sword arm for them, & have at least struck, (I hope) a stalwart blow or two.

To Cable also, the ——— little creature "coming right across my hawser"—as a sailor would say, I have paid my respects.[3] What I first wrote was so *spitefully bitter*—Mrs H. declared, that, reluctantly, tho my reason was convinced of the correctness of my wife's strictures, *reluctantly* I toned down the two pages of scorn to a few paragraphs.

Please write me when you *can*. We wish so much to learn of the results of the recent lectures, in a *material way*. Of their brilliant success otherwise, the papers have assured us.

I fear I *fear* that you have been defrauded. If so, "by the splendor of God," or rather by the *darkness* of Satan! It—will be—but language fails me here![4]

Our love to *Mrs Gayarré*. How often we think of her, an image of sweetness, patience, constancy & faith in a world not worthy of such pure spirits. Ah God has blessed us both in our wives. Without *mine* I should simply, as the *Scotch express* it, "die."

Ever affectionately,
Paul H Hayne.

1. See Letter 123, n. 2. The installments appeared in June, July, and August.

2. Characterizing the book as defective in structure and execution, Hayne is rather forthright in his criticism, but Gayarré was equal to the situation. "I'm glad," he wrote on April 24, "that you have thrown a shade over the light." "The fact is," he continued, "I wrote at random with no other plan in Fernando de Lemos than that of treating solely of moral and religious questions as they happened from time to time to present themselves to my mind. . . . Hence, as you correctly observe, a lack of harmony in the parts, or adjustment in the wheels. It is a string of episodes rather than a connected and compact whole. It is well that you pointed it out and did not grant me more than I claim. . . . I am satisfied that you have done me a great deal more than justice."

3. Hayne has left the blank unfilled. He "pays his respects" to Cable in relatively mild language: "Mr Cable's talents are hardly of a kind to grapple successfully with difficult race problems. Let him stick to the light artillery of fancy" (n.s., II [August, 1886], 174).

4. For the "material" response to Gayarré's lectures, see Letter 122, n. 3.

125

To R. D. Blackmore[1]   MS Duke

22nd April 1886.

My Beloved Friend:—

I continue very sick, which must excuse writing in pencil.

Let me say how delighted we, (my wife & I) are with your opening Chapters of "Springhaven"! 'Tis in your best style. Full of beauty & that peculiar subtle humor, which can't be defined, but to me is irresistible.

I write *from the heart*; with no arrière-pensée as to the "dedication," & its ineffable sweetness to my spirit.

Perhaps I may never see it, for altho, I try to conceal my real condition from my wife, I feel assured that the end cannot be far off.[2]

But ah! my friend, whom I do love & honor,—*we shall meet somehow*, somewhere; and as for *Death* I'll endeavor to meet *him* in the temper & with the faith outlined in my poem called *"Face to Face"* in the May *Harper.*[3]

But it is awful to part with those we love, & among them, *you* have (in my affections) an exalted place.

I think it has truly come to this, "*Moriturus* nos saluto" !![4]

Remember me tenderly to Mr*s* Blackmore. Should the cloud pass—
well!—if *not* there is sunshine beyond it!—

> God be with you & yours;
> *Ever affectionately & loyally*
> *here & hereafter—*
> Paul H. Hayne
> Copse Hill Geo
> 22nd April 1886

1. Hayne and Blackmore (1825–1900), the well-known English author of *Lorna Doone* (1869) and other novels and poems, had corresponded for a number of years and had become good friends. They exchanged plants and books and agreed on many subjects. Blackmore, for example, supported the Confederacy during the war and continued to express himself in favor of the South thereafter. He read Hayne's *PCE* and wrote of his admiration of the poems, and Hayne characterized Blackmore as the best of living British novelists. There was indeed mutual affection between the two writers, and the expressions of that affection in Hayne's sonnet to Blackmore (*Harper's Weekly*, December 10, 1884) and in Blackmore's dedication of *Springhaven* (1887) to Hayne are undoubtedly genuine. See also Blackmore's letter of May 7, 1886.

2. The first five chapters of the novel appeared in *Harper's Monthly* in April, but the book and the dedication, of course, would not appear until 1887, too late indeed for Hayne to see.

3. The last stanza reads, in part:

> Far voices of fond acclaim
>   Thrill down from the place of souls,
> As Death, with a touch like flame,
>   Uncloses the goal of goals;
> And from heaven of heavens above
>   God speaketh with bateless breath—
> My angel of perfect love
>   Is the angel men call Death!

4. Though there are several slips of the pen in this Latin, Hayne apparently has modified the old Roman gladiatorial cry, *morituri te salutamus.* He presumably wishes to say, "About to die, I salute you."

126

To Charles Gayarré   MS Duke

> *"Copse Hill," Geo*
> *Wed 28th April 1886.*

My Very Dear Friend;—

I am a little, a *very little* better, & *must,*—during this breathing space—write to you, in special answer to your last characteristically cordial communication of the 24th in*st.*

Both my papers upon your genius as "Statesman" & "Author" are in Knott's hands; & I have—as previously stated—his *emphatic* promise that the 1*st* will appear next month (*June*).[1]

About the "*wealthy ladies*" of N. Orleans—and their embarrassment touching the non collection of the *miserable* stipend promised you, & then their application to *Tulane*, thro Poché—, I can only observe that—unless there are circumstances behind the curtain, of which I am ignorant—, the entire affair is contemptible![2] By God why didn't one or two of these "*embarrassed ladies*" sell a bracelet or brooch, or string of pearls, rather than *countenance*, or at all events, bring about a Correspondence which besides being in execrably bad taste so far as its publication is concerned reflects upon them, one and *all*, in a manner *most unfortunate*?

These women, I don't hesitate to affirm, have *disgraced themselves*, but, *my Friend*; you are a thousand times over right in taking your dues, or rather your dues, *minus* an *entire fourth*!![3] *Dear me*! if I could only have room enough to express my indignation, what Gargantuan "*anathemas*" would explode from the surface of this paper!!

I see, as indeed I knew that I would—, how absolutely you comprehend my purpose in being candid concerning a few questionable "lapses" in "*Fernando de Lemos*." *Yours* is a genius which does not claim—as mediocre talents often do—*infallibility*![4]

Apropos, I expect to be assailed, perhaps *violently* assailed, because of my uncompromising language in regard to the Louisiana Democracy, its present Leaders &c, touching your claims & magnificent past-services; & the abominable neglect wherewith you have been treated. *So be it*!

I don't care the snap of my finger for anything they may say or do.

How glad I am that you offered Knott your article upon "*Marie Stuart*;" and be sure to let me see—*if I am living* at the time—your new essays upon the Lafittes.[5]

I *cannot* think that the Harper's will refuse your "*Sugar estate of the old regime*" in La![6]

As for "*The Century*," you are right in having nothing to do with them. As for the Northern periodicals I would advise you to contribute to, as prominent paying ones, let me mention, in N. York.

Harper's Monthly

The Independent (a "weekly" strictly republican, & yet ready to receive So articles at times)

Harper's "Weekly" &c

in Boston

"The Atlantic"—narrow & sectional; still, if you wrote some of your great historical essays—they might be accepted—

in *Philadelphia*

"Lippincott's Magz"—

Mrs. [Thacker Kaye] did me *also* the honor of noticing me in *"Lit Life"*—an article *well-intentioned*; but as in *your case* exceedingly deficient on many points. Her notice of *you* in truth is by far the best of the two, despite its *"bob-tail-ed-ness."*[7]

These scribblers are a horror to me. Would to God they could be induced to let us alone.

My ill-luck is quite on a par with yours, referring to likenesses— Glancing over the pages of two *large-octavo* vols—edited by *Jno James Piatt*, called "[*The Union of*] *American Poetry & Art*" [1880]—I find myself represented as the most atrocious of wooden-headed donkeys; a Son, or, twin *brother* of the immortal Capt Buzzby [*sic*] in *"Dombey & Son."*[8]

And now adieu! for the present, my *beloved friend*!

My wife joins me in affectionate regards to Mrs G; and pray believe me   Ever

> *Your faithful & devoted friend,*
> *Paul H Hayne.*

1. The first installment appeared, as promised, in the *Southern Bivouac* for June, and the second and third parts followed in July and August.

2. For Gayarré's honorarium for the six lectures he delivered in February and March, see Letter 122 and n. 3 under it.

3. Gayarré received, as he reported to Hayne on April 24, four hundred dollars of the five hundred dollars due him; consequently he lost a fifth of what had been promised, not a fourth.

4. For Hayne's criticism of *Fernando de Lemos* and Gayarré's response, see Letter 124 and n. 2 under it.

5. Knott rejected the article on Mary Stuart for the *Bivouac*. On June 11, 1886, Gayarré sent his essay on the Lafittes to Knott, who accepted it for publication in August, 1886.

6. "A Louisiana Sugar Plantation of the Old Regime," *Harper's Monthly*, LXXIX (March, 1887), 606–21.

7. Hayne's brackets. Emma Thacker Kaye, a southern journalist living in the Midwest, contributed these two sketches to *Literary Life*, a new monthly established in Chicago. For Gayarré's ironic comments on her and on her sketch of him, see his letter to Hayne of April 24, 1886.

8. Buzzby, of course, is a slip of the pen for Bunsby.

127

To Charles Gayarré   MS Duke

May 29th 1886

My Very Dear Friend;

Your tender solicitous letter of inquiry to my wife, reached here last ev*ng*.[1]

Were I *dying*, which I am not *yet*, be assured—, I should have tried to answer that loving communication. Yours of the 3*rd* May, with the "C.[*atholic*] World" arrived just upon the eve of our starting for Macon; whither I had been long before earnestly asked to come by the chief literary society of the place. My Doctor said the change might prove beneficial; and therefore, with my wife—who had been formally invited too—, we set off, & arrived safely at, the most delightful City to my mind in all Ge*o*. It is a conservative town, prosperous, and wonderfully loyal to old Confederate memories. Every man treated me like a *brother*,—every woman seemed a sister. If I get stronger, someday, I'll describe their magnificent reception.[2] Such kindness made me feel better for some days; but a re-action set in upon our return, & moreover, I have been assailed by a most debilitating sort of dysentery. Too bad, eh? Yet, I am no puling Valetudinarian, & shall fight *Disease* as if it were a personal foe.

You shall hear how the contest goes, & if it should be *against* me, at all events, I have succeeded in doing my illustrious friend some slight justice in "*Bivouac*." O! but *slight indeed*! Pardon my errors in consideration of the author's feebleness, that physical depression which attacks the mind.

2*nd* Paper is to appear in July.[3]

You don't know how delightedly I would hail one of your characteristic letters. Write me, my friend! write to me![4]

Our tender love to Mr*s Gayarre*—whom may God bless for all her gentle sweetness. How does the likeness of yourself in June "*Bivouac*," please her?—I like it much.

Ever most affectionately,
Paul H Hayne.

1. Gayarré had written on May 26 and enclosed a "postal card" for Mrs. Hayne to indicate Hayne's condition, since he did not wish to disturb the poet himself.

2. Hayne and Mrs. Hayne had been invited by the Athenaeum Club to attend an

affair in his honor on May 20. See Letter 119, Hayne to Marston, February 7, and n. 12 under it.

3. Hayne's essay on Gayarré for the *Bivouac* appeared in June, July, and August.

4. Gayarré did write—on June 10 and 11—but Hayne was not able to answer. The dysentery worsened, and in June he had a stroke which led eventually to his death on July 6, 1886.

128

To Richard Fraser Michel[1]   MS Duke

Excuse pencil!   *8th June 1886.*
Dear Dick;

For 14 days I have been *very sick*, struggling with such a strong bowel complaint as I don't remember ever having encountered before; (3 & even 4 passages a day).[2]

But with exquisite & continual care on my wife's *part* & under the advice of my beloved friend, D*r* [Henry] Campbell, I am much *better*, (altho *not out* of the woods)—

Death! he is *everywhere*! At each idle laugh of ours, some human spirit passes away—*whither, who knows?* And Dr. *Baldwin* too has departed! I know how you were attached to him, & sympathise with your sentiments.[3] And for myself; he never failed whenever I wanted M[cdicine], to be exceptionally kind, & attentive. I pray that he may pass thro the river of purifying mercy to the Place of Beauty, reconciliation, & love.

"Soft by the City of the Saints of God"!

There is no man to whose soul faith may not come, at last. At a signal he may be transfigured mentally & spiritually.—Let *us hope for all*, oh, my brother!! *Christ* died for *all*! *Don't* talk to me of theological dogma. Unless the *spirit*—not the nice *letter* of the bible be worshipped, *"hope farewell"*! I have fought with many a literal beast at Ephesus, but beyond their miserable gabble have beheld the Metropolis of S*t* John, & the Palms along the Stream of life immortal!

Love to all! Kiss Annie & my poor little, *Sue*, with the arrow from Heaven yet burning her heart! Still, let the child *remember* that there is balm upon the shaft, & destined in due season to cure the wound which it in its mysterious course created![4]

To D*r* B's family give my heart-felt sympathy.

Write me Dick,

I continue very sick—, and with difficulty hold my pencil. Love from Minna & Willie—

Affectionately
Paul H Hayne.

P.S. Thanks for the paper about D*r* Baldwin and poor Miss Farley! You have my sincere sympathy in the death of the former: W. H.[5]

1. Michel, a physician in Montgomery, Alabama, was Hayne's brother-in-law. Shortly after receiving this letter he went to Hayne's bedside, but he had to return to his own practice before Hayne died on July 6, 1886. Middleton Michel, Hayne's other brother-in-law and a physician in Charleston, had been injured in an accident and could not come.

2. It will be remembered that Hayne had observed to Gayarré on May 29 (Letter 127) that he "had been assailed by a most debilitating sort of dysentery."

3. Dr. Baldwin was a close friend and colleague of Michel's who had died recently in Montgomery. Hayne had met him there on his various visits to Michel's home.

4. The references to Annie and Sue are to Michel's wife and daughter, Mrs. Fred Hammond, who had recently experienced a death in her own family.

5. The postscript is written in the hand of Hayne's son, William Hamilton Hayne. This is the last letter Hayne ever wrote. He subsequently suffered a stroke, lasped into a coma, and died of "congestion of the brain" on July 6, 1886. See *PHH*, 29–30, 171.